A History of the
Church of St. Laurence,
Church Stretton

A History of the Church of St. Laurence, Church Stretton

A Rural Parish through a Thousand Years

by

Douglas Grounds

Logaston Press

LOGASTON PRESS
Little Logaston Woonton Almeley
Herefordshire HR3 6QH

First published by Logaston Press 2002
Copyright © Douglas Grounds 2002
Copyright illustrations © Douglas Grounds 2002,
except as otherwise acknowledged

ISBN (paperback) 1 873827 43 1
ISBN (hardback) 1 873827 73 3

Set in Times by Logaston Press
and printed in Great Britain by
The Cromwell Press, Trowbridge

For Elaine and Adele

I gather up the fragments of the years,
here, where the coloured sunlight paints
the rainbow's promise on the timeless stone.
Here, in this warp of time, all time is one.

(The opening lines of Roy Coad's poem,
Communion at St. Laurence,
by kind permission)

Contents

Foreword

This is a splendid book, wide-ranging in its survey of national and local history, and of politics and economics and church life of the past thousand years in Church Stretton and the neighbouring villages. Douglas Grounds has, by painstaking research, built up a fascinating picture of the history of the Church in this part of Shropshire near the Welsh Border, a place whose history goes back at least to Roman times, and whose attractive and fertile landscape has continued to attract people to live and work here, not least in recent years.

Most of the earliest chapter has, of necessity, to be speculative, but there are important fragments of evidence which point to the existence of a Christian Church in Stretton from the Dark Ages onwards. The Church of St. Laurence, as we know it today, would certainly be recognisable to our medieval forebears, although it has been much altered and improved, particularly in the past century. The Victorian restorers laid heavy hands on the fabric, but there are still places—such as the north side by the doorway to the ringing chamber—which have a wonderful feeling of antiquity and continuity.

As society has changed over the centuries, so has the life of the Church ebbed and flowed, and we have reason to be grateful to Douglas Grounds for his faithful investigation of the past, his clear and honest assessment of the present, and his stylish, but highly readable presentation of the enthralling story of the mission and ministry of the Church in the Strettons. I am greatly encouraged by the inspiring and hopeful note on which this book ends, and I wish it every success among a wide readership.

✝John Hereford

Preface

For at least a thousand years the Church of St. Laurence, the oldest structure in the parish of Church Stretton and a Grade One Listed Building, has borne witness to the Christian faith. Yet the full story of the church and its people has never been told.

The end of the second millennium A.D. presents perhaps the ideal opportunity to recount this story, for the parish church was probably founded shortly before the close of the first millennium. It is a story of continual change and development, punctuated by periods of major building work and religious upheaval. Initially, of course, Stretton's church was subject to the Pope in Rome and so remained for over five hundred years. Following the Reformation in the sixteenth century it assumed the Protestantism of the new Church of England. Yet its nearly 60 known rectors have represented many different points on the continuum stretching from the historic Roman faith to the Puritans at the Protestant extreme.

It is a story, too, of the inter-action between the developing local community of the parish and its church. At first the church was the place where the people of the parish worshipped, celebrated the rites of passage that marked their lives, met on formal and social occasions, and even did business. The church was the focus of their cultural identity, with the events of the rural calendar mirrored in the festivals of the ecclesiastical year. As the local economy and social structure evolved, with times of both hardship and prosperity, they were reflected in the church's fabric, decorations, services and activities. Although in our complex modern society the church no longer has the same centrality in the life of the community that it enjoyed for so long, there are few local families untouched by its ministry.

From another angle the parish church tells the story, in microcosm, of the Church in England, illustrating its changing role in national life and the theological currents that have, under God, helped shape its development.

These are the themes—the evolution of the church building, the varied contributions of its clergy, its relationship to the development of the local community, the impact of major national events on its life, and the broad ecclesiastical and theological changes that have influenced it over the centuries—that I have tried to weave together in this history.

The church building itself is, of course, the greatest treasure for its history. That apart, the materials from which this story has been compiled have been quarried in a variety of places. It is fortunate that for centuries the manor of Church Stretton and the patronage of the church were in the hands of the king or one of his great nobles because references to the church occur in their records. On the other hand, as the lords of the manor did not reside in the parish, the church perhaps received less financial assistance than many other churches and lacks the striking memorials that make some unique. A great debt is owed to the painstaking transcriptions of late nineteenth-century researchers—many of them clergymen—and above all to the Rev. R.W. Eyton who illuminated our county's medieval history in the pages of his monumental *Antiquities of Shropshire*. The records of the diocese of Hereford are a mine of information, with the bishops' registers going back to the thirteenth century. In more recent times material is more readily available in the deposits at the County Records and Research Centre, in the church's own archives, and in the pages of the *Shrewsbury Chronicle*, the *Church Stretton Advertiser* and other newspapers. For almost the last hundred years surviving copies of the parish magazine and the minutes of the Parochial Church Council provide a wealth of detail. And recollections of more than half a century are lodged in the memories of our oldest parishioners.

There remain periods in the more distant past when almost nothing is known, when the course of the church's history flows through subterranean channels only to reappear suddenly a little further on. The task of the historian then becomes more that of the explorer, searching for evidence of the on-going course of his quarry before attempting to produce a general and coherent map. That search has led me far and wide—to the Public Record Office, numerous county record offices, university and college libraries, reference libraries, the church archives, longstanding members of the church and residents of the parish, many other churches, and even to France to track down some of our thirteenth-century rectors.

I am pleased to record my thanks for their gracious and helpful assistance on my frequent visits in the last six years to Tony Carr and his colleagues at the Shropshire Records and Research Centre, to Miss Hubbard and her staff at the Herefordshire Record Office, and to the staff at the Church Stretton Library. Among university and college libraries I have worked in I particularly wish to thank the staff at the Bodleian Library at Oxford, and the Librarian of St. John's College, Cambridge.

I am grateful to the late Henry Horrocks and to David Bilbey whose booklets on St. Laurence's first aroused my interest in its history. David Bilbey has also kindly allowed me to use some of his already published drawings.

I am pleased to acknowledge my debt to George Baugh, one of the editors of the *Victoria County History of Shropshire*, who has provided me with a number of references, and to Dr. Sylvia Watts for her help in deciphering and translating some early documents. Keith Stanley, a former colleague, also assisted in translations from Latin.

For provision of illustrations, I wish to thank Tony Carr of Shropshire Records and Research Centre for provision of photographs of illustrations on pages 95, 146, 148, 152, 157 176, 216, 224, 225 and 235 and also for permission for their use, with the exception of those on pages 146 and 176 where permission is kindly given by the Shropshire Archaeological and Historical Society and that on page 148 where permission is given by the Rector, Jonathan Millard; to Hereford Record Office for provision of the material and the Bishop of Hereford for the use of those on pages 90 (Woodard 9/2/7), 110, 112 (HD 5/11), 125 (HD 2/15/1), 132 (HD 5/14/164) and 155; to the Bodleian Library, University of Oxford, for the illustrations on pages 91 (MS. Top. Salop. c. 2, fol. 458r) and 143; for that on page 2 © Crown Copyright 1947 / MOD reproduced with permission of the Controller of Her Majesty's Stationery Office; to David Bilbey for the illustrations on pages 31 (lower), 131, 181 and 193 (upper); Church Stretton Town Council for that on page 179; Dr. M.J. Cressley-Evans for the photograph of the entry in Henry Maurice's diary on p.118; Ann Amos for the copy of John Mainwaring's letter on p.145; and Logaston Press for the illustration on page 59. I wish also to thank Phillip Crowcroft for the illustration of the church used on the front cover.

I wish to express my gratitude to the Bishop of Hereford, the Rt. Rev. John Oliver, who graciously agreed to write a foreword, and to Bishop John Saxbee, now at Lincoln, who showed great interest in the project when he was at Ludlow. The Ven. Mark Wilson kindly assisted me with memories of his father's time as rector in Stretton, and Preb. John Woodger and his wife Rose generously shared with me their recollections of their years in Church Stretton. To Preb. Michael Stedman and Gill I owe a great debt for their ministry in my first seven years in Stretton, for discussing in detail their knowledge of the parish and for their encouragement. Their successors, the Rev. Jonathan Millard and Jill, have given me every support as they have themselves 'written' the final pages of this history.

Among the many friends at St. Laurence's and in the town who have dug deep into their memories to answer my questions are Ron and Jennie Bennett, Helen Bower, Norma Brewer, Helen and Patricia Davidson, Pete Faulkner, Leslie Harrison, Sister Winifred Henry, John Hughes, David and Loveday Janes, Gladys Lewis, Ian and Leslie Penny, Gordon and Joyce Skinner, and Fred and Nan Weaver. Roy Coad kindly let me use some lines from his poem, *Communion at St. Laurence*. Susan Beale's advice on geology and building stone was most valuable. Nancy Cleaton and Mervyn Williams have given practical assistance on many occasions. I thank them all sincerely.

To Tony Crowe I am particularly grateful for he has generously shared with me his extensive knowledge of Stretton history and given me access to his unrivalled collection of local photographs.

My special thanks go to Dr. John Leonard for his informed comments on various aspects of St. Laurence's architecture, for his personal encouragement, and for introducing me to Logaston Press. I owe a great debt of gratitude, too, to Andy Johnson, who has been a most helpful publisher with his constructive criticisms and personal kindness.

My warmest thanks must be to Rosaleen Whately, daughter of a former rector, whose personal knowledge of the parish goes back 65 years and who has given constant encouragement, lent and given me books, and read through almost the whole of my text before being struck down by illness; and to Preb. Francis Palmer, who has taken a close interest in the project from the beginning, read the whole of my first draft, offered valuable advice and given generous encouragement.

Needless to say, the responsibility for the final form of this history rests squarely with me.

My final and deepest thanks go to my late wife, Elaine, who lived long enough to retire with me to Stretton and to urge me to write a history of our church, and to my present wife, Adele, who throughout the later stages of this enterprise has been as constant in her support as she has been perceptive in her comments. It is to them both, for their love and encouragement, that I dedicate this book.

Douglas Grounds
Church Stretton, June 2002

1
THE SAXON AND NORMAN CHURCHES

Church Stretton's very name declares the prominence of the parish church in its history. The first documented appearance of that name, no doubt to distinguish it from All Stretton and Little Stretton, is not until the mid-thirteenth century, but it is known from Domesday Book that it had had a church nearly two hundred years before then. What is uncertain is when the first settlement was established at Stretton, when and how the Christian faith first arrived there, and when the first church was built.

That there had been movement and settlement in the surrounding area in early centuries is testified by the Portway and Bronze Age burial tumuli on the Long Mynd and by the Iron Age forts on Caer Caradoc and probably at Bodbury Ring. The Romans had then built the southern spur of Watling Street from *Viroconium* (Wroxeter), the fourth largest city in Roman Britain, to *Bravonium* (Leintwardine) and on to *Magnis* (Kenchester) through the Stretton Gap. There is no evidence that there was a settled community at Church Stretton at that time, although it has recently been suggested that most of the settlements that subsequently developed into parishes are likely to have been in existence throughout the Roman period and probably for centuries before that.[1]

The name Stretton is Anglo-Saxon, meaning the '-tun' or settlement near the 'street', or Roman road, its site close to but not actually on Watling Street. Yet in spite of the scarcity of pre-English names for natural features — 'Mynd' is an exception — initially Anglo-Saxons were anything but numerous in the central Marches. In the sixth century they had advanced deep into the country from their landings in the east but probably did not get as far as 'Shropshire', where the obscurity of events in these years has been described by a modern historian as impenetrable.[2] What probably happened was that the area, which had formed part of the territory of the Romano-British Cornovii people, was absorbed into the Welsh kingdom of Powys. The next century, however, saw the Saxons establish the central kingdom of Mercia. One of their earliest kings, Penda, probably in alliance with the ruler of Powys, was powerful enough to defeat Oswald, king of the rival kingdom of Northumbria, at the Battle of *Maesbyrig*, generally believed to be Maesbury, near Oswestry, in 642 A.D. He went on to

An aerial view of Strettondale from the north, with the Stretton Hills on the left and the Long Mynd on the right. The Roman road, Watling Street, stands out clearly. (Cambridge University Collection)

extend his authority over the border tribes in the eastern region of Powys, including what is now Shropshire. In the eighth century Mercia under its even more powerful rulers Aethelbald and Offa became the dominant kingdom in the land, its western boundary briefly marked by Offa's Dyke before the kingdom pushed yet further to the west. It was perhaps at this time, as piecemeal forest clearing proceeded, that an earlier settlement at Stretton was consolidated and that this name came into regular use. Modern Shropshire has an exceptionally large number of places with names ending in '-ton', which did not become a fashionable place-name element until about 750.[3] If the name 'Stretton' originated at that time the settlement itself is likely to have been peopled not just by Anglo-Saxons, by then perhaps the dominant group, but also by those of British descent who locally continued to form the main stock of the population.

The original settlement at Stretton, as local historian David Bilbey came to believe,[4] was almost certainly sited near the foot of the Burway, where the Old Rectory stands, taking advantage of the secluded position, the fresh water of the Town Brook, cultivable land, and the defensible position on the bank of Longhills in the event of attack. An early nineteenth-century antiquarian believed that a Celtic 'twm' and later a Saxon fortification had stood on this eminence near the site today of Bank House and the war memorial.[5]

By the time the name Stretton had come into use, Christianity was firmly established in the Anglo-Saxon kingdoms. The faith had first been planted in

Britain in the Roman era, although in the west archaeology has uncovered fewer signs of Christian activity than in the more Romanised east and south. After the Roman withdrawal the British Church survived, and at *Viroconium* some modern researchers have found evidence of a church and believe there may even have been a British bishop there.[6] Indeed, it has recently been argued that the British Church did not merely survive, but that 'an evangelical fervour seems to have swept part of the countryside. For the first time, Britain can be said to have become a Christian land'.[7] Physical evidence of the British Church is hard to identify, but is thought to be found in circular raised churchyards as at Easthope and Diddlebury. It has even been suggested that in Herefordshire church dedications to St. Lawrence could be an indication of early church communities in sub-Roman Britain.[8]

Probably the best evidence for the continued existence of an active British Church is found in the period after the Anglo-Saxon invasions. After reaching the West Midlands late in the sixth century, they quickly colonised the whole region. The invaders were pagans who worshipped a whole pantheon of gods headed by Woden and Thor, yet there are no clearly identifiable pagan burial sites with grave goods west of the Severn. The most likely explanation is that they had come into contact with organised Christianity—but this was happening before Augustine's mission from Rome arrived in Kent in 597. In the West Midlands 'it was the British Church which converted the immigrants. It left the missionaries from Canterbury and Iona little to do'.[9] Dr. Margaret Gelling considers there may have been only one generation of English paganism in the sub-kingdom of the 'Magonsaetan' of north Herefordshire and south Shropshire.[10] She does, however, point out that the suffix in Whittingslow, subsequently part of the early manor of Stretton, may indicate an early heathen burial place.[11]

It seems, therefore, that the majority of the newcomers may have been converted soon after their arrival in the west, especially if they came as small groups seeking land to farm rather than as conquering warriors. Certainly when Edfrith, a missionary of the Columban Church in Northumbria (which had its roots in Iona) arrived among the Magonsaetan his task may have been 'not so much outright conversion as the rekindling of the waning flame of Christian faith'.[12] Nonetheless, their king, Merewalh, had to be converted. According to their traditions incorporated into the later *Life of St. Milburga*, the king founded the double monastery at Much Wenlock and made his daughter Milburga its first abbess in about 680. But already by that time the authority of Rome, rein-troduced by Augustine, was being asserted by Archbishop Theodore, following the decisive Synod of Whitby in 664. It was he who created the diocese of Hereford, roughly coterminous with the territory of the Magonsaetan, at about the same time that Milburga went to Wenlock, and perhaps less than a hundred years before the settlement at Stretton adopted its English name.

It should be realised, of course, that early commitments to the Christian faith were often shallow and that paganism was not immediately eradicated. 'Even after the seventh century, the clergy and the king lived in a world where superstition, magical practice and the observance of pagan beliefs existed in parallel with Christianity and the secular establishment'.[13] The 'sheila-na-gig' in the north wall of the Norman nave at Stretton confirms that there were still those who put at least some of their trust in other deities.

Precisely when and how Christianity reached Stretton is unknown. The few and probably scattered settlers in Strettondale will have included Britons, who may have heard the gospel from their native Church, and, from the seventh century on, some Anglo-Saxons who could have learned of the faith from their neighbours or from itinerant preachers. But there could have been no regular worship and no depth of understanding. The permanent establishment of the faith in Stretton, as elsewhere, was most likely achieved through the outreach of one of the large minster churches that were then founded. The clergy carried the Word of God out into the scattered settlements of their *parochia*, preaching in the open air, baptising and perhaps conducting burials as they developed a pastoral ministry. They may also have invited the converted to the mother church, often miles away, for these rites of passage and to observe the cele-bration of the Mass, especially on the great Christian festivals.

'The parochial organisation of central Shropshire bears clear hallmarks of the system of minster churches set up in England in the seventh century'.[14] But which minster church counted Stretton among its spiritual progeny? It is thought that Leominster was a major centre of Christianity from at least the late seventh century, but it is nearly 30 miles distant from Stretton and its *parochia* did not extend

Map of Shropshire in the Anglo-Saxon period

4

beyond the northern boundary of what became Herefordshire.[15] Another possibility is that preaching canons came from the smaller but nearer collegiate foundation at Bromfield, whose influence came to extend as far north as Wistanstow,[16] but it is doubtful if it was collegiate early enough to have been the source of Stretton's conversion. Much Wenlock would appear more likely, for its priests were active in the nearby Severn Valley and Corvedale, and Stretton later became part of Wenlock Deanery. But Much Wenlock is 14 miles away, and Wenlock Edge forms its natural western boundary. There exists, however, a still more likely candidate. Condover was almost certainly a sub-minster of St. Andrew's, Wroxeter, in Lichfield diocese, but it had a sphere of influence that extended far to the south. 'The area of this former minster parish (and of Condover "hundred" at the time of Domesday Book) has a dramatic geographical unity, a semi-circle of lowland hemmed in by the northern end of the Long Mynd, Wenlock Edge and other similarly high ground'.[17] If Condover's *parochia* came that near it is hard to believe that its preachers did not venture into Strettondale, even if it then lay just over the diocesan boundary. And today Condover, rather than Wenlock, is the centre of Stretton's deanery!

From whatever community they came, priests visiting the little settlement at Stretton may have erected a cross at the place where they preached and which later became the site of the church. 'The provision of minster churches had been appropriate to the period of conversion, but once Christianity was established the need was felt for a more immediate clerical presence with churches and priests in local centres'.[18] Such churches, or rather chapels or field-churches, were sometimes built by the minster clergy who evangelised the countryside on their more or less distant lands, although they could not always spare a priest to serve them. Stretton's first church may have been one of these. It is more likely, however, to have been a 'patronal church' founded later when the minster system was beginning to decline, a development which coincided with the fragmentation of vast royal estates into self-contained local manors. This gradual but major change in society saw some field-churches taken over but, more frequently, new churches built by the lesser nobility.[19] It is probable that the first church in Stretton was founded by the local 'thegn' or leading landholder, for whereas many minsters had been associated with the larger administrative units called 'hundreds', the newer churches often coincided with the emerging manors. According to Professor Pounds, 'It is generally agreed that the majority of parish churches in rural England today derive from the patronal churches of Saxon thegns or Norman lords.'[20] Indeed, for a thegn the village church became essential to his status and part of his capital value, because as owner of the 'advowson' he appointed the priest and came to have an interest in offerings and tithes (whose payment became compulsory from the late tenth century), although in time the Church asserted its control by insisting that candidates had to be approved by the bishop. Such a benefactor was concerned, too, for the spiritual benefits of prayers in his lifetime and intercessions after his death. In many places the local thegn not only built the church but also provided a 'glebe', or land-holding, and a site, usually large enough to become a burial place—an acre, 'God's Acre', came to be the standard. It was the possession of a churchyard which came to distinguish a parish church from a field-church. The provision of a priest, certainly a literate one, may have presented a greater problem; sometimes one peripatetic priest may have served several churches on his lord's different estates. In many villages, perhaps including Stretton, the tenants will have welcomed and probably contributed to the building of a local church as it saved them long journeys, especially in winter, to a minster. The new system of rural parishes which slowly succeeded the larger minster *parochiae*, as more and more places established parochial independence, crystallised between the eleventh and the thirteenth centuries.

It is known from the Domesday entry that there was a church at Stretton in 1086, but the Norman building, some of which remains today, was almost certainly constructed later than that. The original church, therefore, was erected in the Saxon period, quite possibly in the mid- to late tenth century, a time of religious revival, associated with Archbishop Dunstan and other monastic reformers, and of greater peace after the Viking attacks of the ninth century and the gradual re-conquest of the Danelaw by King Alfred's successors. Churches at this time seemed to be springing up 'like mushrooms in the night'.[21] According to Dr. John Blair, 'Excavation of ordinary rural churches is producing a rapidly growing number of stone or timber phases of the tenth or eleventh century, but strikingly few of the eighth or ninth. The signs are that small private churches were still rare in 900, whereas by 1000 a church was something that any prosperous ceorl aspiring to thegnhood might be expected to have'.[22] The likelihood is that Stretton's late Saxon church was situated where the church stands today as that is hard by the original settlement. Since another modern authority considers that 'most parish churches were founded by local lords who often built them next to their place of residence',[23] Stretton's first church may well have been on land given by the local thegn close to his dwelling, for the site of the later Hall (near today's Scout Hut) could also have been where an ancient manor house stood. A wooden church building is probable as such constructions were general at that period, there was plenty of local timber, and the local community could provide the necessary skills. The interior walls are likely to have been plastered and painted with religious scenes to assist the understanding of the illiterate. However, short of discovering the original foundations, which could lie near or under the present church, we cannot be sure whether the first church building in Stretton, small and simple as it must have been, was made of timber or stone.

*

Stretton was fortunate in that it was remote enough to escape the Danish conquest of the ninth century and the marauding Viking army which reached as near as Welshpool and Bridgnorth in the 890s. It may not have been so fortunate with attacks from the Welsh. The threat from the Welsh in Powys had led the Mercian king in 853 to request help from the King of Wessex in regaining land in what became Herefordshire and Shropshire, and the English King Athelstan in 927 summoned five Welsh kings to Hereford and forced them to surrender to his power.[24] Fighting in the Welsh marches reached a new peak in the eleventh century when Gruffydd ap Llewelyn, king of Gwynedd and Powys, began to climb to supreme power in Wales. In 1039 he defeated a Saxon army near Welshpool and in 1055, allied with the English Earl Aelfgar and some Vikings, pillaged and set fire to Hereford. The warrior Bishop of Hereford was killed on an expedition against the Welsh the next year. Llewelyn's own defeat and death in 1063 were followed by a short time of peace.

The crises of 1066 were precipitated by the death of the childless King Edward the Confessor in January. When Harold Hardrada, king of Norway, invaded the north of England to challenge the new English king, Harold, formerly Earl of Wessex, he was confronted near York by Edwin, the young Earl of Mercia (and lord of the manor of Stretton) and his even younger brother, Morcar. The brothers' lack of military experience compared with that of their foes contributed to their crushing defeat at Fulford. Among the many who fell are likely to have been some of the Mercian thegns and landholders from Shropshire (county divisions had been created in the tenth century and the *Anglo-Saxon Chronicle* referred to the king's visit to Shropshire in 1006). Even Stretton, which was large enough to provide one warrior, could have appeared on the casualty list. The invaders were in their turn defeated days later by King Harold at the battle of Stamford Bridge. But the English losses, followed by the long march south, were critical factors in their defeat at Hastings on 14 October 1066 by William Duke of Normandy.

The Norman victory was to prove a turning-point for the country and for Stretton, too, although that was not to become apparent for a few years. Initially Edwin, who had survived Fulford, was allowed to remain Earl of Mercia and therefore lord of Stretton, although he was forced to stay with the new king's court. His later resistance to the Normans, however, was to lead to his downfall. There were outbreaks of rebellion in many parts of the country: in Shropshire the leader, in Edwin's absence, was Eadric the Wild whose estates included land at Hope Bowdler. In 1069, when there was a major rising in the north, sympathetic revolts in Staffordshire and Shropshire led Eadric with his Welsh allies to burn Shrewsbury and besiege its newly-built castle. William's response was uncompromising. The north was devastated and depopulated, and in January 1070 it was the turn of Cheshire and Shropshire to be similarly laid waste. Eadric submitted and was pardoned, but his home county, including Stretton to judge from the catastrophic fall in its value recorded in Domesday Book, suffered severely. Its Saxon church, however, would seem to have escaped destruction.

When Earl Edwin, who had taken no part in the rising, fled from the court in 1071 and was killed on his way to Scotland, the king lost no time in replacing him by one of his leading Norman barons. All over the country Normans and Frenchmen were being appointed to top secular and ecclesiastical positions as the upper echelons of English society virtually disappeared. Mercia itself ceased to exist. The man appointed Earl of Shrewsbury, with immense possessions and powers in the central Marches, was Roger de Montgomery. His appointment was of great significance for Stretton and for its church because he became lord and patron. As a favourite of Duke William and an experienced soldier, Roger was also rewarded with lands in Sussex while, of course, retaining his vast estates in Normandy. It is unlikely that Stretton claimed much of his attention. He was occupied in managing his lands, ruling for the king in the middle March, and holding the Welsh as far back as Montgomery, named after him and where he built the early Hen Domen castle. Thousands of motte and bailey castles were being thrown up all over the country, but nowhere more thickly than in Shropshire and Herefordshire; there is, however, no mention in Domesday Book of a castle at Stretton.

It was in Roger de Montgomery's years as Earl of Shrewsbury that King William took his historic decision of 1085 to have a survey made of the whole country. The information compiled in Domesday Book is invaluable for Stretton as for so many places. The entry for Stretton[25] reads as follows:

It was therefore a 'demesne' manor, held by Earl Roger himself and not granted to a vassal; as such it was not assigned to a particular 'hundred' within the county of Shropshire. Twenty years earlier it had been held by Earl Edwin, as it had probably been held (as Wistanstow was) by his father Earl Aelfgar and by his grandparents Earl Leofric and Lady Godiva. It was an area still largely forested. 'It is scarcely too much to say that more than one half of the county, including almost the whole stretch of Shropshire south of the county town ... was forest under the early Norman rule'.[26] The manor of Stretton included, in 1086, four berewicks or outlying hamlets which can probably be identified as All Stretton, Little Stretton, Minton and Whittingslow. It contained eight hides of land, perhaps about a thousand acres.[27] On the demesne land, which produced directly for the lord, there were three ploughs and six male and two female slaves, the males probably serving as three plough teams, so reducing the labour services of the villeins.[28] The two females may have been maidservants, implying that this great earl had an occasional residence within the circuit of the manor where he stayed when hunting in the Long Mynd forest. The community also included 18 villeins who held a landed stake in the village fields, and eight bordars, the small-holders and craftsmen; between them they had twelve ploughs. With 35 males specifically mentioned, the total population could have been between 140 and 175.[29] There was a mill and in the woodland five 'hayes' or hedged enclosures for the capture of game, usually roebuck, for royal hunting. It was reckoned that there was sufficient land for a further six ploughs. The fall in value since the Conquest was striking: from £13 to £5, presumably the result of Welsh raids and the punitive devastation of 1070. Of Minton it was recorded: 'Was and is waste'.[30]

What is of special interest is the information that there was a priest and a church,[31] for it is the first documentary reference to either in Stretton's history. The priest was included with the villeins and bordars: he, too, worked in the fields, for the church probably enjoyed a small endowment. He may well have been married. The church, as already suggested, was of Saxon origin and perhaps a hundred years old. It seems highly improbable that the Norman church, partly visible today in the nave of St. Laurence's, had been built by 1086. For some years after the Conquest the Normans had been stretched to impose their authority; when they did begin to build, their first priorities, after defensive castles, were imposing cathedrals, abbeys and great churches. 'Before the end of the eleventh century most of the larger English churches had been pulled down and were being re-built in the Norman variety of the Romanesque style',[32] such as can be seen in the monasteries of Jumièges and Caen. Roger de Montgomery, whose second wife, Adeliza, was renowned for her piety, built Shrewsbury Abbey in his last years. Shortly before his death in 1094 he took his vows there as a Benedictine monk.

It was the sons of his first marriage, however, to the notoriously selfish and cruel Mabel de Bellême, who succeeded him in the earldom, first Hugh and, on his death, Robert. Perhaps fortunately for Stretton, Robert de Bellême became involved in the baronial rebellion early in the reign of Henry I and was in 1102 deprived of all his English estates. The earldom of Shrewsbury disappeared and, by escheat, Stretton became a royal demesne manor, which it remained for most of the next two centuries.

*

The patronage of Stretton's church also passed to the crown, although it is not for more than a hundred years that the first known rector emerges. The outstanding development in the parish in the twelfth century was the building of a stone church. In Dr. John Leonard's judgement, 'It is probable that in the twelfth century at least 150 parish churches were built in Shropshire, an impressive record for a sparsely-populated, impoverished county, remote from the power-centre of the country'.[33] It is not possible to state certainly that the new church in Stretton was erected on the same site as its Saxon predecessor, although in a small settlement it cannot have been far away. Nor is it possible to allocate a precise date to the Norman building. The middle years of Henry I's reign, say between 1110 and 1130, seem most probable. It was at this time that the chronicler William of Malmesbury wrote that one might see 'churches rise in every village'.[34] By then the Welsh border was quieter, the civil war of Stephen's reign lay in the future, the country was growing in population and prosperity, and masons were mastering the new technology and style of Norman architecture.

Not that the new parish church at Stretton required a mason of great experience for it was a simple structure; but the appropriate stone had to be chosen and particular care taken with foundations, doorways and roof. The design was almost certainly a basic two-cell one — nave and chancel, very similar to but slightly larger than the one that can still be seen at Heath Chapel in Corvedale and dating from the same period. The nave can be described with some confidence as much of it stands today, though significant modifications have been

Heath Chapel in Corvedale

The north wall of the Norman nave, with flat buttress

made to the original. The walls, now stripped of later plaster, may be like they were when first raised—although Normans, too, plastered interior church walls and decorated them with religious scenes except for the modern pointing which emphasises the irregular courses. They are four feet thick, with rough courses of undressed stone known as 'rubble'. Much of the sandstone of the nave walls is Hoar Edge Grit from east of the Lawley; it is buff, brown or pale grey-white in colour.[35] Large dressed blocks form the typically Norman flat buttresses that protrude on the corners of the west wall. Other stone includes Chatwall sandstone, most likely from Soudley, and some ancient pre-Cambrian rubble probably from the local quarry at All Stretton, besides the occasional pebble turned up by the plough. The infilling of the walls was almost certainly local, perhaps even from the quarry on the north side of the lower Burway.

The main entrance to the church was the south door, whose exterior is now concealed from view by the vestry. The characteristic semi-circular arch, however, stands out, and closer inspection in the vestry

The south door of the church, the main entrance for seven centuries. The Scripture was probably added when a porch was erected

The ornamental western capital of the south door

reveals that the door is flanked with one order of shafts and a Norman buttress on the west side only. The western shaft capital has a square abacus ornamented with volutes. The text, 'Reverence my sanctuary', from Leviticus 19:30, over the doorway on what was its outside was probably added when a porch was erected to shelter the door.

The north door is even more interesting. Although the inside was bricked up in the Victorian restoration, the arch stands higher than on the opposite side. It is the exterior that catches the attention. The doorway is unmistakably Norman, recessed in a thickened wall and with two rolls to the arch. The abaci on the west side are carved with rosette, cable and round billet ornaments. The capitals opposite are not the original ones but have been replaced, in a botched repair, by a much later piece of stone which Dean Cranage, in his *magnum opus The Churches of Shropshire*, surmises is 'apparently a Perpendicular basement moulding turned upside down!' The whole is quite plain,

The north door, blocked up 200 years ago. Above left the Sheila-na-gig can just be seen

12

with less elaborate sculpting than at Heath Chapel or Holdgate. The door itself looks rather ancient but, like the door to the tower, was probably inserted in the early eighteenth century. What attracts most visitors today is not the doorway but the 'sheila-na-gig' above it which features in the guide-books. Although it has been thought that this figure might be of St. Nicholas and Cranage considered it 'a quaint representation of a human figure', there is no doubt that it is an early fertility figure, though not so well preserved as those at Holdgate or at Kilpeck in Herefordshire. 'This curious piece of ancient sculpture from ignorance and want of taste [or awareness of what it represents] has been smeared over repeatedly with the chuchwardens' brush of obliv-ious purity', as one antiquarian records.[36] No-one is sure of the age or origin of

The Sheila-na-gig

the sheila-na-gig. It seems most likely that it was inserted into the original Norman wall, probably by builders who retained some belief in the old pagan practices, for popular religion was still 'informed by pagan festivals and deeply coloured by superstitions with which the Church had compromised'.[37]

The nave is eighteen feet wide and was probably nearly double that in length, giving an area of over six hundred square feet, rather smaller than average for churches of this period,[38] but able to accommodate more than a hundred standing—at least half the population. If the chancel was built in the same proportions as at Heath Chapel, which it seems reasonable to assume, it would have been about twenty feet long and thirteen feet broad. The east end, which might have featured a semi-circular apse, another characteristic of contemporary ecclesiastical architecture, would therefore have been about where the front pews now stand, for there was, of course, no crossing, just a simple semi-circular arch separating nave from chancel.

Heath Chapel also provides the clearest indication of what the windows would have been like, for there only one later window has been inserted. There are likely to have been lancet windows, narrow on the outside but deeply splayed on the inside (like those in the transepts added in the later extension, except that those are pointed), two on each side of the nave and of the chancel,

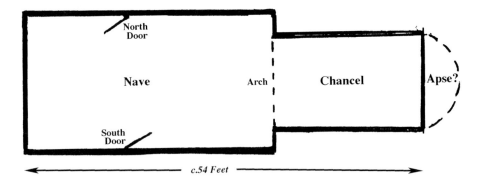

Plan of the two-cell Norman church

and perhaps one at the east end and west end. Initially they may have been without glass. The interior would have been dark, lighted only by candles. The present roof of the nave goes back to the thirteenth century; we can only assume that its Norman predecessor was similarly if more simply finished, with perhaps a thatched roof.

Who made the decision to build a new church or provided the funds remains unknown. As one of many royal manors it is unlikely to have received great financial help from the king whose local steward would perhaps have been more concerned to raise money for his master than to spend it. Possibly the initiative came from the Bishop of Hereford, keen that the churches of his diocese should be built of stone and in the new style. Very probably its construction owed most to the local community, which wanted a church commensurate with its size and dignity. The financial contributions of the more wealthy could have been supplemented by a royal donation, perhaps in the form of a gift of land to extend the churchyard or enhance the endowment. The bishop would surely have consecrated the new church, though whether it was originally dedicated to St. Laurence is again unknown. Certainly it was an episcopal responsibility to visit the parish. Bishops who were conscientious, and not too involved as advisers of the king, will have included Stretton in their perambulations. Robert de Béthune, bishop from 1131 to 1148, would have been gladly welcomed because he was a man of holy life, whose corpse was reputed to have worked miracles on its way back to Hereford after his death at the Council of Rheims. On his visitations the bishop would perhaps have preached, confirmed boys and girls, and generally overseen the condition of his flock. His occasional visitations may already have been supplemented by those of an archdeacon whose area of responsibility was often made to coincide with the boundaries of a shire; an archdeacon of Shropshire is mentioned in a mid-twelfth century document. At this early date we do not know who held the living of Stretton, but initially at least the parish priest was likely to be a local man, ordained and instituted by the bishop. Stretton was perhaps fortunate that it escaped impropriation by a monastery which was the fate of many parish churches. In such cases the monastery usually received the great tithe of corn, leaving the lesser tithes to a vicar who was appointed to undertake the parochial duties. All who bred animals or raised crops were bound to pay a tenth of the yield to the church to be divided into three parts, one for the maintenance of the fabric, one for the poor and one for the ministers of the church—though the first two progressively lost out to the clergy. As a royal manor, however, Stretton may not have been much better off than impropriated parishes, for the king tended to use his patronage to reward officers in royal service, they in turn regarding their parishes simply as a source of income. Many rectors were therefore absentees who pocketed the greater share of the income of the living and, like the impropriating religious houses, left a vicar or chaplain to perform their duties. Such vicars augmented their meagre incomes by working on their share of the land.

The instituted rector, or his vicar if he was an absentee, received the cure of souls and was required to minister to and instruct the people. His duties included prayer, pastoral care, anointing the sick, hearing confession, administering penance, celebrating mass daily, perhaps preaching (though that was rare at this time), preparing candidates for confirmation, and administering the eucharist to the faithful, usually three times a year—at Christmas, Easter and Whitsuntide—and to those near death. He conducted the rites of passage—solemnising matrimony, baptising, and burying the dead. He may have charged for baptism because he had to pay for chrism (the oil used in that rite and for anointing the sick), which he fetched from the cathedral after the bishop had consecrated it each Maundy Thursday. Burial in the churchyard required the gift of part of a dead man's chattels, a due known as soul-scot or, later, 'the mortuary'. By the twelfth century the parson may have been celibate for the Church had made periodic, though often vain, efforts to end clerical marriage. His social position remained low, his economic status approximately that of a villein. But because of the small size of the community and his detailed personal knowledge of all his parishioners, the conscientious parson could perform a most valuable function in teaching the faith, comforting the needy, restraining violence and civilising manners. Unfortunately many did not live up to this ideal. Yet the good priest will have been regarded by his flock as a learned friend and counsellor. He may not have known much Latin and possessed few books, but he could teach his people the Lord's Prayer, the articles of the faith and something of the meaning of baptism and the Mass, which they could stand to watch through the narrow chancel arch. He may have touched their imagination or stirred their moral sense with tales of the saints. He was also the likeliest person to have taught their children to read and write and perhaps the elements of Latin grammar. And yet, as one of only rudimentary education, isolated from the minster and the Church hierarchy, but living and working daily alongside his simple neighbours, he is likely to have practised and inculcated a popular form of Christianity, in which Scripture, liturgy and moral teaching interacted with local folk culture and echoes of pagan practices.

As for their new church, so solid beside their rude dwellings, Stretton parishioners will have valued it not only as their place of worship, but as their meeting-place, community centre and refuge in the event of attack. Such multiple use would not have seemed incongruous to them, for the church was as much a part of their lives as the oxen pulling the plough or the bucks in the king's forest on the hills. The Christian faith and the practices of religion were by now integrated into the life of society. The Church taught the importance of living in community, the special duty owed by Christians to the poor, the obligation to give alms, to feed the hungry and to care for the sick. The very seasons that governed rural life were reflected in the Church's year: Christmas festivities, Lent when supplies ran low (but when plough alms had to be paid), and harvest celebrations. And when life ended, the churchyard, ever a sanctuary, offered a final resting-place.

2

THE CRUCIFORM CHURCH

S tretton begins to emerge from its obscurity half a century after the completion of its Norman church. Administrative records, which improved with
the development of royal government in the reign of Henry II (1154-89), illu-
minate the changes taking place in national life and even shed a little light on
the remote manor of Stretton since it was part of the royal demesne.

The Rev. R.W. Eyton's heroic labours on these early documentary sources,
which provide the substance of his massive *Antiquities of Shropshire*, have
been a blessing to many who have delved into the history of the county.
Although his account of Stretton-en-le-dale, as it was then known, opens with
the Domesday entry, he advances at once to the accession of Henry II in 1154.
The manor then, according to the Pipe Roll, had the reputed fiscal value of £4
per annum. That was the amount for which the Sheriff of Shropshire, who
'farmed' the manor (i.e. collected payments for the king) was accountable to
the royal exchequer. At that time the whole sum was paid directly to Engelard
de Pitchford (later known as Engelard de Stretton), until 1177 the castellan of
the royal fortress in Strettondale, now known as Brockhurst Castle. This was
probably of recent construction, possibly even in the first year of Henry's reign,
as Hugh de Mortimer, with castles at Wigmore, Bridgnorth and Cleobury
Mortimer, was still defying his authority in the Middle Marches. Engelard, who
was 'a man of great importance in his day',[1] lost his position through tres-
passing on the royal forest. His successors as custodians of the castle in the
following half century were Simon fitzSimon (1177-89), William fitzAlan
(1192-97) who was also the sheriff, and Cassivellaunus fitzOen (1197-1208).
William and James fitzSimon, sons of the former custodian of the castle, seem
to have been considered as lords of the manor from 1192 to 1194, as was
Cassivellaunus during his term as castellan. He was probably dismissed
because as the half-brother of Gwenwynwyn, Prince of Powys, he was
involved in the latter's rebellion and ravaging of the central March in 1208, for
which King John, at Shrewsbury, deprived him of his estates.

Sadly the records of the second half of the twelfth century contain no reference to Stretton's church. However, by this time it had become established that

only one church—the parish church—could have responsibility for the cure of souls of a group of inhabitants. 'Burial rights, baptismal rights and tithes became the normal definition of a parish church'.[2] This led to the stricter definition of parish boundaries and the annual practice of 'beating the bounds'. In Stretton, as in many places, the parish was roughly coterminous with the manor. The first known description of the parish boundaries appears in the records of the manor court dated 15 January 43 Elizabeth I (1601).[3] Using natural features like hills, streams and hedges to delineate the confines of the parish, it begins:

> From Hopegate to Bentley's Green, and so following the borders of the Cwms to the end of the Hope Way over against Cornbatch Cross; and from thence crossing to the Cwms' head, and from thence right over the Caradoc Hill to the Marches wall, and so following the water to the Watling Street to Botwood, and so to a forked oak in Brown Hill's hedge, the parish compassing the township of Botfield...

The parish so defined formed a rectangle roughly five miles north-south and three miles east-west and encompassed about 10,000 acres. It stretched from Womerton in the north to Hamperley in the south, and from the Portway on the top of the Long Mynd on the west side to the eastern slopes of the Stretton Hills. In an anti-clockwise direction from the north its neighbouring parishes were Leebotwood, Woolstaston, Smethcott, Ratlinghope, Wentnor, Norbury, Wistanstow, Acton Scott, Hope Bowdler and Cardington.

The priest who served this large parish was still one of the people, but the nature of the faith he proclaimed and perhaps its expression in worship were changing. In the early twelfth century an intellectual and religious revival in Christendom gathered momentum, spreading from scholars, monks and priests ultimately to affect all people. 'There were significant shifts in the objects of popular worship. Awe of God the Father was almost replaced by a Christocentric piety, strongly re-inforced by a cult of the Blessed Virgin Mary. Christ ceased to be depicted on the cross as the triumphant God, eyes open, serene, without pain. Instead He became the dying and suffering Lord, a piteous creature'.[4] The advent of the Cistercians—their great abbeys were founded at this time—popularised this more gentle and mystical faith, with their greater reverence for the Virgin Mary, their patron saint. At about this time the position adopted by worshippers in prayer started to change. 'Originally, Christians had prayed standing, with arms raised high to heaven. Now they began to assume the posture taken by feudal vassals when performing fealty to their lord, on their knees with hands joined together before their bowed heads'.[5] But it was not all peace and piety within the Church. The Papacy's determination to emancipate the Church from lay

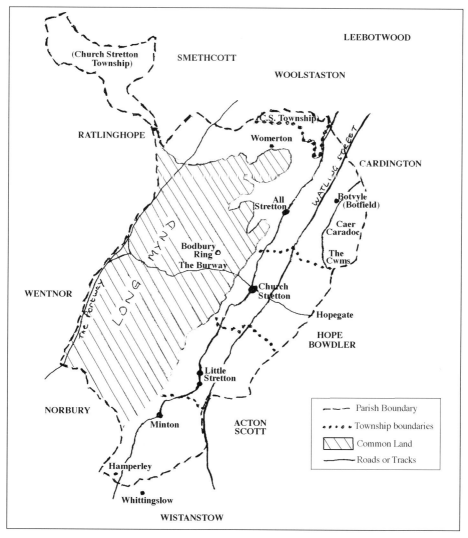

Map showing the parish and its neighbours

control provoked clashes with rulers in England and on the continent. The bitter struggle between Henry II and his archbishop, Thomas Becket, culminated in 1170 with the murder of the latter near the altar at Canterbury. The folk of Stretton may not have understood the conflicts over lay investiture or criminous clerks, but they would have heard from travellers of the quarrel between the king and the primate and its terrible sequel.

It is safe to assume that Stretton's population at this period was slowly growing for in England these were in general years of peace and increasing prosperity. In the century since Domesday Book the national area under the plough had expanded steadily and the animal population even faster. This was particularly true of sheep, valued for their milk made into cheese, their skins for parchment and, above all, their wool as the raw material for cloth. Most villages produced their own home-spun cloth and towns still more, but it was the value of wool for export that accounted for the expanding flocks of sheep. English wool was prized as far afield as Florence and was the staple of the cloth industry of Flanders. And of the small, short-wool mountain sheep, whose fleece could be carded into soft woollen yarn, the best and most valuable clip came from the Welsh border. Strettondale, its surrounding hill pastures extending as forests were cut back—Eyton refers to the community being fined in 1209 by the Court of the Forest for such an 'assart' or forest clearing—must surely have been among the beneficiaries from this demand. This does not mean that all members of the community shared in the growing prosperity. Some had nothing more than a few goats, but these they could pasture on the unwooded hills, 'a privilege enjoyed by even the poor people of the manor of Stretton in the time of every king, and which indeed constituted their liveli-hood'.[6] The livestock of even the better-off were too frequently lean beasts of poor breeding. As for cultivation, the practice had changed little, the farmer's day was long, the tools still basic, and the land often under-nourished. Moreover, villagers still had to work some days each week on the king's demesne, with heavier demands at harvest-time, in addition to paying rent. With Stretton so close to the Welsh border there were also occasional raids, perhaps with loss of life or violation of person, apart from looted homesteads, damaged or blackened fields and animals driven away.

Eyton remarked on the disclosure in the Pipe Rolls that of five tallages (charges levied on the royal demesne) of Henry II's reign only one , that of 1177, was assessed upon Stretton. This is unlikely to be explained by senti-ment, yet even less likely by poverty, for in Strettondale these were good times, prosperity enhanced by the proximity of the royal castle with its additional demand for food, handicrafts and trade. Indeed, David Bilbey believes that it was early in the next century that Church Stretton began to assume the basic layout that is still apparent today. 'This was a peak period in the plantation of medieval towns, and Stretton does exhibit many features which suggest that it was moved from Town Brook valley to the present position at about that time. The skeletons of burgage plots, a wide market street, a back lane, and what seem to be the remains of the "aratral curve" of the open fields on which the town was built can still be traced'.[7] The open field would have been the Overfield, later called the Hollenfield, which extended up what is now Rectory field. The other fields were Ashbrook (then Nasbrook) Field and Snatchfield on the east side of the dale beyond the water meadows. Bilbey's view is supported by the writ of King John (1199-1216) which was dated 26 June 1214 ordering the Sheriff of Shropshire to advertise a weekly market to be held on Wednesdays at the king's manor of Strettondale, and also a yearly fair to be

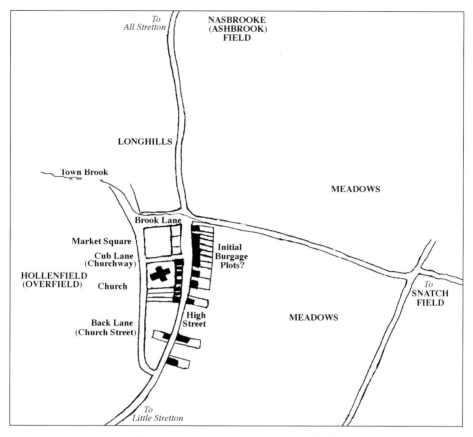

Plan of the town and the open fields

held on the feast day of the Assumption (15 August), so long as the market and fair did not injure any neighbouring assemblies of like character.[8] This was a significant event in the history of Church Stretton, although there is some evidence that the market failed to establish itself permanently. Whatever length of life it enjoyed, the market is likely to have been held in the present market square for 'market places are often found next to churchyards in small market towns which grew up in the twelfth and thirteenth centuries'.[9]

Six years before Stretton's market first opened, King John's quarrel with Pope Innocent III over the choice of Stephen Langton as Archbishop of Canterbury had led to England being placed under an interdict. This meant the suspension of all church services, except the baptism of infants and penance for the dying. There could be no confirmations, no Christian marriage, no church-yard burial, no Mass, no absolution of sins, and no consecration. Even the church bells were silenced. For the people of Stretton, as elsewhere, this was a grievous blow. 'The pious were left without comfort and ordinary men and women without the familiar ceremonies'.[10] Yet life went on. It was more than six years later, on 2 July 1214, that the interdict was finally lifted—just six days after the announcement of Stretton's market and fair. Approval for such an innovation could be given only by the king, who at this time was in his French dominions campaigning against his arch-enemy King Philip Augustus of France. The king, of course, conducted the business of state wherever he was, but Stretton's market can hardly have been of the first importance in the midst of a campaign that was to end disastrously with John's defeat at Bouvines only a month later. He must have delegated the decision to his officers of state in England—or had a special desire to reward one of his courtiers.

It is surely no coincidence that in 1214 the manor of Stretton was in the hands of one of the king's close associates, Hugh de Neville. It seems that he had been castellan there since 1209, as the sheriff, when drawing up accounts at Michaelmas 1212 for the previous three years, assigned '£12 in Stretton to Hugh de Neville for custody of the castle', and stated that 'Hugh himself ought to render an account of his trust'. No such account is preserved, nor do the Pipe Rolls of 1213-14 assign the £4 annual revenues of Stretton to Neville or any other. That he still held land there in 1214 is, however, vouched for by his assessment for 40s. to the king's war chest in respect of 'one knight's fee at Stretton, which had once been Engelard de Stretton's'.[11] Stretton itself was assessed at 10 marks, or £6 13s. 4d., for a tallage. Although both payments remained in arrears against Hugh's name in 1219, he explained that the money had been spent on works at Stretton Castle. None of this is surprising for Hugh was a great man, one of King John's henchmen and a favourite gaming companion.[12] He was, indeed, the king's Chief Forester, a role he had taken over from his uncle Alan who had held the office under Henry II. He is unlikely to have done more than pay occasional visits to Stretton because the royal forests were very extensive and he also held Marlborough Castle, his master's favourite haunt.

At a time when many nobles were disaffected, King John must have valued Hugh de Neville's loyalty and friendship. It seems quite probable, therefore, that it was at his instigation, though no doubt originally at the request of the leading inhabitants of Stretton, that King John, or one of his chief advisers, gave the royal approval for the market and fair in June 1214. A weekly market afforded a valuable opportunity for local exchange; an annual fair could attract buyers and sellers from much further afield. Since Stretton now became the smallest settlement in the county to enjoy these privileges, its importance and chance to prosper were greatly enhanced.

What more natural, then, than that in praise to God for His goodness it should be proposed to extend and embellish the hundred-year-old parish church? This would both accommodate the growing population and create a structure worthy of a new market town. There is no documentary proof that it was at this moment that the decision was taken to transform the Norman building into a cruciform church, but Dean Cranage is quite clear from the architectural evidence, that 'considerable alterations took place at the end of the twelfth century or very early in the thirteenth'.[13] Since, in Dr. Moorman's opinion, 'The early years of the thirteenth century saw little church building for the times were unsettled and the interdict crushed any such enterprise',[14] the other periods possible for the extension of Stretton's church are the reign of Richard I (1189-99), when the fitzSimon brothers were lords of the manor, or the opening years of John's rule. There are three reasons why the beginning of the reign of Henry III (1216-72) is to be preferred as the most likely time for the rebuilding. First, the introduction of Gothic features into church buildings, initially mixed with Norman in the Transitional period, is likely to have reached so distant a part of the kingdom later than in the economically more advanced south and east. Second, Holy Trinity Church at Wistanstow, which, as Sir Stephen Glynne observed,[15] bears a striking resemblance to Stretton's church, was surely the work of the same team of masons. Which was built first? We do not know, but the inclusion of some round-headed lancet windows in the north transept at Wistanstow suggests the earlier start. If this were so, one can imagine the interest and envy with which the people of Stretton watched the building of this neighbouring church. Their inevitable response was to invite the masons to transform their two-cell Norman building into a similar cruciform church. The third reason is that by 1214 Stretton had a rector, as well as a lord, capable of pulling strings and perhaps also of making a substantial donation to the construction costs. This, Stretton's first known rector, was Ralph de Neville, nephew of Chief Forester Hugh, who held the castle and manor of Stretton for the king. Ralph was himself an officer in the royal Chancery sufficiently senior to expedite his own presentation to the living at Stretton, and to another at Ludgershall in Wiltshire, also on 6 May 1214[16]—just a few weeks before the market and fair were announced. Stretton, at this significant moment, had friends in high places, friends capable of persuading local landowners to donate timber or grant access to quarries.

It would seem unlikely that construction started during 1214, or during the next two turbulent years. The baronial revolt that led to King John's acceptance of the terms of Magna Carta in June 1215 may have passed Stretton by, but when mutual distrust still led to civil war, and the king sought the active support of his allies on the Welsh border, the people of Stretton did not escape involvement. On 2 August 1215 John fitzAlan, possibly the son of William fitzAlan, castellan at Stretton in the 1190s and a former sheriff, was reported to have seized the castle as an act of rebellion. The king ordered its immediate return to William Barat, an officer of Hugh de Neville. On 19 August, however, the king directed Hugh to surrender the castle to Hugh de Mortimer, the great Marcher lord whose power was centred on Wigmore in Herefordshire, and who was to hold the fortress in Strettondale at the king's pleasure. Whether or not this indicates Hugh de Neville's fall from favour, or merely a consolidation of the royal hold on the middle March under one lord, it is impossible to say, but when in May 1216 the king was in retreat after the French invasion in support of his rebellious barons, his long-term friend Hugh de Neville did desert him. John's subsequent loss of his treasure train in the Wash and his death in October brought his reign to an ignominious end.

*

The decision not to build an entirely new church in Stretton was almost certainly due to inadequate financial resources. 'In most parishes fund-raising was a slow or fitful process. Few could manage the sudden outlay that was required for a complete re-building'.[17] Whatever the reason, the church of today is what it is because the agreement then was to leave the nave standing but to pull down the chancel and replace it with a lofty crossing opening out to two transepts and a larger chancel and surmounted by a central tower. The retention of the nave at least left somewhere to worship while work went on.

If we are uncertain of the date of the extension, we may readily describe what was done because the church in 2000 is substantially the church of the early thirteenth century. Its total length is 100 feet, the greatest width 67 feet. In addition to the Hoar Edge Grit stone as used in the nave, the builders of the extension chose Grinshill dressed blocks for the corners and door- and window-jambs, and the walls show widespread use of fine- to medium-grained sandstone almost certainly from Soudley, where it is 'beautifully banded purple, brown and green'.[18] Also evident are thinner 'Chatwall flags'.

The outstanding feature of the interior is the crossing with its four beautiful arches

Transitional arches

of cream-coloured Grinshill stone which support the central tower. They exhibit a mixture of Norman and Early English characteristics, described by the architectural term 'Transitional'. The abaci, or flat slabs, on the capitals of the supporting piers are square and moulded in the usual Norman manner. On the other hand, the arches are pointed in the Gothic style, clearly different from the semi-circular arched doorways of the Norman nave. Other Early English features include the fillets on the columns, the water-hollows and square plinths of the western columns and, on the capitals of the eastern respond of the south arch, the stiff-leaf foliage carving.

The beautifully carved heads, four females and one male on the

Water hollow at the base of the south-west pier

Carved heads on the eastern respond of the north arch

Carved heads on the eastern respond of the south arch

eastern respond of the north arch and three males in the same position on the south arch, present acute problems of dating. Hardwick considered that they were 'exquisitely finished in the ornamental *style* [my italics] of the reign of Henry III',[19] but whether any of the heads were actually carved at that time is doubtful. In Pevsner's view the capitals and heads are 'much renewed'.[20] Certainly the southernmost head on the north arch is smaller and different in character from the others, with an awkward junction of the neck and capital,

Two volutes in the crossing, with square abaci above

26

while the male head on the north side protrudes less and wears a painful grimace. The three central heads on the north arch are much more damaged than the three on the opposite side of the chancel arch, which may be explained by David Parkes's note on his drawing of the church in 1808[21] that 'a capital on *one* [my italics] side of the cross aisle is curious' and his separate sketch of the heads from the north arch only. Since Cranage mentions the heads on both arches, it seems likely that a nineteenth-century rector, most probably Robert Pemberton, had a complementary group of heads in the medieval style added on the south arch. The heads, whenever fashioned, are shown in medieval head-gear, one perhaps wearing a crown. The opposite responds and all the capitals of the east and west arches have ornamental volutes, though not all of the same design, possibly on account of subsequent restoration. The columns of the north and south arches now terminate some distance above the floor, probably truncated when pews were erected.

Above the crossing there is now a late twentieth century memorial attached to the floor of the ringing chamber. Originally, with a shorter tower, there would have been no such floor, and the increased height, illuminated by the narrow windows now in the ringing chamber, would have greatly enhanced the impressiveness of the crossing.

North and south of the crossing rose the new transepts. Each had a door granting access from the outside. The doorway of the north transept, in its north-west corner and now blocked up as it leads only to the aisle added in the nineteenth century (today the Emmaus Chapel), is clearly Early English. The south transept doorway was not originally situated in its present central position in the south wall but in its western corner; it was

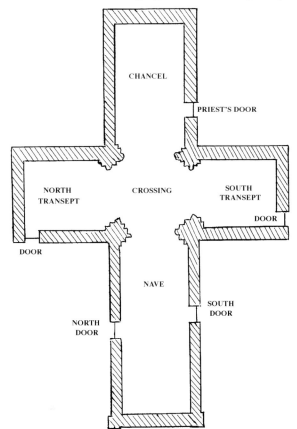

Plan of the cruciform church

Lancet window
in the south transept

moved in 1827 when the wall needed repair. Its exterior identifies it as Early English in style with hood moulding added later. The existence of these doors is strong evidence that the transepts were from the start side-chapels, a supposition apparently confirmed by a 1227 reference to a chaplain, and by the gift of land at Hodghurst beyond All Stretton to endow a chaplain by the later thirteenth century.[22] The chapels would have been very dark, the only natural light coming from splayed lancet windows of which one survives on the east wall of each transept. These became the Hesba Stretton and Dixon windows in the early twentieth century. The side-altars would have been positioned so that the light from the lancets fell directly on them. Similar lancets faced them on the west walls, lancets that were moved at the Victorian restoration to the west walls of the new aisles—one now in the Emmaus Chapel and the other the Wimberley window. The internal masonry of the north wall of the north transept

Thirteenth-century priest's
door in the south wall of the
chancel. The hood moulding is
probably seventeenth century

*The recess in the chancel
south wall—possibly an
aumbry, but more likely
once used as a piscina*

clearly reveals even today where two other lancet windows were situated (see p.52), matched no doubt in the south transept, before the large windows were inserted, most likely in the next century. The solitary corbel on the east wall of the north transept, perhaps the sole survivor of a pair in each transept, will probably have supported an image behind the altar. The roof timbers of the north transept are ancient but probably not the original; the south transept roof is later, perhaps early seventeenth century.

On the east side of the crossing was erected the new, larger chancel. It is 34 feet long and, like the transepts and nave, 18 feet wide. It came to be separated from the rest of the church by a rood screen, but that may not have been in place till the fifteenth century, although a great rood or crucifix may have been

suspended from the ceiling. On the north side may be seen the shouldered or Caernarvon arch where a door then gave access to the tower staircase. Another door on the north side, visible in the water-colour by John Homes Smith painted before the organ chamber was built (see p.192), led into a tiny vestry which was possibly part of the original building. On the south side is the priest's door giving him direct entry to the chancel, which was his domain and his responsibility.

*Two-lght window in the
south wall of the chancel.
The hood moulding is probably
of the seventeenth century*

Cranage believes this doorway is the original one as it has the heavy roll moulding often used in the thirteenth century, but again with later hood moulding. In the south wall of the chancel today is a stone recess, around which the later carved reredos has been fitted. Its date is uncertain but its proximity to the altar suggests that it was a either a piscina for the priest to wash the chalice and his hands, or an aumbry, (a recess to hold the sacred vessels), although these were usually on the north side. The glass and most likely the tracery of the present east window was inserted in 1819, although Pevsner dates the tracery from before 1639. Its predecessor is likely to have replaced three lancet windows similar to those still to be seen at Wistanstow. Further lancet windows on the side walls were replaced by the present double-light windows. The two small windows on the south side nearer the chancel arch probably belong to the later Perpendicular period when perhaps the rood screen and loft were installed. The chancel walls, as was common in that period, slope slightly inwards at the bottom. The medieval roof timbers are probably not as early as

The tower as it is today, extended in the Perpendicular period

those in the nave. The floor of the church may not yet have been paved but remained compacted, flattened earth.

Above the crossing was the tower. In the early thirteenth century it was not the tower we see today for it was extended in the Perpendicular period, though at what date is one of the most difficult questions to answer about the church's history. The first tower was certainly more squat. Looking at the tower from the outside one can readily discern the rubble walls extending as high as the apex of the roof, with some light admitted through slit windows into what is now the ringers' chamber. The change from rubble to dressed stone is very striking when seen

The change in walling as seen inside the ringing chamber

An imaginative reconstruction of the original cruciform church
(by kind permission of David Bilbey)

from the inside just below the ceiling. From the outside, seven or eight courses of this dressed stone or ashlar are visible but with a surface that appears more worn than the ashlar of the top stage and battlements. This is the present clock chamber and presumably the bell chamber of the original tower. Its windows, one on each face, are of Early English lancet style, contrasting sharply with the larger Perpendicular louvred openings above. It seems probable that the first tower was finished with a pyramidal roof, or even a mini-spire, foreshadowing the roof of today but without the battlements.

The completion of the extended church was a fitting event to mark the establishment of the first market and the new layout of the town. Within half a century there appear the first recorded references to the dedication of the church to St. Laurence and to the town's new name of Church Stretton.

3
THE CROWN AS PATRON :
THE FIRST KNOWN RECTORS

During the thirteenth century the crown's patronage of the benefice of Stretton-en-le-dale was exercised more to the advantage of the king than of the local congregation. The first known rector illustrates this well, even though he may have played a valuable part in the rebuilding of the church. At the time of his presentation in May 1214 Ralph de Neville, who came from a baronial family in the north-east, was a senior clerk in the royal Chancery, a position he may have owed to his kinsman, Hugh de Neville, the King's Forester. By this time he was important enough to process his own appointment; he may indeed already have been Keeper of the Great Seal under the Lord Chancellor, Bishop Peter des Roches. He would not have taken such action without the approval of the king, whose own treasury was not depleted if he could reward his leading servants with ecclesiastical preferment. Neville was certainly doing very well in this respect: in April 1214 he had been made Dean of Lichfield and the next month acquired not only the living of Stretton but also that of Ludgershall in Wiltshire. Other benefices followed: Ingham and Meringthorp in Norfolk later in 1214, Penrith in 1215, Hameleden and a prebend in London in 1216. With his back to the wall in his struggle with his rebellious barons, King John rewarded loyalty liberally—particularly at the expense of the Church. Ralph de Neville duly collected the income due to the rector from tithe and glebe and paid a priest, perhaps only a pittance, to serve in his place. He may never have even come to Stretton, unless it was to ensure that he was getting all that he should,[1] to appoint a steward to superintend his lands and revenues, and to check that the vicar was performing his ministerial functions. But, as has been indicated, he may have used some of this income to help build the new church, and later, as a bishop, it is known that 'he was a benefactor to his church and see, expending much on the repair of the cathedral'.[2]

When appointed rector, Ralph de Neville was still probably only in minor orders for it was not until 1220 that Pope Honorius III relieved him of the ecclesiastical disabilities consequent upon his illegitimate birth. By 1218 he was

Vice-Chancellor, in 1221 acting Chancellor, and in 1226 he was finally appointed to that great office, granted for life the next year. By then he was no longer rector of Stretton, having surrendered his other benefices when he became Bishop of Chichester in 1222. 'Neville was typical of a large class of bishops who were really, by training and inclination, civil servants and statesmen rather than ecclesiastics'.[3] Yet he had already achieved higher honours than any subsequent rector of Stretton and still greater only just eluded him. He was chosen in 1231 by the monks of Canterbury as the next arch-bishop, an election approved by the king but quashed by the Pope who was advised that Neville was 'swift of speech and bold of deed', capable of taking an independent line in relations with Rome. Seven years later he was elected bishop by the monks of the great see of Winchester, only to fail again as the king wanted the see for his brother-in-law. Ralph de Neville proved himself not only a great administrator but also a skilful political operator, holding on to his office until his death in 1244 through years of turbulence occasioned by the king's changing favourites. 'Since Neville on several occasions resisted irre-sponsible acts of the king and generally discharged his office in an even-handed manner, his whole career broadcast the value of great officials of state appointed in this way'.[4] The contemporary chronicler Matthew Paris described him as 'a steadfast pillar of loyalty and truth in state affairs',[5] rendering equal justice to all and especially the poor. He also built up the endowments of the dean and chapter of Chichester. He was, however, always a king's man, starting as a royal clerk and going on to become effectively the head of the civil service. He lacked the saintly qualities of his successor at Chichester, later canonised as St. Richard, the author of the well-known and lovely prayer which concludes:

> O most merciful Redeemer, Friend and Brother, may I know Thee more
> clearly, love Thee more dearly, and follow Thee more nearly. Amen.

As Neville's successor at Stretton the king, in a Patent writ addressed to the Bishop of Hereford on 18 November 1222, presented Walter de Brackley (or Brackele), another royal servant:

> Walterus de Brackele, clericus, habet litteras de presentacione ad eccle-
> siam de Strattundel, que vacet et est de donatione domini Regis, et diri-
> guntur littere Herefordensi episcopo.[6]

Although various references exist to his activities in the king's service at Westminster, a tenure roll records that he was still holding the church of Stretton by the king's gift in October 1227. The next month, however, another Patent writ refers to the resignation of Walter de Brackley, now Joint Clerk of the Royal Wardrobe (in effect Treasurer of the Royal Household) from the parsonage of Strettondale on his consecration as Bishop of Meath in Ireland. In 1233 he was translated to the see of Ossory.

In the absence of these early rectors, others served the church in Stretton on their behalf, some of their possible names emerging from contemporary documents. In the early years of Henry III's reign, probably before 1224, and therefore in Neville's last or Brackley's first years as rector, a certain Walter, son of Walter of Stretton, is recorded in the Cartulary of Shrewsbury Abbey[7] as having given to the abbey kitchen a messuage in the town of Shrewsbury. His gift was witnessed by Gilbert, reeve of Stretton, and Hugh, clerk of the same town. Hugh may be the first known priest actually to minister at the parish church. A few years later, when Walter de Brackley resigned, the Patent Rolls record on 14 November 1227 that the king gave the church of Stretton in Strettondale to William Friland but limited his share of the income to 25 marks per annum as the 'parsonage'. The remainder and the 'vicarage' were to go to one Walter, chaplain of Strettondale, who in the Charter Roll of 1228 is named as Walter de Mora. Eyton's view was that Brackley had been both rector and vicar. It seems inherently unlikely that Brackley personally came to Stretton on account of his commitments at Westminster. What most probably happened was that the chaplain, Walter de Mora, who may have served in Brackley's place, now acted as vicar with the guarantee of a greater share of the church's income. This was probably the consequence of the decision of the Lateran Council of 1215 that 'since it is not lawful to muzzle the ox that treads the corn, but he who serves the altar should live of the altar, we have ordained ... a sufficient portion be assigned for the priest'[8] — who should also become a perpetual vicar, not an 'annual chaplain'.

Whoever was serving its church, important developments for Strettondale were imminent. Real power in the country under the king was in the hands of the Justiciar, Hubert de Burgh, who was carving out for himself an extensive lordship in the Welsh Marches. In a royal charter dated 18 October 1229 the king granted 'the manor of Stretton, in the county of Salop, together with the advowson of the church, to Hubert de Burgh and his heirs to hold in fee, at a rent of £16, payable at the Exchequer'.[9] Whether or not the Justiciar exercised his right to present a rector is not disclosed by the records, but in the summer of 1232 he fell dramatically from power and all his possessions were forfeited, including the great new castle at Montgomery and, of course, the manor of Stretton which became again part of the royal demesne.

The situation on the Welsh border remained extremely volatile. By a Patent writ of 1233 the men of Strettondale were informed that the king had given to Richard de Muntone (Minton) and Walter, Provost of Stretton, custody of the dale to defend it against the king's enemies. The real threat came from the Welsh prince, Llewelyn the Great, who was in alliance with the Earl of Pembroke, leader of the baronial opposition to the Poitevin ministers who had ousted Hubert de Burgh. In a bitter war the March was desolated, the Welsh insurgents penetrating as far as Stretton, probably aiming to raid manors in the dale or to ambush merchants or drovers on Watling Street, which 'was still a major artery in the thirteenth century'.[10] But the defenders were ready for them in substantial force,[11] for no fewer than 57 Welshmen were killed in a foray in the dale.[12] They were rewarded when on 14 June 1233[13] the Sheriff of Shropshire was ordered by the king to pay 57s. to Richard de Muntone and his troops as 'head money'—the slain intruders were decapitated to prove death and as a brutal deterrent.

*

The next we hear of the church is from the entry in the Patent Rolls on 2 August 1237 which records the presentation of William de Pinu to the church of Strettondale. The description of the new rector as Archdeacon of Vézelay in Burgundy is a reminder of England's remaining interest and possessions in France at that time, despite John's loss of Normandy. Yet again, for political reasons, the living had been given to one who already held a significant position in the Church and who, with greater responsibilities as far away as Vézelay, was certainly not intending to reside in Shropshire. Other matters of interest are the date of the appointment and the rector's surname. Only the previous year King Henry III had married Eleanor of Provence whose uncle, William of Savoy, became for a time the leading royal councillor. The Savoyard influence led at once to an increase in the number of aliens presented to English benefices. William de Pinu seems to have belonged to a prominent family in Gascony, the only remaining province of the Angevin Empire and one in which Queen Eleanor was to take a considerable personal interest.

Nothing more is known of William de Pinu, but a member of his family, William Reimundi de Pinibus, Lord of Caumont in the Gironde, was a witness to Henry III's agreement in 1242 to aid the Count of Toulouse against the King of France. Another member of the family was Arnald de Pinibus, Bishop of Bazas, also near Bordeaux in the Gironde, whose nephews loaned the king 5,000 shillings to relieve his precarious financial state during the campaign of 1242. In these events there lies the explanation of the presentation, by a Patent writ of 11 February 1246 and addressed to the Archdeacon of Salop, of one Bonettus de Pinibus to the church of Stretton. It is again highly unlikely that a foreign rector was ever resident in the parish. Indeed, there is evidence of others holding the vicarage. Such details are available to us only because Stretton was in the patronage of the king and appointments to its church were noted in the records of the central administration. On 12 December 1252, according to the Calendar of Patent Rolls, Ralph de Cestreton was granted the vicarage of Strettondale on the order of the king to Peter de Aigueblanche, Bishop of Hereford—another Savoyard intruder.

Ralph de Cestreton had little time to enjoy the rights of the 'vicarage' which then, like 'rectory', meant not just a house to live in but a number of rights and a stipulated share of the income. On 3 July 1253, the king, on the eve of his departure to confront a new outbreak of rebellion in Gascony, dispatched a writ to his brother Richard, Earl of Cornwall, and Master William de Kilkenny, Archdeacon of Coventry and Keeper of the Royal Seal. Its subject was Ralph de Cestreton, described as Kilkenny's chaplain. Ralph had apparently resigned the Stretton vicarage at the request of the king who wished in his place to promote the nephew of the Prior of Le Mas in Aquitaine. It comes as no surprise that William, the Prior of Le Mas d'Agenais, was another member of the Pinibus family whom the king was clearly so anxious to have on his side.[14] Henry III's conscience was now troubled by this treatment of his own appointee, Ralph de Cestreton. He therefore commanded his brother and the archdeacon 'to confer upon the said Ralph £20 yearly of rent out of ecclesiastical benefices in England in the king's gift, when they fall void, lest the liberality of the said Ralph be to his harm, and the king incur sin thereby'.[15] Such

an income is evidence of the king's real concern for it was way above a vicar's stipend at a time when the rector was expected to take the lion's share of the income of the living, said in 1255 to be 40 marks (£26-13-4), the highest estimate in the next two centuries. In that year one Gilbert, Dean of Pontesbury, was vicar at Stretton[16] — could he have been the prior's nephew? It seems more likely than ever that though persons were classed as vicars, they, too, were absentees and that the church was actually served by an impecunious chaplain.

The Priory Church of Le Mas d'Agenais in Gascony

In the meantime the rector, Bonettus de Pinibus, appears to have been with the king in Gascony. On 27 September 1254, at Bordeaux, he and two others were entrusted with the king's letters, together with letters from Simon de Montfort, Earl of Leicester, and his unrelated colleague Peter de Montfort, to deliver to the castellan of the fortress of Mehun-sur-Yevre in central France. These ordered him to hand over two members of the de Pinibus family whom Simon de Montfort, then the king's seneschal in Gascony, had imprisoned after their capture in earlier fighting at Bordeaux. The earl was given a bond for 500 marks as ransom.[17] Henry III was concerned to secure their immediate release because it was at the request of Alfonso, King of Castile, whose sister was about to be married to Henry's son, Edward, later Edward I. So, in just over a year, both the rector and the vicar of Stretton found themselves involved in matters that received the personal attention of the king.

Significant changes were taking place in the parish in the absence of its rectors. The area of forest, the home of wolves, as well as roe and red deer, was shrinking, as the Long Forest survey of 1235 revealed. The oaks of the Long Mynd and Ragleth were well kept, but in the north oaks had been felled to improve defences against the Welsh and for repairs to the castle, while encroachments on the forest by local landowners and religious houses were to continue through the century. It is in reports on forest offences that the name 'Church Stretton' is first met—in 1250 'William de Chirlestretton' and in 1262 'William fitzGilbert of Chirch Stretton' were both fined.[18] The manor itself was assigned by the king in 1238 to Henry de Hastings and his wife, but was repossessed for the king in 1245. By the late 1250s the men of Stretton were themselves responsible for the rent of £24 per annum and were probably cultivating the demesne. The weekly Wednesday market, which perhaps had not been successfully established and the one day fair each August initiated in 1214, were superseded in 1253, the Close Rolls reveal, by a weekly market on Tuesday and a four day fair on the eve and day of the Feast of the Holy Cross and the two days following (2-5 May)—the original May Fair. The Hundred Roll of 1255 is particularly informative.[19] The manor was said to be an independent jurisdiction, with its own community responsible to the crown for its ordering. The Provost in that year was named as Henry and the six jurymen who assisted him to answer the questions were also named. Their account included the various encroachments on the demesne, the valuation of the manor at £24 per annum, and the sale of the fish in the king's vivary which the sheriff had ordered should be dried out—although 20 years later the stock of fish was augmented by the arrival of a hundred female bream from Ellesmere. As they also reported that there was no castle at Stretton, the conclusion that it had been abandoned or destroyed before 1255—possibly in the Welsh incursion of 1233—seems inescapable.[20] The construction of the great stone castle at Montgomery begun in 1223 as the outpost of English control had rendered many castles further east semi-redundant, and Stretton was already changing in character from a manor with a royal fortress to a market town. Though the

Hundred Roll contains no detail about the church, among the jurors of the 1256 Assizes, after Henry Provost, were Robert fitzPriest, perhaps the son of the vicar, and Philip Clerk, possibly the chaplain.

Apart from the grant of the manor in 1259 to Peter de Montfort, Sheriff of Salop and Staffordshire since 1257, nothing is known of Stretton in the years of baronial rebellion, reform and war which ended with Simon de Montfort's defeat and death at Evesham in August 1265. Only three months later, however, a Patent writ announced the presentation of a new rector on the death of his predecessor. The rector who died is named as Poun del Espineye, whom Eyton considered to be one and the same as Bonettus de Pinibus, a claim impossible to verify or contradict. With either name he would have been vulnerable to the popular hostility to aliens, including alien clergy, that swept the country in the early 1260s. His successor, named on 22 November 1265, was Richard de

The figure of St. Laurence on the south-east corner of the tower

Radeclive, chaplain, who had been presented by the king to the vicarage of Whitchurch the previous year. Since his successor at Stretton was named a mere four days after his own presentation, it would seem either that there had been a mistake or he arranged an immediate move, a supposition strengthened by a reference to him as parson at Bradford shortly afterwards. Either way he scarcely merits inclusion in a list of rectors. Nonetheless, his presentation is of value because it was expressly to 'the church of St. Laurence, Strettondale',[21] the first time the dedication of the church is documented and almost exactly a thousand years after the saint's martyrdom.

Church Stretton is one of four places in the county whose church is dedicated to St. Laurence: the others are Ludlow, Burwarton and Little Wenlock. St. Laurence, who was born in Spain, had been one of Pope Sixtus II's seven deacons in Rome in the early days of the Christian Church. The persecution unleashed by the Emperor Valerian reached a peak in 258 AD, when the Pope and six of his deacons were martyred; Laurence suffering the same fate four days later, on 10 August. The historical reliability of the accounts of how he paraded the poor, sick and handicapped before the Prefect of Rome as 'the treasure of the

Church' and of his slow roasting on a gridiron is suspect, but there is no doubt that he became one of the most venerated martyrs of the Roman Church. The Emperor Constantine, converted to Christianity 60 years later, built the first chapel on the site of the present Church of St. Laurence-outside-the-walls of Rome. Before the Reformation there were 228 English churches dedicated to him, including the famous Anglo-Saxon church at Bradford-on-Avon.

Richard de Radeclive was succeeded by William de Ippele whom the king presented to the Bishop of Hereford by a writ of 26 November 1265; unfortunately the church was in error referred to as St. Andrew's in Strettondale. William de Ippele was probably another king's clerk, or became one, because the Patent Rolls use this description in 1276 and again in 1280, the year in which he was presented to the living of Acton in the diocese of London which was also in the king's gift. After the battle of Evesham Henry III had bestowed the manor of Stretton on Mereduc, son of Ress, for two years, and then on Hamo le Strange, one of the bosom companions of his son, the Lord Edward, who went with him on crusade in 1270. Before he left, Hamo made a conditional assignment of the manor to his sister Hawise, the wife of Gruffyd (Griffin) Gwenwynwyn, the Prince of Powys. At the Assizes of 1272 the Stretton jurors avowed that the king had also given Hamo le Strange the advowson of the parish church. It is possible that William de Ippele resigned in the early 1270s and that Hawise presented her own son as rector: all we know is that 'David, son of Griffin' resigned the rectorship in late 1276,[22] not how long he had been there nor whether he followed William de Ippele. Hawise certainly had a younger son called David, who was in holy orders.[23] When news of Hamo's death on the crusade was received, the sheriff was told to seize the manor for the king as Hamo's assignment to his sister was without royal approval, although subsequently Hawise was allowed to receive its full income during her lifetime. The king clearly kept the patronage of the church in his own hands. This was to prove of great importance in the following years when the resignation of 'David, son of Griffin' precipitated one of the most fascinating episodes in St. Laurence's early history.

*

The individual who now became rector was Walter, son of William the physician. What was unusual was that he was only 16 years old. Bishop Thomas Cantilupe of Hereford sequestrated the income of the benefice until Walter, only an acolyte, promised in January 1277 that when he reached his 18th year he would proceed to his next orders as sub-deacon.[24] This was the minimum age for ordination as a sub-deacon.[25] The presentation of a minor was unprecedented at Stretton, but by no means unknown.[26] In the meantime, Walter's tutor, Master Philip le Waleys, who according to the Patent Rolls was presented as rector on

6 February 1277, was given corporal possession of the church as its custodian by the bishop on 27 March 1277 during the bishop's pleasure. Philip seems not to have been satisfied with a temporary appointment, for on 12 April 'Magister Philippus dictus le Waleys' was instituted as rector. He did not, however, proceed to ordination as priest since the rector of Stretton is one on a list of over 80 who failed to present themselves at Leominster on 18 September 1277.

No sooner was Master Philip the Welshman—or Philip Walsh—established as incumbent than his loyalties were put to the test. King Edward I, intent on forcing the submission of Llewelyn, Prince of Wales (and grandson of Llewelyn the Great), summoned the feudal host to meet at Worcester by late June 1277. Strettondale is hardly likely to have escaped the marshalling of local levies by the sheriff, the impressment of woodsmen, carpenters and diggers, and the collection of all manner of supplies. So successful was the ensuing campaign that Llewelyn came to terms by the end of the year. As relations between him and the king improved, a meeting was arranged the next year at Rhuddlan where a new royal castle was being completed. It was on his way there from Gloucester that King Edward stayed for two days at Stretton, writs being dispatched from there on 26 and 27 August 1278.[27] He is likely to have been the guest of his steward, but even if he did not stay at the parsonage, which was probably adjacent, his entourage, especially clerics, will have done, and the king himself, a devout Christian, surely attended mass at the parish church. This assumption may well be vindicated by the following entry in the Calendar of Close Rolls dated 8 September 1278:

> To Roger de Clifford, justice of the forest this side Trent. Order to cause
> the vicar of the church in Strettondale to have seven oak trunks ('robura')
> in the forest of Strettondale, of the king's gift.

Cranage's belief that the timbers of the fine trussed-rafter roof of the nave of St. Laurence's may date from the thirteenth century is surely proved right by this gift of the king to his hosts, even though the parishioners may have been responsible for the upkeep of the nave by this period. Possibly the timbers of the chancel and north transept roofs date from the same time. It seems that the king's attention was drawn to the need for better roofing and that this was his response. The encounter was beneficial for the rector also, for in February 1280 Philip le Waleys was chosen to accompany overseas Richard, Abbot of Westminster and Treasurer of the Exchequer, who had been appointed as the king's envoy.[28]

The rector was to be grateful for the king's friendship when Bishop Thomas de Cantilupe, later canonised as St. Thomas de Cantilupe, died and a new Bishop of Hereford was appointed in 1283. Richard de Swinfield had been consecrated less than a week when he began a correspondence in Latin with the king about the parish of Stretton.[29] In a letter dated 14 March he advised Edward I that at Gloucester, five days earlier, the Archbishop of Canterbury, John Pecham, had declared the living of Stretton to be vacant. Bishop Swinfield was no doubt trying to impress his superior, just as the archbishop was following the instructions of the Pope that the canons of the Council of Lyons, 1274, should be enforced in England. So Bishop Swinfield requested the king as patron to provide 'a suitable person who is willing and able to relieve our burden by personally residing there and caring for men's souls', especially as the church had earlier been vacant for a long period—perhaps

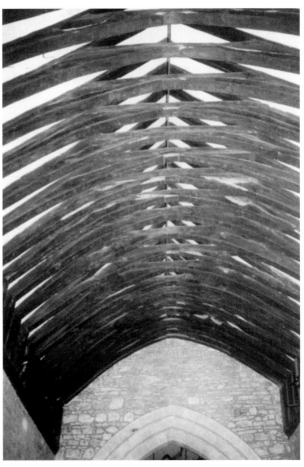

The thirteenh-century roof of the nave

William de Ippele had been absent or had been rector only briefly.

The king's prompt reply, perhaps explained by the rector's presence with the Court, was sealed at Aberconway on 17 March. It was crisp and to the point:

> When you informed us that the Venerable Father, the Archbishop of Canterbury, had declared the church of Stretton in Strattonesdale, in your diocese and within our gift, by law to be vacant, you omitted to give a clarification of the law and also the reason for this vacancy, about which it would be fitting for us to be informed before we go there. We ask you, Father, to inform us quickly, clearly and openly in your letter about the law and the cause of the aforementioned vacancy so that we shall thus see, in our council, what should be done.

The bishop's response was almost as quick. In a letter dated 23 March he was brave enough to aver that it was not customary to explain the reason for vacancies, but, out of respect for the king, he agreed to do as he was asked. He asserted that Master Philip had *de facto* taken possession of the church at Stretton and 'acted illegally in the worst way by supplanting his own pupil who had held the post rightly beforehand'. Furthermore, the rector had failed over a period of five years to proceed to priest's orders, although the Council of Lyons in 1274 had laid it down that an incumbent should be 'priested' within two years of his institution. 'The Lord Archbishop, with the highest authority of the Council, declared the church to be vacant and that Philip had no rights within it'.

When the king sent his answer on 30 March he chose to stand on his royal dignity. He simply declined to accept that benefices in his patronage were subject to rules made by the Council of Lyons as to proceeding to priest's orders. Bishop Swinfield was not made of the stuff of martyrs, and appears to have pressed the matter no further, influenced perhaps by his awareness that the king was in the area pursuing another campaign against the Welsh. Prince Llewelyn had been killed in December 1282 and his brother David condemned by the Parliament which met at Shrewsbury in October 1283 to be hanged and quartered. King Edward was again in the area the next year when the adjourned Parliament met at Acton Burnell, the home of his great Chancellor, Bishop Robert Burnell. It is not surprising, therefore, that in 1285 Bishop Swinfield decided to licence no vicar in Stretton, leaving the whole benefice in the hands of Rector Philip.[30] This seems to have marked the end of the practice of reserving part of the income for a vicar. Henceforth an absentee rector had again to ensure that there was a priest to serve the living and what stipend he should receive. Six years later the Taxation Assessment of 1291 valued the 'church of Strattonisdale' at £15 per annum, after Wenlock the highest in the Deanery, and the following year the Stretton jurors valued it, perhaps more realistically, at 40 marks (£26 13s. 4d.).[31]

The dispute between king and bishop was but the last in a series of occasions during the century when the parish of Stretton had exhibited some of the weaknesses of the contemporary Church. The pluralism of Ralph de Neville may be defended as providing a ladder of opportunity for a really able man to reach the higher echelons of Church and State, but the continued absence of Neville and then Walter de Brackley on royal business meant that the parish was in the care of a poorly paid vicar or chaplain. Matters were worse still during the rectorships of William Pinu and Bonettus de Pinibus because they were out of the country, probably never even visiting the parish. Yet there would have been no shortage of others to serve the church in their place. It has been calculated that in the late thirteenth century there were about 9,500 parishes in England[32]—342 in the diocese of Hereford—but perhaps as many as 40,000 secular, that is non-monastic, clergy. The consequent competition for places may have produced some able and committed men as vicars: nationally,

Dr. Moorman reckoned that about 80% of them had been ordained to the priest-hood, compared with only 20% - 25% of rectors. 'Where there was no vicar the spiritual responsibilities were borne by a parish chaplain, paid by the incumbent, but with no rights and little security'.[33] Most vicars, including Stretton's, were provided with a house and received £4 to £5 a year from which they often had to pay an assistant priest or clerk, and provide for church repairs and charity. They may have been able to supplement their income from freewill offerings— 'Mass pennies'—and from small payments for conducting baptisms, marriages and funerals, witnessing wills, and sometimes from a gift from a dead person's estate after the lord had exercised his right to take his best animal.

Richard de Radeclive may be an example—and perhaps William de Ippele and David son of Griffin are others—of rectors who moved on quickly when better prospects presented themselves. Walter, son of William the physician, illustrates the appointment of minors to livings, and perhaps Philip le Waleys the actions of the ambitious or unscrupulous. The quality of spiritual example or service given by vicars such as Walter de Mora and Ralph de Cestreton or by unknown clerks will have depended on their individual faith and conscien-tiousness. The dedicated priest will have conducted Matins before the morning Mass and Evensong (often poorly attended), celebrated Mass on weekdays as well as Sundays, and administered communion (offering consecrated bread but no longer wine) usually only once a year at Easter. He will have heard confes-sions, obligatory once a year for all Christians since the fourth Lateran Council of 1215—and more frequently under zealous bishops. There was little preaching, but he would also have baptised infants, taught and catechised the children, conducted marriages, visited the sick and buried the dead. Many of these tasks will have been neglected by the ungodly, corrupt, lazy or absent vicar, and left to a chaplain or other clerk anxious to augment his earnings. But 'the standard of manners and morals among the vicars and clerks was not very high',[34] and some kept poor company. An inquest was held on 25 October 1285 into the following case:

> William de Tuttebury and John de Arderne, chaplain, came together from the tavern of Stretton; they quarrelled at the town end of Hope [Bowdler] and William drew his sword and tried to kill the chaplain, pursuing him to his own house. The chaplain's household, seeing this, raised a hue and cry and all the men of the town came hastily thereto. And William, seeing this, ran against Richard, son of Richard de Cimiterio of Hopebudlers, who was coming with the rest, and would have struck him with the sword. But Richard fled, pursued by William, into a corner outside the churchyard, constantly begging the king's peace. William struck him on the left arm, and Richard, in fear of being killed, drew his knife and held it between himself and William. But he, trying to strike a second blow, ran on to the knife.[35]

The inquest found that Richard acted in self-defence.

Since Sir Maurice Powicke considered that 'on the whole the English bishops in the thirteenth century were able and respectable',[36] we may ask why they did not act more effectively in their parishes. Of Hereford's four bishops in the second half of the century, Peter de Aigueblanche (1240-68) was a notable exception to Powicke's generalization. He has been described as 'a fat and ugly Savoyard' who made no attempt to administer his diocese in person, preferring to live abroad, and whose memory, according to Matthew Paris, 'exhales a foul and sulphurous stench';[37] John le Breton (1268-75) was a judge as well as a bishop; Thomas de Cantilupe (1275-82) was an outstanding prelate who, in spite of being excommunicated by Archbishop Pecham and retiring to Italy where he died, was later canonised; and Richard de Swinfield (1283-1317), as we have seen, endeavoured to carry out reforms, maintained two poor scholars at Oxford and, like his predecessor, conscientiously visited his parishes. Yet even Thomas de Cantilupe, in the year before he became bishop, was Archdeacon of Stafford, a canon of Lichfield, Precentor of York, a prebendary of both St. Paul's and Hereford, and rector of at least ten parishes! And the register of Bishop Swinfield, who took his episcopal responsibilities seriously, contains only one reference to confirmation in 25 years of active diocesan work and the institution to benefices of 17 men out of 76 who had not been ordained priest.

Yet there were signs of improvement. Scholastic standards were rising: Stretton's rector Philip le Waleys, for instance, is entitled 'Master' which indicates completion of the Trivium and Quadrivium, a seven-year university course. There were revered archbishops like St. Edmund of Abingdon and reformers like John Pecham; there were saintly bishops like Thomas de Cantilupe, great reformers like Robert Grosseteste of Lincoln, and vigorous leaders such as Richard de Swinfield. There is little evidence in the see of Hereford of diocesan synods, used by some bishops to educate their clergy and disseminate good practice, but much could be learned from detailed questionnaires sent out before visitations inquiring about property, competence, and the morals of clergy and laity. Of one such visitation, by Bishop Swinfield in 1290, some details have been preserved.[38] He set off from Colwall in early April, travelled north, usually spending only one night in each parish, and reached Wenlock after 12 days. On 27 April he slept in the manor-house at Stokesay and the next day, a Friday, dined on cod and salmon at Wistanstow. After a day at Eaton-under-Heywood as the guest of the Prior of Wenlock, the bishop and his party reached Stretton 'in its beautiful dale' on Sunday, 30 April. It seems certain that he attended a service in St. Laurence's, but no record remains. The conversation at dinner would have touched on the wedding that day in Westminster Abbey of the Princess Joan with the Earl of Gloucester. More interesting for us would be what passed between the bishop and the rector,

Philip le Waleys! All that we do know is that the rector placed his rick and garner at the service of the travellers' 35 horses, and that the guests' fare included bread, wine, ale, beef, pork, poultry, eggs, milk, vegetables and salt.[39] They left early on Monday, 1 May, in order to reach Pontesbury 'over a country mountainous and intricate and not to be traversed without a guide'. The bishop returned to Hereford after a journey of six weeks.

In October 1292 the Stretton jurors reported that Philip de Valence was the incumbent of their church, but this is surely a slip of the pen or a Normanised form of the Welshman's name. That Philip remained rector is triply confirmed by an entry in the Close Rolls in 1286 when he stood surety for another parson accused of harbouring a criminal; by a writ of 1288 in which he acknowledged his debt of 11 marks to the executors of Master William de Radenoure which were to be levied, in default of payment, 'on his land and chattels in County Salop'; and, most interesting of all, by a royal message to Bishop Swinfield in February 1303. This concerned the charges, or procurations, demanded in lieu of hospitality, on the occasion of a bishop's visitation:

> Request that he will desist from the exaction of twelve marks in the name of procuration, by reason of his visitation upon three occasions, to wit four marks each time, from Master Philip le Waleys, rector of the church of Stretton in Trattonesdale, in that diocese, which is of the king's patronage, as the king learns from Philip that the bishop exacts this sum in the name of procuration by reason of his visitations, although other bishops visiting their dioceses and also archbishops visiting their provinces have been wont from time out of mind to exact procurations from cathedrals and collegiate churches and from religious houses only, and not from parish churches, as the king learns from many people.[40]

So the rector was still at loggerheads with the bishop and still being defended by the king. But it was not to be for much longer. Philip le Waleys must have died in 1309, for on 28 August that year the new king, Edward II, presented William de Cleobury to the church of Stretton.[41]

4

NEW PATRONS—THE EARLS OF ARUNDEL

Only three weeks after his presentation of William de Cleobury to be rector of the parish of Stretton, King Edward II made a decision momentous for its future. On 17 September 1309 he granted the reversion of the manor of Stretton to Edmund fitzAlan, Earl of Arundel, lord of Oswestry and Clun castles, when the existing tenant for life, Hawise de la Pole, the elderly widow of the Prince of Powys and sister of Hamo le Strange, should die. Five weeks later, on 26 October, the earl was also granted the advowson of the church at Stretton.[1] He did not have to wait long to succeed to the manor nor to receive the advowson for Hawise died in November 1310. Apart from a significant break at the end of Edward's reign, the Arundels were to remain the church's patrons for the next 260 years.

Ironically for Arundel, William de Cleobury seems to have been recommended to the king by Roger Mortimer of Wigmore, Earl Edmund's great rival among the Marcher lords, for in 1310 Rector William was in Ireland with Mortimer, having appointed as his attorney one Thomas Ace of Ludlow, Mortimer's clerk. It is of interest that Mortimer had complained twice in the previous year that Roger Foliot and William de Sparchesford, with others, had assaulted Ace in Stretton and taken from him Mortimer's deeds and charters that were in his custody.[2] Nothing more is known of William de Cleobury, although clearly he was not always resident in the parish.

Stretton was a valuable manor and advowson to acquire; indeed, Earl Edmund had been so eager to gain possession of Stretton that he had sought to surrender his manors of Wroxeter and Upton in exchange.[3] A royal commission of 1309 had valued the manor—rents (including the site of an ancient manor), pasture, timber, mill, fisheries and the profits of justice—at £20 per annum; the church was also worth £20 per annum.[4] There was considerable traffic as the toll on carts passing through the manor produced 20s. a year. According to the Lay Subsidy Roll of 1327 there were eleven inhabitants of Church Stretton sufficiently wealthy to pay this tax, six in Little Stretton, and 11 in All Stretton where the leading landholders were rather better off than in Church Stretton and included John Cambray of the family that was to marry into the Leightons, linked in the future with St. Laurence's.

It was six years before the earl had an opportunity to exercise his rights as patron. Even then there was still a challenge to his presentation of a new incumbent. Either the king's officials had forgotten he was no longer the patron or Edward was anxious to appoint one of his closest aides, for on 12 February 1316 he presented Master Thomas de Charlton, clerk, Doctor of Civil Law.[5] Such a nominee was doubly unacceptable to Earl Edmund: not only did he now own the patronage, but the Charltons were a powerful rival family in Shropshire. It is a remarkable co-incidence, nonetheless, that it was on the very same day that Charlton's name was put forward by the king that Roger de Kynlet, priest, presented by the earl, was instituted by the Bishop of Hereford.[6] It is almost certain that Kynlet transferred from Hopesay where one of the same name and with the same patron had been installed in 1313.

Roger de Kynlet is another of whom we know nothing else, although as a priest he may personally have ministered in the parish. The benefice became vacant again in 1321, and the bishop's register records that on 10 October that year Ralph de Snelleston was admitted to the church at Stretton as the candidate of Earl Edmund. (Again the king nominated a rival in the person of Robert de Tong, clerk, but not till 2 November. Tong was unsuccessful, but was found another preferment in London four years later.) It is interesting that the bishop who instituted the new rector was Adam de Orleton who gained the see in 1317 after the royal nominee—Thomas de Charlton again—was vetoed by the Pope.[7]

It is a pity that we do not know if Ralph de Snelleston was in the parish when Edward II paused there on 25 January 1322 while campaigning against Mortimer in the Marches. What is known is that the new rector was soon off on his own travels, granted a dispensation by the bishop for absence from April to Michaelmas 1322 to be in attendance upon Sir John Peche.[8] His final departure in 1327 may have been precipitated by the dramatic events in the national struggle for power.

King Edward II, who had not learned from his earlier mistakes over his favourite Gaveston, and weakened by his defeat by Robert Bruce at Bannockburn, made what proved to be his fatal error by heaping rewards upon his new favourites, Hugh Despenser and his son also named Hugh. Even his wife, Queen Isabella, turned against him and in 1326, supported by her lover, Roger Mortimer of Wigmore, she returned from exile in France. London turned against the king who fled to the West Country. The Despensers were captured and executed, the king imprisoned, and—most important for the church at Stretton—the Earl of Arundel captured in Shropshire by his arch-rival John Charlton and beheaded without formal judgment in November 1326. Arundel, who had opposed the king earlier in the reign, now paid with his life for supporting him. The king himself was murdered at Berkeley Castle the next year.

Though the king's 14-year-old son was proclaimed as Edward III, the real ruler of the country was Roger Mortimer. His seizure of power was to have immediate consequences for Stretton's church. On 26 June 1327, with the Arundel estates in the king's hands, William son of William de Hardishull was nominated to the church by royal letter and instituted later in the year.[9] The previous rector, Ralph de Snelleston, had presumably chosen or been encouraged to move to a new living in the Worcester diocese. William de Hardishull was probably only in his teens for he was not ordained sub-deacon until September 1328 and was then almost at once granted a dispensation by the bishop (now Thomas Charlton) for non-residence for two years to pursue his studies. In April 1330 the bishop was ordered to ensure that Hardishull presented himself before the justices at Westminster to answer the plea that he owed £10 to a certain William de Wiggeley of Ludlow.[10]

While the rector was playing the role of the impecunious student, important events occurred in Stretton and on the national stage. For his services to Queen Isabella and the young king, in November 1327 Roger Mortimer was granted for life the manor of 'Stretton in Strettonesdale' and the advowson of the church. Early in 1330 Mortimer, who had by now become Earl of March, was further granted 'the advowson of the church of Stretton in fee simple in enlargement of a prior grant for life to him of the same with the manor of Stretton'.[11] This grant constituted a grave threat to the future of the Stretton church for within a fortnight he had obtained a licence to alienate 'the advowson of the church to ten chaplains to celebrate divine service daily in the church of St. Mary, Leintwardine, for his soul and the souls of his ancestors and successors'.[12] Had Mortimer lived and put this intention into effect the story of the church in Stretton could have been very different. But his days were numbered. He had over-reached himself and the end came quickly. Opposition grew, he was seized by the king, and his peers in Parliament sentenced him to be drawn and hanged as a traitor. The sentence was carried out on 29 November 1330.

The patronage of Stretton's church reverted again to the king. In January 1331 he presented as the new incumbent a second William de Hardishull, son of John, rector of Stylton in the diocese of Lincoln, who exchanged benefices with the first William de Hardishull of Stretton, surely a relative of his.[13] Certainly the second Hardishull displayed some of the characteristics of the first: in July 1332 he acknowledged that he owed 100s. to Thomas de Wynnesbury the younger and £10 to none other than Ralph de Snelleston, now parson at Whatecote, Worcestershire.[14] He was also eager to move on. In September 1332 an exchange[15] was arranged with Adam de Bridlington, king's clerk, who held a prebend in Canterbury, but the deal fell through. The next year he must have been travelling in the king's service for he was granted royal protection for a year. It is also recorded that he paid through his proctor four marks as procuration for the bishop's last visitation at Stretton—Philip le

Waleys would not have approved. Another proposed exchange, this time with the parson at Ness, near Shrewsbury, also failed.[16] At last, however, he got his move for on 28 March 1335 he exchanged the living at Stretton with John de Watenhull, rector of Kingsley in the diocese of Coventry and Lichfield.[17]

John de Watenhull was presented as rector of Stretton on 9 April 1335. What proved to be the last royal appointment to the church—apart from one odd exception in the sixteenth century—was of another clerk in the king's service. Before his arrival (one presumes that such rectors did actually visit the parish) John de Watenhull had already been active in the area for the king. He and two others had been dispatched late in 1330 to seize the possessions of Roger Mortimer for the crown, and two years later he had visited bishops and abbots in Shropshire and Staffordshire to raise a subsidy for the marriage of the king's sister.[18]

As we know that his predecessors had frequently done, the king rewarded Watenhull for his services by appointing him to benefices in the king's gift so that he could enjoy the revenues while another served the parish. When rector of Stretton he seems to have continued as a canon of St. Mary's, Shrewsbury, and perhaps as a prebendary at Bosham in the Chichester diocese. So he was a pluralist as well as non-resident, with benefices granted to him until their combined revenues amounted to what the king judged an appropriate income. And he continued to take on greater commissions for the king:

> To the mayors, bailiffs, communities of towns, masters of ships, mariners of the Cinque Ports, and others from the mouth of the Thames towards the west. The king sends to them John de Watenhull, his clerk, fully informed upon certain things close to the king's heart, ordering them to give credence to what he shall say, as they wish to avoid the king's indignation.[19]

This was dated December 1336 when there were rumours of a great French armada. And in 1337—in response to movements of the French fleet at the beginning of the Hundred Years' War—he and another were appointed

> to arrest thirteen of the largest and stoutest ships of the Cinque Ports beyond the number which the king has ordered to be taken up in these ports for his service, and to have these equipped with all speed with men, mariners and munitions of war; with power to imprison until further order anyone resisting them in the execution of the premises.[20]

It is even recorded that in 1345 John de Watenhull was to deputise for the admiral of the fleet, none other than his ecclesiastical patron, Richard, Earl of Arundel![21]

As well as conducting financial transactions and other business for the king, Watenhull, like his predecessors, was always borrowing money. In particular he owed increasing amounts—the huge sum of £60 by 1345—to John de Wodehouse, Clerk of the King's Hanaper. The parson at Ludlow was in debt to Wodehouse, too, so perhaps there is nothing exceptional about Watenhull's loans, as may be confirmed by the growing number who owed him money.

It was while Watenhull was rector that there were two very significant developments in Stretton. In the Calendar of Charter Rolls it is recorded that on 16 March 1336 Edward III made a

> gift for good service rendered with the assent of the prelates, earls, barons and other magnates of the present Parliament, to Richard, Earl of Arundel, of the manor of Stretton, co. Salop, to be held by him and his heirs together with the knights' fees advowsons and all other appurtenances by rendering to the king one sore (in its first year) sparrow hawk at the feast of St. James.[22]

So the Arundels, already restored to favour in the person of Richard, eldest son of the executed Earl Edmund, returned as lords of the manor of Stretton and patrons of the church. Their patronage was to continue virtually unbroken until the reign of Elizabeth I. A further favour was granted in June 1337 by the king's special grace to Earl Richard and his heirs of 'a weekly market on Thursdays at their manor of Chirchestretton, co. Salop, and a yearly fair there on the vigil, the feast and the morrow of the Exaltation of the Cross'[23]—that is, the 13, 14 and 15 September. The weekly market on Thursday is still a feature of Stretton life, and the annual fair in mid-September was only discontinued in the twentieth century. The fair, according to Miss H. Auden, a distinguished local historian in the early twentieth century, came to be the highlight of the year. 'Almost every village and each town had its fair days when velvet and silk from Italy, linen and fine cloth from Flanders, wines from France and Spain, and even the produce of the Far East, were to be bought from travelling merchants. To the young people the fairs were the great days of excitement and amusement, while to their elders they were the chief business days of the year'.[24]

The taxation inquiry of 1341—the 'Inquisitio Nonarum'—assessed the parish at £4 13s. 4d., the reduction from 50 years before probably explained by the omission of some elements from the levy.[25] This information apart, the story of the church at Stretton in the early fourteenth century would have been no more than the record of incumbents' names in the bishops' registers—and it is fortunate that these have survived for seven hundred years —had its patrons not been the king and an earl closely involved in the political and military struggles of the period. Such patronage ensured that records were preserved in the royal Chancery. But of the nature of worship in the church or life in the parish nothing specific is known, although the former can be assumed to conform to contemporary practice. Evidence from the buildings that have survived until today is also tentative. Cranage considers that some of the windows of St. Laurence's may have been inserted in the four-teenth century as they contain Decorated stone tracery, with its characteristic double ogee 'S' shape on the jambs, but that their coarseness may indicate a date early in the seventeenth century. 'Perhaps the true explanation may be that they [referring to the two large windows at the ends of the transepts and to the west window] were put up in the fourteenth and repaired in the seventeenth century'. The evidence for the seventeenth-century origin of the west window is strong, but a four-teenth-century date for the transept windows is more likely; the posi-tions of the earlier lancet windows in the end wall of the north transept are visible to this day. Cranage points out, too, that the picture of

The north transept window. The stones marking the positions of the earlier lancet windows can be seen to right and left and under the window

the east window featured in Eyton's *Antiquities of Shropshire* appears to have Decorated rather than its present Perpendicular tracery; it could be therefore that the large east window was another embellishment of the fourteenth century, although David Parkes's drawing of 1808 shows a different Perpendicular tracery from that of today.[26] In Pevsner's judgment the present tracery dates from the 1630s, but this is surely mistaken. As it seems that the building of the cruciform church took place soon after King John's order to advertise the town's first market, so it could be that the large Decorated windows in the transepts, and maybe the original east window, were inserted soon after the granting of the third market by Edward III in 1337—perhaps with some financial help from the Earl of Arundel in gratitude to God for the restoration of his family's estates and fortunes. A still more likely benefactor was Sir Walter Collins, steward in Stretton successively for Edward II, Edward III and the Earl of Arundel. His daughter married Watkyn Cambray who succeeded him as the earl's steward. Cambray's daughter in turn married Edward Leighton of Stretton's leading family in the fifteenth century.[27]

Rector John de Watenhull's brief appointment as deputy to the admiral of the fleet proved to be the summit of his career for he then fades from the Chancery records. There is, however, one final interesting reference in the bishop's register in 1347 when the Bishop of Coventry and Lichfield was asked to inquire into an exchange of livings 'between Roger, rector of Bangor, and John de Wodenhull, rector of Stretton, in the patronage of Richard, Earl of Arundel'. Probable dates for his successor suggest that Watenhull made a move or died, but there is no evidence that Roger of Bangor was ever presented.

Instead, in all likelihood Watenhull was succeeded by one 'Sir' John Sprot, whose resignation in 1358 was recorded in the bishop's register but not his institution. The title 'Sir' was accorded to one who had probably been educated at university but had not taken a Master's degree. An earlier register records that a John Sprot had been ordained priest in 1330, and one of this name is described in the Patent Rolls in 1347 as the Earl of Arundel's chaplain. By 1349 he was named as the parson at Stretton when he served on an inquiry into the earl's lands.[28] All in all it seems justified to assume that John Sprot was rector of Stretton from 1347 to 1358.

It was during these years that the Black Death swept through the land. The dreaded pestilence spread north through the Welsh border counties and was at its height in Shropshire in the summer of 1349. What the effects were in Church Stretton is unrecorded, but nationally about one-third of the population died. Faced with such disaster people will have turned to the Church. Bishops advised prayers, litanies and penitential processions round market places and through churchyards. In Hereford it was claimed that the epidemic was checked by carrying the shrine of St. Thomas of Cantilupe through the streets.[29] Whatever clergy were resident in Stretton—and John Sprot is the only one we know of—must have been torn, as elsewhere, between ministering to their suffering people and saving their own skins. The full fury of the plague in any locality lasted only three to four months and, where details are known, social recovery seems to have been astonishingly rapid. Nonetheless, the appalling loss of life disrupted communities and had important economic and social consequences as land was left untended, wages rose and prices fell. At a deeper level, too, people must have been unsettled, with shock, doubt, gloom, crime, profligacy and depravity all evident in a destabilised society.

When John Sprot resigned as rector of Stretton in 1358 the country was returning to something like normality after the plague, although there were to be serious recurrences, as in 1361. Sprot's successor was Nicholas de Chaddesden, described as clerk and Professor of Civil Law. He was admitted on 7 December 1358 on the presentation of Richard, Earl of Arundel,[30] and at the age of about 28. The bishop asked the Dean of Wenlock to induct him. Chaddesden was only in minor orders and was given a dispensation for study absence at an English university for three years. He was told to proceed to sub-deacon's orders within a year from his preferment. No doubt he was aided in the early stages of his career by his uncle, Henry de Chaddesden, who had risen in royal service to be keeper of the regent's seal in 1347 when the king was in

France after the battle of Crécy. Nicholas resigned from Stretton in October 1361 after only three years, but what followed provides an astonishing example of a careerist in the Church of the fourteenth century.[31] His moves were too numerous to reproduce here but within the next ten years he was linked with no fewer than nine other benefices; at various times he was a canon of Lichfield, Hereford, Southwell and Lincoln and ended as Archdeacon of Lincoln, one of the most lucrative positions in the country. In 1361, when his association with Stretton ceased, he became Chancellor of the Archbishopric of Canterbury and was Dean of the Court of Arches for many years. At the time of his death in Rome in 1390 he was a member of the Roman Curia. He left a silver cup and cover bearing the arms of Warenne (the family of the former Earl of Surrey) bequeathed to him in 1372 and a magnificent bed 'cum papejays et draconibus' that had belonged to his uncle.

The story of the church at Stretton in the next 40 years is almost wholly dependent on the only partially complete records of the bishops' registers.[32] Chaddesden was followed as rector by Robert de Astmede, admitted on 13 November 1361, and presented to Church Stretton by Richard, Earl of Arundel. He exchanged the living three years later, on 5 July 1364, with William de Wolverton, rector of Ness. Wolverton, who had been there only two years—and had previously held the living at Shrawardine nearby for the same length of time—probably did not remain rector for long, though long enough to be named as a pluralist in 1366.[33] One of his name was presented to Westbury in 1369, but the next reference to Stretton is 20 years later. This is to a 'Sir' Richard, named as rector of Stretton in 1386. His surname was probably Cloppe as a Sir Richard Cloppe was instituted at Shrawardine on 22 May 1388 on the resignation of Robert Pobelowe – who, on the same day, was presented to Stretton-en-le-Dale by the earl. The references to Shrawardine are interesting because the castle there was up to this time the favourite Shropshire residence of the Earls of Arundel. Earl Richard, who had been restored to favour after the downfall of Roger Mortimer in 1330, had lived there until 1375, and served as Sheriff of Shropshire from 1345 onwards. This was the golden age of the fitzAlan family. Earl Richard had acquired further land and title on the death of his uncle, John Warenne, Earl of Surrey, in 1347. He now had massive estates and the largest flocks of sheep in the Marches. 'The Marcher lords waxed rich; many of them waxed even richer during the course of the fourteenth century ... None did better than the house of fitzAlan'.[34] Earl Richard was reputed to have a stock of 100,000 marks in cash on his death. The earl himself was surely rarely seen in Stretton, but Richard Brugge, Abbot of Haughmond, the key figure in the management of his estates, would have been a more frequent visitor. However, the earl, and his son and successor, another Richard, would have taken a personal interest in appointments to the churches of which he was patron, because this was an economical way of rewarding those in his service as clerks or private chaplains—or of consolidating good relations with the local gentry by favouring their aspiring sons who might also be members of his household.

Stretton's succession of short-stay incumbents was uncommon in the diocese at this time.[35] Pobelowe who, like Wolverton, had served only two years at Shrawardine before the Stretton appointment, probably again left soon afterwards, for the next recorded resignation, five years later, on 9 March 1393, was of William Baron who arranged an exchange with Walter Clyfford, rector of Boyton in Salisbury diocese. All we know of Baron is his resignation, and Walter Clyfford is not much better: presented in March 1393, he exchanged the Stretton living on 24 November 1395 with William Smythecote, rector of Hanmere in the Lichfield diocese. This last name suggests a local man and there is one crumb of evidence that he stayed longer than some others for his estate as parson of Stretton-en-le-Dale was ratified in a long list in the Patent Rolls dated 3 February 1399. Smythecote was therefore the rector when the bishop made his visitation of the diocese in 1397. Sadly the records for the Wenlock Deanery have not survived. We can only wonder if Stretton, like neighbouring Wistanstow, was famed for sexual incontinence even among chaplains or, like Wentnor over the hill, its incumbent was criticised for slip-shod leadership and frequenting inns day and night; almost certainly, as at them both, the churchyard fence would have needed repair.[36]

Clyfford and Smythecote were the last rectors presented by Richard, the fourth Earl of Arundel (and Earl of Surrey) who had taken the title on the death of his father in 1376. Whereas the father had been the close friend of Edward III, the son became the bitter enemy of Richard II and was executed for treason in 1397, when his younger brother, Thomas, the Archbishop of Canterbury, was sent into exile. The Arundel lands, including the manor of Stretton, which together with the forest of the Long Mynd was in 1395 valued at £22 per annum (and the advowson of the church at £21), were again confiscated by the king.

Yet the Arundels once more bounced back. The earl's son Thomas and his uncle, the archbishop, joined Henry Bolingbroke, John of Gaunt's son, in Paris and supported his invasion of England in 1399. Richard II hastened back from Ireland and made his way to Conway Castle in North Wales. Bolingbroke, joined by an increasing number of other magnates, marched north through the Welsh Marches and almost certainly passed through Stretton on his way from Ludlow to Shrewsbury in August 1399; no doubt this meant trespass and spoli-ation for the local people. The next month King Richard was forced to abdicate and then Henry Bolingbroke was crowned king as Henry IV, the first of the Lancastrian line. The support of the Arundels was rewarded by Thomas's recognition as Earl of Arundel with the family estates restored, and by the rein-statement of his uncle as archbishop.

It therefore fell to the new earl to present the next rector to Stretton. Perhaps William Smythecote had stayed long enough to see in the new century as the episcopal registers record that on 28 September 1402, one Alan Thorpe was presented by Earl Thomas. It is very likely that this is the same Alan Thorpe who in 1388 had exchanged his living as rector of Llanarmon, in the St. Asaph diocese, with the rector of Clungunford, another Arundel benefice.

The patronage of the Earls of Arundel in the fourteenth century seems to have brought little benefit—and certainly no continuity—to the church at Stretton; rather, like the king before them, they used it to reward those in their service. The rectors themselves tended to treat the living as a stepping-stone to something better. In his *The English Clergy and their Organisation in the Later Middle Ages*, Professor Hamilton Thompson wrote: 'In the course of the fourteenth century the custom of exchanging ecclesiastical benefices had reached serious proportions',[37] and by the end of the century it had become a flagrant abuse. There were brokers who facilitated these exchanges and bishops regularly collaborated:

> One of the ordinaries (bishops) concerned issues a commission to the other to carry out the business and institute to both churches; this done, the ordinary who has expedited the exchange sends his certificate to the other, to whom the new rector of the church in his diocese reports in person or sends his proxy to do obedience ... There are many instances in which a man exchanges one church for another, and then, a day or two later, or even on the same day, exchanges this for a third. The obvious explanation is that the first of these exchanges is a transaction with a middle man who negotiates the second.[38]

It is easy to see why an incumbent wanted to obtain a more lucrative benefice; the reason why there were others willing to make an unfavourable exchange was that it enabled a needy clerk to acquire capital from the difference between the living he surrendered and the one he received.[39] 'There is evidence of a fairly active market in benefices, sometimes organised through brokers known as 'chop-churches''.[40] The practice had become such an abuse, as what happened in the church at Stretton confirms, that Archbishop William Courtenay, a former Bishop of Hereford, denounced the brokers in a strongly-worded mandate of 1392 as 'accursed consorts in guilt of Gehazi and Simon Magus'.[41] In the following century there is evidence that this forthright condemnation helped bring about a decline in the exchange of benefices, an improvement reflected in the parish of Church Stretton.

Ecclesiastical corruption could not be wholly stamped out and in the next century, which was dominated politically by dynastic clashes, calls for reform continued. But, it has recently been argued,[42] the popularity of established religious forms and imagery, and 'the voracious appetite for religious literature' — not to mention the many magnificent Perpendicular churches erected across the length and breadth of the country—are testimony to the continuing vitality and vigour of the 'old faith'.

5
THE LAST YEARS OF THE OLD FAITH

S hropshire and the Welsh Marches figured so prominently in national affairs at the turn of the century that life in Stretton cannot but have been affected. Richard II summoned the Parliament of 1398 to Shrewsbury, Henry of Lancaster pursued Richard north through the border counties the next year, and 16 September 1400 signalled the start of Owain Glyndwr's revolt against the new king, Henry IV, with his proclamation at Glyndyfrdwy of himself as Prince of Wales. He immediately attacked local towns, including Oswestry and Welshpool. Henry IV's army, marching south from Scotland, was diverted to Shrewsbury which became his base for a punitive campaign into North Wales. The rebels' capture of Conway Castle in 1401 showed that Glyndwr's revolt was no mere flash in the pan, and the Welsh victory at Pilleth near Knighton, in June 1402, threatened the English in the Marches as Welshmen in the border lordships flocked to his cause. The Earl of Arundel, who was put in command of the defence of the Northern Marches, stationed a large garrison in Montgomery Castle. 1403 saw the emergence of a still greater threat to the stability of the area in the revolt of the Percies, led by Hotspur and his uncle the Earl of Worcester. Henry IV and the young Prince Hal, however, crushed the rebels at the Battle of Shrewsbury on 22 July 1403; Hotspur was killed and Worcester executed. Glyndwr's revolt was, nevertheless, still very much alive and 'there were genuine fears that Welsh rebels would extend their raids into Shropshire, Cheshire and Herefordshire'.[1] These fears were realised in 1404 when attacks on Arundel manors only a few miles west of Shrewsbury left a trail of burnt villages and fleeing tenants. Early in 1406 Bishop Mascall of Hereford reported 52 churches damaged, including Wentnor on the other side of the Long Mynd.[2]

How were Stretton and its church affected by these dramatic events? The most direct impact will have been through the recruitment of soldiers by the lord of the manor, the Earl of Arundel, the commandeering of food and stores by the army, and probably pillage and plunder. Perhaps displaced or fearful relatives or other refugees from the warfare made their way to Stretton. More generally, 'the property damage, the fighting, the coming and going of armies, and the dislocation of economic and social life arising from the troop move-ments and from the rebellion must have made conditions in the county unset-tled and put considerable strains on the agencies charged with the administra-tion of justice and the maintenance of law and order'.[3] This had a longer-term effect: at the Parliament of 1414 it was reported that 'conditions in Shropshire were worse than anywhere else in the country, homicide and rape being offences mentioned as particularly common'.[4] Documents reveal that on Whitsunday 1395 John, son of Thomas Wetenhull of All Stretton was pardoned for the death of Richard Downton,[5] that on the eve of St. Bartholomew's Day in 1400 David Wright of Stretton feloniously killed Ralph Williams, another local man, at Church Stretton, and also that the justices at Shrewsbury in 1414 dealt with two cases of cattle theft from Stretton householders.[6]

In times of war and social breakdown people still turn to the Church; at the beginning of the fifteenth century this would have been even more true. The rector to whom Stretton parishioners may have turned (if he was resident) for comfort, assistance and prayers was, as has been mentioned, Alan Thorpe, instituted in 1402. He was not, however, rector for long because Bishop Mascall's register records that on 12 February 1405 William Corf, clerk, was presented to Stretton-en-le Dale by Thomas, Earl of Arundel and Surrey. Under both rectors many of their duties would have been performed by poorly-paid, unbeneficed and, for us, unknown clergy.

William Corf or Corve (and therefore probably from a local Corvedale family) was an academic churchman, a Fellow of Oriel College, Oxford.[7] Only a month after his institution he was granted ordination 'to all orders'—in fact most probably as deacon, as his ordination as priest was recorded in December 1405. It seems unlikely that he lived for long in Stretton for in February 1406 he was given a dispensation by the bishop for study leave for a year, and he is recorded as renting a room in Oriel College in 1409 which he still had two years later. By 1409, too, he was Master of Arts and Doctor of Theology. Together with the Abbot of Shrewsbury and others, he was ordered by the king in December 1413 to look into two impoverished prebends of St. Mary's, Shrewsbury; his reward was the prebend of Coldehall in Pontesbury—presum-ably not an impoverished one—on the presentation of Edward Charlton, Lord of Powys. His career was now approaching its zenith. In 1414 he acted as Archbishop Chichele's Proctor at the Roman Curia and then at the Council of Constance, summoned by the Emperor in that year. In March 1415 he was elected Provost of Oriel College.[8] He was given further reward the next year by his appointment as rector of Hanbury, Staffordshire.

William Corve was thus a distinguished churchman, though guilty of both pluralism and non-residence. The Council of Constance, where he represented the Archbishop of Canterbury, had been called to resolve a much greater scandal in the Church. Since 1378 there had been two rival Popes, at Rome and

The Hus memorial in Prague

Avignon, and the Council's purpose was to end this Great Schism, which it did by forcing the rival Popes to resign and electing Martin V as Pope of the whole Catholic Church. The Council also conducted the trial of John Hus, a theologian from Prague who had urged reform in the Church. Stretton's rector, Master William Corve, 'represented the English nation on the commission appointed to deal with Hus's case after the papally-appointed commission had lost its authority because of Pope John's flight'.[9] The other nations represented on the panel were Italy, Germany and France. William Corve is recorded as questioning Hus on the doctrines of predestination and, particularly, transubstantiation, comparing him with John Wyclif, the Englishman who had urged similar reforms 50 years earlier. At one point Corve interjected: 'Wait! He speaks evasively, just as Wyclif did. For he conceded all these things that this man concedes, yet nevertheless he held that the material bread remained in the sacrament of the altar after consecration'.[10] Hus denied this, but was still burned at the stake as a heretic in July 1415.

Whether or not Corve returned to England we cannot be sure, but he died at Constance in 1417 and was buried at St. Stephen's Church in that city; the Bishop of Lincoln, Richard Flemyng, gave the funeral oration. In his will he left his books on the Blessed Gregory and St. John Chrysostom to Oriel College which still holds them, and a bequest of £10 5s. 0d. 'for the building [presumably repair] of the nave of the church of Stretton'.[11] This is the first recorded gift to the church and, indeed, apart from the Domesday Book references, the earliest documented mention of the building. The legacy was a very substantial sum and suggests strongly that William Corve had spent some of his rectorship in Church Stretton and had a special affection for the place, as there are no similar bequests in his will. Yet it is surprising that his bequest was specifically for the nave, as for over a century it had been increasingly recognised that the upkeep of naves was the responsibility of parishioners.

Corve was rector of a parish in a diocese home to a number of Wyclif's followers (after his death in 1384 called Lollards). Some of Wyclif's early attacks on the 'Caesarean clergy', by which he meant those churchmen who neglected the cure of souls to do the king's business, would, if known, have been greeted sympathetically by Stretton inhabitants with long memories, but his later theological and philosophical writings would have gone over their heads. Even the appearance of the first English Bible, translated by Wyclif and his followers, could have meant little to illiterate country folk – that is, if anyone could have afforded a manually produced copy. But delivered in the language of ordinary people, the subsequent Lollard attacks on clerical pretensions, confession to priests, papal indulgences, tithes and the worship of images—and even the expression of doubts about the nature of the eucharist— could have found the odd listener in Stretton, although they seem to have been more heeded by tradesmen and artisans in the towns. However, the authorities in Church and State felt sufficiently threatened by these humble preachers and 'Bible men' to get Parliament to pass a statute in 1401 making death by burning the punishment for obstinate heretics. Yet the preaching continued and on 17 March 1407 one William Thorpe,[12] in a sermon at St. Chad's, Shrewsbury, so troubled the congregation that he was handed over to Archbishop Arundel. The most prominent figure in later Lollardy, Sir John Oldcastle, came from Herefordshire, and after the fiasco of his attempted coup in London in 1414— the year in which Stretton's rector was off to Constance to challenge John Hus—he went into hiding and was eventually caught near Welshpool in 1417.

One man who perhaps brought to Stretton personal knowledge of these last events was its next rector, for in that same year of 1417, when the news of William Corve's death reached England, Thomas Oswestre from the border country was presented to the Stretton living. The Earl of Arundel was probably in France with King Henry V on the campaign that followed the victory of Agincourt, because the presentation was made by his four feoffees (trustees); the Dean of Wenlock was asked to induct the new rector. Thomas Oswestre is described as 'clerk' in the bishop's register, but he was apparently only in minor orders, for the next August he is recorded as an acolyte on being ordained 'to all the sacred orders'. In one particular, however, Oswestre excelled his predecessors because he remained as rector for the next 22 years until his death in 1439. Unfortunately nothing more is known about him, although he must surely have officiated on an important occasion in 1428. This was the funeral of John Leighton, who, 45 years earlier, had married Maud, daughter and heir

The coats-of-arms in the Leighton window

of Watkyn Cambray of Stretton-in-the-Dale. Whether immediately after the wedding in 1383, or some years later, Leighton had moved to the Cambrays' manor house which became the Leighton family residence for some generations. John's death is commemorated by the date 1428 and by the Leighton coat-of-arms impaling Cambray in the Leighton window at St. Laurence's — although that was not inserted until 1899 and then to commemorate a nineteenth century artist!

On Thomas Oswestre's death, John Fox, chaplain, was presented to Stretton-in-the-Dale in September 1439 by William, the new Earl of Arundel. It was natural that he became friendly with John Leighton's son, Edward, at the manor house. Fox's ownership of land in Ludlow — he was almost certainly one of the Fox(e) family who by the middle of the next century had become the richest and the most powerful family in Ludlow[13] — is mentioned in Edward Leighton's will made in 1444 but not proved until 4 March 1455. Edward's death is also commemorated in the Leighton window by the date 1455, by a request to pray for his soul, and by the Leighton arms impaling Stapleton, for Edward had made another astute marriage — to Elizabeth, daughter and co-heir of Sir John Stapleton, of Stapleton, Shropshire.

It was something of a freak chance that the Leighton window was ever placed in St. Laurence's, yet these much earlier Leightons could have been among the church's principal benefactors. There is little doubt that they were the leading family in the parish. Edward Leighton's eldest son, John, was able to capitalise on the shrewd matrimonial alliances of his father and grandfather. In 1460 he became an M.P. for Shropshire and was three times sheriff of the county in 1468, 1474 and 1482. He was also at various times the bishop's Steward of Bishop's Castle, Guardian of the estate of Lord Powys, Constable of the Arundel castle at Oswestry, and Steward for Montgomery under Richard, Duke of York.[14] These were the years of the Wars of the Roses, another period of military action in the Marches, which witnessed battles at Ludford Bridge and Mortimer's Cross. From their stronghold at Ludlow the Yorkists sought to raise troops, but Stretton may have been beyond the area of York family influence. It will have been at risk, however, from the bands of armed men who roamed the countryside. As an official of the Duke of York, John Leighton might have been expected to support the Yorkists, yet at the decisive Battle of Bosworth in 1485 he fought on the side of Henry Tudor. He was yet another Leighton who married an heiress—Ankoret, daughter and co-heir of Sir John Burgh of Wattlesborough. On his death in 1493 he was succeeded by his son Thomas who followed his father as an M.P. and sheriff, and became a 'knight of the body' to King Henry VII. He continued to live at the great house in Stretton-in-the-Dale, but after his death in 1519 his son, Sir John, probably moved the family seat from Stretton to the ancient Corbet estate of Wattlesborough, west of Shrewsbury.

These details are relevant to the history of St. Laurence's because the Leightons were the family with the wealth and influence to make a major contribution to the further restoration of the church building. Rector John Fox's will was proved in May 1454 and Edward Leighton, *armiger*, was one of the administrators named.[15] Edward's own will was proved in March 1455 and expressed his wish to be buried in the church. Relations between the leading family of the parish and the next rector, however, are unlikely to have been so close, for Richard Norys, presented by William, Earl of Arundel, on 24 October 1454, was soon away at Oxford studying Civil Law, receiving his master's degree in 1459. His non-residence was matched by other irregularities that would have been seized upon by reformers: though rector from 1454 he was not in priest's orders until 1458 and the next year he was granted a papal dispensation to hold an additional incompatible benefice. In 1459, too, he exchanged the living of Stretton with Master David Haliwelle, rector of St. Nicholas, Guildford. In his time, at a meeting of the manor court on 6 May 1461 the lands and tenements at Botvyle in Stretton of a certain William Botvelde were passed to his son Richard and his heirs, with remainder to his married daughter and her heirs, and finally, if their lines failed, to 'the Church of Seynte Laurence to susteyn a prieste'[16]—almost certainly a chaplain to say mass in the Lady Chapel. It was Richard Botvelde's son, John, who first assumed the name of Thynne and from whom the future patrons were descended. Haliwelle himself resigned in October 1465 and was replaced by 'Sir' William Hugyns, again presented by Earl William.

Hugyns appears to have come from a local All Stretton family as the will of a John Hugyns in 1468 named his executors as his wife, Joan, and his son, Sir William.[17] It seems probable, therefore, that he would have been a resident rector. What is more, William Hugyns was already a priest and remained as rector until his death in 1514, a period of 49 years. He immediately appealed to the bishop for action to remedy defects in the church building which resulted in John Greneway, a magistrate, being asked to inquire in March 1467 into the state of the chancel and the rectory.[18] Both were the incumbent's responsibility and had probably been neglected by the succession of non-resident rectors, with David Haliwelle named in the bishop's response. Stretton's trouble was far from unique. 'Allegations of neglect were common', writes a church historian of this period, 'but by far the most frequent manifestation of this was the decayed condition of the chancel of the church or of the parsonage'.[19] Nothing is known of the parson's house in these years, but it would have been a substantial building, for as early as 1324 the buildings judged 'proportionate to the estate of a vicarage' at Condover were 'a hall, two chambers, a cellar (storehouse or larder), a kitchen, a stable, a brewhouse and other buildings'.[20]

William Hugyns needed generous support to repair the dilapidations in the chancel and parsonage, which parishioners might say were not their responsibility. Fortunately, as a native of Stretton, the rector had better prospects of raising funds than absentee predecessors, and the increasing wealth and eminence of the Leightons could have been of vital importance in effecting restoration and perhaps other developments. Yet it was not a poor parish: when Henry VII was granted a clerical subsidy by Convocation in 1488 Stretton's share of 40s. bore comparison with Ludlow's 54s. 4d., and in a grant of 1505 Stretton's share of 15s. was the largest in the Wenlock Deanery.[21] Nor would Stretton people have wanted their church to compare poorly with those of other local parishes. As for the Leightons, they would have wished to give glory to God—and probably themselves—for their improving fortunes. Their importance had already been recognised by the permission granted by the bishop in 1481 to John Leighton to have an oratory or private chapel in his house. Such requests were less frequent than they had been, as gentry had come to favour instead the founding of chantries where masses could be said for their souls— as John Leighton's son was to do —but it is possible that the Leightons' 'great house' was in All Stretton, and therefore distant from the church.

Not all that went on in William Hugyns's time was as edifying as the repair and development of the church. The rector would have conducted the funeral of John Hughes who was killed in Stretton in an infamous incident a few days before Christmas in 1491. An inquisition by the coroner[22] the next day recorded that, according to eyewitnesses, Hughes was attacked by three men 'lying in wait and with premeditated assault'. Their leader, who was on horseback, rode at Hughes and struck him a fatal blow in the chest with a lance; the others joined in with a sword and a bill-hook. The leader was none other than Humphrey Kynaston, 'Wild Humphrey' as he became known, from a landed Shropshire family, who became celebrated as an outlaw and highwayman living in a cave at Nesscliffe until pardoned by Henry VIII.

*

At the end of the fifteenth century the main structure of St. Laurence's had not changed since the cruciform church had been erected nearly three hundred years earlier and, indeed, would still be recognisable today. The interior, however, although embellished by new roofing timbers and larger windows, would have been markedly different from its present appearance.

It is quite likely that by 1500 a south porch had been erected,[23] for they were popular places for conversation and even business deals. On entering through the Norman south door (there was, of course, then no west door) the first thing that would strike a modern visitor—apart from the smell of damp walls, incense and burning candles—would be the comparative darkness. Several windows had been enlarged, but there was no big west window, the Norman walls continued up to the crossing, and the light from the east end was partly blocked by the rood screen. The dimness was relieved, however, by the light cast by the candles burning on the screen and before the images. Such light would have revealed colourful paintings on the plastered walls—probably St. Christopher opposite the south door, because it was believed that the sight of this saint gave protection for the day against sudden disaster, and on the west wall, where they were still visible at the end of the eighteenth century, a full-size figure of a skeleton and a representation of Time.[24] In winter months the church would have felt very cold since there was no regular heating syatem.

In all probability there would have been no seating, for it is doubtful if any of the box pews, replaced in the nineteenth century by today's pews, had yet been installed, and the only seating available for those unable to stand would presumably have been some seats against the walls of the nave—the origin of the phrase 'the weakest go to the wall'—and possibly some benches near the front. In 1500 the congregation stood, squatted or knelt during services, and it seems likely that on the well-beaten earth of the floor, or possibly newly-laid flagstones then coming into vogue, were spread straw or rushes to make kneeling more comfortable. Fresh straw or rushes were brought in before major festivals. The open area of the nave would have been very familiar to the people of the parish for as well as being the place of worship it was also, as the only large, enclosed public space there was, the venue for meetings and social gatherings like the 'church ales', which a Stretton document of 1595 describes as of ancient origin. These were festivities designed for Christian fellowship, to raise money for the church and to provide opportunities for enjoyment. In midsummer the music, dancing, games, eating and drinking would have been out-of-doors in the church-yard, unencumbered by tombstones until probably the seventeenth century, but at other times in the nave itself. Weddings, baptisms and 'wakes' after funerals or on the eve of special saints' days provided other occasions for social celebration.

Almost opposite the main entrance to the church was the north door used, as it had been for centuries, for the entry of funeral processions, some making their way down from the hamlets to the east along what is still, five hundred years later, known as the 'coffin path'. The north door was also called the 'devil's door' as by

The font

tradition it was left open at baptisms for the devil to fly out. The font stood near the south door and in 1500 was surely the same font as today since its Perpendicular style suggests it dates from the fifteenth century. It is of stone, octagonal in shape, with some simple sculpting on three of its faces—two with unmarked shields and one in the centre with a regular floral pattern. The font has a lead lining to prevent water seeping through the stone. Today's cover is modern; in 1500 it would probably have been more ornate and kept locked to stop people taking away the holy water.

But the feature which would have arrested one's attention was the great rood screen between the eastern piers of the crossing. It may have been the screen, which separated the chancel from the nave, that needed repair when William Hugyns became rector and found the chancel in a bad state. It could since have been replaced or extended as new timber screens, more elaborately carved, were a popular and relatively inexpensive improvement at that time. The dado or lower part of the screen would most likely have been of solid wood, possibly with pictures of the saints in panels and a few peep-holes to enable those kneeling at the front to see the celebrant at the altar. The upper part would have been open tracery. Above the screen was the rood-beam, surmounted by a large crucifix or rood, with the crucified Christ between the figures of the Virgin Mary and St. John. It was customary for the space between the top of the screen and the apex of the chancel arch to be filled in, probably with a wooden tympanum on which was painted the Doom, the Day of Judgment, with lurid depictions of the tortures of the damned. At Stretton, however, this may have been painted on the wall to the sides of the chancel arch and above it where the space was more extensive than it is today because the floor of the ringing-chamber did not then exist. The reason for the probable absence of a tympanum, or one of smaller size, is that there was an extension eastwards from the roof-beam to form a rood-loft. This was reached through the shoul-dered arch in the chancel and up the tower stairs, and gave access to the lights and lanterns along the beam and facilitated the covering of the rood during Lent. In some churches the loft was used as a storage place. But St. Laurence's exhibits a very unusual feature:

> At Church Stretton there is an altar-drain in a most abnormal position, viz., in the sill of a window, high in the south wall of the chancel. The window-sill, in which the basin of the drain is hollowed, is at a level of about 11 feet 6 inches above the present floor of the chancel. Situated where it is, near the western extremity of the chancel, this drain could only have served for an altar in the rood-loft, but the latter must have extended eastward, contrary to general usage, some considerable distance into the chancel.[25]

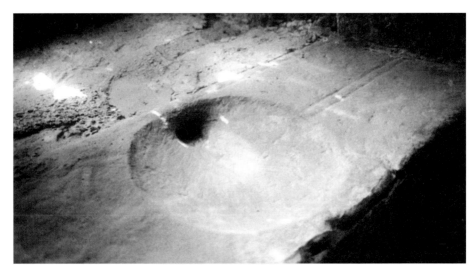

The piscina in the sill of the upper side window

If this drain did serve an altar in the rood-loft then St. Laurence's was unique among Shropshire churches, although there was another at Little Hereford, just over the county border. The roughly circular shallow basin has a large drain-hole on the south side. In Cranage's view it was not moved to its present place as there is no other 'nave or chancel window continued low enough to a sill which would have accommodated a piscina'. This is as near as we can get to proof that there was an altar in the loft which provided an additional place for the celebration of Mass. Illumination for the loft came from the lights on the rood-beam and from the small rectangular window high on the south wall of the chancel near its west end (with the piscina in its sill) which appears to have been knocked through in the late fifteenth century. There are no clear signs of where the loft was fixed, but the evidence of the high side window and piscina is supported by the existence of a low side window (see illustration on p.218), apparently from the late Perpendicular period, surely formed to provide light under the loft, perhaps also for ventilation, and possibly to ring the sanctus bell for the benefit of those in the churchyard.[26] That this lancet-shaped window was shuttered can be deduced from the marks on the jambs. The dripstone has a shallow hollow and terminations in the form of a shield charged with a cross; the signs are that it was repaired in the early seventeenth century.

The transepts acted as side-chapels, the one on the south side dedicated to the Virgin Mary as revealed by Edward Leighton's will of 1444 which expressed his wish to be buried 'in the chapel of St. Mary in the Church of Stretton'.[27] It is likely that the other was dedicated to St. Laurence, for in his will of 1535 John Coke asked that he should be buried in the church of St. Laurence and that of the torches surrounding the bier at his funeral two were for St. Laurence, two for Our Lady and two to burn 'in my lampe', probably one on the rood-beam or before the altar that he had maintained in his lifetime.[28] The remainder and eight tapers were donated to the churches at Hope Bowdler and Ratlinghope. It seems very possible that these churches were served by those, including perhaps Coke himself, who were chaplains at Stretton. Most likely there would have been statues on either side of the screen, of the Virgin Mary and the patron saint. A document of 1572 from the reign of Elizabeth I[29] (when property given earlier to churches was being sold by a government with Protestant sympathies) lists lands in Church Stretton, and even more in All Stretton, whose rents had been given to maintain 'the Lady priest' who served in the Chapel of St. Mary in the parish church of Stretton and for lights before 'divers images, the roode and the crucifixe'. It refers to pastures in both Church Stretton and All Stretton known as 'Our Lady Meadow'. A further gift of a 'leasowe' in Botfield was for the maintenance of a stipendiary priest, a lamp and a taper in the church at Cardington or Stretton.

Beyond the screen lay the chancel and sanctuary, the domain of the priest. There was, of course, no organ and no choir-stalls, but the present aumbry in the south wall may well once have been a piscina serving the high altar. Sacred vessels and altar plate would have been safeguarded in a locked chest. The eye would have been led irresistibly, however, to the high altar, probably with a stone slab top and bearing a cross and two candles with a colourfully embroidered frontal. Suspended above the altar there may have been a pyx of silver or ivory containing the sacrament. Ordinary parishioners who would have been buried in the churchyard liked in their wills to make a small bequest to maintain a candle at or near the high altar to hold them in remembrance close to the blessed sacrament: John Bright 'of Lytill Stretton' would leave 4d. for this purpose in 1556.[30]

Above the crossing in the central tower there were five bells, in addition to a sanctus bell, according to an inventory of 1553 in Edward VI's reign.[31] These would have summoned worshippers and notified local people of the imminence of baptisms, marriages and funerals, as well as celebrating national events. But what of the tower itself? The original cruciform church, already described, almost certainly had a squat central tower as at Wistanstow, where it was also later, but more modestly, extended. All who have written about St. Laurence's have commented on and praised the Perpendicular style of the upper part of the tower, but have attributed this to very different periods—or to none at all. Henrietta Auden's introduction to the printed version of the early parish registers maintains that 'in the fourteenth century the upper storey was added to the tower', and in an article of 1903 on 'Shropshire 500 years ago' she claims that several churches in the county show fifteenth-century work in their towers, but she does not instance Church Stretton although she lived there. Her brother, the Rev. J.E. Auden, however, in his *Little Guide to Shropshire* wrote of St. Laurence's tower 'the upper part of which is fifteenth century'. This is also the period assigned to the building of the upper tower in the Department of the Environment's Listed Buildings. On the other hand, the architect who carried out the Victorian restoration of the church refers in a written note on his drawings to the 'upper stories of Tower late Perpendicular 16th century'. Cranage hazards no date but gives a detailed description:

> The fine Perpendicular work above is the most striking sight outside. The Transitional walls appear for some distance above the roof, but the whole of the upper part is Perpendicular. The ornamentation is rich and effective. The windows are cusped and pointed under square heads. The gargoyles, unfortunately, are considerably decayed, but they are still unusually fine and grotesque. The upper part of the tower is rather narrower than the lower, and has slight diagonal buttresses at the corners. In the south-east buttress is a figure of the patron saint, St. Laurence, with the usual accompaniment of the gridiron.

Another view of the tower

There was then no pyramidal roof as later paintings show (see illustrations on pp. 176 & 192). Pevsner in his *Buildings of Shropshire* emphasises the difference between the lower and upper parts of the tower. He points out that there are lancets in the lowest stage visible outside (the ringers' chamber is inside) and continues, 'This is followed by a change from rubble to ashlar, yet there are again lancets here and the fenestration turns Perpendicular only one stage higher'. David Bilbey, in the introduction to his illustrated book on Church Stretton and in his valuable short guide to St. Laurence's, follows Cranage and probably wisely desists from allocating the extension of the tower to any particular period. Yet the original tower must have extended above the ridges of the roof, and the lancet windows that Pevsner alludes to in the lower ashlar stage (where the clock chamber is inside) suggest that the thirteenth-century tower may have been of that height. Perhaps that section of the tower was rebuilt in ashlar later—possibly, as some of the ashlar blocks appear a little more worn than in the upper stage, in the fifteenth century, with the final section completed in the early sixteenth century or even, as some believe and as will be examined in Chapter 7, early in the seventeenth century.

*

Any reconstruction of the forms of worship observed in St. Laurence's in 1500 must depend not on surviving local documentation, for there is none, but on our knowledge of the universal practice of this time.

'At the centre of the life of the medieval catholic church, and of the religious experience of all orthodox believers, stood the Mass.'[32] In Church Stretton, as elsewhere, Mass was celebrated every Sunday at the high altar and, as all priests had to celebrate Mass daily, on some or all week days at dawn in the 'morrow Mass' for the benefit of those on their way to work. At St. Laurence's week-day Masses could have been celebrated at one of the side-altars in the transepts or in the rood-loft. Parishioners actually received communion—and that meant just the bread, the Body of Christ—only once a year on Easter Sunday. That does not necessarily mean that at other Masses they were merely passive spectators: the fundamental requirements for the laity at Mass were 'to kneel quietly without idle chatter, saying Paters and Aves, to respond to certain key gestures or phrases by changing posture, above all at the sacring'—to which they were alerted by the ringing of a bell immediately before the priest held the consecrated element aloft—'to kneel with hands raised in adoration, to gaze on the Host, and to greet their Lord with an elevation prayer'.[33] That the Mass was conducted in Latin was probably of less significance than it seems as the priest often said the service silently to allow the congregation to say their own prayers, and people were familiar with the sequence of the liturgy. After he had received communion using, in Stretton, the silver chalice recorded in the inventory of 1553, and the paten not recorded, the priest recited from the last gospel the first 14 verses of John's first chapter. To encourage the laity to remain to the end of the Mass, in many churches indulgences[34] could be gained by kissing a text or an image at the words, 'The Word became flesh'.

Although these Masses were for some a truly spiritual experience, and for many a spectacular and colourful drama, reformers pointed to superstitious attitudes that could develop. The Lollard preacher, William Thorpe, in his sermon at Shrewsbury in 1407, condemned those who ran from one altar to another to catch a glimpse of the Host, and Archbishop Cranmer was later to question the spiritual understanding of those who expressed their faith in sentiments like, 'I cannot be quiet unless I see my Maker once a day'.[35]

The parish high Mass on Sundays was a more elaborate occasion. It began with a procession round the church, with holy water sprinkled on the altar and on the congregation. Another additional ceremony was the 'bidding of the bedes', prayers for the Church, those in authority, people in need, recently deceased parishioners and those on the roll of benefactors of the parish church —which encouraged gifts of lights or ornaments. At Sunday Mass also, the pax, a disc bearing a sacred emblem, such as the Lamb of God or the Crucifix, was kissed by the priest and then taken outside the screen to be kissed in turn by the parishioners. This was clearly a substitute for the reception of communion, as was the distribution, at the end of the service of a piece of bread to members of the congregation from the loaf presented each week by a different householder of the parish and blessed by the priest.

There were also Masses for the souls of those who had left bequests for this purpose. Stretton does not appear on the lists of churches with chantries, but the side-chapels owed their on-going existence to bequests from well-off local people who wanted to ensure that prayers continued for them after their death. In his will of 1519 Sir Thomas Leighton would direct his executors to 'finde an honest and wel disposed Prist to say Masses and other suffrages affore our Blessed Lady in the Parish Churche of Stretton, therfor to pray for my Sowle, the Sowles of my Father and Modyr, and the Sowles of all mine Auncestors, and all Crystyn Sowles, yevyng to the said Prist for hys Salary and Wages viii Marks by the yere'.[36] And in 1535 John Coke was to leave 20s. to a Mass-priest for the same service. Behind their desperate desire for intercessory Masses lay the doctrine of Purgatory, formulated in the twelfth century, that there was an intermediate place between Heaven and Hell. In Purgatory souls might be cleansed of the guilt attached to sin committed during life according to a graduated scale of divine punishments. Their suffering, too, might be shortened by the prayers of the living and especially by Masses and, above all, by Masses for one soul in particular. This helps us to understand why in the late Middle Ages there was such a preoccupation with death. There was also great concern about the place of burial: Edward Leighton had specified the chapel of St. Mary, John

Coke said the church—the chancel and near the high altar were especially prized burial places, but generally limited to the clergy and the patron—and John Bright simply said the churchyard, where a grave near the parish cross was deemed most desirable.

It was the priest's duty to hear confession, and the duty of everyone to confess to the priest once a year and to complete any penance ordered, so that communion might be received on Easter Day. Confession helped the priest to fulfil another role, instructing the people in the articles of the faith and the divine precepts, because he could discover at the confession if his people knew the Ten Commandments, had committed any of the seven deadly sins, or had engaged in any of the seven acts of mercy. Sermons would have been unusual, but the conscientious priest might occasionally have addressed his flock in English. On the other hand, the cure of souls meant a demanding pastoral ministry, visiting the sick, reconciling those who had quarrelled, and trying to get people to live together in peace and harmony. The sacrament of extreme unction produced the frequent sight of the priest hastening to bear the Host to the dying.

Ritual stood at the heart of parish life. The passage of the agrarian year corresponded to and was marked out by the festivals and fasts of the liturgical year. Advent climaxed in the celebration of Christmas, and on 2 February Candlemas featured a procession of all parishioners bearing candles which were presented to the priest at Mass; other candles were blessed to take home to ward off sickness and to comfort the dying. As the long fast of Lent neared its end, Holy Week was heralded by the great Palm Sunday procession in which the congregation, bearing branches as palms, gathered at the churchyard cross while anthems were sung; sticks were brought to church to be made into crosses while the narrative of the Passion was read. On Maundy Thursday the altars were stripped in preparation for the solemn commemoration of the Passion on Good Friday, when a crucifix was brought into the church and clergy and people crept barefoot and on their knees to kiss the foot of the cross. A previously consecrated host was placed in the Easter sepulchre, usually a simple wooden container put on the north side of the chancel. The sepulchre was guarded by a trustworthy parishioner until Easter Day, when the Host was removed as a symbol of the Resurrection, the great Paschal candle lit, and all received communion in the triumphant Easter Mass. The Rogationtide processions and beating of the bounds took place on the three days leading up to Ascensiontide. Everyone was expected to turn out for them, and the wealthier parishioners provided food and drink for their poorer neighbours. All the church banners and processional crosses were carried through the parish, accompanied by bell-ringing and singing, to drive out the evil spirits. At the centre of the ritual was the solemn reading of portions of the Gospel at points on the parish boundary sometimes marked by wayside crosses. Beating the bounds must have been a demanding physical exercise in a parish as large and hilly as Stretton. Then there were the traditional bonfires to mark saints' days in the summer. In Stretton there would have been a special celebration of St. Laurence's Day on 10 August, but all major saints' days were marked by a fast on the preceding day and a holiday on the day itself. Finally, at Harvest time the service of Thanksgiving was followed by games for the children and a joyful feast for all.

*

In October 1512, towards the end of William Hugyns' time as rector, the Lady Chapel received additional financial support when, at the manor court, 'John Ryton one of the wardens of the Blessed Mary the Virgin of Church Stretton was admitted to a messuage and one acre of land lying in Dudesley and a cottage with the appurtenances in All Stretton to the use of the service of the Blessed Mary the Virgin'.[37]

William Hugyns died in 1514, nearly 50 years after his appointment. In spite of an apparent difference in spelling, it is hard not to conclude that his successor, Edward Higgons, was a relation, especially as Bishop Mayew's register records: '1514 – 12 December – Edward Higgons, dec. doc., presented to Stretton-in-the-Dale by Richard Hyggons, on a grant of the presentation *hac vice* from Thomas, Earl of Arundel, and through his proctor Peter Hygyns, on the death of William Higgyns' — which displays four different spellings of what was surely the same surname. More important, it appears that the earl, no longer resident in the area, had granted a turn in choosing the rector to a substantial local figure, Richard Hyggons, a practice that was to lead to dissension a century later. The new rector, Edward Higgons, had already ascended high on the ladder of ecclesiastical preferment: a graduate of Oxford University, he had been ordained priest in 1501 and is recorded as receiving his Doctorate of Canon Law in 1511. He became Principal of Burnell's Inn on the site of the Oxford college soon to be founded by Thomas Wolsey as Christ Church. In 1505 he was registrar of the Bishop of Hereford, the next year he is described as 'notary public', and in 1512 he was appointed a Master in Chancery. For his services to the law he had been rewarded by a succession of no doubt increasingly valuable benefices and prebends, particularly in the diocese of Salisbury. His admission as rector of Church Stretton may well have been the consequence of his being appointed Dean of the College of the Blessed Virgin Mary at Shrewsbury in 1513 as well as of his relative's timely death. He was rector of St. Laurence's for only five months before resuming his ecclesiastical promotion, now chiefly in Sussex, where he went on to become Master of Trinity College, Arundel, and a canon of Chichester, finally becoming a canon and prebendary in Lincoln diocese. He died in 1538, leaving a collection of musical settings to masses to Caius College, Cambridge, and his one known published work, *Geographia*.[38] It was in his time that John Thynne's son, Ralph, who had married the daughter of John Hygons, 'was interred with great solemnity at Church Stretton'.[39]

Edward Higgons' resignation was followed quickly by the Earl of Arundel's presentation of George Dycher to the church at Stretton on 25 May 1515. The new young rector had supplicated for the degree of Bachelor of Canon Law at Oxford only two years earlier; he was already in priest's orders. He was destined to serve as rector through the tumultuous years of Henry VIII's breach with Rome.

All that is known of George Dycher's rectorship, however, suggests that local issues remained more important than national in a country parish far from London. In 1521 the Bishop of Hereford charged the rectors of Stretton and Wistanstow with the task of pronouncing the excommunication of the unknown boys who had broken down the fences and gates of the bishop's meadow called 'Old Church More'[40] at the southern extremity of the parish—a heavy-handed response indeed. Rector Dycher seems to have made several exchanges of land to consolidate the church's properties, one of them with a Thomas Rawlins.[41] On another occasion, known only through an appeal to the Earl of Arundel preserved in the Blakeway MSS, the two men seem to have fallen out. It reads:

> Sheweth and complaineth unto your good mastership your Orator [i.e. petitioner] George Dycher, clerke parson of the parish church of Stretton. Whereas your said orator and his predecessors have been seased [i.e. possessed] of one acre of land lying in Dalacre in the township of Church Stretton time out of mind as in the right of his said church whereof my Lord of Arundel is patron, so it is good master that one Thomas Rawlyns of the same town, of his extort power and covetous mind hath entered into the said acre. In consideration whereof and for as much as the patronage is in my Lord of Arundel that it may please your mastership to see that your said orator may be restored to his right and your said orator shall daily pray for your good mastership.

There is no evidence that this obsequious appeal was successful or not. George Dycher would regularly have prayed for his patron in any case; as for Thomas Rawlyns, he seems to have made his peace with the church as he (or his son) was one of the churchwardens who signed the inventory of 1553.

An outsider's view of Church Stretton is given by John Leland in his celebrated *Itinerary*. On a journey from Ludlow, probably in 1538,

> I left the Egge [Wenlock Edge] and the Longe Forest, 2 great wodds havynge roe deer, on the right hande coming to Stretton. Thens I rode a 3 miles by well woddyd ground to Streton, a prati [pretty] uplandishe

townelet, where by the church one Brooke a lawyer hath a praty howse, and here rennythe a broke (the same, as one told me, that goeth by Stretford).

This townelett is the chefist buildinge that is in Streton Dale; Streton Dale is inclosyd with grete hills, well woodyd in some places. It is in length but a 3 miles, and in it be 3 Stretons, Little Streton, Great Streton and Old Streton. This Streton Dale longgith to the Erle of Arundle.

From Streton to Libot Woode a thorough faire 3 miles, by hilly and woody ground.[42]

It is interesting to find a reference to the church and to lawyer Brooke's house nearby, for Francis Brooke had succeeded the Leightons as steward of the manor for the Earl of Arundel. Later Brookes lived in Bank House, Longhills, but 'by the church' suggests the 'prati howse' may have been where the Hall was subsequently situated, nearly opposite the church. It is interesting, too, that the wooded nature of the area impressed Leland as much as the hills. But for the road from Ludlow to Shrewsbury running through the town, Stretton would have been very remote.

It was still financially a good benefice, however. The *Valor Ecclesiasticus* of 1535,[43] a national survey of clerical incomes to determine the product of a 10% annual tax under the terms of the Act for First Fruits and Tenths, contains the details of the Stretton Rectory. The glebe was annually worth £1 6s. 8d., the corn and hay tithes £9 6s. 8d., and other tithes £5 6s. 8d., a total of £16 per annum.

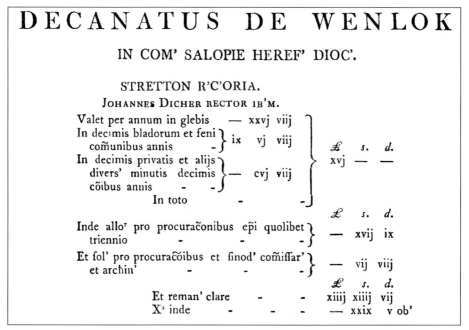

Stretton's entry in the Valor Ecclesiasticus *1535*

From this had to be paid the annual portion of the bishop's triennial procurations (the original burden of entertainment on the bishop's visit long commuted to a yearly charge), which amounted to 17s. 9d., together with 7s. 8d. for the annual procurations and synodals of the commissary and archdeacon. This left the rector with a net income of £14 14s. 7d., exceeded in the deanery only by Rushbury and Munslow. The next year, in answer to the king's writ demanding to know the annual value of all ecclesiastical benefices, the bishop's response gives Stretton-in-the-Dale as £15 10s., less than Wenlock Priory and Munslow, but still in value in the top 25% of livings in the country.[44]

George Dycher died in 1549. It would not be true to say that with him there passed the Roman Catholic era in the history of St. Laurence's. Yet the publication of the first Prayer Book in English in the year of Dycher's death was a moment of great significance in the Reformation. Its appearance will have brought home to ordinary parishioners, even in a rural parish in the Welsh Marches, that a wind of change was blowing through the Church.

6
PROTESTANT REFORMATION

It is likely that while George Dycher remained rector the parish of Church
Stretton was largely sheltered from the gusts of change that were buffeting
the English Church during the later years of Henry VIII's reign. There is no
detailed knowledge of Dycher's doctrinal position, but he had already been
rector for 20 years when the king's assumption of the title of Supreme Head of
the Church in England in 1534 opened the door wider to reformist ideas, and
as the nominee of the strictly orthodox Earl of Arundel he would have been
committed to the Mass and to the doctrines which underpinned it. Moreover,
Stretton's remote situation in the Welsh borderlands meant that its inhabitants
were 'much behind the king's subjects in the south', as a new bishop wrote of
his people in the nearby diocese of Chester.[1]

Nevertheless, some changes in devotional practice as well as in worship will
have been apparent at St. Laurence's. For instance, in 1535 the first English
Primer was published. The Primer, or Book of Hours, was a scriptural prayer-
book with liturgical extracts and popular devotions, related particularly to
Christ's Passion and the Virgin Mary. In its Latin form it had reached a much
wider readership since the invention of printing. The first English version
omitted some of the popular features and attacked what it regarded as superstitious practices. Reformist sympathies were also revealed in the King's Primer,
again in English, published ten years later. These changes, however, will have
touched only the literate members of the Stretton church. Ordinary parishioners
will have been alerted to what was happening by news filtering through of
clashes between the proponents and opponents of change in other parts of the
country—clashes over relics (Bury St. Edmund's, for example, claimed to have
the coals that roasted St. Laurence), the worship of saints and images, creeping
to the Cross, Purgatory, intercession for the dead, 'lights', processions, pilgrim-
ages and indulgences. Henry VIII's own position was ambiguous: he decreed
in 1536 that any saint's day falling in the summer months should be celebrated
at the beginning of October—in order to stop interruptions during harvest-
time—but then, the next year, himself observed St. Laurence's Day at court in
August. However, this merely reflected the uncertainty and conflict within the

country: bishops included traditionalists and reformers, the clergy were divided, and there were numerous instances of dissension, even violence, within parishes between 'papists' and 'heretics'. One suspects that Church Stretton may have been among the more traditional parishes where abrogated feast-days were still observed, where the clergy resisted the royal injunction to teach the Pater, Ave and Credo in English, and where images, if taken down, were not destroyed. If so, the parishioners will have felt relieved to hear of the more conservative Six Articles Act of 1539 and the fall of Thomas Cromwell, the king's chief minister, in 1540. Yet the government's order of 1538 that all churches should provide 'one book of the whole Bible of the largest volume' in English for public reading, reaffirmed three years later, was to prove of greater long-term significance. As Edward Fox, Bishop of Hereford, told his fellow bishops in 1537: 'Make not yourselves the laughing-stock of the world; light is sprung up and is scattering all the clouds. The lay people know the scriptures better than many of us'.[2]

By the time of Henry VIII's death in 1547 probably little had changed in the church at Stretton, but George Dycher's last two years as rector witnessed the start of a turbulent period of reform in the country precipitated by the accession of the young Edward VI under the influence of Protestant advisers. New injunctions condemned the recitation of the rosary and the veneration of images. Lights on rood-lofts as well as before images were prohibited and the destruction of the images themselves ordered; all processions were banned. Commissioners were appointed to tour the land to see that the injunctions were obeyed. All over the country, even in staunchly traditionalist areas, there were outbreaks of iconoclasm accompanied by the suppression of familiar devotional customs: no Candlemas ceremonies, no Palms, no creeping to the Cross, no Easter sepulchres, no Paschal candles, no blessing of the font, no Rogationtide processions. Then, from Whitsuntide in 1549, Cranmer's first English Prayer Book, authorised by an Act of

THE

BOOKE OF THE COMMON

PRAYER AND ADMI-

NISTRACION OF

THE

SACRAMENTES, AND OTHER

RITES AND CEREMONIES OF

THE CHURCHE AFTER THE

USE OF THE CHURCHE

OF ENGLAND.

Londini in Officina
Edouardi Whitchurche.
Cum privilegio ad imprimendum solum
Anno Do. 1549, *Mense* Martii.

From the first
English Prayer Book of 1549

Uniformity, became the sole legal form of worship. It introduced not only regular congregational Communion services wholly in English, but swept away the time-honoured features of Sunday Mass—the parish procession, the elevation of the Host, the kissing of the pax, and the sharing of holy bread. It abolished the observance of most saints' days. The reaction was hostile in many areas and there was a rising in the West Country. Yet bishops were ordered to destroy or deface Catholic service books so that they were no longer usable, and local officials and churchwardens had to ensure that all images and sacred paintings were destroyed under threat of fines and imprisonment. In 1550 it was ordered that all altars should come down and be replaced by communion tables. It was while radicalism was at its flood-tide that the second English Book of Common Prayer was authorised and introduced in 1552. It sought to purge the Church of the last vestiges of the traditional ways of thinking and worshipping. In place of the Mass, the Holy Communion or the Lord's Supper was introduced, to be administered by a minister wearing a surplice, at a table set in the body of the church, and at which all partook of the wheaten bread and wine.

The dissolution of the chantries and the series of inventories of parish valuables demanded by the Crown in 1547, 1549 and 1552 alerted local congregations to the danger of the confiscation of their treasures. In parishes where records have survived there are details of sales of sacred vessels and vestments. Some bought objects they had grown to love, perhaps in the hope that one day they might be needed again. Sales helped to finance the removal of images, roods and altars, the filling of niches and whitewashing of walls and, more positively, the construction of parish chests, pulpits and communion tables, and the purchase of Bibles and Prayer Books. In place of the painting of the Day of Judgment in the chancel arch, it became standard practice to have paintings of the royal arms (though the first reference to one in St. Laurence's is not until 1742), the Commandments and other Biblical texts. In strongly traditional churches, however, the inventories were sometimes falsified or precious items concealed in the walls—to be discovered when building work was undertaken in later centuries.

Unfortunately, St. Laurence's records, with one exception, have not survived from this period, and it is necessary to try to piece together its story from odd scraps of evidence and by observation of what happened elsewhere. Because people were conditioned to do what the Crown commanded, it must be accepted that by the end of Edward VI's reign in 1553 the church in Stretton, as in other places, would have lost its rood-loft, its altar and its images; the churchwardens' accounts confirm that this had happened at Ludlow. The one Stretton document to have survived is the response to another inventory demand in 1553:[3] it records that St. Laurence's had five bells, a sanctus bell and one silver chalice—probably other vessels and vestments, and perhaps images, had been discreetly disposed of (again, records reveal the sale of images at Ludlow). The English Prayer Book would have been introduced and Mass superseded by the Holy Communion service. The walls should have been whitewashed to conceal the sacred paintings, although, as has already been observed, two were still visible at the west end of the church at the close of the eighteenth century.

These dramatic changes, of course, do not necessarily reflect the wishes of the parishioners of Church Stretton nor what they believed in their hearts. The reference in the 1553 inventory to the sanctus bell suggests an attachment to traditional practices. Further indication of their real beliefs may be revealed in the preambles and dispositions of their wills, although these have to be treated with caution. John Coke's will of 1535 bequeathed his 'solle to all mighty god and to his blessyd mother seynt mary and to all the holy company of hevyn', and proceeded to give instructions about the distribution of the torches and tapers at his funeral. There is no doubting his Roman Catholic beliefs, but at

John Bright's Will (HRO)

the time of his death the king's breach with Rome had only just occurred. John Bright's will of 1556 bequeathed his 'soule unto almighty god my maker and redemr to be associate the copany of our blessed lady the virgin and all the holy saynetes of heaven', but left only small conventional bequests to Hereford Cathedral and the high altar of the parish church of Stretton. There is no sign of Protestant influence here, but that could have been because the Catholic Mary had then succeeded her Protestant half-brother on the throne. This cannot be the case, however, with Catherine Bowdler whose will is dated 1565[4] and who bequeathed her soul to God and 'our blessed lady Saint Mary' in almost the same words as John Bright (which suggests the wills were drafted by the same person—surely the curate, John Felton, who witnessed both).

No will of George Dycher has survived, but his death in 1549 led to the presentation as rector of John Marett by Henry, Earl of Arundel, on 1 August in that year. The earl's imprisonment later in Edward's reign, his rehabilitation under Mary, and his later intrigues with Mary, Queen of Scots, strongly suggest that his choice of rector would have been a man sympathetic to the old faith. For such a man it was not an easy moment to be instituted since the first English Prayer Book had been introduced only weeks before. But if the proposed dating of a document[5] in Archbishop Parker's MSS at Cambridge is correct, Marett was a man of over 40 and therefore with parochial experience elsewhere. He is confirmed as parson at Stretton in the return to the 1553 inventory inquiry, which also gives the names of the first churchwardens in the church's history who can be identified, although the office of warden had begun to appear late in the thirteenth century. Those named were Thomas Walker and Thomas Rawlyngs, and two other parishioners, Richard Beddow and John Hayle, possibly the previous or succeeding churchwardens. A Clergy List for the Archdeaconry of Salop[6] preserved in the Lansdowne MSS at the British Library also names John Marret—as usual, spellings vary—as rector in 1563, and the return to the Parker inquiry, tentatively dated in 1567, adds revealing detail: 'Stretton-in-le-Dale. John Maret (inst. 1549), priest, rector, 60 years old, is not in residence here but is vicar of Nether Wallop in the diocese of Winchester'. He was one of only four absentees in the Wenlock Deanery. Diocesan records at Winchester, though not complete, show John Marett as vicar at Nether Wallop between 1567 (in which year this last Roman Catholic rector of Church Stretton is said to have conformed)[7] and 1578; he may have gone there in 1560 when his predecessor is last mentioned, and probably died in 1579. The curate who served the parish of Stretton in his absence during the important early years of Elizabeth I's reign, or at least some of them, was John Felton.

But John Marett had been in all probability resident at Stretton during the dramatic reversals of the reign of Mary. Edward's half-sister, a devout Catholic, was the daughter of Henry VIII and Catherine of Aragon. With the aid of Cardinal Pole, the Papal Legate, she set about re-establishing traditional

Catholic forms of worship and devotional practice. The Latin Mass almost immediately reappeared with its accompanying vestments, vessels and service books. Procession, pax, holy water, holy bread, the cult of the saints, intercession for the dead and the old ceremonial all came back again. In St. Laurence's, as in other churches, a stone altar would have been re-erected, images replaced and, when money allowed and craftsmen were available, a rood screen rebuilt. If the judgment is right that the parish of Stretton had been reluctant to see traditional forms of worship abolished, their restoration by the queen will have been welcomed, except for the cost involved. But in the Church as a whole not all the changes of the previous 25 years were undone: the Catholicism restored was that of the last years of Henry VIII, with fewer saints' days, new English Primers, an English Bible sanctioned, parochial preaching encouraged, and the clergy exhorted to teach the Lord's Prayer, the Hail Mary, the Creed and the Ten Commandments in English.

News of the other side of the Catholic restoration—the hunt for heretics, the burnings at Smithfield, and the martyrdom of Archbishop Cranmer and Bishops Ridley and Latimer at Oxford—are likely to have been greeted more with satisfaction than horror in Church Stretton for 'Foxe's Martyrs' were identified with unpopular reform. But when Elizabeth succeeded to the throne on Mary's death in 1558 and the subsequent religious settlement reverted virtually to the position under Edward VI, the local mood must have changed to one of bewilderment. The altar was dismantled again, images destroyed and, if the rood had been replaced, it was once more taken down. The Latin Mass and all that went with it were again abolished, and the new Act of Uniformity reintroduced the English Prayer Book, a communion table and communion in both kinds, bread and wine. One significant change, suggestive of the queen's desire that the settlement should be a comprehensive one, was the combination of the words of administration from the 1549 Prayer Book, 'The Body of our Lord Jesus Christ which was given for thee preserve thy body and soul unto everlasting life'—which some Roman Catholics had felt able to accept—with the clearly Protestant, 'Take and eat this in remembrance that Christ died for thee and feed on Him in thy heart by faith with thanksgiving', from the Prayer Book of 1552. This clear compromise was preserved in the 1662 Prayer Book and is at the heart of what became a much-loved service. The Elizabethan Settlement also banned processions except at Rogationtide when it became more a perambulation of the parish boundaries in Ascension week, with no banners or stops at wayside crosses. Once again commissioners toured the country to enforce the new injunctions; they were particularly zealous in unearthing hidden images.

Resistance to reform, particularly in funeral practices and Rogationtide rituals, was widespread, but there is evidence that in the Welsh Marches people clung more generally to the old ways: in 1569 the churchwardens at Ludlow paid for a cross to be unstitched from an altar-cloth still in use for the communion table, and a further payment the next year reveals that the stone pedestals on which images had stood had still to be removed. As late as the 1580s Hereford was one of the dioceses that were still inquiring from parishes about the use of beads and primers and the survival of altars, images and vestments. Even in 1590 John Harrington of Stretton-in-le-Dale bequeathed his soul 'to the mercy of God and to our Lady and all the blessed company of heaven to pray for me', at a time when the more usual ascription had become 'to almighty God my maker and redeemer' (e.g. Edward Harries in 1587).[8]

But attitudes and loyalties were gradually changing. As had happened earlier with the sale of the lands of the dissolved monasteries and chantries, vested interests in the maintenance of the Protestant Church—its redistribution of the Church's property, if less certainly its reformed doctrines—were becoming more firmly established. The document of 1572, which confirmed that the church at Stretton had had its rood-loft, crucifix, images, lights and Lady priest in pre-Reformation days, was actually drawn up to record the transfer by the Crown to two named gentlemen of the yearly rents from literally hundreds of earlier gifts of land and money made to maintain Catholic worship in churches all over the country. Protestantism came, too, to be more closely identified with national sentiment after the Pope's excommunication of Elizabeth in 1570 and the consequent threat to the kingdom from Catholic Powers. The disappearance from churches of all vestiges of traditional worship, gradual though this may have been in Church Stretton, and the required regular denunciations by clergy of popish superstitions were likewise slowly transforming attitudes. There was also a new generation growing up unfamiliar with and not wedded to the old ways. Even more significantly, the new ways were imperceptibly putting down roots in people's lives. The English Bible became more familiar and, in time, more treasured, as something of the old sense of the sacred was transferred from sacramental ritual to the Scriptures. Reading the Gospels for himself brought home to the man of open mind the striking contrast between the simplicity of the lives of Jesus and the apostles and the power and wealth of the late medieval and Renaissance Church. The Prayer Book was even more instrumental in effecting the gradual acceptance of the Elizabethan order: through its provision for the rites of passage such as the churching of women (thanksgiving after the safe delivery of a child) and burials, and the retention of the sign of the cross in baptism, it absorbed something of the practice of traditional religion and made parishioners less reluctant to use it. Indeed, the extent to which local communities like Stretton began to discover in the Prayer Book what they had clung to in the missal and manual is reflected in the increasing hostility of the Puritans to the Prayer Book as years went by.

*

This progressive 'Protestantisation' during the 1560s and 1570s was contemporaneous in Stretton with two other significant events. The first was a change in the church's patrons. The line of the fitzAlan Earls of Arundel who, with only a short break, had held the advowson since 1310, was coming to an end with Henry, the nineteenth earl, who had no son to succeed him. His younger daughter married Thomas Howard, Duke of Norfolk, and passed the Arundel title to their son Philip. The duke himself was executed in 1572 for plotting to marry Mary, Queen of Scots, but the title was restored to the Howards in 1662 and they are Dukes of Norfolk and Earls of Arundel to this day. When Earl Henry's other daughter, Jane, married John, Lord Lumley, he settled upon them the manor of Stretton. We know that Lord Lumley was lord of the manor in 1566[9] and soon afterwards he and his wife joined the earl in conveying the estate to Sir Rowland Hayward, a Shropshire man and probably a native of Bridgnorth, who had made his fortune in cloth in London, where he was sheriff of the City in 1563 and Lord Mayor in 1570 and again in 1590. He was described as 'one of the wealthiest citizens of London'.[10] Sir Rowland has the distinction of being the first named on the church's Roll of Benefactors[11] now in the vestry. To assist the maintenance of a schoolmaster—the first known reference to a school in Stretton—he bequeathed the sum of £1 13s. 4d. (five marks), yearly payable out of certain lands in the parish.

One of Sir Rowland's daughters, Joane, in 1575 married Sir John Thynne of Longleat, great-grandson of the John who had first assumed the name Thynne and ancestor of the present Marquesses of Bath. On her father's death she brought to her husband the lordships of Stretton and Caus, for Sir Rowland had purchased many of the Arundel estates in Shropshire.[12] The Thynnes were originally from Stretton, or more precisely Botvyle, where the wills of several persons named 'de le Yn' or 'of th'Inn' were registered in the early sixteenth century; the

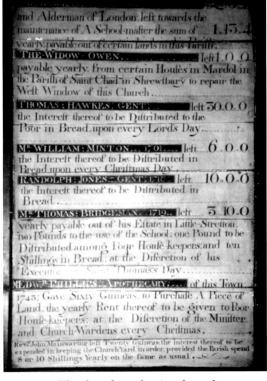

The first benefaction board
(now in the vestry)

name derived from their residence at the inn in Stretton. What is uncertain is if the advowson of the church was also bought by Sir Rowland Hayward and passed to the Thynnes on his daughter's marriage or at his own death. According to one source:

> It is apprehended that the patronage of the church at Church Stretton upon the attainder and execution of Thomas Howard, Duke of Norfolk, father of Philip (both strenuous defenders of the Romish Church) on 2 June 1572 vested in the crown and on 2 May following the rectory of Stretton and all lands, tenements, tithes and hereditaments with the appurtenances to the same belonging were granted by the Crown to Edward Dyer, he paying ten shillings yearly, which on 22 December 33 Elizabeth (1591) he disposed of to William Typper and Robert Dawe of London Gent., two traders in church property who shortly afterwards disposed of the same.[13]

Sir Rowland's daughter was later to contend in the Court of Chancery[14] that her father had given the advowson to herself and her husband in about 1579, although John Hayle maintained that he had bought the right to make the next appointment in 1592—which would fit nicely with the first account.

The male line of the fitzAlan Earls of Arundel finally failed in 1580 on the death of Earl Henry. It was almost certainly in the previous year that John Marett, the only rector that the earl had presented to Stretton (and that 30 years before) had died. His successor was appointed, not by Sir Rowland Hayward, but by the queen—which may confirm that the Crown had assumed the advowson when the earl had been imprisoned for intriguing with Mary Queen of Scots. The Calendar of Patent Rolls records the royal presentation thus: '11 April 1579 William Harrys to the rectory of Stretton Sugwas, Hereford diocese, by approval of the Bishop of Rochester'. So they had the diocese correct but the wrong Stretton! Although the diocesan registrar was also confused and called the living 'Sutton-in-the-Dale', it was certainly to Church Stretton that William Harries—which is how he spelled his name—was instituted on 23 May 1579. He is the first rector to appear in the earliest Call Books (records of licences produced at the bishop's visitation) of the Bishop of Hereford, initially in 1586, and from these we learn that he had been ordained priest on 23 March 1571 by the Bishop of Chester—although, in the later dispute about the patronage of the living, Sir John Thynne's widow, who was also Sir Rowland Hayward's daughter, alleged that Harries had never been properly ordained and should therefore never have been instituted to the benefice.

Properly ordained or not, Harries was probably a local man as there had long been a family of this name in Stretton. A Clergy List in the Lambeth Palace archives[15] accords him no degree but describes him as a scholar, which probably means that he had had a grammar school education before ordination or that he had been at university without proceeding to a degree. This latter possibility may be supported by an Oxford University record of a 'Harries William, of Salop, minister, who matriculated on 28 April 1587, aged 34. Mr. Case's scholar'.[16] If the date is correct, and it is our man, the age is probably wrong or he would have been only 18 years old at his ordination. The Lambeth Palace document describes him as of good character — 'honest conversation' — and resident. It also provides the name of his curate at St. Laurence's, one William Childe, also described as a scholar, resident and of honest conversation, who had been ordained by the Bishop of Gloucester. After the absenteeism of John Marett, Stretton parishioners must have been amazed to have two resident clergy. The benefice was still valued at £15 10s., but all that William Childe received as a stipend was four marks (£1 6s. 8d.) per annum. He probably supplemented this inadequate sum by acting as schoolmaster. William Harries himself became Stretton's first rector to take a wife when he married Margaret, daughter of Peter Higgyns and widow of Edward Hayle of Stretton.[17] It is likely that he was also Stretton's first Protestant rector for he had been appointed by the queen, proceeded to marriage, and later was licensed to preach.

William Harries had the daunting task of restoring harmony to a church where probably many had only reluctantly adopted the reformed faith. There would also have been the usual neighbours to be reconciled and personal relationships healed. Indeed, it has been suggested that the primary social task entrusted to a rural parish priest was that of a settler of conflicts. Some details of what disturbed parish life have fortunately been preserved in a fragment of the Stretton Court Roll covering part of 1566 and 1567[18] when Lord Lumley was lord of the manor and John Marett the absentee rector. Among the Stretton families of this time who appear in the Roll or who are known from other sources are the names Leighton, Brooke, Eymes, Hayle, Harrington, Hughes, Harries, Scaltocke and Bright. Presiding over the court were Richard Mytton, the lord's steward, and Francis Brooke, the under-steward. Most of the cases they dealt with were minor and resolved by small fines — for illegally selling ale, assaults and fights (where both parties were charged with assault), no doubt often the consequence of consuming the ale. Some evidence of how leisure time was spent, and what kept some away from church on Sunday, emerges in the case of John Colley of Church Stretton who, besides breaking the regulations governing the sale of ale, had 'used unlawful games, namely cards and tables in his house'. Twenty years later the schoolmaster of the day, one Walter Burrie, was up before the church court on 8 September 1589 'for setting forth playes and enterludes on the sabothe daye'.[19] Back in the manorial court of 1566-67, there were numerous charges and counter-charges for trespass and some cases of debt. Four members of the Bowdler family at All Stretton were fined for entering a property 'with force of arms' and assaulting the householder, Richard Tewe. The most serious incident was the theft of four bullocks from the under-steward, Francis Brooke, by a butcher called John Smyth. He was hanged for the felony and all his possessions forfeited to the lord of the manor.

We are reminded of the essentially agricultural nature of life in sixteenth-century Stretton by the contents of the first known terrier of the church's lands[20] which also belongs to this period. It is undated but must have been compiled in William Harries's early years as rector because he, the churchwardens and sworn men of the parish acknowledged Sir Rowland Hayward, knight, alderman of London, to be the patron. The document provides the first surviving description of the then rectory, situated where the eighteenth-century Old Rectory now stands. It comprised 'a decent hall, two parlours, two butteries, five chambers, a kitchen, a boulting-house and a malt chamber, a stable and ox-house all under one roof'. Clearly a spacious dwelling, it was very much a farmhouse as well as a rectory with its store-rooms for liquor and provisions, brewing facilities and shelter for horses and cattle—not to mention the boulting-house where flour would have been sieved. Standing detached, and perhaps forming a farmyard, there were a sheepcote of five bays (the right to graze sheep on the common land was acknowledged) and a barn of five bays that could have been the old Tithe Barn, which still stood in 1830 not far from the churchyard.[21] What part Stretton's rector personally played in the farming activities is not known, but Professor Dickens considered that 'for many a country parson life on six days of the week was not markedly different from that of a substantial yeoman'.[22] Certainly he will have had overall responsibility for and a personal interest in the effective exploitation of the 'glebe' lands of the church. In addition to the garden on the south side of the house, probably used to grow vegetables, there were substantial areas of cultivated land and meadow scattered about the parish: ten acres on the west side of the house, perhaps in the upper part of what is now the Rectory Field; 17 acres in four separate 'closes' or enclosed fields;14 acres of pasture and meadow; and several acres in holdings in the open arable fields—about 50 acres in all in 1614. Yet Harries was brought before the manor court in 1613 for cutting firewood in Womerton Wood—though he seems to have ingratiated himself with the lord of the manor three years later, offering to pay for all court dinners for the rest of his incumbency.[23]

This rural parish was still thinly populated with scattered farmhouses, a tiny hamlet at Minton, small settlements at All Stretton and Little Stretton, and a compact little market town in Church Stretton. That some building was taking place in the late sixteenth century is attested by the stone set in the wall of what was until recently The Hotel in the centre of Church Stretton and which declares that the old malthouse that previously stood there was 'Erected by Copper and W. His Sonne Ano Dni 1587'. Most of the dwellings would have been timbered or half-timbered with thatched roofs, and fire was always a hazard. Wolverhampton had been seriously damaged by fire in 1590, and there was clearly a major fire in Church Stretton three years later according to a manuscript dated 25 November 1593.[24] This is an appeal on behalf of 'the inhabitants of the towne of

The stone commemorating
Copper's malthouse, 1587

Church Stretton who by misfortune of fier of late had their dwelling houses and goods consumed and burnt to their great losse and hindrance'. The town was then little more than the present High Street as far as Cunnery Road and fire would have spread quickly through properties set close together. The church, with the churchyard acting as a fire-break, seems not to have been damaged. The rectory, too escaped unscathed. The appeal to 'the town and liberty of Salop' was issued from Ludlow Castle by the Queen's Council in the Marches of Wales who were 'moved with pitie' for the poor estate of the people of Church Stretton. Such appeals were by no means unknown—one had been made at Nantwich in 1583—but Stretton was helped by the fact that two members of the Council who signed the order for the collection, William Leighton of Plaish and Sir Henry Townshend of Cound who had married a daughter of Sir Rowland Hayward, had family links with the town. The collection—amount unknown—was received on behalf of the town and of all who had suffered loss by William Posterne.

The rebuilding was in timber-framing, 'some of which still hides beneath Georgian and Victorian exteriors', according to local historian David Bilbey. The Buck's Head dates from earlier, but the King's Arms, Tudor Cottage and perhaps the Old Barn date from this period. Other buildings erected in the late sixteenth or early seventeenth centuries have survived in All Stretton and Little Stretton.

The rector to whom it fell to nurse the people of Church Stretton through the trauma of the fire and its aftermath was still William Harries. He was not a man afraid to stick to his principles, even if these involved some unpopularity. At the court of the lord of the manor, Sir John Thynne, on 18 March 1595, he appeared before the deputy steward Richard Halewell and a homage jury of Richard Leighton Gent, Richard Haille, Thomas Huygyns (alias Hughes), Thomas Mason, John Harrington, Richard Huggyns jnr., William Chelmyck,

William Wilkes, Stephen Streete, Richard Wylding, Thomas Okes, Thomas Rawlins, Thomas Scaultock, Edward Lewes Gent., Richard James and John Mason—no doubt the leading parishioners of the day. In their presence he ended for ever 'the very old but improper practice of ale drinking in this church at Easter which had doubtless been the custom in the early days of Christianity'—perhaps as a fellowship meal. It was acknowledged that 'there hath been and used and is a custom the time whereof the memory of man is not to the contrary, that the parson and incumbents of the said parish have used yearly to bestow and make for the said parishioners and inhabitants of the said parish a drinking of ale, bread and cheese called the Easter drinking in the said church upon Easter Day immediately after Evening Prayer'. With the full consent of the lord and patron and of the homage jury on behalf of the inhabitants, the rector now promised for himself and his successors that instead of the Easter ale he would pay yearly to the churchwardens a rent of 20s. for 'the use of a school and schoolmaster there to be kept to instruct the children within the said parish'. If he or a successor defaulted on the payment, the Easter drinking custom would be revived.[25]

On 17 July 1605, 26 years after his institution and two years after the death of Queen Elizabeth I who had presented him, Harries was licensed to preach by the new Archbishop of Canterbury, Richard Bancroft. Such licences were being issued more frequently as the consequence of a sustained drive by John Whitgift, Archbishop 1583-1604, to improve the education and quality of the clergy. This was a considerable achievement at a time when the Elizabethan Religious Settlement had been and still was under attack from both Roman Catholics, who wanted to restore the old faith (the Gunpowder Plot was discovered only months after Harries received his licence), and from Puritans, who thought the settlement did not go far enough. Some Puritans wanted to get rid of the surplice, kneeling for communion, and the sign of the cross in baptism because these were seen as remnants of popery; others went as far as demanding the abolition of episcopacy and the establishment of a Presbyterian system of church government. What united the Puritans was the primacy they gave to the Scriptures: services, sacrament and sermon were all to embody the living Word of God. Preaching, the exposition of the Word, was therefore for them the supreme task of the minister; in a few places, indeed, the Prayer Book was displaced by sermons. The award of a licence to preach to William Harries, however, does not mean he had become a Puritan. About half the clergy now had such licences,[26] and Archbishop Richard Bancroft, who had headed the Court of High Commission's measures against the Puritans for the previous two decades, would not have given his licence to one whose churchmanship was suspect. That the future High Church bishop, Roger Mainwaring, was born in Stretton in 1590 is further evidence that the church's teaching was orthodox.

Part of the Jacobean pulpit, now at the west end of the church

The introduction of regular preaching may, nevertheless, have triggered important developments at St. Laurence's. It seems probable that the Jacobean carved pulpit, which stood on the south side of the chancel arch until it was superseded by the present one on the north side in 1880, was erected at this time; a nineteenth-century authority[27] dates it from the reign of James I (1603-25). Part of it may still be seen displayed on the wall near the west door of the church. It was an impressive three-decker structure, with a high pulpit, a reading desk for the Scriptures and the Prayer Book services below that, and at the base a pew for the parish clerk who led the responses and any singing. More frequent sermons also increased the need for seating. Some benches may already have been in place, but it is likely to have been in this period that the box pews, which were only removed in the Victorian restoration, were progressively added to the church. Certainly there was seating before 1639 when it is referred to in Jane Norton's will. Pews were probably installed piecemeal, first for the better-off members of the congregation, with their position determined by the demand for proximity to the preacher. With later ones added whenever individuals could afford them, or as demand grew, it is not surprising that by the early nineteenth century they needed to be reordered.

How different the church will have looked from its appearance in pre-Reformation days. The emphasis was now on simplicity and plainness rather than elaborate ritual and colour, on hearing the Word rather than observing the celebration of the Mass. The church will have been much lighter with the walls

T.F. Dukes' painting of the interior of St. Laurence's. It dates from the mid-nineteenth century, but shows the three-decker pulpit on the south side of the chancel arch, the box pews and the plastered ceiling. (Bodleian Library, Oxford)

whitewashed, the rood and perhaps the screen removed, and plain windows where there had possibly been stained glass. The introduction of the three-decker pulpit and pews will have transformed the interior. Some idea of what it looked like can be gained by a visit to Stokesay Church which also exhibits the seventeenth century wall paintings of the Ten Commandments, the Lord's Prayer, the Creed and various Biblical texts which will similarly have embellished the walls of St. Laurence's at that period. How this 'auditory church', designed for hearing the Word, appeared in 1842 can be seen in T.F. Dukes' water-colour of the interior. There are likely to have been more tombs, commemorative slabs and plaques than were later recorded because of the 'obsessive concern with the provision of physical memorials to the dead'[28] in the century after the Reformation. A 'comely partition' at the entrance to the chancel may have remained as the Royal Order of 1561 required, and the Commandments perhaps appeared on the east wall, in accordance with Archbishop Parker's 'Advertisements' of 1566. As in many churches the wooden communion table probably stood at the east end of the chancel, set altarwise, except when moved for Holy Communion into the body of the church for the convenience of those gathered for the ministration of the sacrament. The two Jacobean chairs with arms, now in the vestry, may have stood inside the sanctuary on either side of the communion table. During the celebration of the Lord's Supper the table was covered with a 'fair linen cloth', at other times with a 'decent covering' perhaps made from former vestments. Ornaments were few, candles used only for illumination. The only other items required in services were a copy of the Prayer Book, the large English Bible, a silver communion cup and paten, 'two comely pots of pewter' for the wine and water, and a surplice with large sleeves for the minister.

The services matched the new simple, plain setting in which they were conducted. The offices were said and lessons read from the new reading desk, or 'convenient seat', erected at St. Laurence's beneath the pulpit. The Prayer Book liturgy, particularly Matins and Evensong, and the rites of passage provided the core of parish Anglicanism. Parishioners were required to receive communion three times a year, but it was usually offered quarterly at Easter, Whitsuntide, Michaelmas and Christmas. The authorities tried to ensure that there were four sermons a year, with one of the appointed homilies read at other times, but when William Harries received his licence, sermons at St. Laurence's were surely more frequent. The religious teaching of young people was not neglected. The incumbent was expected to catechise the youth of the parish every second Sunday, usually before Evensong. 'Above all this was an age of catechising', writes Professor Collinson.[29] The training offered through the catechism helped the religious people of the new generation to understand the Bible and listen to sermons, the twin pillars of the Protestant Church. Yet Stretton's remodelled medieval church in which the new services were held was a constant reminder of the continuity with the past, just as Anglicanism itself came to blend the new with the old.

7

THE PARISH IN AN AGE OF
COMMERCIAL GROWTH & CIVIL WAR

Evidence that in the early years of the seventeenth century Church Stretton was recovering from the effects of the fire of 1593 and that rebuilding had proceeded apace is provided by the initiative to obtain royal permission for a weekly market. Presumably the market which Edward III had granted the right to hold nearly three hundred years before had fallen into desuetude. The news that Church Stretton wanted a market was greeted with alarm by the bailiffs and burgesses of Bishop's Castle. They believed that their prosperity depended on the trade in cattle from Wales and the delivery to Wales of corn 'from Shropshire, Corvedale and Herefordshire', and that 'the erecting of many little markets tends to destroy them all'. They therefore appealed to the Earl of Northampton, the Keeper of the Privy Seal, who was their lord of the manor and had a personal interest as he derived £10 a year from their market tolls. In 1609 they sent him a letter of thanks with a gift of a gilt cup for dispelling an approaching great evil 'by stayinge a determined and almost optayned erection of a superfluous market' at Stretton.[1]

Their relief was premature. In the same year, on 14 June, the Sheriff of Shropshire held an inquisition which concluded that a market at Stretton would not cause loss to the king or others. Yet it was not until seven years later, on 13 January 1616, that King James I granted a charter for a market at Stretton.[2] The preamble, originally in Latin, reads:

> Whereas lately we have heard upon testimony of belief that the town of Church Stretton, in our county of Shropshire, which is an ancient and popu-lous town, being a place convenient, useful and adapted not only to hold and keep a market for the commerce and business of our people, but also requiring and affording inns and lodging houses for the convenience of our subjects passing through the town and receiving guests at seasonable times …

There then enters upon the scene one of the leading characters in the history of Church Stretton and perhaps its church:

> By reason of which our beloved and faithful subject, Bonham Norton, of Church Stretton aforesaid, Esquire, and other inhabitants of the said town have humbly supplicated us … From our royal munificence we have vouchsafed to grant to the said Bonham Norton, Esquire, being possessed of the two greater parts of the landed possessions within the town, that he … and his heirs for ever hereafter may have and hold … a market on Thursday each week in the same place.

A pie-powder court was to be established to dispense justice at the market, enforcing reasonable tolls, dues, stallage and customs rights. That Thursday market continues to this day.

Who was this Bonham Norton? As the royal charter reveals he was the leading landowner in Church Stretton; he also owned substantial other estates in Shropshire. Much of this he had inherited from his father, William Norton, who came from an Onibury family and endowed a school in that village, but who 'left 40s each to the poor of Onibury, Ludford, Ludlow, Stottesdon and Cleobury Mortimer in all of which parishes he owned property'.[3] William had made his money in printing. He was one of the original freemen of the Stationers' Company named in the royal charter granted in 1555 and one of the first six admitted into the livery of the company in 1561. In that year, too, he received his licence to print.[4] He married Joan, only daughter of William Bonham, another of the original freemen of the Stationers' Company; their only son, born in 1565, was given his mother's maiden name of Bonham. William rose to be Master of the company three times before his death in 1593. He left 'a large fortune in real and personal estate' which his son inherited. By this time Bonham himself had married Jane, daughter of Thomas Owen of Condover, one of the judges in the Court of Common Pleas from 1594 to 1598.[5] Bonham, too, went into printing, was admitted as a freeman of the company, and grew rich through the grant of monopolies at a time when printed books were in greater demand than ever before. Together with Thomas Wight he was granted a 30-year patent in 1599 for the printing of law books. 'If Shakespeare had written in law he could not have got the first printer he met in Cheap to have printed his book; but he must have gone either to Richard Tottle or Charles Yetsweirt, or to their successors, Thomas Wight and Bonham Norton'.[6] Under James I he was granted a further patent to print and sell books in the Latin, Greek and Hebrew tongues and to print the Bible in Latin with notes. The right to print the Authorised Version of the Bible was granted by King James in 1611 to Robert Barker, the King's Printer. The expense of the undertaking was so great, however, that Barker went into partnership with Bonham Norton and his colleague John Bill, another rich stationer who hailed from Much Wenlock. They advanced Barker thousands of pounds. The agreement was sealed by the marriage of Norton's eldest daughter, Sarah, to Barker's son, Christopher.

As one of the county's wealthy landowners, Bonham Norton served as Sheriff of Shropshire in 1611 and received a grant of arms. Late in the next year he succeeded as Master of the Stationers' Company, on the death of the serving Master, his cousin John Norton, yet another wealthy stationer who left him a further legacy. In 1613 he was elected to continue as Master for a year. At what was perhaps the height of his wealth and influence, in 1617, the year after the grant of the weekly market, Bonham Norton paid for the erection of a fine timber-framed Market Hall in what is now The Square in Church Stretton. Sir Henry Townshend generously contributed 25 trees 'to help to build a market house, school house and court house in Stretton' [7] We know no more of the two last unless the court-house was the upper room of the Market Hall—but a drawing of this handsome building, which may have replaced one destroyed in the fire, still exists. The hall itself was pulled down and a new one erected in 1839.

It has always been assumed that the date 1619 high on the west wall of St. Laurence's indicates when Bonham Norton's wife, Jane, financed the insertion of the large west window, but were there other developments at that time? It will be recalled that it seems probable that the first great extension of the church followed King John's order to advertise a weekly market and annual fair in 1214. Similarly, a number of large windows at the east end and in the transepts may have been inserted after Edward III's renewal of those rights. It is not surprising that on those two occasions of a significant upturn in the community's fortunes the townsfolk wanted to express their gratitude to Almighty God and to celebrate their new status by extending or embellishing their church.

Bonham Norton's Market Hall built in 1617 (SRRC)

Did the same happen in the second decade of the seventeenth century as the town rose again from the ashes of the 1593 fire? Cranage believes that the end windows in the transepts, inserted in the fourteenth century, were repaired early in the seventeenth. Jane Norton's west window is different—Eric Mercer points out that it has fillets on the mullions and slightly looser cusping beneath rather broader heads[8]—supporting the evidence of its origin in 1619. Cranage also takes the view that the work in 1619 'included the coarse hood-mouldings to windows on the north and south sides of the chancel' and the double lancet windows without cusps which 'are almost too broad to be original thirteenth century insertions'. The ceiling of the south transept is also 'probably Jacobean',[9] and may have formed part of the improvements in about 1619, though some think it is sixteenth century. It has collar-beams and a tie-beam at the north end, together with one tier of wind-braces ornamented with quatre-foils. The discovery of a Flemish coin of the time of James I in the foundations of the south porch in the nineteenth century may indicate that that too was erected or repaired in these years.

The nature of Jane Norton's gift is readily understood if the assumption is correct that Bonham Norton built or extended The Hall (described as 'a large timbered mansion after the fashion of the old Market Hall'[10]) as his seat in Stretton, for it was opposite the end of Cub Lane (now Church Way) and there-fore nearly facing the west end of the church. Park House may have been the lodge for the 'park-keeper'; its site was later said to have been the stables of the old Hall, and the old barn 'where strolling players fretted and strutted' was the barn for the Hall. Jane, whose will shows her to have been very devout, may have persuaded her husband to help fund the work on the other windows. (St. Laurence's would not be the only church that could number Bonham Norton among its benefactors, for Cranage records that he built the chapel at Loughton near Brown Clee Hill in 1622.) Of still greater interest is the possibility that the Perpendicular section of the tower was added at this time. The most widely supported view is that this extension was completed at the end of the fifteenth or the beginning of

The west window, the gift of Jane Norton, 'the widow Owen', with the Owen coat of arms in the centre

'The tower is a massive and pondrous building finished with battlements and pinnacles at each corner having a variety of singular figures projecting from the parapets of its walls, which attaches to the whole fabric an air of antiquity, respectability and solemnity'[12]

the sixteenth century, in the days of Rector William Hugyns and prior to the Reformation. Richard Morris points out, however, that as early seventeenth century masons used the same tools and methods as their medieval predecessors, it is very difficult to distinguish between work of the fifteenth century and that of the age of the Stuarts if they chose to build in the Perpendicular style.[11] Many church towers may have been wrongly assigned to the earlier period, and at Stretton there are some features which suggest a date of about 1620. Certainly the necessary financial resources would have been available from those who had prospered as a result of the resurgent commercial activity and, of course, from Bonham Norton.

These were tempestuous years in Bonham Norton's personal fortunes. The partnership with the King's Printer, Robert Barker, had brought him wealth and prominence, but when still greater riches beckoned the temptation proved too strong. Norton and John Bill, 'being imployde in the said office of printing as aforesaid and perceiving great profit and benefit to arise and come thereof, and being desirous to enrich themselves thereby',[13] claimed that they had purchased Barker's rights as the King's Printer. (From 1617 to 1619 publications from the king's printing house in fact bore their joint imprint.) Barker disagreed and brought a suit in Chancery which found in his favour and against Bonham Norton (but not John Bill); Barker was restored as King's Printer together with Bill. Norton, however, who has been characterised as 'a hard, calculating and grasping man',[14] ousted Barker again and held the very lucrative office with Bill from 1621 to 1629. These were apparently good years for Norton who became an Alderman of the City of London and was re-elected Master of the Stationers' Company in 1626 and again in 1629. Then disaster struck. In that latter year a further series of law-suits brought by Barker in the Court of Chancery were finally determined in Barker's favour. Bonham Norton reacted by calling the court corrupt and accusing the Lord Keeper, Sir Francis Bacon, of accepting a bribe. For this he was hauled before the Court of Star Chamber,[15] heavily fined and imprisoned at the king's pleasure. A letter from him in London in April 1630 suggests an early release. Two years later, at the age of sixty-seven, and with John Bill in his grave, he seems to have begun to put his affairs in order: no fewer than 98 book titles were assigned by him and Bill's executor to Mistress 'Joyce' (Jane) Norton and another.[16]

There seems also to have been trouble in the family over the Norton copy-hold lands in Stretton which the rent roll of the manor in 1664 shows had been very extensive.[17] Bonham and Jane Norton had seven sons and four daughters. One son became a freeman of the Stationers' Company and another ran a publishing business, but a breach developed between Bonham and his eldest son, Arthur, who was to die in the same year as his father. A letter dated 30 June 1629 from Francis Phillips of Wistanstow to Hugh Hill, steward of the manor of Church Stretton for Sir Thomas Thynne, states that Bonham Norton had surrendered (transferred with the approval of the lord of the manor) his lands in open court held in the church to the use of Mr. George Norton and others. The letter supposes that Arthur Norton would receive compensation for the sale of lands in Stanton Lacy that would have been his. In another letter to Mr. Phillips dated in London on 17 April 1630 Bonham Norton writes of his 'thank-less heir' and says he will not stay to defend himself against 'that scurrilous question to know in what alehouse I passed my surrenders'.[18] Perhaps this quarrel with his eldest son and his own imprisonment also damaged the rela-tionship with his wife, for on his death in April 1635 Bonham was buried in St. Faith's, London, near his father, though Jane was later buried in Condover. That the arms of her own family, the Owens, rather than those of Norton, appear in the west window of St. Laurence's was not, however, her choice; they were most likely inserted in the early nineteenth century.

*

The alterations to the church's windows and perhaps the tower may well have been completed in the last year of William Harries's incumbency. After over 40 years as rector—years of continual change in town and parish church—he died in late 1620 or early 1621. The bishop's Call Book in 1621 shows his name crossed out and 'R. vacat' inserted. It was 70 years since an appointment had been made by the Earl of Arundel back in 1549, as Harries himself had been presented by Queen Elizabeth when the church was in sequestration. The lord-ship of the manor and the ownership of the advowson had changed hands several times and in 1610 this had led to a dispute over the patronage of the living.[19]

Dame Joane Thynne, widow of Sir John and daughter of Sir Rowland Hayward, complained to the Lord Chancellor that although her father had conveyed the manor and the advowson to her husband and herself 'about thirty years past'—at about the same time that William Harries became rector—a certain John Hayle of Church Stretton was claiming that he had the right to appoint the next rector. She wanted Hayle to be summoned before the Court of Chancery. Hayle himself contended that although Sir Rowland Hayward had conveyed manor and advowson to the Thynnes, he had 18 years before (in 1592) granted to his servant William Smyth the right to make the next appointment to the rectory and parsonage of Stretton. Hayle, who had become William Harries's step son through the rector's marriage with his widowed mother, maintained that he had bought the right of the next appointment from William Smyth for £58. He insisted therefore that when the living became vacant he would present 'a suffi-cient and fit person both for life and doctrine', as documents in his possession proved he had the right to do. Dame Joane countered that Harries had never been properly ordained and so should not hold the living and that the advowson had been conveyed to her husband and herself long before any grant that Hayle was claiming. There is perhaps a hint in Hayle's reference to 'doctrine' that the dispute was about more than rights. Harries may have encouraged his step-son to try to ensure that his successor would maintain his own churchmanship—very probably preserving some elements of the old faith in conservative Stretton. This seems the more likely when we find that the man presented by Sir Thomas Thynne displayed Puritan sympathies. The Court of Chancery's decision in the case is not known, but when 11 years later the living did fall vacant 12 clergy and 12 laymen were appointed, on 13 April 1621, to inquire who was the patron of the Stretton benefice. Among the laymen were Francis Jencks of New Hall, Esq., Thomas Chelmick of Botfield, Gent., John Powell of All Stretton, Gent., and Richard Thin of Plash, Gent. 'The matter was apparently decided in favour of Sir Thomas Thynne who presented'.[20] The clergyman he named was unsurprisingly a native of Wiltshire as Sir Thomas's seat was at Longleat. Anthony Hawkes was duly instituted as rector on 28 June 1621.

Hawkes was an Oxford graduate who had matriculated at New College on 11 November 1608 at the age of 19, and been awarded his B.A. from St. Edmund Hall in February 1613 and his M.A. in May 1616. The Register of Clergy Titles records that he was ordained 'deacon and presbyter' on 25 February 1621. He was, therefore, one of the new breed of younger well-educated clergy, very different from those in another part of the county in the 1620s immortalised by Richard Baxter:

> These were the schoolmasters of my youth … who read Common Prayer
> on Sundays and Holy Days and taught school and tipled on week-days,
> and whipt the boys, when they were drunk, so that we changed them very
> oft. Within a few miles about us were near a dozen more Ministers that

were near eighty years old apiece, and never preached; poor ignorant Readers, and most of them of scandalous lives.[21]

However, even in backward dioceses 'graduate recruitment was the norm by the second quarter of the seventeenth century'.[22]

Certainly at Stretton, as the Call Book entries, though irregular, still reveal, the curates — who probably also acted as schoolmasters — were now young men of education who after a few years moved on to a living of their own, more after the modern practice.[23] In 1621 William Haile, recorded as 'curatus', was almost certainly the one of that name from Salop who matriculated aged 17 at St. John's College, Oxford, in June 1610 and supplicated for his B.A. four years later. His name is of particular interest: was he the son of John Hayle and the one his father and William Harries hoped would be the next rector when the latter died? If he was, it is unlikely that he stayed long after Anthony Hawkes's arrival, although the next 'curatus' does not appear in the records until 1626-27. This was Thomas Hennant from Herefordshire, who matriculated aged 18 at Trinity College, Oxford, in 1619 and was awarded his B.A. in 1623. He was ordained in 1625 and later served as Vicar of Thame, Oxon, for over 30 years. John Swetnam, who appears under Stretton-in-le-Dale as ordained deacon in 1629 and priest in 1630, is likely to be the one of that name who was the son of Thomas, priest of Westbury, Salop. He matriculated at All Souls College in 1625, aged 17, and gained his B.A. in 1629. Thomas Taylor, named as curate in 1636, presents more of a problem because his name is more common: he could be another Oxford man who hailed from Alvechurch, matriculated aged 16 at Brasenose College in 1631 and went on to gain his B.A., later returning to Worcestershire as a rector, or he could be the first Cambridge man to minister at St. Laurence's, for another Thomas Taylor matriculated aged 16 at Christ's College in 1627 and graduated B.A. in 1631 and M.A. in 1634. It is intriguing that Peile's *Biographical Register of Christ's College* records that one of this name was Vicar of 'Sutton-in the-Dale' in 1650 when it may be recalled that that very place name was incorrectly attributed by the Hereford Diocesan Registrar to William Harries on his institution in 1579. It is also interesting that only two of these curates were natives of Shropshire which sent relatively few students to Oxford in the late sixteenth and early seventeenth centuries,[24] although Shrewsbury School had a link with St. John's College, Cambridge.

Graduates they may have been, but were these young clergy trained and prepared for their vocation? Professor Collinson says that 'a training in the schools was some preparation for the pulpit, and prevalent religious values virtually reduced the ministry to a pulpit function'.[25] But were they able to communicate with simple country folk and how were they equipped for the pastoral ministry of counsel and reconciliation? How did they deal with Thomas Bright who in 1621 was before the archdeacon's court 'for keeping

John Oakes out of his pew in church'?[26] Some of these skills can only have been learned through experience, supported by a semi-formal in-service training. The bishops' Call Books contain some record of visitations and clerical synods involving bishop or archdeacon that must have provided opportunity for the discussion of topical issues and social intercourse as well as the customary formal charge or injunction. Local clergy must also have exchanged visits or attended larger gatherings with the rural dean: Church Stretton at this time was in the Wenlock Deanery which included several parishes within easy riding distance. It is hard to believe that Anthony Hawkes, who was later to be acknowledged as a fit Presbyterian minister, was not in touch with Sir Robert Harley, the renowned Puritan lord of Brampton Bryan, of whom it was said at his funeral in 1656 that 'his planting of godly ministers and then backing them with his authority, made religion famous in this little corner of the world'.[27] The Harleys' own minister, Thomas Pierson, organised a monthly 'combination lecture' at Leintwardine supported by eight preaching clergy and licensed by the bishop; another was founded at Bishop's Castle, and 'exercises' on Christian basics were arranged in various places in North Herefordshire and South Shropshire. No evidence that Stretton's rector was involved has come to light, but the assumption that he was seems justified since he was later sufficiently well-known to be included with leading local Puritans in the list of acceptable ministers at the end of the first Civil War. He was certainly near enough to Leintwardine to be part of the network of ministers who used to meet for dinner together followed by a debate on some controversial question or difficult passage of Scripture.

As happened in some other parishes, Anthony Hawkes may have gathered around him within the congregation a small godly élite, but it is very doubtful if the generality of local people shared the spiritual aspirations of Puritan ministers and laity, for Puritanism combined a desire for plain worship with 'an intense emphasis on the godly behaviour of the individual'.[28] Certainly in Stretton there will have been some who still hankered after the old religion. They are likely to have been theologically unsophisticated but had been brought up in families which continued to cling to older patterns of piety, perhaps treasuring some ancient primer, vessel or image, perhaps occasionally burning a candle on the feasts of the Virgin Mary or a favourite saint, telling their beads, or making the sign of the cross. Had they understood its significance they would have been heartened by the enthronement of Augustine Lindsell as Bishop of Hereford in 1634, for he was one of the growing number of Arminian bishops appointed under Charles I. The Arminians rejected the prevailing Calvinist doctrine of predestination and asserted the free will of all men to obtain salvation. These High Churchmen stressed the sacraments as sources of grace and sought to reduce the emphasis on preaching; they believed in the divine institution of the episcopacy, coupling that with the divine right of kings. In the practices and services of the Church they stood for good order and what Archbishop Laud, their leading protagonist, called 'the beauty of holiness'. While Laud insisted that the communion table should be at the east end and railed off, his opponents saw this as a device to restore the Mass, especially when he encouraged bowing to the altar. Stretton had links with Arminianism through Roger Mainwaring who was born there in 1590 and after graduating and receiving his doctorate at Oxford was made a chaplain to King Charles. Preaching in this capacity before the king in 1627 and declaring the royal right to tax without Parliament's consent, he outraged the leaders of the Commons and was fined and given a suspended prison sentence by them. In 1635, however, he was consecrated by Laud as Bishop of St. David's.

There will have been yet others in Stretton who were indifferent to religion, with no time for Puritans or Arminians. No doubt they welcomed King James's Declaration of Sports, reissued by his son, which commended such Sunday recreations as dancing, maypoles, ales and archery. Yet while this infuriated the Puritans who were ardent sabbatarians, it did not go far enough for those who resented having to attend church and preferred (in another parish) to 'sit at cards on the Sabbath by a hot fire, than to sit at a sermon with God in a cold church'.[29] They found more congenial company in the ale-house or dancing. Of course, strictly, parishioners were obliged to attend divine service, but churchwardens probably reported only habitual absentees.

Nonetheless, attendance at St. Laurence's had been encouraged by the improvements carried out around 1619 and especially by Jane Norton's rebuilding of the west wall with its present large window 'and the seats adjoining'. It seems probable that these were intended for the poorer parishioners, as the more affluent would have had their pews nearer the pulpit. Bonham Norton must often have been away in London—or in prison—but he will surely have been present in 1633 when his daughter Mary was married to Thomas Edwardes, a Shrewsbury gentleman of means. We can be even more confident that Rector Hawkes would have presided at this family wedding of his most munificent parishioners. We know of their friendship because six years later, in her will dated 5 November 1639,[30] and witnessed first by the rector, she bequeathed 'to Anthony Hawkes clerk parson of Church Stretton and Dorothy his wife twenty pounds to buy them mourninge blacks requesting him also to preache my funerell sermon'. Keith Thomas says that 'Puritans objected to ritual mourning … they condemned funeral sermons because only the families of the rich could afford to have them',[31] but country customs die hard. Jane's will is notable for its expression of her piety and Biblical faith. She was also solicitous for the poor: 'I give to soe many poore women as I shall bee yeares of age att the tyme of my decease twenty shillings a peace for my executors to buy them mourning blacks for my funeral, twenty of the said women to be of the parish of Cundover [where she was born], twenty of the parish of

Stottesden [where she and her husband had property and were well-known and liked], and the rest to bee of the parish of Church Stretton where I dwell'. As she died in June 1640 at the age of 70, the mourning contingent from Stretton would have numbered 30. Jane Norton, or the Widow Owen as she is called on the Roll of Benefactors, also bequeathed two messuages to her daughter Mary and her son-in-law Thomas Edwardes to pay, among others, 'yearly the some of xx shillings for keepinge in repaire the west window and seates adiogninge in the west end of the said Church of Stretton (wch yt pleased God to give me leave to build). And the overplus and Residue of ye said xx shillings yf any bee, to be paid yearlie to the use of the poor there for ever'. She also left £100 to be expended on a monument in Condover church to her father, her brother, her husband and herself, which fortunately can still be seen today. Her generosity and compassion are evident in the bequests of two years' wages to her servants and ten shillings annually for life to each of the daughters of Roger Phipps — Mary who was blind and Grace who was dumb.

*

Perhaps it was as well that Jane Norton died when she did for the country was shortly to be plunged into the Civil War in which her family would be sharply divided. At her death in June 1640, however, civil war was neither imminent nor inevitable. Two months earlier the king had called the Short Parliament after 11 years of non-Parliamentary rule, but he had dissolved it after three weeks. In November 1640 Charles had to summon Parliament again, the famous Long Parliament which released Puritans and imprisoned Archbishop Laud and other bishops including Roger Mainwaring, the Stretton-born Bishop of St. David's. The next year Parliament debated the Root and Branch Petition for the abolition of all bishops, and the gulf between King and Parliament widened. The crisis of the 1640s, of course, was not only about religion, but one modern historian considers that 'religious poles are the ones around which most other discontents formed',[32] and another, writing of the Harleys and their influence in North Herefordshire and South Shropshire, believes that, 'It cannot be over-emphasised that religious differences were primarily responsible for the polarisation which occurred in their county after 1640'.[33] Lady Harley, in a letter to her husband in 1643, related how Ludlow people going through Brampton Bryan on market day called for all Puritans to be hanged.[34]

Local gentlemen began to take sides in 1642 when they had to decide whether to respond to the King's Commissioners of Array or to Parliament's Militia Ordinance. The king finally raised his standard at Nottingham on 22 August 1642. A fortnight earlier 'The Declaration and Protestation of the Gentlemen of Salop' had been signed by many who were ready to 'adventure their lives and fortunes in the Defence of the Royal and Sacred Person of the

King'.[35] The county clergy followed suit with a resolution in support of Charles I on 24 August, but only seventeen signatories are known and they do not include the rector of Church Stretton.[36] These expressions of loyalty were sufficient, however, to attract the king to move west to Shropshire and he arrived in Shrewsbury on 20 September. For most people this was not good news. By 1 October it was said that, 'All the country over within twelve or fourteen miles of Shrewsbury are full of soldiers'.[37] Houses were taken over or plundered, corn and cattle requisitioned. The great majority of the county gentry were Royalists but there were pockets of Parliamentary support and many families were divided. Jane Norton's nephew, for instance, was the Parliamentary commander Sir Thomas Mytton, her daughter Mary was married to Thomas Edwardes, a staunch Royalist, and her brother, Sir William Owen, was a Commissioner of Array for the king who, nonetheless, 'kept up a constant communication with the Parliamentary commissioners at Wem and divulged the intended movements of the Royalists'.[38]

The generally Royalist character of the county is likely to have been reflected in Church Stretton, although there may have been some Parliamentary sympathisers, possibly including the rector, Anthony Hawkes, in the light of his later approval as a Presbyterian minister. His marriage to Dorothy, daughter of John Thynne of Little Stretton, great-grandson of the second Sir John Thynne of Longleat (who had married Sir Rowland Hayward's youngest daughter), however, suggests he moved in the same social circle as his near neighbour and ardent Royalist, Thomas Edwardes.

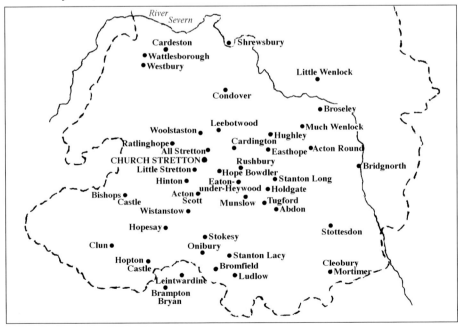

Map of the south Shropshire area in the seventeenth century

It was Edwardes, living almost certainly in Bonham Norton's former house, who drew Church Stretton more deeply into the conflict. His first wife, Mary Norton, died in childbirth in 1641 and he married again the next year to Cecily, daughter of Edward Brooke and referred to as Mary's servant in Jane Norton's will. On 20 December 1642 Edwardes signed 'The Ingagement and Resolution of the Gentlemen of Salop to raise and maintayne troops for the king at their own charge'. Two months later he was writing to his brother-in-law Sir Francis Ottley, the Royalist Governor of Shrewsbury, that he was busy raising dragoons in Stretton and its neighbourhood. This is unlikely to have been welcome to local people who would have been incredulous to find their country in the throes of civil war and wanting most of all to avoid involvement. Yet this was the fate of Shropshire's more rural areas. The largest towns, capable with additional fortification of becoming defensible centres, suffered more physical destruction; smaller communities had to endure the hardships of billeting soldiers, forced service for some of their able-bodied men, and the commandeering of crops, livestock and possessions. Stretton's situation deteriorated in January 1644 when Prince Rupert assumed the command of the royal army in Shropshire and the adjacent counties. Thomas Edwardes, who had just become High Sheriff of the county, was still at Stretton and 'engaged now in the thankless and not always successful task of collecting levies of money and provisions from an already much impoverished neighbourhood'.[39] His difficulties increased as Prince Rupert had a large force scattered in Shropshire and the border area, and 'it was the High Sheriff's disagreeable duty to plunder (for it could be called by no other name) for the support of the troops'[40] at the expense of his own poor and much oppressed friends and their tenants and dependants. In a letter to Sir Francis Ottley from Stretton dated 10 May 1644, Edwardes wrote:

> Good Brother, This evening was brought before me one William Phillips of Lentwardine who being tipling in this Towne and discovered to have the letters inclosed. I examined him whence he had these letters and he saith they come from the Lady Harley and were delivered him by a tenant of hers one Lokere that lyves in Lentwardyne, hee would not confess any more, but he hath byn noted to pass this Towne as a common Intelligencer from that castle into these parts ...[41]

Perhaps the High Sheriff hoped that his co-operation would lead to a reduction of the Royalist demands because the next month he and the gentry of Salop petitioned the king:

> The distressed condition of this county is such, the rebels having so great power in it and in the adjacent parts, that the money which may possibly be raised out of this county cannot in its proportion sufficiently supply the necessary charges of the army now under Prince Rupert, and the sum

required, £4,410, being greater in all probability than this county can afford in money or plate, we pray Your Majesty to give orders that the moneys required from the gentry of this county by Privy Seal and Royal letters may be assigned to Prince Rupert for support of the army in these parts, with power to moderate the sums required from persons who shall appear unable to bear it, and to impose the deficit on other persons of ability in that county, to whom no Privy Seals or Royal letters are directed, also that His Highness may take the same partly in provisions.[42]

The appeal fell on deaf ears. On one of his journeys through Shropshire in 1644 Prince Rupert found that Edwardes had fallen short of collecting the assessment of £9,000 laid upon the county. With nine troops quartered within a little distance of Church Stretton, the prince sent the High Sheriff an ultimatum that the next day he should deliver to the Royalist headquarters £500 and such provisions as he could raise—or face the prince's displeasure. All Edwardes' endeavours to raise that amount failed and a hundred musketeers were consequently ordered to his house opposite the church. We are told that they carried the threat into execution, presumably by shooting out his windows or worse.[43]

Thomas Edwardes may have been a little mollified by the king's award of a baronetcy in February 1645. Certainly his loyalty was unshaken for he was with the royal forces in Worcester when they surrendered in July 1646 at the end of the First Civil War. It was then Parliament's turn to take its revenge: the Sequestration Commissioners levied on him a fine of £2,060, an 'exceedingly heavy one in proportion to the size of his estates',[44] although his older brother Humphrey, an M.P. for Shropshire, was a Roundhead and would eventually be one of the signatories of Charles I's death warrant.

The attack on the Edwardes' house was probably the nearest Church Stretton and St. Laurence's got to warlike action, but depredations continued as soldiers moved frequently through the Stretton Gap, the most direct route between the Royalist strongholds of Shrewsbury and Ludlow. In February 1645 Parliamentary forces captured Shrewsbury and four months later Lieutenant-Colonel Reinking with a force of 500 foot and 300 horse headed south, foraging again on their way along Strettondale, and successfully demanded the surrender of Stokesay Castle. The Royalists rallied and collected an army of 2,000 men but were defeated by Reinking's smaller contingent near Wistanstow.

Such an encounter only five miles away must have had repercussions in Stretton as defeated Royalists sought to evade capture or triumphant Parliamentary troops returned to Shrewsbury. It is difficult to see how anything approaching normal life could have been maintained then or indeed right through the central years of the war. Fortunately St. Laurence's may have been considered too small as a billet for troops and so escaped the damage from this cause suffered by the churches at Bishop's Castle, Clun and Stokesay, all of which were closer to military action. Anthony Hawkes seems to have remained as rector but would have had his work cut out to sustain the religious life of the parish. There can have been little guidance from ecclesiastical superiors and few opportunities for contact with other clergy. He would have done well to conduct regular services and to meet the pastoral needs of his people suffering so much from the effects of war. We have no way of knowing the effect on the parish church when the Westminster Assembly of Divines, which began to meet in July 1643, made an early resolution, approved by Parliament, that all altars or tables of stone should be demolished, communion tables moved back from the east end into the body of the church, communion rails removed and chancels levelled. A petition to the King and Parliament in 1642 from nearby Wistanstow[45] had protested against the proposed abolition of episcopacy and the Prayer Book, but Anthony Hawkes would have welcomed the eventual disappearance of the Prayer Book and its replacement by the Presbyterian Directory of Worship. For as the Presbyterian system was gradually introduced into some parts of England after Parliament's victory in the Civil War, there is evidence, in a document in the Bodleian Library at Oxford, that he had adopted a Presbyterian position. The document, dated 29 April 1647, when it was autho-rised by the Parliamentary Earl of Manchester, is entitled *The Severall Divisions and Persons for Classicall Presbyteries in the County of Salop. Approved by the Right Hon. Committee of Lords and Commons for Judging of Scandals.*[46] By this the county was divided into six 'classes', with Church Stretton named first among 34 parishes in the Sixth Classis. Six ministers were named as 'fit to bee of the Sixth Classis' and Anthony Hawkes was one of them, along with the incumbents of Clun, Mainstone, More, Hopesay and Chirbury. Twelve laymen were also named in the Sixth Classis, among them Samuel More of Linley, Esquire, famed for his defence of Hopton Castle three years earlier and the sole survivor when the Royalists butchered the garrison. 'In face of the failure of most English counties to put the scheme into practice, this success in Shropshire argues the presence of a vigorous Puritan element already in existence some years earlier'.[47] That Hawkes was named alongside such well-known Parliamentary supporters as More and so staunch a Puritan minister as Thomas Froysell of Clun must be regarded as a strong indication that he had been in contact with Sir Robert Harley's network of godly clergy and lay people, that he at least had Puritan inclinations, and possibly that he had been sympathetic to Parliament's cause. The national Presbyterian system did not last long for 'Pride's Purge' in 1648 ejected 'Presbyterians' from the Commons and left only the more radical 'Independent' M.P.s. In Shropshire 57 ministers opposed to the extension of toleration to Independents signed 'A Testimony to the Truth of Jesus Christ and the Solemn League and Covenant'.[48] Two of the approved ministers in the Sixth Classis signed, Froysell at Clun and Barkley at Mainstone, but the significance of the absence of Hawkes's signature is uncertain. When the Classes were abolished a state of chaos and ecclesiastical anarchy spread over all Church government.

It is both disappointing and galling that over the following years, which witnessed the Second Civil War, the execution of the king and the establishment of first a Commonwealth and then a Protectorate, virtually nothing is known of life in Church Stretton or of what was happening in its parish church. Yet these were years of extraordinary religious and political ferment. 'A religious laboratory was created; and in it religious experiments were conducted of a type and diversity which has not been seen at any other time in the history of the country'.[49] When the use of the Prayer Book was forbidden, followed by the abolition of bishops, the monarchy and the House of Lords, there was ushered in a period of religious liberty that saw the growth of Independents (later Congregationalists) and Baptists, the beginnings of the Quaker movement and an astonishing proliferation of millenarian sects. Pamphlets advocating an extraordinary range of religious and political opinions poured off the presses. Oliver Cromwell wanted to preserve religious toleration, but he was under pressure on one side from those who feared such freedom would threaten property rights and the social order, and on the other from those who opposed any sort of religious authority and believed that the 'inner light' was the only true guide.

Unlike the hundreds of clergy who were ejected from their livings rather than abandon the Prayer Book, for example the rector of Wistanstow, it seems certain that Anthony Hawkes would have welcomed the Presbyterian Directory of Worship since it neither prescribed a set liturgy, nor left the form of worship entirely to the individual minister or congregation, but offered general guidance. It also encouraged the preaching of the Word, 'being the power of God unto salvation'. But after his inclusion in the list of the Sixth Classis in 1647, Hawkes, then aged 58, had only a few years to live. There are no ecclesiastical records in this period, no bishops' registers, no complete lists of institutions and no Call Books. Moreover, as Foster's *Alumni Oxonienses* confuses Hawkes with Anthony Hawles, Miss H.M. Auden's belief that Hawkes went on to become Archdeacon of Salisbury in 1658, canon in 1660 and a canon of Windsor in 1660 before his death in 1664 is mistaken. In fact, as the records of the Prerogative Court of Canterbury disclose, letters of administration were granted on 24 March 1652 to Dorothy, widow of Anthony Hawkes, who had died intestate. His death must have occurred late in 1651 or early in 1652. A few months later Dorothy's mother, Susanna Thynne, also died. Her bequest of 'my best broadcloth gown laced with gold lace' was scant consolation for one who had lost husband and mother so close together. These personal items apart, during the years from 1647 to 1660, a period of unprecedented turbulence and radical change in the land, all we hear from Church Stretton is a resounding silence.

8
ANGLICAN SETTLEMENT

The 11 years without a king in England came to a sudden end with the restoration of the Stuarts in the person of Charles II in 1660. On 29 May, his 30th birthday, the king re-entered London amid scenes of great rejoicing. As these were replicated all over the country, no doubt there was jubilation in Shropshire, with its royalist traditions, and in Church Stretton. Across the country surviving churchwardens' accounts 'almost invariably record the ringing of the bells at the king's return, and contemporary observers concur upon the fervour of celebration in both town and country'.[1] Bonfires were lit on hills and maypoles suddenly reappeared.

For those closely associated with the previous regime, of course, the prospects looked decidedly less promising. Just as hundreds of Prayer Book clergy had been forced out of their livings during and after the Civil War, so the Restoration saw many of these return and their supplanters summarily ejected. Some of these joined the 'gathered churches', individual congregations attached to a particular minister, which had sprung up during the years of religious ferment. Yet with a third of the parish churches, in a national survey of churchwardens' accounts, still in possession of the illegal Prayer Book, and another quarter with the new Directory of Worship, some comprehensive settlement appeared desirable, and 'it could be expected that a revived traditional Church, which embodied some of the reforms and tolerated others in individual parishes, would be well received at all levels of society'.[2] The king himself favoured a degree of toleration. But the gentry in the provinces and the young M.P.s in the Convention Parliament, which greeted Charles's return, generally pressed for the return of bishops and the Prayer Book, and these attitudes were even more strongly represented in the next Parliament. There is again no evidence available of how Church Stretton fared in the first year after the king's return, but in Wistanstow the Presbyterian minister of 1647 retired in 1660 and was replaced by the parson ejected from St. Alkmund's in Shrewsbury in 1644.

One of the first targets of the Cavalier Parliament elected in 1661 was the re-establishment of an Episcopalian Church with traditional liturgy. 'The old religion was in effect returning with the maypoles'.[3] The Convocation of

Clergy, also elected in 1661, rapidly accomplished the well-prepared revision of the Prayer Book, with 600 generally minor alterations agreed in the course of a month, and this was the text presented by the Act of Uniformity passed in May 1662. The importance of the Prayer Book was that it demonstrated what the Church believed, for the Reformation in England had not constituted a distinctive reformed Church with a confession of faith as on the continent, but had retained a purified medieval Church proclaiming a vaguely reformed doctrine. As a result the Church of England had pursued a middle way between the Catholic and the Reformed and in consequence been subjected to continual attack from both sides. Yet whatever the circumstances of its origin and subsequent revision, the 1662 Prayer Book has stood the test of time. It displays Cranmer's mature mastery of language, selection and arrangement, his splendid gift of phrase, and his flair for culling ideas from a range of sources. Its timeless quality has ensured that it is still widely used today.

There can be no doubt that the Act of Uniformity which imposed the Prayer Book on the Church was strongly partisan. 'Instead of healing the nation's divisions and easing the path to conformity for moderate Presbyterians, this "sharp Act" virtually ensured that they would be forced out of the national Church'.[4] The Act came into force on St. Bartholomew's Day, 24 August 1662. It provided for the deprivation of every minister who by 'Black Bartholomew', as the nonconformists called it, did not testify to his acceptance of the entire Prayer Book, denounce the Presbyterian Solemn League and Covenant,[5] and abjure the principle of resistance to royal authority. Those who were prepared to subscribe in the diocese of Hereford were required to put this in writing and to add their signature. Some read their declarations of conformity publicly in their parish church. Suddenly Church Stretton re-emerges from the mists of obscurity, for among those who appear in the Subscription Roll is its rector. The entry is as follows:

I Peter Dormer Rector of Church Stretton in ye County of Salop and chaplayne to ye right hon Henry Earle of Dover doe willingly subscribe to ye abovesayd declaration or acknowledgment.

August 21, 1662   Witness my hand   Peter Dormer.

Who was Peter Dormer and how long had he been rector? Only one Peter Dormer features in the records of Oxford and Cambridge Universities in the mid-seventeenth century, one who matriculated at Magdalen Hall, Oxford, in May 1632, aged 16, was awarded his B.A. in October 1633, M.A. in June 1636, and D.Med. in April 1648. Also recorded is that he was baptised on 7 May 1614 and was 'of Gray's Inn, 1637'.[6] The contradiction of his stated age in 1632 by the date of his baptism is resolved by the entry in the parish register of Quainton, Bucks, which shows that he was actually baptised on 7 May 1615 and therefore just 17 on matriculation. He was the son of Sir Fleetwood Dormer, a barrister knighted by James I and with estates in Buckinghamshire and Northamptonshire.

Given his medical and legal background, he does seem an unlikely figure to have been rector of Church Stretton in 1662. There are three reasons, however, for believing that this is our man: first, he is elsewhere referred to as 'Magister' and there is no other Peter Dormer at that time with a master's degree; second, the Blakeway MSS, compiled nearer to the time of Peter Dormer than to our own, have a pencilled insertion that he was 'the uncle of Judge Dormer'—and Peter Dormer's nephew was indeed a Justice of Common Pleas from 1706 to 1726; and third, his son was buried in St. Mary's, Shrewsbury, and his youngest daughter married Thomas Dawes the late seventeenth-century rector there,[7] establishing a family link with Shropshire. So in August 1662 Peter Dormer was 47 years of age with a varied track record but perhaps one explained by the extraordinary events that had convulsed the country in the two previous decades.

Peter Dormer was married to Anne Shepherd of Rollright, Oxon, and their first three children were all baptised, as he had been, at Quainton in 1639, 1641 and 1642, but the baptism of the youngest in February 1645, in the middle of the Civil War, was registered at St. James's, Clerkenwell, London. There are no original sources which reveal when he was ordained or when he came to Church Stretton, but he was clearly the incumbent at the time he subscribed to the Act of Uniformity in 1662 and not appointed as the result of another's unwillingness to conform under the Act. But how long before 1662 had he become rector? The living was vacant on Hawkes's death in 1651/2, but Stretton does not feature among the twelve Shropshire benefices to which appointments were made between 1648 and 1659 and listed in the Composition Books in the Public Record Office; nor is it in the list of ministers appointed between 1651 and 1659 preserved at Lambeth Palace. Yet from the silence of these years in Stretton faint whispers were picked up and recorded.[8] A far from complete list of rectors has Peter Dormer, M.A., taking up the position in 1654, making him in those confused years a possible successor to Anthony Hawkes. His presence in Stretton in 1654 is confirmed by his appearance with his servants before the lord's Court Baron on 23 October for cutting turf on the

The presentment of Richard Williams & Edward medhroot Church wardens of the pish of Church stretton Anno Dom 1662

Titul

1) Our Church & Chancell is in good repare
2 Ther is nothing imbesoled as we know of
3 Ther is a font of stone wth a Comunion Table wth a Carpet of woll Cloth & a nother of finne linnen we haue 2 fayer Comunion Cups wth to Couers for them
4 we haue both Cloth & Cushion for the pulpet
5 we haue a larg Surplice
6 we haue a Register Booke
7 we haue to other Bookes wth a Chest Locke & key to keep all necessaries in

Titul 2 Our Church yard is well repaired
our ministers house is in good repare for ought we know
And ther is none that hath entrocched upon his Glibe for ought we know
Ther hath none of the Glebe lands bine Exchanged for as we know
Our minister is lawfully ordained & Inducted for ought we know

Tit 3 To this Article we haue not any thing to present
3 He is a minster according to the Laws of the Church of England
4 He hath bine absent since we presented last but he came home this week
5 But he hath a Curate wch is nevy Diligent in his absence wch is in holy Orders
6 He observeth this Article for ought we know
7 He weareth the Surplice so doth his Curate
8 we haue Sirvice upon holy dayes
9 If he be sicke or absent his Curate doth visit the sicke
10 They doo instruct by Catechising
11 Ther is now Infant unbaptised through his default as we know
12 He doth not preach Schismaticall Doctrine wch we know
13 He hath not presumed to marry any wth out Banes asked for any thing
14 wth in our pish ther is no Lecturer
15 He hath no privat flocks nor offerings as we know of
16 He is no Gamester neyther doth he incorage suts or debate as we know

Tit thet 4 Tho Sankey his wife & Eliz: the wife of Tho Callier cometh not to our Church & they are reputed Anabaptis or the like
2 by John Sankey the yongtes & his wife for liuing incontinently befor they were maried
3 Ther is no shops kept open on saboth dayes as we know of
4 Ther are none but doe abide quietly in the Church for ought we
5 They do put of ther Hats & so sit or knile
whether al House kepers do instruct ther families is more then we knew

Part of the churchwardens' return in 1662 (HRO)

Long Mynd.[9] This seems conclusive, though one would have thought Dormer more likely to have been instituted in 1660 when bishops were restored and because as chaplain to Henry Carey, Earl of Dover, who was a former Speaker of the House of Lords in 1641 and a colonel in the king's army, he must have been of Royalist sympathies. Perhaps he had been welcomed by Stretton's traditionalists and royalists after the demise of the Presbyterian Hawkes. Dormer's generous contribution of 40 shillings to the 'free and voluntary present to His Majesty' in August 1662,[10] one of the largest gifts from the clergy of the Wenlock Deanery, may have no particular significance as Thomas Froysell, the old Puritan rector of Clun, also contributed although he had to leave his living when he refused to subscribe under the Act of Uniformity.

In the autumn of 1662 the bishops went on a visitation of their sees and sent out articles of inquiry to all churchwardens. The response of the wardens[11] at St. Laurence's, Richard Wilding and Edward Medlicott, constitutes the earliest surviving description of the state of the church and parish and is therefore of the greatest interest. The first article solicited information about the building and its furnishings. The wardens replied that the church and chancel were in good repair. There was a stone font, and the communion table was covered with 'a carpet of woollen cloth and another of fine linen'; the two 'fair communion cups' had covers. The pulpit had both cloth and cushion. They reported that there was a Register Book, two other books, and a chest with a lock and key to keep all necessaries in. Under the second article they recorded that the church-yard fence was well repaired, as was the minister's house as far as they knew, and that there had been no encroachment on the glebe nor any exchange of glebe lands to their knowledge. The third article concerned the incumbent and his role. The wardens believed their minister to be lawfully ordained and inducted according to the laws of the Church of England, but ominously reported a long absence: 'he hath bine absent since we presented last but came home this week'. Fortunately he had 'a curate which is very diligent in his absence which is in holy orders'. The rector or, when he was away, the curate visited the sick and instructed by catechising.

The good state of the building, furniture and church property will have reas-sured the bishop anxious for his diocese after years without episcopal oversight and, in some parishes, without a properly ordained incumbent. But he also wanted to know how far the congregation was obeying Convocation's instruc-tions 'to observe a greater ceremony and sobriety, standing for hymns, kneeling for prayers, bowing at Christ's name and removing hats in church'.[12] This concern for conformity to the Anglican character of the restored church, and a desire to know the extent of sectarian influence and practice, were reflected in further questions. The wardens' responses were again reassuring: both minister and curate wore a surplice, services were held on holy days, and the wardens knew of no infant unbaptised through the minister's default nor any marriage performed without banns called. The minister did not preach 'schismaticall doctrine' nor encourage debate, and no stranger had recently preached in the church. There was no evidence of organised Dissent: no 'lecturer' in the parish 'and no private fasts nor prophesyings as we know of'. In fact the only Dissenters were Thomas Sankey and his wife and Elizabeth Gallier who 'cometh not to our church and they are reputed Anabaptists or the like'. The wardens were able to marshal further evidence of order and decency in the church and its worship: no shops were known to be open on the Sabbath and people were 'quiet and reverent in church ... they do put of theyr hats and so sit or knele'. They knew of no-one who walked around in the church or church-yard at the time of divine service, and no-one put his hat on the communion table (an anti-Roman gesture of some Puritans). They admitted they did not know if all householders instructed their children in the faith, but no-one refused to receive the sacrament kneeling, no-one was excommunicated (although another Sankey and his wife were reported for having lived inconti-nently before they were married), none had refused to pay taxes to the wardens, and none had refused to bury the dead according to Church of England prac-tice. The wardens' 'taxes' were the poor rate and church rate—payment for the maintenance of services and the nave.

The inquiry elicited a few further interesting details. The minister was no gamester, the clerk was reputed to be diligent and a scholar, there was no hospital and no-one practised surgery. Finally, the wardens revealed something of themselves, assuring the bishop that they were chosen by the joint consent of the minister and the parishioners and had been sworn, that their predecessors had handed over their accounts, that there were no sidesmen, and that they provided bread and wine for the communion. They ended by acknowledging that one of them, Edward Medlicott, had erected a pew in the church, 'partly by consent of the parishioners', which was for the use of his wife and after her decease for the use of future churchwardens; they were confident that the parishioners would be happy about it. For us it is confirmation that the occa-sional addition of pews continued.

The same wardens replied to similar articles of inquiry in 1663. Their answers were virtually identical. Once again they reported the minister's absence for at least two months. This time they added a reference to church-ings: 'There is none that refuse to returne thanks after deliverance'. They also reported that there was 'a chapel in the towne of Minton which was very much decayed for there was no service in it of fforty years, as we are informed, and it was converted to that pious use of a scole house in the town of Church Stretton, and there were to [two] Bell but little ones were sould by the inhabi-tants then of Minton'. This chapel, like the one at Womerton, had probably been erected in the late Middle Ages as a 'chapel of ease' for the benefit of those living at the extremities of the parish. For probably at least two hundred years they had been the only other places of worship in the parish, but both had fallen into ruin by the seventeenth century; that at Womerton was said to be 'utterly defaced and the stones thereof carried away' by the 1630s.[13] It seems that the proceeds of the sale of the materials and site of the one at Minton, with any endowment, were given to the school in Church Stretton as a contribution, one assumes, towards the cost of educating Minton children.

The wardens' reference to a Register Book was timely for the parish registers have survived from 1662; unfortunately earlier registers, first legally required in 1538, have perished. Early entries in the new register were sometimes in Latin, sometimes in English, but the details of baptisms, marriages and burials are of prime importance for our knowledge of the parish and its people. The first entry records the burials of James Dee of Little Stretton and James Parker of Church Stretton on 23 March 1662. There is then added in English on the first page the names of three children born to Edward Berry and his wife Elizabeth between 9 August 1653 and 20 March 1660, even giving the time of birth of the second child on 22 October 1655 as between 1 and 2 a.m. The only other occasions that such details came to be recorded were when an incumbent noted the births and baptisms of his own children. It is possible that Edward Berry acted as minister in those blank years between Anthony Hawkes's death and the likely arrival of Peter Dormer, but as he continued to live in the parish —two other Berry offspring appeared in 1665 and 1670—it seems virtually certain that he was the diligent and literate parish clerk commended by the wardens. An analysis of the entries in the register for the first two decades, 1662-1679, reveals an average of 16 baptisms a year, with a peak of 27 in 1676; an average of 13.3 burials a year, with a range from only 4 in 1678 to high points in 1667 (22), 1675 (30, including many children) and 1676 (22), probably years of epidemics; and two or three weddings a year, including as many as eight in 1670 but none in three years. The population was gradually rising, by 49 between 1662 and 1679, assuming there was a balance between movements in and out of the parish.

It seems that in the slowly expanding but still small town that Stretton was in the second half of the seventeenth century the nonconformists constituted only a tiny minority. In Shropshire as a whole they were also less numerous than in many counties, although over 50 ministers failed to subscribe under the Act of Uniformity out of 194 parishes,[14] and others had been ejected two years earlier. Nationally, many of the estimated 1,760 clergy forced to leave their English parishes between 1660 and 1663[15] would probably have accepted a less rigorous conformity, and it was these moderates that Charles II would have liked to include in a broader Church, as well as relieving penalties against Roman Catholics. But Archbishop Sheldon, backed up by a majority in the House of Commons, was too powerful and in 1664 the Conventicle Act was passed. It decreed that any person aged over 16 who attended an unorthodox religious gathering of more than five was to be fined and for a third offence even transported. Conventiclers were hunted down and many, especially Quakers, imprisoned. In 1665 the Five Mile Act laid down that no ejected minister could reside within five miles of his old parish or any corporate town.

These repressive measures were largely irrelevant in Church Stretton. Only three dissenters had been named by the wardens, Peter Dormer was a loyal Anglican, and his curate appointed in 1664, Samuel Paddy, readily subscribed on 27 May. Paddy came from Shrewsbury, the son of a clothier. From Shrewsbury School he had proceeded in 1654 to St. John's College, Cambridge, which had close links with the school. He graduated B.A. in 1658 and was ordained priest in November 1660. He would have been 29 years of age when he came to Church Stretton where he remained until at least 1668. In his first year it is recorded that he preached once at St. Julian's, Shrewsbury, where his father had helped restore the church after the Parliamentary occupation in 1645. On this occasion father no doubt swelled with pride and Samuel was rewarded with 'a pinte of sack, 1s'.[16] The baptisms of twin sons born to Samuel Paddy and his wife, Anne, were recorded in March 1667 but sadly one was buried 11 days later; a daughter was baptised in October 1668.

It is hoped that like his unknown predecessor as curate Samuel Paddy coped well in the absence of the rector. Peter Dormer's earlier absences had been noted by the wardens, but they may have had a different cause from a later more extended period away. An affidavit signed by him, and filed by the Registrar on 21 May 1666, must have come as a bombshell to the diocese:

> Peter Dormer of Church Stretton in the County of Salop Clerke maketh oath that he was a close prisoner in the Marshalsea for debt till about ye month of July 1665, and that he is not yet discharged from ye said prison, and further saith that his two sonns whose company he did frequent lately were visited with the plague, whereof one died, and saith likewise that he had the same distemper which as yet renders him unfit for travell.[17]

The document does not disclose when he had been first confined to the Marshalsea nor when he was eventually released, but his incarceration must have lasted at least a year. He may never have returned to Church Stretton, for after being named as rector in the Call Books of 1664 and 1665 his name is crossed out in 1668; indeed, he must have died in 1667 (perhaps still in prison as he was not buried at St. Laurence's), for his successor was presented in January 1668.

*

The parish sorely needed a committed minister who would stay long enough to establish the new Anglican ways. But it was not yet to be. The candidate presented to the bishop by Sir Henry Frederick Thynne on 22 January 1668 was

George Roberts. In his subscription of 1665, with no parish named, he described himself as Master of Arts and Fellow of Merton College, Oxford. This clearly identifies him as the George Roberts who matriculated at Trinity College, Oxford, in 1652, was awarded his B.A. in 1656, became a Fellow of Merton in 1658, took his M.A. in 1662, and was made a Proctor in 1667. As the son of the Rev. George Roberts who had been deprived of his living in Buckinghamshire in 1647 but restored in 1660 and acted briefly as Archdeacon of Winchester before his death in 1661, and as an Oxford Fellow himself in the 1660s, George was almost certainly a traditionalist in religion. He made a second subscription on his presentation to Church Stretton. Yet he must have resigned within months — he later became a rector in Surrey — for his successor was presented, again by Sir Henry Frederick Thynne, on 3 June 1668.

That successor was Henry Maurice, one of the most interesting of St. Laurence's rectors, although he too was not to bring the period of stability that was needed. Maurice, who was born *c*.1636 and descended from 'a considerable family' in Caernarvonshire, had been a student at Jesus College, Oxford, and is described as Magister in the Call Books, though university records contain no reference to a degree. He was appointed Vicar of Bromfield near Ludlow in 1661 and subscribed the next year. He was married with two sons, but a third, born in Bromfield, lived for only three weeks. A daughter, named after his wife Ellenor, was born in February 1666. He left Bromfield that year heavily in debt (Peter Dormer was not the only clergyman in financial difficulties). Maurice subscribed again on 3 June 1668 when, at the age of about 32 and following George Roberts's departure, he was admitted as Rector of Church Stretton, described by Edmund Calamy in his *Nonconformists' Memorial* as 'a valuable living which had a delightful seat'. The churchwardens reported soon afterwards that they had 'nothing amiss to present touching our minister' and thanked him for his faithful assistance in drawing up their presentment at the bishop's visitation. The next year they wrote, 'Our minister demeans himself and performs every duty relating to his function as a Gospel minister ought to doo'.[18] But Maurice was uneasy in his conscience about his conformity — 'a delayed action Dissenter', as he has been described — and about his wealthy benefice. Although as rector he had an income of about £140 per annum, he had run up further debts of £300, chiefly as a result of annexing some out-buildings to his parsonage house. In 1671 he reached a personal crisis. Calamy reports that when the town was visited with a malignant fever which carried off many of his parishioners (although the parish register shows only average numbers of burials in his three years at Stretton), Henry Maurice was 'much awakened and very solicitous about his everlasting state if he should be seized by death … He could not be easy in his mind till he had taken up a resolution to quit his living'. His wife supported his decision despite their young family and debts. He preached his farewell sermon from Luke 23:3, upon which, according to Calamy, 'the Chancellor of the diocese sent him a citation, charging him with reflecting on the government of the Church'.[19] Worse was to come. He disclosed his personal estate to his creditors who took all away and carried him off to Shrewsbury gaol. After his release he was licensed as a Congregational teacher at Acton Round, and his house at Much Wenlock was licensed as a meeting-place under the terms of the royal Declaration of Indulgence of 1672 which lifted the penal laws.

A diary kept by Maurice in 1672,[20] the year after his resignation as rector, throws valuable light on his spiritual life and his continuing links with the parish, affording us a precious glimpse of the ministry of an erstwhile Stretton rector, albeit untypical, in the seventeenth century. On 13 June 1672 'the Widow Jones's son from All Stretton, the weaver' came to seek his spiritual advice about 'the trembling of the heart'. Maurice recorded that 'I spoke to him about his soul'. Two weeks later, on 26 June, Rowland Gilbert's wife, Mary, from Church Stretton 'came to me to discourse about soul concerns, which

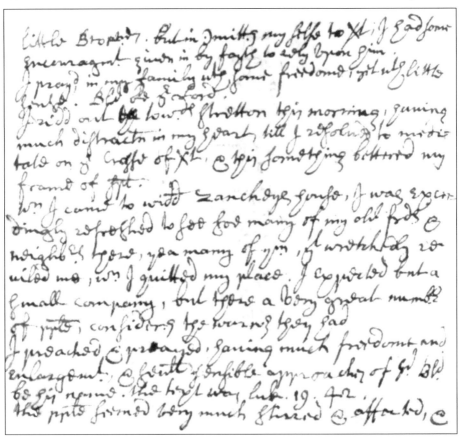

A page from the diary of Rev. Henry Maurice
for 2 July 1672 (see opposite)

made me much wonder. The poor woman seemed to be much concerned and sensible in a measure of the hazard of her soul'. In the following week, on 2 July,

> I rode out towards Stretton this morning having much distraction in my heart, till I resolved to meditate on the Cross of Christ, and this something bettered my frame of spirit. When I came to Widow Zanchey's house, I was exceedingly refreshed to see so many of my old friends and neighbours there, yea many of them, that wretchedly reviled me when I quitted my place. I expected but a small company, but there [was] a very great number of people ... I preached and prayed, having much freedom and enlargement, and several sensible approaches of God. Blessed be His name. The text was Luke 19:42. The people seemed very much stirred and affected, and certainly there was much of God appearing in this meeting.

That same month, on 25 July, he was at Ratlinghope, disappointed that the wet weather had kept away his friends from Church Stretton. But he was back in Stretton on 27 September, only days after being arrested in Shrewsbury on account of his debts and detained over-night in the sergeant's house. 'I came to Widow Zanchey's house in All Stretton where I preached this day from Romans 5:8, having encouragement and enlargement in preaching and praying. Blessed be the Lord God for ever. I came home thence this night'. The Widow Zankey and other nonconformists are considered later in this chapter.

Perhaps it was when financial and political pressure led to the revocation of the edict of toleration after a year that Maurice returned from Shropshire to Wales where his contribution earned him an honoured place in the annals of Welsh Puritanism. He is described as 'famous for his return to us after some little recidivation' — in the Church of England! — 'and his wonderful zeal and indefatigable pains afterwards'.[21] He travelled all over Wales preaching the gospel and vast numbers came to hear him. Morning and evening he expounded the Scriptures in both Welsh and English. Still in debt, he was pursued by the authorities but only once arrested; eventually he discharged his debt shortly before his death in July 1682. He was buried in St. Mary's Church, Abergavenny. His end was hastened by the excessive demands he made on himself which undermined his constitution. In Calamy's judgement Maurice was in the last part of his life 'a person of great humility, meekness, patience and resignation to the Divine Will, and full of compassion to his enemies ... He had a wonderful skill in unravelling the very thoughts and inward workings of men's hearts, and was very particular and convincing as well as affectionate in his applications to the consciences of his hearers'.

Henry Maurice's resignation in 1671 had deprived Church Stretton and South Shropshire of a charismatic preacher. His departure also meant the loss of a rector who through his own experiences would have understood the pastoral needs of parishioners beset by personal problems and who would have dealt sympathetically with local dissenters or backsliders: Abram Broughton and his wife, for instance, cited for non-attendance at church in 1669, promised him faithfully that thereafter they would come to church.

Other local tensions are apparent, this time between local landholders and the lord of the manor, the church's patron. Thirty years before Maurice's rectorship, in a letter[22] dated 6 March 1638 'to the right worshipfull our honoured landlord Sir Thomas Thynne, in Canall rowe in Westminster in London', Stretton tenants expressed their surprise that he had not long since righted himself upon the encroachments on his commons and their hopes that he would soon do so. His humble petitioners also asked their lord 'to graunte us licence to plowe up some little parte of our common wheare formerly yt hath been plowed, and we will in acknowledgment of this favoure, give your worship 20 bushells of otes for your horses every yeare as longe as wee sowe in the comon'. We do not know if this was carried out, but three decades later relations were again under strain between Sir Henry Frederick Thynne and his steward Thomas Harries on the one hand, and Elizabeth Horne widow, William Bowdler, Richard Wilding and other complainants on the other. The plaintiffs, like village-Hampdens withstanding the tyrant of their fields, alleged in Chancery that Thynne and Harries had been refusing to accept surrenders (the transfer of tenancies), had taken some documents out of the church chest, and had been trying to treat copyholders as tenants at will. The rector could not avoid some involvement because the crucial documents were kept in a chest in the church and the protagonists were leading local figures. The matter was eventually resolved by the Lord Keeper of the Rolls who set out the customs of the manor of Church Stretton as they had been recognised 'time out of mind'. The copyholders' rights were reasserted and the steward ordered to record surrenders and admittance on parchment to be kept in the parish church in a chest with three locks, one key to be held by the steward and the two others by customary tenants.

*

Maurice's place in Stretton was taken by Henry Clayton, presented by Sir Henry Frederick Thynne on 11 June 1671; he duly subscribed under the Act of Uniformity on the same day. The churchwardens' visitation return of 20 September 1671[23] recorded that he had 'lately received institution from the Right Reverend Bishop of this Diocese and being inducted accordingly did openly in our parish church read the 39 Articles and declared his assent and consent thereunto'. No-one was to know at the time that Henry Clayton would remain as rector until his death 54 years later, the second longest rectorship in

St. Laurence's history, and would at last introduce that era of stability for which the faithful of the parish yearned.

Henry was the son of Richard Clayton, 'a gentleman of Shropshire'. He was 27 years old, having matriculated at Christ Church, Oxford, in May 1662 at the age of 18, and been awarded his B.A. in 1665 and M.A. from Oriel College in 1669. He had been ordained priest in the Oxford diocese on 26 February 1671. Since Samuel Paddy had already departed—he was to become rector of Southease in Sussex in 1673—a new curate was appointed and appears in the 1671 Call Book alongside the new rector. The curate, who was also granted a licence to serve as the schoolmaster, was Charles Farrer, described as 'magister' though no-one of his name appears among graduates recorded at that time.

The two new clergy faced their first appraisal at the bishop's visitation in September. Henry Clayton was not yet resident but expressed this intention; the wardens' comment was typically non-committal—'he behaves himself well and civilly for all we know'. The curate was in holy orders but as yet without a licence, though he intended to procure one at the visitation. The wardens attested that the church was in good and sufficient repair and 'all things well and decently ordered', with a decent font, a communion table with coverings for it, and a chalice. There was a 'convenient place' for the minister to read divine service together with 'a pulpit and all things thereunto belonging'. A chest contained surplice, register book, churchwardens' account book (now sadly lost) and other books and utensils. The churchyard was said to be well and sufficiently fenced and the parsonage house in good repair. The only 'hereticks and schismaticks' were those already excommunicated. To their knowledge there had been no disorder or misdemeanour in the church nor the minister disturbed during divine service.

If the wardens' returns were accurate the new rector's long innings had got off to a solid start. Now he had to get to know his parishioners. A document[24] dated 3 January 1672, signed by the curate Charles Farrer, is a testimonial for one Jane, the wife of Daniel Jones of Church Stretton, who wished to be recognised as a midwife. Six literate ladies vouched for her ability and understanding to assume the role and her 'honest life and conversation'. They obviously carried weight for Jane Jones is recorded as 'obstetrix' in the Call Book of 1677. She no doubt delivered younger members of the families featured in the 1672 Hearth Tax returns[25] which also give us some idea of the size of the four constituent areas of the parish and the relative prosperity of some of its inhabitants, if this can be judged by the size of their houses. The tax was levied at 2s. per hearth. The Rev. Mr. Clayton, assessed for six, was second equal in Church Stretton with Mr. Edward Brooke, but way behind Mr. Thomas Powell, the tenant of Sir George Norton at the Hall, which had 11 hearths. Thomas Hawkes, out at Botvyle, had eight hearths, but interestingly John Thynne at Minton, the only householder accorded the title of Esquire in acknowledgment of his distinguished family, was assessed for only one. In Church Stretton 37 householders paid the tax, in All Stretton 29, in Little Stretton 12 and in Minton 20, a total of 98 householders in the parish. As in the county 23% were classed as paupers and did not pay the tax, there would have been, if the same proportion applied in Stretton, about 120 households which could represent a population for the whole parish approaching 600, although the poll tax returns of 1666-67[26] name 489 (some children may have been omitted).

Charles Farrer did not stay long for in February 1673 the rector presented John Bowdler to the bishop requesting his appointment as the new curate, at a stipend of £20 per annum, and also to instruct boys in grammar. With the presentment the rector was able to enclose a testimonial[27] in Latin from the Provost and Fellows of Oriel College, Oxford, commending John Bowdler, B.A., as a dedicated student of sober and honest life who had shown his orthodoxy in the Christian religion and held to the doctrines of the Church of England. A further testimonial, again in Latin, signed by Henry Clayton and four other local rectors, attested that John Bowdler's parents who lived in the vicinity—actually recorded as Montgomeryshire—were good and honest, that he had a good reputation for academic study and personal integrity, and that he had always upheld the teachings of the Church of England. This paragon of virtue, who was only 22, was ordained deacon and first appears as curate in the Call Books in 1674, in which year he was also licensed to teach. He was still curate in 1676 but two years later had been replaced by Vincent Hicks, whose family lived near Kington in Herefordshire and who had been a student at Christ Church, Oxford. Both Bowdler and Hicks went on to become rectors in Shropshire, Bowdler at Cardeston from 1688 and Hicks at Rushbury from 1684.

It is from Clayton's early years as rector and from the few years preceding his arrival that the sometimes almost indecipherable records of the diocesan court throw some light on what life was like in Church Stretton and its parish church. The church courts dealt with testamentary and matrimonial matters, ecclesiastical cases, and moral and spiritual offences. It was common for the family of a deceased person to apply to the court for probate; for instance, Jane Griffiths, Elizabeth Tomlins, Thomas Oakes and Maria Pinches all appeared in 1676 after the death of a parent. The most common ecclesiastical cases concerned non-attendance at church, like John Masson of Little Stretton in 1672. A few defaulters were Dissenters, while others pursued their occupations on the Sabbath day like Roger Morris, presented for grinding his mill on Sundays and holy days; even a churchwarden, Thomas Phillips, was cited for burning grounds on the Sabbath. Others preferred their own amusements to going to church: John Cowper of All Stretton was presented for playing at quoits in the churchyard one Sunday.[28] The churchwardens were in an unenviable situation, for if they reported absentees they made themselves unpopular locally, but if they did not they could themselves be brought before the court, as happened in 1675 to Joseph Paddy and Samuel Minton. And churchwardens were regularly in trouble for not keeping the churchyard wall and fence in good repair; occasionally they themselves reported those responsible, as in 1672 when the inhabitants of Little Stretton and Minton were presented for not repairing their sections of the church fence.[29] Churchwardens were frequently summoned, too, for not presenting their accounts to the parish and handing them over to their successors. They must have been relieved that their term of office usually lasted for only 12 months. Other ecclesiastical cases, like those of Edward Lloyd and John Meredith in 1676, were prompted by the failure to pay Easter dues or, on other occasions, tithes or church rates.

But the most common appearances before the courts were for moral failings, usually for extra-marital sex. In 1667 John Botfield and Mary Butler were presented 'upon common fame of living in adultery together'; two years later she was accused of living incontinently with Thomas Howells at Minton. Howells was also cited to answer allegations against him concerning his soul's health and the reformation of his manners. Richard Morgan and Margaret Mornefield were in 1675 before the court 'for committing fornication together by his own confession'. Elizabeth Sherry was reputed to have lived in 1676 with both Thomas Corfield and Thomas Posterne, while William Davies and Matthew Stephens, churchwardens in 1676, were both accused six years later of incontinence with Elizabeth Powell and Martha Urwick. William Minton was presented 'upon a fame of unlawfully begetting with child Elizabeth Morris', Richard Kite for the same offence with Mary Adams of Wistanstow. Pre-nuptial intercourse was the reason for presenting Edward Broome and his wife Eleanora, for although they had been married by licence on 19 May 1677 'she was delivered of a child about a fortnight after Michaelmas following'. One can almost hear the gossip and back-biting that went on. Richard and Alicia Langford were but one couple who had their child before they got married. Illegitimate births were frequent and were not usually followed by marriage: in 1679 Margaret Jordan was summoned for 'being unlawfully begotten with child'—she named Joseph Jones as the father—went to Lichfield but returned and had another child. Sexual immorality was not confined to the lower orders: in August 1680 Dorothy Powell, wife of Richard Powell, Gentleman, and her lover, William Jones, were 'presented for a fame' (public rumour). In a list of excommunicants in Wenlock Deanery in July 1676 there were eight names from Stretton and only three were paying the penalty for religious unorthodoxy.[30]

But not all moral cases were of a sexual character—Thomas Phillips, for example, was accused in 1663 of slander by Thomas Hawkes. As happened with great frequency he failed to turn up, and was therefore declared contumacious and excommunicated. Since the church could only impose spiritual penalties, excommunications were handed out for a variety of offences and so frequently that they lost some of their deterrence. Those excommunicated were not simply excluded from worship and the sacraments, but also disabled from pleading in court or acting as an executor, and denied burial in the churchyard. It is unlikely that the threat of social ostracism was carried out by local people. Sometimes a penance was commuted to a small money payment, but not always—Joseph Jones had to make the following confession in St. Laurence's on Sunday, 23 May 1680, before or after one of the services and in the presence of the minister and two churchwardens:

> I Joseph Jones doe here in the presence of God and this Congregacion confess and acknowledge that having not the fear of God before mine eyes and being seduced by the temptacions of the devil and my own lusts have lived incontinently and committed the foule sinn of fornicacion with one Margery Jordan whereby I have greatly offended Almighty God endangered mine own soule and given an evil example and scandall to good Christians for which offence I am heartily sorry and doe humbley begg pardon of God and this Congregacion for the same and doe here promise God assisting mee with his grace never to offend in the like againe but to live chastly here after beseeching this Congregacion to pray for mee and with mee to say Our Father ...[31]

Criminal offences were tried before the secular courts. The most notorious in this period was a double murder.[32] John Adams lived at Stretton as a hired servant of John Harris, a sawyer, and worked honestly for him for several years. On 13 January 1675 he set off with his master to walk to Cardington but left some of his tools behind and went back, he said, to collect them. He knew that in the previous July his employer had sold two cows for £10, but his story was that the devil put the idea of theft into his mind and that two fiends in black gave him a long knife. He cut the throat of his master's wife, Anne, and then that of their daughter, Sarah. He found the £10 and two gold rings and set fire to the house, but before it was wholly burnt a butcher's boy driving cattle discovered the bodies. Adams, however, stayed in the area lurking in woods and out-buildings, and the next night robbed another house. He was found on top of a hay-rick with the £10 and rings, confessed, was tried at Shrewsbury Quarter Sessions, condemned to death, and hanged in chains.

*

Although Church Stretton had tended to espouse traditional ways in religion, there were, as has been noted, a few Dissenters in the parish. As early as 1662 the wardens had reported that Thomas Sankey and his wife and Elizabeth Gallier did not come to church and were reputed Anabaptists. Henry Maurice when rector would have shielded them, but the young and orthodox Henry Clayton is likely to have felt differently, for within the Church schismatics were generally regarded with horror. Yet he was not given a clear lead by the tolerant Bishop of Hereford, Herbert Croft, who in 1675 had decided that 'he should not be over-zealous in insisting on the surplice',[33] and whose pamphlet, *The Naked Truth*, was a plea for moderation.[34] Thomas Sankey died in 1665, but for years the records contain references to Joanna or 'the widow Zankey' and to Elizabeth Gallier as excommunicants. Briefly in 1672 the king's Declaration lifted the penal laws, which perhaps accounts for the revelation that in that year John Oliver, Edward Higgins and Thomas Medlicott and his wife attended conventicles—but what was not revealed was that the ex-rector Henry Maurice addressed them! Under the terms of the Declaration the widow Zankey's house in All Stretton was on 25 July 1672 granted a licence as a Congregational, possibly Baptist, meeting house—of which, as mentioned, Maurice took advantage two months later. According to the Hearth Tax returns of that year, hers was a substantial dwelling with four hearths. It was one of the 57 meeting places licensed in Shropshire.[35] When the Declaration of Indulgence was termi-

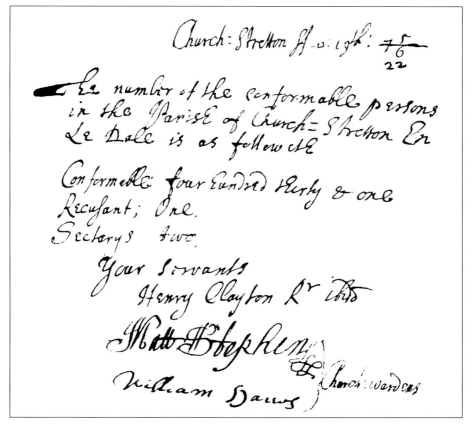

Stretton parish's return to the Compton Enquiry, 1676 (HRO)

nated in 1673 Joanna Zankey and Elizabeth Gallier were again excommuni-cated. No doubt they are the two Dissenters referred to when the rector completed his return for the Compton Census in 1676. This was a national inquiry organised by Bishop Compton of London which disclosed that coun-trywide less than 5% of the population were Dissenters and less than 1% Roman Catholics. Church Stretton's proportions were way below even these figures, for the response signed by Henry Clayton and his two churchwardens, Matthew Stephens and William Davies, records in the parish: 'Conformable 431; Recusant 1; Sectaries 2'.[36] These figures perhaps confirm the estimate of a population for the parish in 1672 of approaching 600, for the Compton Census would have excluded children. The one recusant, or Roman Catholic, was Elizabeth Stephens, the churchwarden's wife. The likelihood of a growth in the number of Dissenters was lessened by two baptisms in significant fami-lies registered in 1677: 29 April—John Gallery (Gallier) of All Stretton, an Anabaptist converted at the age of 21/22, and 27 December—John Sankey of Botfield between 16 and 17 years old. Perhaps Henry Clayton, still in his early 30s, had an effective ministry to the young. By this time, in any case, the pres-sure on Dissenters was being transferred to Roman Catholics. The resignation as Lord High Admiral of the king's brother, James, Duke of York, on the passing in 1673 of the Test Act which exposed his Roman Catholicism, and the king's growing friendship with France, revived fears of Popery that culminated in the Popish Plot and provoked the Exclusion Crisis of 1678.

The attempt to exclude the Duke of York from the succession failed and he became king as James II when his brother, Charles II, died in 1685. Although royal edicts were sometimes read from the pulpit, probably the only event of the new reign that had much impact on Stretton was the king's passage through the parish on 24 August 1687. The tradition is that he asked for a glass of water from a clear stream that crossed the road in All Stretton. What is certainly apoc-ryphal is that All Stretton got its name from the king's witticism that (having passed through Little Stretton and Church Stretton) 'They are all Strettons round here', because the name, derived from Alured Stretton, had been in use for 400 years.

The landing of William of Orange in Torbay on 5 November 1688 precipi-tated James II's flight and led to the offer of the crown jointly to William and his wife, Mary, James's daughter. The 'Glorious Revolution' saw the passing of the Toleration Act of 1689 which allowed freedom of worship but rejected the comprehensive settlement that would have kept many moderates within the Church. This was the deliberate choice of the Anglican leaders because it denied the nonconformists political power. But it was made at great cost. The Restoration Church's '*via media*' between Catholic and Reformed had been a broad path 'wide enough to accommodate those who wished to hug either side or those who yawed from one to the other',[37] while still maintaining the unquestionable authority of the national Church. What the Toleration Act did by rejecting comprehension was to reduce the Church of England from the national to the established Church. Inevitably other denominations emerged and grew in importance. The Church of England itself which had slipped its moorings to the Reformed faith and drifted back since the Restoration towards a renewed emphasis on the episcopate and the sacraments, now became caught up in the political current. It split first into High and Low Church parties, and then witnessed the emergence of Broad Church 'Latitudinarians'.

Of course, variations were apparent between regions and between churches. A newly-arrived minister in Sussex found his parishioners reticent to receive the sacrament: 'In Shropshire I was fain to drive away, here I must use the hook and change my bait'.[38] In Stretton the note that in September 1680 there had been seven sidesmen at the parish church[39] suggests large congregations. Certainly by 1689 Henry Clayton would have known well what services his people liked best for he had lived amongst them as rector for 18 years. In such a small community, with probably only 30-40 houses in the 'town' of Church Stretton, he would have known all his parishioners personally, not only as their minister in church, but also as their pastor and, indeed, as a neighbour and fellow-farmer.

The inventory of Clayton's glebe lands dated 1699[40] makes it clear that the rector lived in the same house as William Harries in the 1580s for it is still said to contain 'a decent hall, two parlours, two butteries, five chambers, a kitchen, a boulting house and a malting chamber, stable and ox-house all under one roof'. The description of its situation between Sir George Norton's land to the south, Coneyborough—now Rectory Wood—to the west, 'the king's highway called the Burway' to the north, and Prill-yard to the east, confirms that it stood where the Old Rectory now stands. A large kitchen garden of three-quarters of an acre lay on the south side as far as the Nortons' fence. The out-buildings, now including cow-houses, and the long list of fields and closes forming the glebe make clear that the rector was still also a practising farmer, though most of the land was undoubtedly leased to tenants. Lying mainly to the west and north of the rectory were enclosed fields called Hollenfield, Becheacre, Nether Hill and the New Inclosure; another called Shippen Hill lay near Watling Street, and on the other side of the old Roman road there was a close named Priest's Hill between 'Hesler Lane' and Snatchfields—about 25 acres in all. On the floor of the valley were areas of pasture—Oldersharve, Winley Meadow and Poole Meadow—surrounded by other farmers' pastures. In Nasbrookesfield, now Ashbrook, the glebe included three acres of arable still farmed on the strip system. Finally there were five acres on Longhills coming down to the brook, and 40 acres of woodland on the slopes of Coneyborough.

Even if the rector only managed his estate he will have been, like other parish clergy, in an awkward position since 'they were both part of the workaday world of their rural neighbours and set apart by their education and spiritual function. Many were work-day farmers whose accounts of seed corn and cattle were jotted in the same note-book as their sermons'.[41] Certainly Henry Clayton will have been on familiar terms with the local farmers through arranging deals and leases and receiving his tithe, while his wife will have mixed with their womenfolk at the weekly market and in the mercer's shop which had been owned by Thomas Botfield till a few months before Clayton's arrival. The inventory filed with Botfield's will[42] lists the stock in the shop which clearly also served as a general store: broadcloths and kerseys, lace, silk and buttons, serges and flannel, black and brown thread, tape and ribbon, buckram and dyed linen, grocery ware, hops, gunpowder, paper, candles, tobacco and pipes, hemp pitch and resin. Botfield's successor, like the sheep-farmers and woollen cloth manufacturers, will have benefited from the Act of Parliament which decreed that from 1678 'the deceased should all be buried in woollen'. Since an affidavit had to be sworn that all burials were in conformity with the Act a new register volume for burials was begun in 1679. No doubt the Claytons also made use of the services of some of the parish's tradesmen which an early eighteenth-century register would reveal included weavers, tailors, shoemakers, tanners, blacksmiths, carpenters, glovers, coopers, a butcher, a sweep and a miller, besides the innkeepers and farmers.

Henry Clayton had married Mary in his early years at Church Stretton and the births of their children are recorded in the parish register: Thomas came first in 1675 followed, at intervals of about two years, by Anne, Catherine, Richard, Felicity, Mary, Sara, Henry and finally William in 1692. Only Anne seems to have died in childhood.

Regular reports by churchwardens that the minister was carrying out his duties and 'behaving himself civilly' suggest that Henry Clayton was a diligent and faithful rector. In 1677 he wrote to the Chancellor of the diocese to request a change of churchwarden. On the advice of his neighbours he had appointed Thomas Hawkes of Botfield but found him 'engaged in multiplicity of business' and without the time to give to his office at a moment when parish concerns were demanding and a warden needed to be 'active in reducing [he surely meant 'conserving'] of our stock which is almost all lost through the incuriousness of former wardens'. But he had found an honest and able replacement in John Postone.

Little bits of evidence culled from documents that have chanced to survive in the diocesan archives give glimpses of a kindly, considerate and tolerant pastor. In 1678 he was writing on behalf of his wardens who had been summoned for not passing their accounts to the parish and not paying in the poor stock: he expressed his confidence that they would give full satisfaction within a fortnight and asked for a stay of excommunication. Another letter to the registrar supported the contention of Edward and Eleanor Broome that their daughter, Ann, who had been baptised on 3 November 1677 and sadly buried the next day, had been conceived in wedlock, although he acknowledged that their marriage licence was dated 1 May. His claim that this met the seven-month deadline set by the church suggests a kind heart or genuine pastoral concern rather than strict accuracy. In 1682 the rector and wardens were themselves cited before the diocesan court for allowing excommunicated parishioners to come to church, especially from Minton. On the other hand, in a letter requesting the postponement of a case as he was 'engaged in a Commission at Wenlock', Clayton denounced Roger Morris the miller, who was presented for working on Sundays, as a 'vile person' from whom he had received base affronts.[43]

*

In the first year of the new century Henry Clayton celebrated 30 years as rector. Old friends were passing away—including Margaret Morgan of All Stretton who died on 2 March 1701 and whose headstone is the oldest in the churchyard of today—but the practice of leaving bequests to the poor or to the school was becoming established. The first such philanthropists in this period were John Jarrett and Henry Richards who, in 1684, left a two acre meadow in Little Stretton in trust to provide relief for the poor. William Minton left £6 in 1701 so that the annual interest of 6s. could be distributed to the poor in 2d. and 3d. loaves on Christmas Day. Thomas Hawkes, who could have been the son or grandson of the former rector as his daughter was baptised Dorothea, the name

The oldest tombstone in the churchyard

of Anthony Hawkes's wife, died in 1704 and left £30 to be laid out in land and the produce sold to buy bread for the poor. His will stipulated that every Sunday eight penny loaves—and 16 penny loaves every first Sunday in the year, Easter Day and Whitsunday—were to be given by the minister, churchwardens and overseers of the poor 'to such poor persons as should frequent the church, and as they should think most indigent (not excluding such poor as should not be able to come to church)'. Four years later the £30 was used to buy a property in High Street, Church Stretton, called Walter's house (nearly opposite the King's Arms), to be used for the poor and any rents used to finance the distribution of bread. Randolph Jones, another former churchwarden, died in 1718. From his estate, which included shares in the South Sea Company, he left £10 to the poor, the interest again to be distributed in bread. Thomas Bridgman, in another will of 1718, left land to provide 40s. a year for the schoolmaster so long as 'he should teach poor children of the parish of Church Stretton till they could perfectly read in the Bible, and then to receive four more, to be nominated by his executors and trustees and the minister of the parish, beginning at Minton and so through the parish'. He also provided for the payment of 20s. to poor householders on St. Thomas's Day, celebrated then on 21 December, and a further 10s. to be distributed on the same day in 20 sixpenny loaves.[44]

Part of another benefaction board

The munificence of some wealthier parishioners was again evident in 1711 in the donation of church bells. Abraham Rudhall, the celebrated bell-founder of Gloucester, cast a ring of bells for the parish church which are still rung today, although nearly two centuries later two were recast and two others added. The bells of 1711 were dedicated and of the sizes and weights as follows:

1. 'A.R. 1711'. Diameter 28.75 ins. Weight 4 cwt, 3 qrs. 23 lbs.
2. 'Don Proavi Ed. Brooke de Strett. Gen. 1711' Diam 30 ins. Wt. 4 cwt. 3 qrs. 23 lbs.
3. 'Prosperity to this place. A.R. 1711' Diam 32.25 ins. Wt. 5 cwt. 3 qrs. 22 lbs.
4. 'Abraham Rudhall of Gloucester, Bell Founder 1711' Diam. 33 .5 ins. Wt. 6 cwt. 3 qrs. 12 lbs. (recast 1890)
5. 'Peace and Good Neighbours A.R. 1711' Diam. 36.625 ins. Wt. 8 cwt. 2 qrs. 12 lbs. (recast 1890 J. Taylor and Co. Founders, Loughborough)
6. 'Mr. Thomas Brookes, Mr. Randolph Jones, Churchwardens 1711 A.R.' Wt. 11 cwt. 5lbs.

What happened to the five bells recorded in the inventory of 1553 is unknown.

A drawing of the shaft of the sundial, or possibly the stump of the old parish cross, supported by a mill-wheel in 1713 (by kind permission of David Bilbey)

Two years later it seems that the churchwardens decided to do something about what today is a stump near the south transept door. It could be the remains of the old parish cross or more likely a sundial erected at that time; whatever it was, a mill wheel was placed round the base of the shaft to keep it upright. On the wheel was inscribed, as we can still read, 'T.W. & J.W.: CW 1713'. The churchwardens of 1713 are not identified in documents but T.W. was almost certainly Thomas Waring, a gentleman farmer who died in 1716, and J.W. was perhaps John Williams or John Wilson who both feature in the parish register in this period.

It is fitting that as Henry Clayton approached the 50th anniversary of his institution, and the end of his life, we should have two detailed reports on the church in the form of written answers to printed Articles of Inquiry sent to all ministers, churchwardens and sidesmen, the first one to be returned at the Primary Visitation of Bishop Philip of Hereford in August 1716.[45] It is interesting that the amount paid in procurations on the bishop's visit, in lieu of hospitality, was £2 13s. 4d.—still the four marks of which Rector Philip le Waleys had complained more than four hundred years earlier!

The wardens reported that the roofs of the church and chancel were in good repair, the windows well glazed, the floors well paved and the inside walls decent and clean. There was a convenient reading desk and a pulpit, the three-decker already described. The communion table was covered with a decent cloth and with a fair linen cloth when the sacrament was administered. The church possessed two chalices, a paten and a flagon, all kept solely for use in the communion service. There was still a decent font, a 'comely surplice' for the minister that was washed and repaired at the expense of the parish, a large Bible 'of the old translation' (was this a Great Bible from 1538?) and a Book of Common Prayer.

Articles of Enquiry.

14. Have you Prayers in your Church twice, and Sermons once every Lord's Day? If not, how often, and at what Hours? Are the Hours conſtantly the ſame?

15. Have you any Chapels within your Pariſh? Have you Prayers twice, and Sermons once, &c. *As in the preceding Article.*

16. Doth the Miniſter always read the entire Service, as preſcribed in the Book of Common-Prayer, without any Omiſſion or Alteration?

17. How often, and at what times, doth he Catechiſe in your Church? Do the Pariſhioners duly ſend their Children and Servants to be inſtructed by him.

18. Doth he adminiſter the Sacrament of Baptiſm publicklickly in the Church, and not elſewhere, except in Caſes of Neceſſity? Doth he in that Caſe uſe only the Office of private Baptiſm, and afterward if the Child recover, receive it publickly into the Church, as the Law requires?

ANSWERS 5

14. We have prayers conſtantly read in our Church here every Lords day and a ſermon once and twice ſaid this hour for the ſervice conſtantly the ſame

15. we have no chapell or chapells within ol pſh

16. o Miniſter do here read the whole ſervice according to the enquiry here made without omiſſion or Alteration

17. o Miniſter Chatechiſeth the whole ſummer quarter in the Afternoon and diligently explains the ſame

18. Our Miniſter doth Adminiſter the Sacrament of Baptiſm according to the Inquiry here made and in the Law required

Part of the churchwardens' return to the bishop's visitation enquiry, in 1716, the first use of a printed from (HRO)

It was admitted that 'a great part of the fence belonging to the church is but indifferently fenced', but the wardens promised it would be repaired in a short time. Notwithstanding this pledge wardens and parishioners continued to be presented regularly for the next 30 years for their failure to keep the churchyard fence in good repair. The register, which the wardens said was maintained, shows that in the previous seven years there had been 18 marriages, 110 christenings and 86 burials, almost exactly the same averages as 50 years before— two or three marriages a year, 15.7 (16) baptisms and 12.3 (13.3) burials. The parsonage was reported to be in good repair.

The return confirms that every Sunday prayers were read twice and one sermon delivered; unfortunately they did not indicate the times of services—

generally Evening Prayer, without a sermon, was read in the afternoon—though they were 'constantly the same'. The minister read the entire service without alteration or omission. He also catechised the children of the parish in the afternoon throughout the summer quarter from Whitsuntide to Michaelmas. He administered baptism publicly in church and as the law required. The Lord's Supper was celebrated at the festivals and on other occasions 'at least twelve times in the year'. The minister was a conscientious pastor, carefully and frequently visiting the sick 'to prepare them for Holy Communion and for their departure into the other world'.

In accordance with Sir Rowland Hayward's bequest the wardens confirmed that £1 13s. 4d. was paid annually for the maintenance of the school or schoolmaster, though there is no reference to the annual 20s. agreed by the rector in 1595 in place of the church ale. The school trustees in 1716 were Thomas Phillips, Thomas Bright and William Davies. The master was said to come to church with his scholars at the time of Divine Service. The Diocesan Subscription Book reveals that John Bowdler, the master in 1674, was succeeded two years later by Robert Taylor, while a tattered page in the Call Book of 1689 has Poole as *'ludimagister'*. This was presumably the William Poole who certified many burials recorded in the register in the 1680s and surely also the incumbent at Leebotwood from 1674 and the one presented by Sir George Norton to Aston Bottrell in 1690. In 1693 he was replaced by Edward Cheese, who died in 1709. There was no hospital in the parish, but from the early years of the century Edward Phillips appears in the Call Books as 'chirurgus' (surgeon) or 'medicus'.

Of themselves the churchwardens said they were chosen every year and their accounts delivered to the parish. The clerk was described as diligent, keeping the church clean 'from dust, cobwebs and other annoyances'. As regards the parishioners the report is perhaps too good to be true: there were no alleged cases of adultery, fornication or incest, though in other years (and throughout the century) people continued to be presented for adultery, illegitimate births or pre-marital sex until action in such cases became more intermittent and they finally disappeared from the records early in the nineteenth century. Nor was there any common swearer, drunkard or blasphemer, and none that 'followed their calling' on the Lord's Day. Jonathan Stringer, a cooper, was named as an Anabaptist and Dissenter, but it is significant that his infant daughter had recently been baptised and buried according to the rites of the Church of England, and that when he himself died he was buried in the churchyard. No meeting for Dissenters was held in the parish, although nine years later, in 1725, an application was made for a licence for Jonathan Stringer's house to be used as a Baptist place of worship.[46] No-one refused to pay church rates and none in the previous 12 months had performed public penance.

Not surprisingly, the responses to the Articles in 1719 were virtually identical to those of 1716, except that the condition of the interior of the church had become 'indifferent'—probably since the clerk was now judged to perform his duties only tolerably well. Richard Bristowe and his wife had done public penance.

Henry Clayton would have been justified in regarding his 'final report' with some satisfaction. He had steered his parish through half a century during which, in some circles, the Church had been under attack from a society ready to scoff and to which nothing was sacrosanct. John Hacket had written in 1675 of 'the ocean of ungodliness breaking in upon us', and Daniel Defoe of 'the present torrent of vice'. Church Stretton, however, was not part of coffee-house society, and generally in rural areas customary religion, with its hatred of innovation, prevailed. Most Anglican churches were medieval foundations and stood in the midst of communities as symbols of tradition, continuity and stability. This was Clayton's world, and at 75 years old in 1719 he had seen enough of change. For many years he had been Rural Dean of Wenlock, heading a Deanery which then included Rushbury, Long Stanton, Munslow, Cardington, Abdon, Hope Bowdler, Tugford, Holdgate, Woolstaston, Church Stretton, Broseley, Acton Scott, Easthope, Eaton, Little Wenlock and Hughley—and presumably Much Wenlock, though it was missed from the contemporary list. He is first recorded as holding the office in 1704, perhaps in recognition of his long service but also because he was a sound churchman. The office would have involved visits to all the churches and reports to the archdeacon or bishop.

In his last years the rector had the pleasure of conducting the weddings of his two youngest daughters, Mary and Sara. He may still have been well enough on 11 June 1725 to celebrate the 54th anniversary of his institution at St. Laurence's, but he died shortly afterwards in the middle of summer and was buried on 30 June. He was 81 years of age and had been rector during the reigns of five sovereigns. With his passing an era came to an end for few could remember any previous incumbent.

Another era had ended during Clayton's time at Church Stretton for across the land the religious passions of the seventeenth century had given way to a new 'Age of Reason', marked by political stability and scientific investigation with a dash of scepticism. In the realm of thought the balance was subtly shifting from what God has revealed to what man has discovered. In the Church the Latitudinarians or Broad Churchmen now predominated; from parish pulpits the weekly sermon praised regular worship, morality and good works, and the Book of Common Prayer was the eloquent expression of a new sense of order and stability. The Church of England, indeed, had gained acceptance as a vital part of people's lives. And as the new Anglicanism slowly took root in the country, for half a century Henry Clayton had gently but conscientiously tended its growth in Church Stretton.

9
CHURCH AND PARISH IN THE 18TH CENTURY

There was a marked deterioration in the condition of Stretton's parish church in Henry Clayton's last years. The rector's age precluded sharp-eyed supervision, the clerk was becoming more negligent in the performance of his duties, and the churchwardens were increasingly lax. In 1713 the clerk was up before the archdeacon 'for not keeping the churchyard gate shut and letting swine get in and dig up the graves'; he had also allowed horses to be led through the churchyard with loads of hay. The wardens had described the interior state of the building as 'indifferent' in 1719; five years later repair was evidently needed as Thomas Waring and John Mitton were summoned to the diocesan court for not paying their assessed rates towards the cost of this repair and for erecting a seat. Worse was to come after Clayton's death. In 1726 the wardens were criticised for a protruding pew and were ordered by the court 'to certify the reparation of the parsonage house presented to be out of repair'; in 1727 they were told to get several of the churchyard 'hayments' (fence sections) restored or to present the persons in default (Thomas Minton and Isaac Prosser were names put forward); and in 1729 the new incumbent was cited for not taking action in the chancel where repair was also required.[1]

The fundamental problem was that during Clayton's long rectorship the welcome stability had bred complacency and, at the last, slackness. Yet something similar was happening in the Church as a whole and, indeed, in society. The neglect at Church Stretton in part reflected contemporary attitudes for there had emerged 'a permissive society in which the decline and fall from Christian standards in all classes of society was universally lamented'.[2] But, immediately, it was the consequence of the appointment of a rector with more pressing matters on his mind. When the Rev. Rowland Tench succeeded Clayton, he was still a master at Shrewsbury School. The son of an ale-house keeper in Shrewsbury, he had attended the school himself before his admission to St. John's College, Cambridge, in 1697 as a sizar, which meant he helped to pay his way by serving fellow students who were socially his superiors. He was awarded his B.A. in 1701 and his M.A. in 1710. Ordained in the year of his initial graduation, he was appointed at once as Third Master at his old school.

He served in this capacity until 1715 when, on the death of the Rev. Oswald Smith, he was promoted to be Second Master. The school's fortunes at this time were at a very low ebb, partly because the teachers supplemented their meagre salaries by taking on ecclesiastical responsibilities. The headmaster, the Rev. Richard Lloyd, who had been appointed in 1687, held prebendal stalls at Hereford and Brecon as well as the vicarage of Sellack in Herefordshire; Tench himself became perpetual curate of Astley, Shropshire, in 1714. During the Michaelmas term in 1717 an 'information' was filed in the Court of Chancery against both Lloyd and Tench for breach of the school ordinance which prohibited schoolmasters to hold parochial or other cures. 'It was stated by the petitioners that the inhabitants sent their sons to other schools in consequence of the masters' neglect and that at the time the information was laid there were only eight boys in the highest school'.[3] In the same term Lloyd was given six months to surrender either the vicarage or the headmastership. He seems to have done neither as he remained in his school post till 1723, and the bishop's register contains no new vicar at Sellack until 1732. The judgment made no reference to Tench, but he took his cue from the headmaster and continued as Second Master and curate of Astley till 1728. It was hardly a propitious record, but on 2 September 1725, a few weeks after Clayton's death, Rowland Tench was instituted by the bishop as Rector of Church Stretton on the presentation of Viscount Weymouth, the title taken by Sir Thomas Thynne on his elevation to the peerage in 1682. This was the first appointment of a Cambridge man as rector.

Tench was pleased to be presented to the living, though more at the financial prospects than the opportunities for service. On 10 September 1725 he wrote from Shrewsbury to Dr. Lambert, a Fellow of St. John's: 'Rev. Sir, Upon the 3rd. instant I was inducted into a living, and such a one as I have reason to believe will afford me a comfortable retirement from this laborious business. I propose to continue here about a year, after which I shall surrender the school freely and in such a manner as shall be agreeable to the College'. Unfortunately for him he had not had a careful look at the rectory, for the next year, on 27 July 1726, he wrote to Dr. Lambert apologising for not having yet tendered his resignation from the school but explaining the circumstances. 'When I came narrowly to view the place I found the building very large and very ruinous and an insolvent widow, in so much that part of the house tumbled down this summer'. He continued: 'I intend to leave as soon as I can get things in order, which I am now doing as fast as I can'.[4] In the event, on account of a long drawn-out legal battle between the Corporation of Shrewsbury and the college over their authority at the school, he did not cease teaching or resign his curacy until 1728. There is no record of a curate at Stretton in these years as entries in the Call Books are very intermittent—negligence in the Church did not stop at parochial level!—but someone must have served on behalf of Tench while he remained at the school. One possible candidate is Reginald Owen whose son was baptised in September 1727 and who is described as 'Cler'(icus) in the register. It is not until 1747 that a curate is named. This was Henry Meredith, the son of a clergyman at Whitton in Radnorshire, who matriculated at Jesus College, Oxford, in 1739 and took his B.A. in 1743 at the age of 23, probably coming to Stretton shortly afterwards.

When Rowland Tench became rector in 1725 he was nearly 48 years old. He had been married 20 years earlier to Anne Plimley, daughter of a mercer in Shrewsbury. They had started a family the next year but had tragically lost their first son before he was two years old and their second son at birth. Three daughters followed but one died at the age of five. As the youngest, Mary, remained single, it must have been a moment of great rejoicing when on 14 April 1740 Tench conducted the marriage at St. Laurence's of his eldest daughter, Anne, to the Rev. Humphrey Parry of St. Mary's, Shrewsbury. It is interesting to recall that Peter Dormer's daughter, too, had married the Rector of St. Mary's back in 1676. Tench was very attached to St. Mary's and was to be buried in the Scholars' Chapel there,[5] the place where he had sat with his young charges during Sunday services for nearly 30 years.

Our knowledge of St. Laurence's in Tench's day is scanty. In the diocesan court the cases continued to be principally concerned with the repair of the churchyard fences, adultery and bastard children. Public penance in the church was still being ordered, as in the case of William Grainger who had appeared before the archdeacon at the Talbot Inn in Stretton in 1733. In the church, memorials which no longer exist were erected to Thomas Brooke and his son Edward and to the local apothecary, Edward Phillips. Initials carved on the back of the door to the tower date from this time: 'J.O. & S.P. WDNS 1737 G.R.' The wardens thus commemorated were probably John Oliver and Samuel Phillips; G.R. indicated that George II was king. Since the door in the south transept and the bricked-up north door are very similar in design and construction it is possible that they, too, were new at this time. The names of John Phillips and Moses Eaton, churchwardens in 1742, were inscribed under the royal coat-of-arms at the chancel arch to commemorate some improvement.[6]

Message on the back of the tower door

An application was made in 1725 for a licence for Jonathan Stringer's house to be used as a Dissenting place of worship. He was the cooper reported as an Anabaptist by the wardens in 1716 and 1719. Baptists were very few in Shropshire, and it is doubtful if the meetings continued in Stretton after his death in 1727. Yet the country stood on the threshold of the great evangelical revival associated particularly with the Methodists. For in 1738, the very year that Thomas Secker, Bishop of Oxford and future Archbishop of Canterbury, had expressed his concern that an open and professed disregard for religion had become, through a variety of unhappy causes, the distinguishing characteristic of the age, John Wesley was to feel his heart 'strangely warmed' as he listened to a speaker describe 'the change which God works in the heart through faith in Christ'. For over half a century such 'enthusiasm' had been out of fashion, and devotion to Jesus Christ replaced by regular worship and moral effort. The evangelical preacher John Berridge had asserted the bankruptcy of this approach: 'Reason has explored the moral path, planted it with roses, and fenced it round with motives, but all in vain ...'[7] John Wesley's conversion and subsequent evangelisation of the country for half a century triggered a dramatic spiritual revival. The Methodists became strong in Shrewsbury but we know of no meetings in the more rural Church Stretton. Nor did the Anglican evangelical revival, preceded by the founding of the Society for the Promotion of Christian Knowledge in 1698, the Church Missionary Society in 1699 and the Society for the Propagation of the Gospel in Foreign Parts in 1701, touch its eighteenth- century rectors.

*

Little may have been happening in its church, but Church Stretton itself could not remain static as the pace of economic change picked up in the country. Although the great days of the Shropshire iron trade did not come till later in the century, Abraham Darby's success in smelting iron with coal already heralded the dawn of the Industrial Revolution. 'He supplied grates, kettles, pots, smoothing irons and similar items to country ironmongers throughout the Borderland', in spite of the formidably high cost of road transport—1s. 8d. for a load from Coalbrookdale to Church Stretton in 1733.[8] Nonetheless, his iron goods would have been found in the homes of the parish, including the new houses like 'Berry's messuage' (17 High Street) facing Bonham Norton's Market Hall in the Square, and the cottages at the bottom of Brook Street, now Burway Road, one of which still displays the date 1733. It was also at this time that a land transaction was completed which was to prove significant for the future: in 1712 Sir George Norton, great grandson of Bonham, had surrendered the family's local estates into the hands of the lady of the manor. After several further transfers, in 1735 these estates—'all of which premises were reputed to belong formerly to the Leightons of Wattlesborough'[9]—came into the hands of William Lutwyche, Esquire, of Lutwyche.

Rowland Tench died in December 1748 and it was six months before a successor was instituted on 2 June 1749 in the person of the Rev. John Mainwaring, again presented by Thomas, Viscount Weymouth. The new rector had been born in 1724 at Drayton Manor in Staffordshire, the son of Gilbert Mainwaring, gentleman, and the third of his 14 children. His mother was the daughter of Thomas Phillips, a Shrewsbury attorney. He was educated at Tamworth under Mr. Prinsep and at Marlborough, and was admitted as a pensioner at St. John's College, Cambridge, in June 1742.[10] He graduated B.A. in 1746 and was elected a Fellow in 1748, before taking his M.A. (delayed for a year because of ill health) in 1750 and being awarded a B.D. in 1758. He was ordained priest in June 1748, just a year before his institution at Church Stretton. He could have owed his appointment to the advice of Tench to choose a promising young man from his old college, or perhaps Viscount Weymouth had some link with St. John's as his own sons were to be admitted in 1752. However he came to be chosen, John Mainwaring was to prove probably the most talented, surely the most extraordinary and, though only by a short head from Henry Clayton, indubitably the longest-serving rector in the history of the parish of Church Stretton. He held the living until his death in April 1807, nearly 58 years later.

It is likely that Mainwaring also holds the record for absenteeism. He was already a Fellow of St. John's when presented at Stretton and became Lady Margaret Professor of Divinity in 1788. Most of his life was passed in Cambridge, but he spent his vacations in Church Stretton and settled there on his retirement. From the standpoint of his parishioners, then, the quality of his curates was even more important than the rector's. There seem to have been only four in his long incumbency. The first was Henry Meredith, inherited from Tench, whom the Call Books show was still there in 1750. He was followed by the Rev. Richard Wilding who first appears in the parish register in 1752. He is no doubt the Richard Wilding of Shropshire who had been admitted as a sizar at Trinity College, Cambridge, in June 1723, graduating B.A. in 1727 and M.A. in 1730. When he was ordained is unknown, but he was instituted at Tedstone Delamere, Shropshire, in October 1739 and stayed for five years. At Stretton he continued to sign the register and to conduct marriages—and, in Mainwaring's long absences, to baptise, read services, preach, catechise and visit the sick—for the next 20 years until his death. He was married fairly late in life, at the age of 48 in 1754, to Elizabeth Oliver, but they had five children before she died in childbirth in 1763; their second son died three years later at the age of eight. If personal experience of tragedy is a valuable qualification in pastoral work, then Richard Wilding, like Rowland Tench before him, would have been welcomed by parishioners in times of personal crisis.

Richard Wilding died in February 1771, and the signature of his successor, Thomas Piazza, who had been perpetual curate at Bettws in Llanfair Waterdine since 1767, appears in the register before the end of the year. He stayed for seven years, but nothing more is heard of him until his death in 1784. Mainwaring's final curate was appointed in 1779 and outlived him. He was another Richard Wilding and, born in 1755, the eldest son and first child of his curate father. He was admitted as a pensioner at St. John's College, Cambridge, where he will have met up again with Rector Mainwaring. After graduating B.A. in 1777 (M.A. 1780), he was ordained deacon at Hereford in 1778 and priest the next year. The year of his ordination also saw him married by John Mainwaring to Mary Luther and then made curate of Easthope—and rector there two years later—on the presentation of William Lutwyche, Esq. Although he held that living for the rest of his life, he acted as curate at Church Stretton from 1779 until the rector's death. He was to become perpetual curate at Leebotwood, 1808-16, and curate of Woolstaston and Smethcott. Curates were not well paid—at Stretton £40 per annum—but such a pluralist would have had a handsome aggregate income, and he was in addition the 'principal landholder among very many proprietors'.[11] Wilding would have been very well-known in the parish, first as a boy and later as a busy minister and farmer and the father of ten children, though three died in infancy. It is fitting that a later rector included his coat-of-arms (see illustration on p.171) in the north transept window at St. Laurence's.

John Mainwaring must have seemed an occasional visitor in the parish. The first time his name actually appears in the register is as the officiant in September 1778—nearly 30 years after his institution!—at the wedding of his curate. But in his periodic sojourns the rector will have been welcomed by local clergy as a renowned theologian and preacher, by those with social aspirations because he was the friend of the famous, by the landed gentry and casual labourers on account of his active interest in gardening, and by the populace at large as an amiable eccentric.

*

As early as his mid-30s John Mainwaring had established a reputation as a preacher in an age still eager for sermons. His style and his subject matter are a far cry from his contemporaries John Wesley and the celebrated evangelist George Whitefield. Mainwaring was an orthodox, academic, charitable Church of England cleric, the very antithesis of an 'enthusiast'. He shared the concern of fellow Latitudinarians that their moderation might be known to all men. In 1780 he published, as an introduction to a volume of his sermons, *A Dissertation on that Species of Composition*. Sermons, he argued, should display Perspicuity, by which he meant they should be well-planned and balanced, Purity in language and grammar, Elegance of style, Pathos or genuine feeling (he instances Jesus's discourse in John chapters 14-16, and Paul's farewell to the elders at Ephesus), Piety, for sermons are neither drama nor lecture, and Eloquence, 'chaste and simple' rather than florid, pompous or theatrical.

His first sermons to be published were delivered to a university audience in 1759. Both took their text from 1 Peter 3:8—'Be pitiful, be courteous'. These human attributes, he believed, were evidence of the divine workmanship and balanced the necessary defects of reason. 'The end and office of Pity is to lessen the miseries of life; … the end and office of Courtesy is to lessen the inconveniences of society'. He deplored the unsociable humour and roughness of university life, the cynicism, ridicule and desire to expose the defects of others. 'The great business of religion and philosophy is to inform the understanding and to regulate the will'. He ended the second sermon with this peroration: 'An habitual attention to please those who are not in a condition to make any returns, to merit their esteem and approbation, and to contribute to their happiness in the least instance, as well as in the greatest; this Quality, whatever be its name, is of such a nature, as will not only endear us to them but to the beneficent Author of all happiness'. Thomas Clarkson and William Wilberforce were not then born, let alone students at St. John's, but it seems certain that when their Anti-Slavery campaign was launched their old college had at least one Fellow whose concern for pity and compassion saw him on their side.

A university sermon of 1764 was dedicated, 'as a public testimony of Respect and Gratitude', to Viscount Weymouth, not Mainwaring's original patron but his son who had been a student at the college ten years before. Another, of 1766, preached at St. Mary's, Cambridge, before the Judges of Assize, was dedicated to his friend, Dr. Powell, the Master of St. John's. In his introduction Mainwaring spoke of his 'regard for the University and College with which I have been so long and so happily connected'. His text was apt: 'Dearly beloved, avenge not yourselves' (Romans 12:9).

Mainwaring's annual sermons in the university church made great demands on him. He told his friend, Joseph Cradock, that they made him ill, 'first, from the apprehension, and then from the consequence of the effort he had made'. When he returned to the vestry he customarily said, 'Thank God, it is over; and I hope tonight I shall get some quiet rest'. Yet, according to Cradock, 'they were admired as polished specimens of their kind', delivered by a man highly esteemed for his classical knowledge and taste. He was conscious that he was not a natural orator and sometimes, because of his asthma, barely audible, and yet he was 'respectfully attended to by the crowded galleries', and never suffered the indignity of being subjected to the scraping of feet by disapproving undergraduates.[12]

Mainwaring liked to dedicate his sermons to his friends. In March 1773 the friend honoured was Lancelot Brown who, with the support of the Master and

Mainwaring, had produced a plan to transform the Fellows' Garden at St. John's into 'The Wilderness'. Mainwaring took as his theme 'The Inequality of Religious Dispensation', with his text from Acts 10:34-35: 'God is no respecter of persons. But in every nation he that feareth Him, and worketh righteousness, is accepted with Him'. The preacher maintained that 'Heathens, Jews and Christians will be tried by the same test —their conformity to the will of God so far as they know or are able to discover it'. He made a plea for charity in our judgment of others: 'Let them leave their brethren to their own consciences, and unbelievers to the mercy of God'.

Two of Rector Mainwaring's published sermons were delivered in St. Laurence's. The first was on the occasion of the bishop's visitation on Thursday, 18 May 1776. It was dedicated to the Rev. Robert Clive, Archdeacon of Salop, who had been an undergraduate in the same college and year as Mainwaring, and to the clergy before whom it was preached. It is the first sermon preached in Stretton's parish church to have survived to this day. He took his text from Mark 9:50—'Have salt in yourselves and have peace with one another'. His own middle-of-the-road theology was evident in his criticisms, on the one hand, of those 'who from ill-informed zeal have so dignified human nature that they have lost sight of our fallen state', and, on the other, of those whose opinions on grace and election left no room for liberty or personal righteousness. Some of his comments on the clergy of his day will have delighted many in his audience: 'There are but two roads that lead to eminence—popularity and court favour; and to speak ingenuously, the footsteps of virtue are seldom to be traced in either … What good effects can possibly arise from an extreme disparity between persons of the same profession, all educated alike, all invested with a public trust, and directing their labours to one common end?' Peace with one another, he maintained, could not include those who abuse the faith—'To urge, or impose anything, as such, which the Scriptures neither avow nor acknowledge, is fraud or folly'. But as the life of Jesus was 'one continued lesson of humility, so a modest and peaceable disposition is a great asset'. He concluded with a plea for true faith and Christian unity:

> The effect of religion when pure and rational is to promote peace and happiness; but when enthusiastic or perverted it renders discord more bitter, and error more pernicious. If the clergy are worldly or divided, the adversaries of religion will improve the opportunity. If they are uncorrupt, and unanimous, believers will be the more strongly confirmed in their faith, and infidels will examine with less prejudice the evidence upon which it is founded. That our holy religion, through its own transcendent purity, and the exemplary lives of those who teach it, may triumph over all opposition, and unite in the same sentiments men of all denominations, let us implore the divine grace and assistance in the

words of our liturgy: 'O Lord, we beseech Thee, let Thy continual pity cleanse and defend Thy church'.

That sermon was preached a few weeks before the American Declaration of Independence; Mainwaring's other sermon at St. Laurence's to have come down to us was delivered a month before the fall of the Bastille, though neither contained any reference to unfolding events in America or France. The occasion of the second sermon, which must have lasted for the greater part of an hour, was the primary visitation of the new Bishop of Hereford on 17 June 1789. This time the rector spoke with all the authority of the Lady Margaret Professor of Divinity in the University of Cambridge, the seat to which he had been elevated the previous year. His text from Acts 10:25-26, Peter's meeting with Cornelius, prompted a learned and robust defence of the Christian religion. He argued that if the Christian revelation had not been granted, mankind would still be lost in sin and idolatry. He surveyed the great

S E R M O N S

ON

SEVERAL OCCASIONS,

PREACHED BEFORE THE

UNIVERSITY of CAMBRIDGE;

TO WHICH IS PREFIXED, A

DISSERTATION

ON THAT

SPECIES of COMPOSITION.

By J. MAINWARING, B.D.

FELLOW OF ST. JOHN's COLLEGE.

CAMBRIDGE,

Printed by J. Archdeacon Printer to the University;

For T. Cadell, in the Strand, London; and
T. & J. Merrill, in Cambridge.
MDCCLXXX.

*The title page of John Mainwaring's
book on sermons
(Bodleian Library, Oxford)*

figures of the classical world, Socrates, Plato, Cicero and others, to consider whether reason could have dispelled the darkness and corruption of Natural Religion, but came to the conclusion that 'to enlighten the minds of men, and to correct their depraved dispositions, nothing less than the divine grace and assistance would or could be of any avail'. He warned against confusing the 'awful and sublime truths of the gospel' with the fanciful inventions of men's own brains. He concluded with a blast against 'heretics, enthusiasts and opposers', for he believed 'the good sense of mankind begins to be offended at the bold excesses of unprincipled scepticism … Let us defend religion with dispassionate and manly zeal'.

*

It is certain that his Stretton congregation was given something more down-to-earth in his sermons during vacations, but Rector Mainwaring was a man of erudition and culture. In 1760 he published anonymously the first biography of Handel, only a year after the composer's death, under the title *Memoirs of the Life of the late George Frederick Handel, to which is added a Catalogue of his Works and Observations upon them*. He had probably largely written it during a sabbatical year—'year of grace' in the college records—from 30 June 1757. Surprisingly he deals only briefly with Handel's later years, when the author must first have heard his works, particularly at the composer's annual concerts in aid of the new Foundling Hospital. He defends Handel against the criticisms of those who preferred Italian music and found the German's compositions lacking in elegance and correctness. He especially praises the great anthems and choruses, above all in 'Messiah' when 'the ear is filled with such a glow of harmony as leaves the mind in a kind of heavenly ecstasy'. Although he concedes that there are great inequalities in Handel's music, he believes that his abilities will place him on a level with the greatest masters. This early tribute helped to establish Handel as a popular composer. There is no indication that Mainwaring ever met the composer; nor does the work throw light on the author's life.

The rector's cultural pursuits extended beyond music to literature and art. He belonged to a circle in Cambridge which included Thomas Gray, of Churchyard Elegy fame, William Mason, poet and musician, and Joseph Cradock, author of *Village Memoirs*, who gives a delightful portrait of Mainwaring and through whom he met Oliver Goldsmith, Samuel Johnson and David Garrick. Cradock records that John Mainwaring was a refined scholar, 'greatly respected by them all; and they willingly confessed that his style was as pure and correct as that of [Joseph] Addison', the renowned essayist.[13] In 1798 Professor Mainwaring published at Cambridge his *Remarks on the Pursuits of Literature in a letter to the Author*, which was in effect a 68 page critical review, displaying his familiarity with academic debate and his wide knowledge of literature, contemporary and classical. He was also interested in art and tempted to publish his views, but realised that the market was already over-stocked. He did, however, indulge his delight in painting and sculpture in frequent visits to the continent—he was given leave in the summers of 1773, 1774 and 1775, when Church Stretton probably saw little of him—and on an extended tour in about 1787, in the company of the Rev. Dr. Fisher, another Fellow of St. John's, tutor to a royal prince and future Bishop of Salisbury. In Rome they encountered Gray and Samuel Whitbread on their travels, and 'all the learned and elegant English frequently met at Cardinal Bernis' palace'. Mainwaring, who had an apartment in the Piazza di Spagna, appeared at the cardinal's table 'dressed in a handsome suit of velvet, with bag-wig and sword'. It is an extraordinary coincidence that while he was in Italy he met the well-known English social hostess Mrs. Piozzi,[14] for the nephew of her second husband became virtually her adopted son and certainly her heir and, as Sir John Salusbury Piozzi-Salusbury married the cousin of one of Mainwaring's nineteenth-century successors as rector of Church Stretton and fathered the next!

It was landscape gardening that provided the bond between Mainwaring and his friend Lancelot 'Capability' Brown. In 1772, after he had submitted plans for the St. John's College garden, Brown went on a tour of Herefordshire and the West Country. The rector looked forward to welcoming him to Church Stretton during the long vacation, but Brown spent more time than expected at Lord Clive's estate at Oakley Park and had to write to postpone his visit. In his reply of 21 August[15] the rector expressed his regrets, but hoped for another opportunity in the future: 'Tho' Fortune has so ordered it now, that you could not cast a look at my little mansion, she may be less cruel another year, and your kindness, I know, will ever be the same'. He rejoiced that his friend would transform Oakley Park into the glory of the county, and added: 'Two of Lord Clive's sisters are now at my house, and my lord himself did me the honour to call on me two days ago, but I was so unlucky as to be from home'. A visit from so famous a figure as Clive of India would have created a moment of excitement for the local inhabitants, but the letter refers to a more important and less fleeting development. Rector Mainwaring's eagerness for his friend to view his 'little mansion' confirms that the former rectory, which dated back at least to Elizabethan times and whose condition had so shocked Rowland Tench, had recently been replaced by what we now know as the Old Rectory, although it was subsequently extended. Another of the rector's friends, Archdeacon Joseph

Extract from John Mainwaring's letter to 'Capability' Brown

John Mainwaring's rectory, now called the 'Old Rectory' (SRRC)

Plymley, attests in his visitation records that Professor Mainwaring had 'at very considerable expense' made the parsonage house 'elegant and convenient'. There is no doubt that it was erected on the same site as the former rectory, and almost certainly incorporated part of it. Plymley added that the rector 'had laid out the ground that is contiguous with great taste' and had 'planted and adorned an adjoining valley with much propriety'.[16] In these words are revealed the

origins of the beautiful walk through the Rectory Woods, then known as Coneyborough, whose corrupted form still lives on in Cunnery Road.

Joseph Cradock was another interested in landscape gardening, but what drew him to his friend's home in Church Stretton was his fascination with the legend of Caractacus, for the rectory was close to Caer Caradoc. 'An enchanting spot' was his verdict on Mainwaring's estate. By the kindness of Viscount Weymouth, Mainwaring had been able to 'extend his walks near half a mile through a forest by a trout stream to a natural waterfall'. Another of the rector's friends, Dr. Richard Hurd, later Bishop of Worcester,

The walk through the Rectory Woods

146

confessed, 'I like your place in general, but methinks it tastes a little of the savage'.[17] Capability Brown, however, whom Cradock met at the rectory in 1775, considered that the whole was laid out to great advantage, while Dr. Powell, Master of St. John's, left his friend £200 to make additional improvements.

Cradock recorded his surprise that neither Mainwaring nor Brown, though both asthmatic, seemed to feel any detriment from the neighbourhood of the Welsh mountains. Yet some of the rector's eccentricities were occasioned by his fear of ill-health. 'I dare not dismiss my flannel breast-plate till the spring is over, and shall do it by degrees and with great caution', he wrote. Bishop Thurlow later recounted that he had followed him in a curacy 'and frequently showed my friends how ingeniously the air in every creek or window was stopped by cork; that there were a hundred little inventions; for I found my predecessor was, or many parts were, hermetically sealed'. In a letter dated 12 December 1782 Mainwaring told Cradock he would not be able to visit him because 'I cannot ride on horseback so far and dare not venture in an open chaise at this time of year'. Later, according to another friend, 'You see the old Professor looking every hour at the thermometer, and sending for his clogs, lest a stone floor should strike chill to his feet'.

Parishioners will have enjoyed exchanging gossip about their rector's idiosyncrasies. What will have taken their breath away was his marriage. As a Fellow he had had to remain single, though enjoying collegiate luxuries; when he became Professor he could resign his Fellowship and forsake his bachelor existence. The wedding was celebrated in St. Laurence's on 12 November 1788, when the Rev. John Mainwaring married Anne Wilding, sister of his curate Richard. What caused astonishment was that he was 64 and his bride 25! Joseph Cradock reported that a clerical friend of his, who had met Mainwaring many times over the years, 'expressed nothing but amazement at the hypochondriac Professor and his blooming lady; and, indeed, the whole University of Cambridge equally expressed their surprise at this wonderful contrast'. The young wife voiced her apprehension when presented to Bishop Hurd that his lordship would censure his old friend for taking a wife so late in life, but the bishop's gallantry was equal to the occasion. Marriage revitalised the ageing rector, for an old friend, the Rev. Thomas Twining, with whom he had conducted an erudite correspondence on classical Greek music back in 1760, wrote to his brother in 1793: 'I supped with my old friend Professor Mainwaring and his young lady. I never saw him look so well in my life'. Another friend gave a lovely description of their domesticity in Stretton: 'Here he regularly takes his nap after dinner, and in the evening is trotting about the hall for exercise, while his accomplished lady is singing Jackson's duet of "Time has not thinned my flowing hair" with a musical party in the parlour'. Sadly, their bliss was not to last. Mrs. Cradock told her husband that though Anne Mainwaring appeared so florid and full of health, she perceived in her strong symptoms of consumption. In June 1795 the rector wrote to the Cradocks telling them of his increased anxiety over the past 18 months about his wife's state of health. Having praised her patience, fortitude, piety and resignation, he went on: 'They who are acquainted with her worth may form some estimate of my loss, should it please God to take from me the greatest support and comfort of my declining years … In that dreadful case my sentiments, I trust, will be what they ought to be; but my strength under such a trial must totally fail me without that aid, which Christians who ask it with sincerity, and strive to deserve it, may hope to obtain'. He concluded that his daily prayer was that she would be well enough to visit them in the autumn, 'but my hopes are almost extinct, and my reasons for fearing the worst as great as they well can be'.

In these circumstances, the sermon he preached before the University on 3 May 1795 in Great St. Mary's was almost certainly valedictory, dedicated as it was to members of the university as a testimony of the speaker's esteem and gratitude. His final message was a warning against the abuses of reason and learning and what he termed 'the dangerous, domineering influence of a presumptuous, self-sufficient, free-thinking philosophy'. He advised the younger generation to take particular care 'to keep separate and distinct the respective provinces of Reason and Faith'. With a final attack on the perversion of the liberty of the press, he was gone. The next month, only two days after he wrote his sorrowful letter to the Cradocks, his wife died at Cambridge on 11 June 1795, aged 32. She was buried in the churchyard of St. Benet's.

It was probably another death, that of his dear friend William Mason, that saw Mainwaring back in Cambridge in April 1797 when he wrote to Sir Edward Littleton saying he had had a tedious illness which had

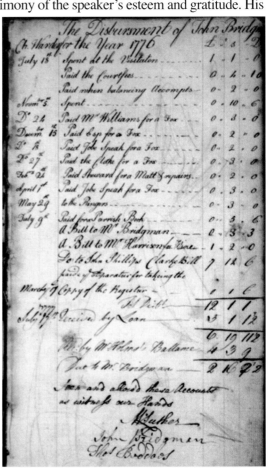

The first page from the churchwardens' accounts, 1776 (SRRC)

forced him to abandon even going out to tea. He wrote of his life of repose and tranquillity and of 'the little time I can expect to last'. In fact, he lived for exactly ten years more and this time was spent in Church Stretton.

*

Church life in the parish as seen through the pages of the Churchwardens' Accounts,[18] which date back to 1776, is very different from the picture presented by the rector's activities. Like all such accounts they are terse, repetitive but revealing. On one page are details of expenditure by the wardens in the course of a year; on the facing page the income from the church rate is set out, with occasionally a full list of rate-paying parishioners in Church Stretton, All Stretton, Little Stretton and Minton, their rateable value, and the amount each had to pay. The actual rate, euphemistically called a loan, was fixed each year at the Easter Vestry—it was 5d. in the £ in 1776 —according to the level of disbursements in the previous year. In 1776 the product of the rate was as follows:

Church Stretton...........£5-11-0
All Stretton................£5-19-7
Little Stretton.............£2-13-0
Minton....................£2- 8-2
TOTAL...........£16-11-9

The ringers' instructions, 1773

The annual cost of servicing and maintaining the church was met from this sum. The account reveals that All Stretton's fewer inhabitants were in aggregate wealthier than those of the larger Church Stretton.

The church bells were a recurring charge on the rates with the need for new bell ropes, oil and repairs. They were obviously well used. In the ringing chamber today there is a plaque dated 1773 listing instructions to ringers:

If that to ring you do come here
You must ring well with hand and ear
And if a bell you overthrow
4d. to pay before you go
And if you ring with spur or hat
6d. you must pay for that
Or if in this place you swear or curse
12d. to pay – pull out your purse.

By an ancient custom the 'pancake bell' was rung on Shrove Tuesday[19] to summon Christians to shrive themselves by penitence and prayer at the approach of Lent. We know also that the bells were rung each year on 29 May to commemorate Charles II's return, and on 5 November, the anniversary of the Gunpowder Plot and of the landing of William of Orange in 1688. They were also rung on occasions of national rejoicing, at which times the accounts show that the ringers were treated, probably to liquid refreshment. There was a clock in the tower, which seems to have needed frequent minor repairs, and a weather-vane with the cardinal points of the compass (see illustration on p.157).

Of course there were costs involved in the provision of church services. Payments for bread and wine for communion tended to be large but irregular. The communion cups were mended at Shrewsbury in 1786, and a flagon purchased for 4s. 9d. in 1790. Some light is thrown on the nature of services by entries recording the purchase of books for a General Fast in 1797, when the country was at war with France, and of specially printed thanksgiving prayers after Nelson's victory at the Battle of the Nile the next year. Archdeacon Plymley's Visitation notes[20] record that in 1792 there were Morning and Evening Prayer every Sunday and on Saints' Days, and prayers on Wednesday and Friday mornings except between All Saints' Day and Lent, 'an alteration that has taken place from want of a congregation in the winter season'. A sermon was preached every Sunday and the sacrament administered every month and twice at Easter. The average number receiving communion 'might be thirty', with as many as 75 at festivals and never fewer than 11. These figures sound very low, but national research has shown that between 1738 and 1811 the number of communicants was generally only about 5% of the popu-lation.[21] The reason is not that church attendance had collapsed, but that churchgoers were happy with Matins and Evensong, and many, especially among the less educated, were never confirmed and so never participated in the monthly celebration of the Lord's Supper. The reference in the accounts to the expenditure of 17s. for the rebinding of psalm books hints that there was congregational singing, but they were more likely for a psalm-singing group; there is no evidence of the use of hymns, even the great ones flowing from the pens of Isaac Watts and Charles Wesley. It is possible that an organ, moved from the chancel in 1819, was installed in Mainwaring's time.

The maintenance of the church and churchyard was the principal expense. The parish clerk who kept the church clean was paid £5 a year. Thomas Phillips was probably the clerk from 1760 as he signed as a witness at virtually every marriage at St. Laurence's from then till his death in 1767; indeed, he may have been clerk as far back as 1736 when the baptism of Richard, son of Thomas and Anne Phillips, was recorded in the register in unusual detail. On his death he seems to have been succeeded by another son, John, who acted as witness to marriages between 1767 and 1816. The annual payment from Jane Norton's bequest in 1640 for the upkeep of the west window is regularly recorded, but the repair of other windows cost £1 1s. in 1783, and the outlay on glazing was so great in 1800 that a number must have been replaced. Iron bars were fitted to the north window in 1803 after the glazier was paid £1 13s. 3d. Every year they paid for the erection and dismantling of the archdeacon's seat used at the visitation; lost keys were always being replaced; and 6lbs. of candles were purchased annually for the bell-ringers. One year they laid planks in the tower, perhaps a new floor for the ringers' chamber. The upkeep of the churchyard was, as we have seen in earlier centuries, a constant headache: payments were made for cleaning up, clearing the snow, gravelling the paths, repairing the fences and, in 1785, putting up a new gate-post and hanging a new gate. Two references to 'repairing the church bridge' are unfortunately not explained — perhaps it was the one that crossed the Town Brook by Burway House.[22]

The churchwardens' accounts incidentally reveal some features of contemporary church and community life. Guy Fawkes' Night was celebrated every year, not only by ringing the bells but also by feasting and drinking and probably by fireworks as 2s. was spent on gunpowder in some years. The psalm-singing girls were rewarded with ribbons financed from church funds. Various people were frequently paid 3s. 'for a fox', presumably for killing one on church land — as many as five are accounted in 1788.

The first reference to a Sunday School in the accounts is in 1798 when a payment of £2 1s. was registered; this was to become an annual item. We know, however, from Edward Lloyd's bequest in 1790 of £3 3s. per annum, chargeable upon his estate called The Bank — an earlier Bank House — in Church Stretton, that a Sunday School was almost certainly conducted by that time if not earlier. The Sunday School movement, which grew out of catechising on Sunday afternoons, was inspired by Robert Raikes of Gloucester and spread very rapidly in the decade after 1780. In Stretton, Lloyd's bequest was paid to the trustees of the charity school who benefited from his will in other ways: half the interest on a funded gift of £100 was paid to the school-master to augment his salary and half was applied towards financing two scholars aged 14 to undertake apprenticeships. There had been a school in Stretton for at least two centuries, but the schoolhouse at Burway House was apparently built in 1779 on the site of the former school, and the Stretton Enclosure Act of 1788 confirmed that the former waste land on which it stood should be held by the rector and nine others in trust for the school. This Act also allocated 27 acres of land at Lower Wood to provide income. In 1792 it contributed £15 per annum to the upkeep of the school, supplementing earlier bequests from Sir Rowland Hayward and Thomas Bridgman, and soon to be augmented by Edward Lloyd and John Mainwaring himself. In that year the school had 16 scholars. The archdeacon noted that there were several dame schools in the parish.

Burway House, the home of the school from 1779 (SRRC)

A visitor to Stretton in 1772 considered it was 'an exceeding neat town, having many good houses, and the streets are broad, open and well-paved'.[23] Most inhabitants had gardens behind their houses. The Thursday market displayed 'great plenty of provisions' and there were fairs on 14 May and 24 September. Archdeacon Plymley's Visitation record of 23 November 1792[24] fills out this picture with details of Stretton two hundred years ago and in John Mainwaring's last years as rector. In the four townships there was a total of 166 houses — 87 in Church Stretton, 42 in All Stretton, 26 in Little Stretton and 11 in Minton, with a further two in Botvyle and some cottages on the wasteland. There were 87 proprietors, but only 49 of them were resident. By the time of the first census in 1801 there were 199 families with 462 males and 462 females, a total population of 924. The industrial development in the east of the county had had little impact on Stretton, but the creation of turnpike roads had begun to open up the parish to the outside world. Owen and Blakeway's *History of Shrewsbury* records that a journey by coach from Chester to London in 1740 took six days, by 1753 it was down to four, and by 1764 the 'Flying Machine' could do it in two days in summer; when Mainwaring got married in 1788 the journey could be done in 24 hours. The roads from Stretton to Shrewsbury and Ludlow were turnpiked from 1756, the Stretton-Wenlock road after 1765.[25] An advertisement in the *Shrewsbury Chronicle* in 1772 invited bids for the turnpike tolls for the next ten years, including 'the tolls arising on the roads leading from Coleham Bridge to Church Stretton'. By 1776 there were daily mail coaches from Shrewsbury to Hereford and back, no doubt changing horses in Stretton at the Crown.

The development of roads brought more visitors, yet Church Stretton remained a small market town, with agriculture still far and away the principal form of employment. In 1801, of those in work, 142 were engaged in agriculture and 66 were classed as 'mechanics'. Labourers earned only 1s. a day and poverty was widespread. The main diet of the poor was bread and potatoes. 'They seldom buy flesh meat', the archdeacon noted, and they had little butter and cheese. But they must have consumed plenty of beer as there were five alehouses and the coaching inn in Church Stretton, in addition to those in All Stretton and Little Stretton.

Support given through the poor rate under the Elizabethan Poor Law of 1601 had been supplemented by charitable bequests for many years. The first known to the nineteenth century Charity Commissioners was the gift in 1684 of a two-acre meadow in Little Stretton by John Jarrett and Henry Richards for the relief and succour of poor people in the parish. The eighteenth century was the golden age of philanthropy. In Stretton donations had become common in the time of Rector Clayton—bequests from William Minton, Thomas Hawkes, Randolph Jones and Thomas Bridgman and then the gift of Street Meadow in 1735 by Edward Phillips, the apothecary. In 1708 the bequest of 1684 and that of Thomas Hawkes had funded the purchase of Walter's House in High Street for the use of the poor. When the 1788 Enclosure Act was passed the Little Stretton and Street Meadows were disposed of to Mr. John Robinson, mercer, in return for his building two or three almshouses adjoining the poor house—near where the Silvester Horne Institute now stands. By 1839 four such almshouses had been built. Edward Phillips junior, an apothecary like his father, left £30 in his will of 1781 to be invested and the income spent on bread for the poor. Edward Lloyd, in addition to his

Part of the third benefaction board

bequests to the school, in 1790 left £21 on trust so that the interest could be paid to 'sixteen poor parishioners of Church Stretton not receiving pay' every year on St. Thomas's Day, and Thomas Harrison left a further £10 in 1794 for the unemployed. Two years later John Bridgman's will directed that £100 should be paid on his death to the minister and churchwardens and the interest paid out every 28 March 'to such poor housekeepers of the said parish as they should think proper'. The harsh solution of the Poor Law Amendment Act still lay in the future. Whatever personal actions on behalf of the poor were prompted by their own Christian compassion, the minister and churchwardens had major responsibilities for the proper investment and equitable distribution of these many benefactions.

*

The needs of the poor constituted a pressing problem for the Rev. John Mainwaring and the church, as well as for the local community. The same cannot be said of the spread of Nonconformity. As already noted, a licence was granted back in 1725 for dissenting services to be held in Jonathan Stringer's house, but there is no evidence of a renewal after his death two years later. The Evangelical Revival, particularly associated with the Methodists, swept the country in the next 40 years, yet on 12 September 1767 Mainwaring was able to write to the bishop in his very clear hand: 'In pursuance of the order I lately received at the Visitation at Ludlow, I have made a careful enquiry, and I find that we have no Papist, or reputed Papist, or Dissenter of any Denomination within this parish'. John Wesley had passed through, as his journal records, on a very cold day in 1762, on a journey from Hereford to Shrewsbury. When he reached Church Stretton his horse 'lay down and could go no farther'. He gave no sermon, however, because he was in too much of a hurry to get to Shrewsbury, which became something of a Methodist stronghold. Madeley was another such centre in the next county. The vicar there, from 1760 to 1785, the celebrated John Fletcher, was a godly man and did not limit his proclamation of the gospel to his own church; indeed, had he not predeceased Wesley, he might have succeeded him as the leader of Methodism. John Mainwaring probably knew Fletcher, but he would have had more sympathy with Dr. Adams, the Rector of St. Chad's in Shrewsbury, who, after the Evangelical William Romaine had preached the gospel there, felt obliged to preach a sermon to refute his Methodist ideas.

Mainwaring was familiar with many leading Evangelicals for the heart of the movement in Cambridge was in St. John's: Henry Venn had entered as an undergraduate on the same day as Mainwaring, though he soon moved to Jesus College, and Rowland Hill from Hawkestone was later in trouble as an undergraduate for preaching in the villages near Cambridge. As to Mainwaring

John Mainwaring's letter to the bishop (HRO)

himself, his familiarity with 'enthusiasm' bred something close to contempt. In 1780 he published his *Remarks on the Postscript of Dr. Halifax's Preface to the Sermons of the Revd. Dr. Ogden.* In it he expressed his belief that in the seventeenth century the unlicensed preaching of Predestination and Justification by Faith had produced a 'frenzy' which ended in the subversion of all order in society. 'The great change in the face of affairs at the Restoration, although it removed this frenzy, produced another, of a very different complexion indeed, but not less fatal to morals and religion. For now the Saints were succeeded by Wits, Free-Thinkers and Sceptics … shallow dupes of their boasted reason'. Unfortunately, as he viewed it, the defence of Christianity and the scheme of redemption 'betrayed many respectable writers into the cant and jargon of Methodism'. He developed this theme the following year in his *Essay on the Character of Methodism.* 'This sect', he wrote, 'like most others, sets up a claim to superior sanctity and professes a more than ordinary severity of life and manners'. He acknowledged that some Methodists may have been very sincere, but castigated them for requiring their followers 'to commit themselves to the guidance of the Spirit, with an utter contempt of reason and all human learning'. He argued that their 'favourite and constant topics are Grace and Assurance, Predestination and Original Sin' and that they excluded other parts of religion and even morality itself. He accused them of 'uncharitable severity and censoriousness ... chiefly directed against the regular clergy'. He was particularly incensed, as a scholar and theologian, at the Evangelical habit of quoting passages of Scripture out of context: 'Imagine sentences of the Sacred Books, pluckt from their natural order and connexion in the context, planted at random in compositions fashioned, of course, to our taste and manners, and presented to the hearer in scraps and fragments'.

The rector, like the egregious Parson Woodforde, would have agreed with the memorable judgment of the modern historian of the Church in the eighteenth century, Professor E.G. Rupp, himself a Methodist:

> More influential than the Evangelical Revival was the continuing life of the Church of England ... Within the walls of its parish churches the greater part of the nation was baptised, married and laid to rest. Through all the changing scenes of life, in trouble and in joy, thither the tribes came up in national crisis or in private need, to reckon with their Maker. Whether the priests were faithful or unfaithful, the liturgy went on, Holy Scripture, prayers, the Word and the sacraments.[26]

In Stretton, too, the parish church was still a focal point of the life of the community. Through the churchwardens' accounts, the archdeacon's visitation records and other surviving documents, a picture emerges of the state of the building at the end of the eighteenth century and of the impact of John Mainwaring's permanent settlement in the living for the last years of his life. The visitor who recorded his impressions of the town in the *Shrewsbury Chronicle* in November 1772 had described St. Laurence's as 'an ancient gothic structure, with a lofty tower, and in it are several ancient monuments'. Most of these were lost in the Victorian restoration, including one to the Wilding family. We know of this only through the childhood recollections of a doctor's wife who later recorded that when Henry Wilding died in 1835 he was interred in the church, the last to be given this privilege. 'The vault, which was a large one, was just under the chancel steps. I was allowed to go down the steps into it and saw several coffins—his mother's, his first wife's and his brother's'.[27] Fortunately other memorials were recorded by visiting antiquarians. Hardwick gives details of a memorial slab in the chancel floor that read: 'In memory of Sarah and Edward Appleyard. She died 5th May 1726 in the 29th year of her age. He died 2nd November 1726 in the 42nd year of his age. They left issue 4 sons and 3 daughters'.[28] And when Edward Williams visited the church on 2 May 1796 he made a note of several other monumental inscriptions now missing.[29] Against the east wall of the chancel on the left-hand side of the window was a marble memorial inscribed:

Edward Williams's painting of St. Laurence's in 1786; this is the best picture of the church at that time and shows the south porch (SRRC)

> Underneath are deposited the bodies of Thomas Brooke, Gent., who died 20 May 1742 aged 70. Also of Elizabeth Brooke relict of the said Thomas Brooke who died 8 February 1758 aged 85. Also of Edward Brooke the only son of the said Thomas and Elizabeth Brooke who died 6 September 1731 aged 19.

Against the north wall of the chancel was a hatchment with the Brooke coat-of-arms. They were the descendants of the lawyer Brooke whose house near the church had been admired by John Leland in 1538; they had moved to Bank House later in the century when the Nortons bought up much of the former Arundel estate, including the site almost opposite the church where the Hall was built.

Upon a slate slab in the chancel was inscribed:

> In memory of Edward Phillips Apothecary who departed this life June the 15th. 1740 aged 73 years. Also here lieth the body of Mary the wife of Edward Phillips of Acton Burnell who died May ye 28th 1770 aged 65.

This first Edward Phillips had been recorded in the bishop's Call Books of the early eighteenth century as 'chirurgus' or 'medicus'. His son obviously moved out to Acton Burnell, for in the 1760s Samuel Matthews and George Munday were named as surgeons, and another stone slab in the chancel read:

In memory of Mr. Edward Phillips Apothecary late of Acton Burnell who departed this life 2 October 1785 aged 76.

Edward Williams also noted a slate slab within the communion rails which read: 'Mrs. Sarah Parkes died 3 June 1785 aged 71 years'. Strangely, slate memorials which today feature on the east walls of the north and south transepts to Thomas and Ann Phillips who died in 1760 and 1798 and to Richard Phillips who died in 1786, and the memorial to the surgeon Richard Langslow and his family in the south transept extension are not recorded by Williams. At that time the first Phillips memorial was on the west wall of the south transept, and the Langslow memorial on the south wall of the nave – both were moved when the south aisle was built in 1868. In the south transept, too, there was a later monument 'In memory of Richard Minton and Elizabeth his wife. Richard died January 16th 1807 aged 80. Elizabeth died October 30th

Richard Phillips's memorial in the south transept

1819 aged 84'.[30] Williams does, however, include the interesting information that the benefaction boards, now in the vestry, were then against the east and west walls of the north transept. The public display of such boards was intended to safeguard the generous gifts of local philanthropists from misappropriation. At the time of Williams's visit they were almost new for apparently they were produced in 1793 although the wardens' accounts show that T.Upton's bill for £4 1s. for their painting and lettering was not settled until 1801!

The archdeacon's description of the church was as follows:

> The church is built of stone, spacious and in the form of a cross. The tower is very neat and exhibits on one angle a figure of the patron saint. The walls of the body of the church have been plaistered on the outside as well as within. The state of repair is good and the original architecture not innovated by any repairs that have been made. There is a disagreeable picture of a skeleton as large as nature on one side the western window which ought to be removed, and a figure of Time for its companion not worthy to remain. The gallery in the church does not overhang any part but rises gradually bench by bench. The visitations of the Bishop or Archdeacon for the deaneries of Pontesbury and Wenlock

are usually holden in the church … The inside has been whitewashed and the plaister of the outside repaired and covered with a grey wash.[31]

The wall paintings had survived from the Middle Ages, but the bank of seats at the west end—the term 'gallery' is rather misleading—may have been of recent construction, although the reference in Jane Norton's will of 1639 to 'the west window and the seats adjoining in the west end of the church' could refer to such a structure. The reference to the plastered and whitewashed interior and the plastered exterior with a grey wash confirm the suggested description of St. Laurence's in the early seventeenth century and emphasise how different from today its appearance would have been.

The rector's interest in gardening, or his sense of approaching death, caused him to show a special concern for the state of the churchyard. After centuries of neglect and argument over the repair of the fences, in 1798 a wall was erected 'all round', according to the archdeacon, 'and coped with stone'. New stiles, gates and wickets were also put up. He paid tribute to Mainwaring's personal effort: 'The rector contributed much to the good work by his exertions and his money. He also laid out the churchyard more decent, by cutting gravel walks through it, and levelling it, as much as was practicable'. A visitor in the year after Mainwaring's death commented, 'The churchyard is spacious, planted round with lime trees, and kept very neat'.[32]

The wall with its coping stones still stands two hundred years later. On several dressed stones there is visible a number, in a few instances with the date 1798 and initials. The numbers are explained in a document at Shrewsbury headed 'Hayments of Churchyard Wall – copied from Mr. Bray's paper'.[33] This lists the names of persons who either contributed to the cost of erecting the wall or, more likely, agreed to be financially responsible for the maintenance of a section of it, like eighteenth-century reincarnations of Nehemiah and his fellow-builders of the wall of Jerusalem. The whole parish was involved: 23 such sections, or hayments, plus a wicket gate and stile, are listed under Church Stretton, 24 and a stile under Minton, 20 under Little Stretton, and nine under All Stretton; Botvyle, where there were only two houses, was responsible for the church gate and stile. Sometimes several names were allocated to one section, sometimes one individual had agreed to be responsible for a number of sections. 'The Parish', as such, appears only once, along with G. Corfield and Mr. Bird for section 2 in the Church Stretton list; the sum of 10s. 6d. in the wardens' accounts paid as a 'Subscription towards building a wall round the churchyard' may or may not provide a clue as to the costs involved. The rector does not feature in the lists, which strengthens the belief that they refer to future maintenance rather than initial subscriptions, but the name of Richard Wilding, the curate, appears against two All Stretton sections. The Marquess of Bath, whose family (Thynne) was about to cease to be the church's patrons, agreed to maintain one section. R. Pemberton, Esq, and Lord Berwick, relations of two future rectors, also appear; indeed, Robert Pemberton, who must have owned a substantial estate at Minton, was down for no fewer than seven and a half sections. Perhaps the most interesting entry is William Cheney Hart, Esq, a barrister-at-law from Hope Bowdler, whose name is against five sections in the north-west corner, together with the wicket and stile, because it is in the stones in this area that the date 1798 appears with his initials, and because Bray's list adds 'for the Hall'. This confirms that he lived there, or owned it, and that this was the Bonham Norton residence in the lower part of the Rectory Field just north of where the Parish Centre now stands. When it had been put up for sale in 1785 by Jno. Reynolds, the advertisement had suggested it was suitable for a school or 'if it were in the hands of a Gentleman of Taste it might easily be made a most desirable object in point of beauty'. But by 1798 its days were numbered.

Within the churchyard there were some unusual inscriptions from this period on memorials that no longer exist. A rectangular tomb, now removed but deciphered 20 years ago in a Women's Institute survey, was inscribed: 'In memory of John Gibbon eldest son of Thomas and Mary Gibbon, Midshipman, lost on board H.M.S. Penelope in November 1778 aged 17'. This young man, perhaps a casualty in the War of American Independence, was probably from the Gibbon family of Little Stretton. The headstone of a 27-year-old, Thomas Price, who died on Christmas Eve 1799, seems to have set a new fashion. It read:

> When blooming youth and beauty are most brave,
> Death plucks us up and plants us in the grave.
> Take care young men your precious time to spend;
> Our lives are short, and quickly at an end.[34]

Two similar memorials, also now missing, were fortunately recorded in an early twentieth-century guide to Church Stretton.[33] One commemorated Henry Harrington who was buried on 31 January 1802, at the age of 93:

> Farewell vain world, I've known enough of thee,
> I value not what thou canst say of me;
> Thy smiles I court not nor thy frowns I fear,
> All's one to me, my head lies quiet here,
> The faults thou sees in me take care to shun,
> And look at home: there's something to be done.

Another stone in memory of the village barber probably refers to Francis Hick, who was buried six months after Henry Harrington, on 13 July 1802, and whose friends concocted an even more arresting epitaph:

Here lies the barber Hick,
Who cut and shaved and was so quick.
And now has gone to his long whum [home],
He killed himself with drinking rum.

Twelve years later, after Rector Mainwaring had himself been buried in the churchyard—but whose memorial has not survived—one Ann Cook was interred. On her tombstone may still be read:

On a Thursday she was born,
On a Thursday made a bride,
On a Thursday her leg was broke
And on a Thursday died.

As the eighteenth century drew to a close, John Mainwaring, at 76 years of age, made his will. He may have been ill or simply felt that his life was effectively over. His young wife had died five years before, and almost certainly the Elizabeth Mainwaring, whose burial the register records in June 1797, was his sister, three years his junior. A Charlotte Mainwaring, buried in June 1809, was surely another sister, 15 years younger than the rector. It seems very likely that these unmarried sisters had come to keep house for him in his new parsonage in Church Stretton during vacations and while he was at Cambridge, and continued to live there after his late marriage.

His will, dated 12 May 1800, reveals that the Rev. John Mainwaring was quite a wealthy man. He had been a Fellow of St. John's from 1748, Senior Bursar from 1768 to 1786, and Lady Margaret Professor of Divinity from 1788, a post referred to as 'that lucrative Professorship' in Baker's history of the college.[36] He had been rector of Church Stretton for over half a century, perpetual curate of Minsterley since his presentation by Viscount Weymouth in 1759, and had held another sinecure as rector of Aberdaron, Caernarvonshire, a gift from the college in 1787 after he completed his long stint as bursar.[37] His income as Stretton's rector is known: the archdeacon's visitation revealed that the whole of the parish was titheable to the rector, and that since the 1770s the tithes had been leased for £180 per annum to one man who agreed individual contributions but made considerable profit for himself; in addition the rector drew an income of £45 a year from the 60 acres of glebe land. From his income he paid the curate £40, and presumably he also benefited from paying the curates at Minsterley and Aberdaron only a percentage of his income from those parishes.

Under the terms of his will John Mainwaring left generous legacies, worth at least a year's wages, to all of his servants. He directed his executors, the Rev. Richard Wilding and Richard Bray, the surgeon and apothecary, to invest £50 in the public funds in their names upon trust so that the annual interest could be applied by the minister and churchwardens to the relief of poor householders in the parish, and similarly another £50 to produce an annual sum for the trustees of the school to be applied in support of the Sunday School so long as the parish continued the support it had given since Edward Lloyd's benefaction. To Archdeacon Plymley he left a further £50 to invest on behalf of clergy widows and orphans in the archdeaconry. Of particular interest is the bequest of £21 to be invested to pay John Evans and future gardeners to maintain the churchyard and trees in good order and to keep the paths gravelled. Again the gift was conditional on the parish continuing to pay 8 to 10s. a year, an arrangement which demonstrates his wisdom in trying to ensure that parishioners recognised their responsibility for the churchyard and Sunday School, and did not leave their upkeep to the generosity of a few. The sum of £300 was left to the University Library to purchase divinity books and £200 to the College Library for the same purpose—the College can identify three of the books so purchased but only one could be classed as divinity. The residue of his estate, together with his books, manuscripts and clerical vestments, was divided between a brother, sisters, nieces and nephews.

Four years later he added a codicil. He had obviously been well cared for in his old age and rewarded his servants generously; he also increased from £50 to £100 the legacies to the poor, clergy widows and orphans, and the Sunday school, though this last was now to be used to augment the salary of the master of both day school and Sunday school. The codicil is dated 5 October 1805, two weeks before Nelson's victory at Trafalgar, which would have triggered joyful celebration even at land-locked Stretton.

John Mainwaring lived another 18 months, dying on 15 April 1807, two months short of 58 years as rector. The archdeacon, who attended his funeral, later noted that his grave in the churchyard was surrounded by iron railings and beneath a cedar of Lebanon, but these have disappeared. What have survived are the churchyard wall, the new (now Old) Rectory and the walk through the Rectory Woods, as well as his sermons, sundry writings and his biography of Handel. In their variety and their quality they constitute fitting memorials to a richly talented rector.

10

EARLY 19TH-CENTURY IMPROVEMENTS TO THE CHURCH

Even before John Mainwaring died it was already known who would succeed him. As early as 1799[1] Thomas Coleman, Esq, Town Clerk of Leominster, had paid the first instalment of £2,000 for the purchase of the advowson of the parish of Church Stretton to the current patron, elevated in 1789 from Viscount Weymouth to Marquess of Bath. In 1803 Coleman went on to pay £14,510 for the lordship of the manor, held by the Thynnes for over two hundred years.[2] On the demise of the old rector he completed the purchase of the advowson and presented his eldest son to the living. On 29 June 1807 the Rev. Thomas Bernard Coleman was instituted by the Bishop of Hereford as Rector of Church Stretton.

The new rector was only 25 years old, nearly 60 years younger than his predecessor. The first of eight children, he was born in June 1782, and in 1801 at the age of 18 admitted to Worcester College, Oxford. He graduated B.A. in 1805, M.A. in 1807, and was ordained.

Coleman's marriage does not appear in the parish register, but in November 1809 it records the baptism of Mary Anne, daughter of Thomas Bernard and Anne Gregory Coleman, whose father was John Stackhouse, Esq, of Acton Scott. Three other daughters and a son followed by 1817. To cater for the needs of his growing family, Coleman added to the parsonage and gave it a new front, 'making it a finer house but not so pretty or appropriate as it was before', in the opinion of the archdeacon. The remodelling moved the main entrance, now flanked by Doric columns, to the western side of the house, so that the principal rooms could face south and so enjoy the sun and the view of Ragleth Hill. The dining room was reduced in size to accommodate the vestibule. It was Coleman who had the old Hall pulled down and laid a new drive from the main entrance of the parsonage swinging across Rectory Field, bought by his father in 1801 and 1804, to what was once an impressive gateway in Church Street.

Coleman seems to have been less concerned about the fabric of the church than the rectory. Certainly no major repairs were carried out, though the

The new front entrance to the Rectory

wardens' accounts include the usual items of expenditure, particularly for whitewashing and painting. There is some suggestion of a new emphasis on the sacrament of Holy Communion, because in 1813 a superfine crimson broadcloth was purchased for the communion table, and £1 was spent in 1816 on 'stuffing cushions for Communion', presumably as kneelers.

Evidence from the parish registers suggests that until 1816 Coleman was running the church without an active curate. Yet the impression conveyed by the wardens' accounts is that the church's affairs were not tightly under control. No expenditure was recorded in 1810 and 1811, and the next year many rate payments were uncollected, money was owing to the parish clerk, and the churchwardens' annual dinner in 1814 cost ratepayers as much as two guineas. By 1809 the church rate had risen to 9d. in the £. There must have been shrill complaints because the next year it was down to $2^{1}/_{2}$d! A ratepayers' rebellion was only to be expected when already taxes were high on account of the Napoleonic Wars—although the only references in Stretton to the conflict were the detention of a soldier, probably drunk, in custody on the order of Richard Wilding in 1813, and the purchase of special thanksgiving prayers on the defeat of Bonaparte in 1814. There is no record of further thanksgiving after Waterloo.

Perhaps the demoralising effect of the long war may account for the somewhat negligent conduct of the church's affairs and the lack of attention to the

The Coleman and Pemberton chalices

building, but the more likely cause is the state of Coleman's health. The archdeacon described him as 'an amiable man but of infirm health'. In September 1816 the Rev. John Nunn appears in the register as his curate to assist him in his church duties. The rector's health continued to deteriorate, however, and he died in Liverpool on 3 August 1818, at the age of only 36. The local newspaper called him 'a gentleman amiable, pious and beloved'.[3] He left the advowson which, together with the lordship of the manor, he had inherited from his father, in trust to his brother-in-law, Mr. Thomas Stackhouse, and Archdeacon Joseph Plymley (now using the surname Corbett) to be sold for the benefit of his younger children. The bequest to his wife of his carriages and carriage horses indicates a man of substance.[4] In his memory his wife presented the parish with a paten and a silver chalice, the oldest in the church today and still used on special occasions. It is inscribed:

> The Gift of Anne Gregory Coleman, widow of the Revd. Thomas Bernard Coleman late Incumbent of the living of Church Stretton to the Parish as a token of regard, 6 December 1818.

And on the reverse:

> The Lord gave and the Lord hath taken away. Blessed be the name of the Lord. Job 1:21.

The rector was buried at Leominster, but his old servant William Norcott, who died in 1829 at the age of 91, is commemorated in the churchyard at Stretton as an 'honest and faithful servant of the late Revd. T.B. Coleman Rector of this Parish' on an impressive memorial probably given by Mrs. Coleman, who remained lady of the manor.

*

The advowson was sold to Mr. Thomas Pemberton for the very large sum of £11,000, of which £10,000 had been left by his brother Robert 'to be laid out in purchasing preferment for his son', Robert Norgrave Pemberton. The Pembertons were an old and wealthy family who had moved from Lancashire to Shropshire in the fifteenth century. It is interesting that the great great grandfather of Robert Norgrave Pemberton had married into the Leighton family.[5] Robert Pemberton was born on 7 August 1791, the son of Robert and Sarah; his second name, Norgrave, was his grandmother's maiden name. His father was a lawyer in Shrewsbury and owned an extensive estate. Robert junior was admitted to Christ Church, Oxford, in October 1809. He graduated B.A. in 1814, M.A. 1816, and proceeded to ordination. He spent two years as perpetual curate at Ford, a village west of Shrewsbury, before being instituted as Rector of Church Stretton on 17 December 1818 at the age of 27. Two years later, on 11 November 1820, at Marylebone Church in London, he married Caroline, youngest daughter of the late Augustus Pechell, Esq, of Portman Square, London, of an established Berkhamstead family. On their return to Church Stretton the young couple were greeted in the fashion accorded to Lord Nelson after his victory at the Nile 20 years earlier. 'They were met by the parishioners and townspeople who took the horses from their carriage and drew them to the Rectory; their arrival was greeted with bonfires, sheep-roasting and every other testimony of esteem and affection. Similar demonstrations were preparing at Millichope, Cardington and other places connected with the good and much respected Rector and his family'.[6] Pemberton, who had been living at the Old Bank House, probably out of consideration for the widowed Mrs. Coleman and her young family, now moved to the rectory.

On St. Laurence's church the new rector's impact was immediate. By April 1819 the curate, John Nunn, had left and for the next two and a half years Pemberton himself officiated at virtually all baptisms, marriages and funerals — and presumably services, although no record of these remains. More dramatic were the changes in the interior of the church. The rector was shocked at the cluttered state of the chancel, which was still his domain and responsibility. He determined to get rid of the tiered seating which probably stood on the north side, but the wardens warned him that there would then not be enough seats for the congregation. So on 22 April 1819 a committee was appointed to make a terrier or inventory of the pews. In addition to Pemberton the committee included six representatives from Church Stretton and two each from All Stretton, Little Stretton and Minton. Their first task was to list all the pews and the persons with a claim to a seat or 'kneeling' in them, usually because they were householders in the parish but in some cases because they had bought them. The claims were listed in a note-book,[7] which also contains the bids made when a vacant pew and a number of unoccupied kneelings were sold off at auction. This may or may not have been the customary way of purchasing a seat in the church but, with the aim of raising enough money to carry out some reordering of the pews, the bidding was keen. The first bid for a single place in pew 43, for example, was £2 5s., but it eventually went to James Edwards for £5 5s. With such large sums the payment surely guaranteed the place for life. A decision already made to take down some of the pews in the north transept and all of the pews in the south transept and to re-erect them in a uniform manner was promptly carried out. When James Edwards, the carpenter who had successfully bid for the seat in pew 43, presented his bill for £93 10s. 6d. it was more than covered by the proceeds of the auction. The surplus of £17 went towards the alteration and repair of the rear pews that accommodated the poor. Vacant pews continued to be auctioned in subsequent years: among the lots at the Buck's Head on 15 January 1834 was 'a good pew in the north aisle of the Parish Church of Church Stretton No. 58'.[8]

At a meeting in the church in June 1819 it was agreed that the 'gallery' in the chancel should be removed to the bottom of the west aisle (the nave) and the old 'gallery' there taken down and altered according to a plan approved at the meeting and at the expense of the parish. At the same meeting, of which a report appears in the churchwardens' Account Book, it was decided to move the organ, too, from the chancel to the back of the nave. This is the first mention of an organ, although the singing of psalms, if not hymns, was noted at the end of the eighteenth century. The organist, Mr. Davies, was paid £4 4s. in 1821. It is apparent from plans of the church drawn in the 1820s that the altered 'gallery' at the west end was in fact tiered seating: there were nine steps on each side of the nave rising westward to give access to areas of seating on each side of the organ. Almost certainly the seating will have been benches because the gallery was used by the schoolchildren. Surely, too, the medieval paintings of Time and the skeleton on either side of the west window, illustrations which the archdeacon had regarded as 'disagreeable', would have been erased before the children were allocated the benches in front of them. The wardens' accounts reveal that £4 8s. 9d. was spent on additions to the gallery. One further decision taken at the June meeting was permanently to close the north door, the old funeral door, in front of which at this time stood the font; 50 years later the doorway was bricked up on the inside. A porch door was purchased for the south entrance at a cost of £3 2s. 4d. It is interesting that the only persons recorded as present at the meeting and voting for all these changes were Rector Pemberton and the Rev. Richard Wilding (no longer the regular curate, but whose experience was invaluable to the young rector), though it seems impossible that such potentially explosive issues should have been determined without the agreement of the wardens and the committee.

The seating problem had not yet been solved. An undated plan[9] from about this time gives precise measurements of the dimensions of the church, and an accompanying note suggests that if the depth of the pews in the north transept were reduced to a uniform 2 feet 8 inches, as it generally was in the south transept, an extra pew could be squeezed in on each side. All these pew alterations aroused a great deal of concern. A public meeting was therefore called on 28 October 1819 at which it was agreed that Archdeacon Corbett should be requested to regulate the sittings, pews and kneelings and to make out a terrier of the same. Recognising the independence of this authoritative figure from outside the parish, they gave him full power to alter, exchange and fix the said sittings and pledged that his recommendations should be adopted by the parish in general. Two copies of this terrier have survived, one showing subsequent changes in the persons allocated to the pews.[10] What the documents clearly show is that people of substance sat at the front: Ralph Benson, of Lutwyche, had the large box pews where today's pulpit stands, and Mrs. Coleman, lady of the manor and the late rector's widow, had front pews in the north transept with others from All Stretton; Edward Gibbon, Esq., of Little Stretton had the double-sized front pew in the south transept. There were free seats for 'The Parish', that is the poor, in the pews towards the rear of the

The east window

nave beyond the south door; the children sat behind them in the west end gallery.

The removal of the tiered seating from the chancel gave the rector the opportunity he sought to embellish and beautify the east end of the church. Already at the meeting in June 1819 he and Wilding had agreed that the rector should be allowed to move a window out of the chancel to the north side of the nave and that the parish should alter the situation of a window on the south side of the nave. Both these windows were to disappear in the Victorian extension. What must have given Robert Pemberton the greatest pleasure, though at considerable personal expense, was the new east window. The date 1819 at the base of the window confirms that this was another achievement of his first year as incumbent. A close look at the window reveals that the mouldings and tracery are later insertions in the original aperture. Cranage considered that the view in Eyton's *Antiquities* showed an east window of Decorated character, and David Parkes in 1808 drew a window with five Perpendicular bays, but the present window has renewed Perpendicular tracery and mouldings. It seems, then, that today's east window, tracery and stained glass, dates from 1819. This was the opinion of James Phillips who, 50 years later, wrote in his *Guide to Church Stretton*, 'The present east window is rather a poor specimen of the Perpendicular style, either restored or more probably put in for the first time in 1819'. Miss H.M. Auden, in an interesting article[11] on the window written soon after it had been repaired in 1932, calls it 'an example of the revival of the art of stained glass which began in Shrewsbury at the beginning of the nineteenth century'. She describes how this art, which had been almost forgotten since the sixteenth century, was revived in Shrewsbury by Betton and Evans, the artists of the east window in St. Laurence's, who set themselves to reproduce the jewel-like colours of medieval glass. Their early work was mainly coats-of-arms and heraldry, and examples may be seen in the head of the same window: the four coats-of-arms portrayed are, clockwise from the top left, of Rector

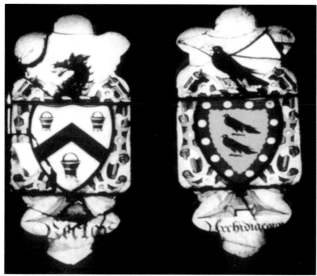

Coats-of-arms in the east window, left Rev. R.N. Pemberton, right: Archdeacon Joseph Corbett

Pemberton, Archdeacon Corbett, King George III and the Right Rev. Dr. George Huntingford, Bishop of Hereford. In the centre of these four is a very small representation, possibly medieval, of an unknown bishop's head, probably again brought from Shrewsbury. The main part of the window 'is in three bays, filled in with well-executed designs in stained glass, representing St. Peter and St. John, with our Saviour in the centre'.[12] A close examination of the glass today suggests that as the head of Jesus has no halo there has been some later repair. In fact it was repaired in 1932 when there were also criticisms from some parishioners of the faces, and a request, not granted, that they should be replaced.[13] The colours of the robes of the principal figures are striking and explain why Betton and Evans' stained glass was later placed in the east windows of St. Chad's and St. Julian's in Shrewsbury. The archdeacon noted Pemberton's gift of 'a handsome painted window'; the verdict of *Bagshaw's Directory* in 1851 was 'peculiarly chaste and elegant'.

Pemberton recognised that what the east end now needed, to set off both the window and the altar, was a reredos. In his short time at St. Michael's, Ford, he had assembled a reredos of carved Jaobean panels with a centre-piece said to be the work of an Antwerp wood-carver of *c*.1530. His acquaintance with the local gentry and his knowledge of their properties now enabled him, at his own expense, to collect more ornately carved oak panelling, which was all the rage at the time. This was tailored to fit behind the altar at St. Laurence's, occupying the lower part of the east wall but high enough to obscure the base of the

The Jacobean reredos. The Pieta is in the centre panel

Coats-of-arms in the north transept window.
That of the Wilding family is at the bottom right

window, and about 11 feet along the north and south sides of the chancel. *Bagshaw's Directory* was enthusiastic: 'The chancel is beautifully ornamented with richly carved oak in antique devices'; the archdeacon merely noted the addition of an 'old carved wainscot to form a reredos'. Sir Stephen Glynne, a renowned early nineteenth-century authority on historic churches, who visited St. Laurence's about 1830 (his reference to a wooden porch at the south door shows it was before 1831), remarked on the 'beautiful wainscoting', the handsome altar, and 'a small wood desk with good carving'.[14] One part of the reredos bears the date 1667, another appears to be the side of a probably sixteenth-century chest with the figure of a fox dressed as a bishop; it has been suggested that as the crook of the staff is turned outwards the bishop held more than one see.[15] The four pillars may have come from a four-poster bed. In the very centre a panel has been inserted with a carving of the Pieta, 'an elegant and well-carved representation of Christ after the crucifixion',[16] in the lap of the Virgin; the inclusion of a crown of thorns and the implements of a crucifixion suggest it came from France or another Roman Catholic country. The reredos remains in position today, although the altar or communion table was brought forward a little in the 1970s.

His personal acquaintance with Betton and Evans—Sir John Betton was Mayor of Shrewsbury in 1816, as Pemberton's father had been in 1808—led the rector to purchase more of their stained glass for St. Laurence's. The upper tracery of the large north transept window contains further coats-of-arms: at the top the Pemberton arms (minus the chevron where, presumably, damage has led to replacement by plain glass) impaling the arms of Augustus Pechell, the rector's father-in-law; below left the arms of the More family, from whom Pemberton's uncle had inherited the Millichope estate in 1792, and whose heir the rector was; and bottom right the arms of the Rev. Richard Wilding, Rector of Easthope but also curate at Church Stretton from 1779, who died in 1820. It seems likely that at the same time as the north window was being embellished, another coat-of-arms was being inserted in the head of the west window. This, of course, was to commemorate the gift of Bonham Norton's

Flemish roundels in the north side window in the chancel

wife, Jane, although the arms are those of Owen of Condover Hall, where she was brought up (she is remembered on the benefaction boards as 'the Widow Owen'), in the heraldic form used to denote a female, that is on a lozenge.

Robert Pemberton's generosity to the church was not at an end. He may have acquired the Flemish roundels in the two chancel windows, but these are described later as they were more likely purchased in the time of the last rector of the century, the Rev. Charles Noel-Hill. In 1823 Pemberton presented a silver chalice to make a matching pair with the one presented by Mrs. Coleman in memory of her husband in 1818 (see illustration on p.165). The new chalice is inscribed: 'The Gift of the Revd. Robert Norgrave Pemberton Rector of Church Stretton. A.D. 1823'. And on the reverse: 'This Cup is the New Testament IN MY BLOOD which is shed for you. Luke 22:20'. An uninscribed silver flagon may have been presented at the same time.

*

So much had happened in the short time since the new rector's arrival that some slackening of pace was inevitable. The appointment of a curate provided relief. Richard Wilding, who had given occasional assistance, died in June 1820. His obituary[17] highlighted his public roles: 'As a magistrate he was possessed of quick discernment, solid judgment and strict integrity. As a clergyman he had an extensive share of learning, and was sincerely attached to the doctrines and discipline of the Church of England'. It also paid tribute to him as a family man, a good landlord and a benefactor of the poor. The next year the Rev. Preston Nunn, brother of the John Nunn who had assisted Thomas Coleman as his health declined, came as curate and conducted his first baptism on 30 September 1821. From then on, as the registers reveal, he officiated at almost all baptisms, marriages and funerals; Pemberton took the occasional one, perhaps when the curate was away. Preston Nunn was to serve as curate for the next 56 years and for much of that time he must have been the minister with whom most parishioners dealt. We have no record of Sunday services from this period, but it seems likely that for the first half of his time as rector Pemberton would have played the leading role.

The respite after the first busy years of Pemberton's incumbency did not last long. In 1823 the wardens had to meet a bill of £7 8s. 11d. for lead and materials for the repair of the tower—which suggests that the flat roof was leaking —and smaller costs for the repair of the clock and, in 1824, for laying a drain in the churchyard. But the real bombshell came late in 1826 when the churchwardens' accounts record that the end wall of the south transept was in a dangerous and dilapidated state. Thomas Corfield was asked to carry out an urgent survey and to make recommendations on action to be taken.

Thomas Corfield's sketch of his repair of the end wall of the south transept in 1827

His report, dated January 1827,[18] offered two possible solutions, one much cheaper than the other. His first proposal was 'to take the stone work of the end entirely down and rebuild it with the same materials as far as they will answer, reapplying the outer part of the stone work of the window by shortening the same to admit the height of the stone work of the present door which would be reapplied under the centre of the window'. This resiting of the door made good sense as the transept was no longer a side chapel but an extension of congregational seating, and the entrance and exit would be made more accessible. It would also allow an additional pew to be inserted, where the passage to the door had been at the back on the west side; its sale would raise £10 towards costs. He advised the rector and wardens that 'the mullions and the Gothic work in the inner part of the window being so much decayed must be replaced with new and be re-glazed'. There were additional costs for an inner door, the extra pew, plastering inside and out, supporting the roof and some retiling. The estimated total cost was £120, reduced by the sale of the pew. If this scheme were deemed too expensive, he said that for about £25 he could move the door under the window by removing its pointed arch, fit an inner door and new pew, brick up the old doorway, replaster and, most important, secure the wall by 'introducing an iron chain and bar one-and-a-half inches in diameter through the wall from the inside of the steeple and continuing the same above the present wood ceiling, secured on the outside by an engine-turned screw and iron escutcheon'.

Figures from the head of the south transept window

The Vestry meeting on 11 January 1827 recognised the seriousness of the situation, unanimously approved his first proposal and invited him to prepare a detailed plan. The wardens engaged local craftsmen to do the work: Ellis's were paid £67 'for repairing the church'; William Lewis, glazier, £7 13s. 4d.; James Edwards, carpenter, £19 19s. 6d.; and Thomas Gough, decorator, £3 18s. 9d. Thomas Corfield's bill was for £6 19s. 5d. The total cost seems to have been about the expected net £110. Even a cursory inspection of the window reveals new tracery, much lighter than in the north transept window. It was surely at this opportunity that stained glass was inserted in the head of the window, for Hardwick[19] described 'the figure of St Laurence the patron saint, and below that of the canonised King Ethelbert of East Anglia' killed by the wife of King Offa in 792, and another figure with mitre and crozier. These figures may still be seen today; the inclusion of King Ethelbert, if Hardwick's identification is correct, is hard to explain—unless it was because of his burial at Hereford. It seems probable that the removal of the wall brought to light the stone coffin that now stands outside near the north door. Slater's *Shropshire Directory* for 1850 states that it was found, with a lid and an alabaster slab bearing an illegible inscription, some years earlier beneath the south transept. It appears then to have been taken to 'The Hermitage' in the Rectory Wood[20] and brought back when the rectory and its lands were sold a century later. One theory is that it is the coffin of the founder of the Lady Chapel in the south transept in the early Middle Ages.[21]

Four years after the rebuilding of the south wall, another Vestry meeting, on 17 March 1831, agreed to build a vestry. Such meetings, in spite of their name, were not held in the vestry, but more probably in the Buck's Head or the room above the Market Hall. No doubt the rector was very conscious of the inadequacy of the tiny room near the tower stairs that had always been the only place for clerical vestments. The new vestry was only half the size of the present one, though when it was later extended the original plaque dated 1831 was attached to the new end wall.

Of course the construction of the vestry necessitated the removal of the old south porch, visible in the earliest paintings of that side of the church. When it was dismantled a Flemish coin of the time of King James I was discovered in the foundations,[22] which may possibly indicate when the porch had been erected or repaired. The important question in 1831 was this: when the vestry was built, what would replace the south door which had been the principal entrance to the church since the erection of the original Norman building? Clearly an answer had been agreed before the vestry plans were drawn up, but with the north door unused, and in any case unsuitable because it faced north, and the west end blocked by the tiered seating which was necessary to accommodate the congregation, it must have involved considerable debate. Robert Pemberton's solution, for which he gained the approval of the 16 persons

John Homes Smith's drawing of the church c.1840
with the first record of the new vestry (SRRC)

present at the March 1831 meeting, was to raise the 'gallery' above head height and create a new entrance in the west wall. The anxieties about cost were allayed when the rector said that the £13 in the Widow Owen's fund would pay for the insertion of a west door and he would bear the cost of raising the gallery, so long as he could have the use of the old materials and personally dispose of the two pews which would be at the front of the new gallery. One of the church-wardens at least, James Edwards, the carpenter, will have strongly supported the rector! He was also given the task of building the new vestry which he thought could be accomplished for £25 — out of the church rates — if, again, he could reuse the old materials. The work went ahead and the Norman south entrance, used by generations of churchgoers for seven hundred years, was replaced by the west doorway that remains to this day. Access to the gallery, with 87 'free sittings', was by means of stairs on each side of the church rising eastwards from the passage left along the inside of the west wall. The gallery was supported by four pillars across the front, two posts and the rear stairways, and decorated at the front with 'a singular figure of a seraphim with a book spread open on the breast' taken from the old vestry.[23]

In the 12 years since Robert Pemberton had come to Stretton, the pews had been reordered, the 'gallery' and organ removed from the chancel to the west end, the east window and reredos installed and other windows embellished, the end wall of the south transept rebuilt and the door moved, a vestry constructed, the gallery raised and a new west door inserted as the main entrance to the church. Yet there were more changes to come. The lighting continued to be provided by chandeliers, first mentioned in the wardens' accounts in 1818, but as parishioners' domestic comforts slowly improved, questions began to be pressed about heating in the church. A small stove was placed in the new vestry and payments for coal began to appear in the accounts, but it was not until the winter of 1841-42 that there is the first evidence of heating in the church itself. This is the payment by the wardens of £2 10s. 7d., plus £1 4s. for carriage, for a delivery of coke, which then cost 1s. a hundredweight. In December 1842 it was agreed that no more than £3 10s. a year should be expended from church rates for the warming of the church. Since there were pipes and gratings before the 1867-68 restoration, it seems clear that from the start the heating was provided by a large stove which heated water for pipes running below the level of the church floor and causing warm air to rise through the gratings. The stove was in the present boiler-house under the vestry but was then approached from the other side, where the south aisle now

The west door today. The entrance was opened in 1831 on the initiative of the Rev. Robert Pemberton

stands. The first payment for fire insurance was made in 1859.

Before the heating was installed other developments took place. At the Vestry meeting on 26 June 1832 it was agreed 'to take into consideration a proposition by the Rev. R.N. Pemberton to add at his own expense a piece of machinery to the organ with barrels containing sundry tunes and therefore dispense with the organist, providing the parishioners at their expense will pay a proper person to attend to the same'. It is by no means certain that this proposal was ever put into effect, or perhaps it did not work well or was disliked by the congregation, because in 1834 it is recorded that Samuel Humphreys was paid 3s.

for blowing the organ and Mr. Edwards for tuning it. Sir Stephen Glynne, at least, had considered it 'a good organ'.[24]

In 1833-34 the north transept was reroofed with new Broseley tiles and the gutters repaired at a cost of about £34, the rector contributing £5. When it was finished the masons and carpenters were treated to six quarts of ale—at 3d. a pint. It was decided in 1841 to reroof the nave, still referred to as the west aisle, again with Broseley tiles at a cost of £40. It was not until 1860 that Broseley tiles were placed on the roof of the south transept. Meanwhile, at the 1839 Vestry meeting on 6 May Pemberton's offer to provide oak boards and joists for a floor in the vestry was accepted; the parish agreed to carry out the work and to pay for new flags in the nave. A few weeks later, after the archdeacon had drawn attention to the need for repair on the tower, further estimates were sought. But after 1841 Pemberton signed no more records of meetings in the wardens' accounts and the impetus for maintenance and development was temporarily lost.

The many changes in the church between 1818 and 1841 led to successive reappraisals of the roles of the non-clerical staff. In July 1822 Thomas Lloyd agreed to execute the office of parish clerk, including the winding of the church clock, cleaning the church, washing the surplices and linen, tolling the bells and clearing snow for £9 a year; Thomas Gough, who had wound the clock, and Mrs. Holmes, who had cleaned the church, lost their jobs. Nine years later, however, the tasks were reassigned, with the roles of sexton and clerk combined for £8 8s. per annum, and Mrs. Hill appointed, at £1 5s. per annum, to clean and air the church. It is interesting that the entry in the accounts includes ringing the curfew, still a practice at the end of the century to advise late walkers on the hills where the town lay. In February 1838 the roles of clerk and sexton were separated: Thomas Lloyd, later succeeded by John Lucas, continued as clerk for £6 per annum plus the usual fees—marriages 1s. 8d., churchings 4d., burials 1s. (non-residents 2s.)—while John Hill became sexton at an annual salary of £3, plus 1s. 6d. for each grave dug (non-residents 3s.). The sexton had to ring the bell for the usual services, wind the clock and act as beadle, 'keeping order and being in attendance in the Church during divine services, and also to obey any orders or directions of the Ministers and Churchwardens'.

*

Robert Pemberton did not confine his activities to the church. He played a prominent role in the development of education and provision for the poor. As one of the trustees of the school, in Burway House since 1779, the rector took a keen personal interest in its progress. The Report of the Commissioners into Charities published in 1839 states that he acted as Treasurer and prepared the accounts for an annual audit at Michaelmas. The school's total annual income, from the sources and benefactions described in the last chapter, amounted to £42 14s. 4d. The schoolmaster, appointed by the trustees, was paid £40 a year and resided in the house free of any rents or taxes; he also taught the Sunday School and no doubt accompanied the scholars to church. In 1840 James and Ann Heighway were master and mistress of the school. There were 60 free scholars, boys and girls, and 11 who paid for their instruction—between 2s. and 7s. a quarter which met the school's costs for slates, books and coal. There were another 15 children who attended the Sunday School only. During Thomas Coleman's incumbency, the archdeacon had reported, 'the Madras system', the 'monitorial' system of instruction developed in India by Andrew Bell, was introduced, and in 1827 the trustees had joined Rector Pemberton in aligning the school with the plan of the Church of England National Society founded in 1811 and using Bell's methods. The commissioners mentioned that, in addition to the 3 Rs for all, the girls were taught sewing in a separate room and that the accommodation for boarders was not used. Archdeacon Corbett, himself a trustee, had no doubt about the value of the contribution of the rector and his wife: 'Through the attention Mr. and Mrs. Pemberton pay to the conduct of the school and through Mr. Pemberton's bounty in money it has now become a very useful institution'.[25] Perhaps the Pembertons' involvement was some compensation for the fact that they had no family of their own. Unfortunately

*T. Mason's picture of Church Stretton from the east c.1830.
The Talbot on the left, the church and the rectory behind it
are all clearly visible. (Town Council)*

the commissioners' warning in 1839 that John Mainwaring's legacies to the school, the poor and the churchyard should be invested in permanent securities, instead of being held by Samuel Wilding (who paid the annual interest), was not heeded. The Commission on Charities for Elementary Education reported in 1906 that when Wilding's business failed, the £100 left for the school by Mainwaring was reduced to £31 12s. 1d. Pemberton himself left £200 in Government Stock for the benefit of the school.

The great majority of the schoolchildren enjoyed a free education because their parents were poor. Most of the menfolk worked in agriculture, and early nineteenth century Directories comment on 'the immense quantities of good wool' chiefly sold to dealers in Yorkshire. The malting business was important in the town, while the poor were 'chiefly employed in the making of coarse linen cloth which is used for the packing of hops and wool'.[26] In 1840 *Robson's Directory* reported 'an extensive woollen manufactory at which employment is

given to a number of hands', and by 1851 it was flourishing, under the name of Duppa, Banks & Co., in a deep valley about a quarter of a mile from the town, 'the machinery being turned by a mountain stream'.[27] This, of course, was the Carding Mill.

After the Napoleonic Wars prices fell sharply and poverty stalked the countryside. Provision for the destitute changed markedly in Pemberton's time. In 1827 the rector and wardens allowed John Robinson, draper, to have the two allotments on Picklescott Hill and the Long Mynd allocated to the poor by the Enclosure Award in exchange for his building, at his own cost, two or three almshouses

The site of the old Poor House,
now the Town Council Offices

*A drawing of the Town Hall which replaced Bonham Norton's Market Hall
in the Square in 1839. It was demolished in 1963.
(By kind permission of David Bilbey)*

on each side of the poor house (now the Town Council office in High Street) to
be occupied by the poor of the parish. When the Poor Law Amendment Act was
passed in 1834 Church Stretton became the centre of a Poor Law Union of 15
parishes. The first thought of the Guardians was to enlarge the existing workhouse, but the site was too small and the townspeople opposed a central situation. They therefore purchased for £280 two acres on the northern outskirts of
the town, a quarter of a mile along the Shrewsbury Road. Here they built a new
workhouse designed to accommodate 120 persons, with four courtyards and
men and women segregated. The one remaining part of the building is today
incorporated in the school swimming bath.

In spite of the widespread poverty the population of the Strettons rose
rapidly. In the first national census of 1801 the parish had 924 inhabitants; by
1821 this had risen to 1,226; and by 1841 to 1,604. The Rev. William Harries,
appointed as a second curate in 1834, compiled some interesting demographic
statistics for the previous 20 years.[28] In that period there were 833 baptisms
(male 397, female 436), 146 marriages and 400 burials (male 198, female 202);
he calculated a total of 98 illegitimate births. With baptisms double the number
of burials the population was growing at a very rapid rate. His analysis of age
at death is of particular interest: it reveals a high infant mortality rate, substan-

tial numbers dying at all stages of life, but more than a quarter of people reaching over 70 years of age. He believed the infant mortality rate was influenced by intemperance. By 1841 there were 860 persons and 183 houses in Church Stretton itself; in All Stretton 454 persons and 88 houses; in Little Stretton 165 persons and 41 houses; and in Minton 125 persons and 34 houses.[29] The most dramatic building development of these years was the erection of a Town Hall in 1839 after the decay of Bonham Norton's Market Hall. The site was purchased by the inhabitants, and the building cost of £1,000 met by the subscriptions of the local gentry. Robert Pemberton himself acted as Treasurer and, along with the Earl of Darlington and the Hon. R.H. Clive, headed the subscription list with a gift of £100. The restriction of the cost to £1,000 may have been unwise as few people have had a good word to say for the design or appearance of the Town Hall.

The population increase also raised the question of the seating capacity of the church. The archdeacon sent out a short printed questionnaire to all incumbents in South Shropshire in 1839. It asked if their church could accommodate 50% of the population or, if not, the ratio of population to seating; how many parishioners lived more than two miles from the church; whether there was enough accommodation for the poor; and what was the state of the church. The rector's responses for Church Stretton are written on the surviving questionnaire.[30] The population (1831) was 1,302 and the church could accommodate 500; 440 people in the parish—over 30% - lived more than two miles from the church; an additional 200 free 'kneelings' would be sufficient to provide for the poor; extra accommodation could be made by altering the pews and building galleries in the north and south transepts; the roof of the tower needed repair, but otherwise the condition of the church, chancel and parsonage was good.

The most noteworthy feature of the replies is the estimation of the seating capacity at 500. The church of today, with its extra aisles but of course no gallery, is more than full with 350. But Pemberton allowed only 18 inches' width per person, so the box pews must have been packed tight and the children (there were 140 in the school) and those poor who came crammed into the 66 seats under the gallery and the 40 in it. The answer to the inadequate capacity 30 years later was to be not galleries in the transepts but aisles added to them. In the long run the problem was solved by the construction of daughter churches in All Stretton and Little Stretton and the gradual decline in church attendance in the twentieth century.

*

By the time of the accommodation inquiry the rector was playing a smaller role in the life of the church and planning to move out of the parish. During the 1820s and early 1830s he had made further improvements to the rectory, raising the height of the large central room with its southern aspect, and probably building a service wing to the east and north of the staircase block. He had leased, and then in 1833 purchased, from Mrs. Coleman further land to add to the glebe surrounding the parsonage. The next step had been to build a brick wall to mark the boundary between his estate and the town, probably at least in part using the old bricks from the former Hall demolished by Coleman because different sized bricks can still be discerned in the lower part of the wall. His extensive purchases of land and property in the parish meant that virtually all the land between the town and the Long Mynd belonged to him. Near World's End a lodge marked the beginning of a carriage drive through Pemberton's new plantations. But in 1832, when his uncle Thomas Pemberton died childless, he also inherited the Millichope estate in Corvedale which had belonged for centuries to the More family and had passed to Thomas Pemberton when their line came to an end in 1792.[31] Robert Pemberton decided to demolish the old house at Millichope and to build the large Italianate mansion which is still standing.

As the rector's time and energy were increasingly absorbed in the management of his estates and the planning and construction of the new hall at Millichope, the momentum for church improvement was lost and more of the

Ashford House, the home of the long-serving curate, Preston Nunn

ministerial duties were performed by others. A second curate, William Harries, was appointed in 1834 to assist Preston Nunn. The rector had a 'neat cottage' built for him near Bank House which he bought in 1835. By 1837 Harries had been succeeded by Sebastian James Gambier, who gave way to Thomas Atkinson in 1841, who in turn was followed by William Day, 1843-48. While these young curates came and went, Preston Nunn continued as senior curate and, as the years passed, in effect as vicar. He lived in High Street at Ashford House, which had been bought and extended by Pemberton. Nunn's two brothers were clergymen, too, and his sister married another; all three took orders after graduating at Cambridge. Preston Nunn himself had been educated at St. Bees' College before ordination, and had come to Church Stretton as curate at the age of 32. He lost his wife in 1848 and only one of his four children remained alive when he died in 1877 at the age of 87. The curates conducted almost all the rites of passage: Robert Pemberton officiated at no marriages after 1838, no funerals after 1844, and at only occasional baptisms in the 1840s. With two paid curates he must have left them to conduct many Sunday services also. He was present at no meetings recorded in the wardens' accounts after 1841, for in that year he ceased to reside in the parish and moved to the new Millichope Hall. It was not uncommon for rectors to be non-resident: indeed, a countrywide survey of 1827 showed fewer than half of the ten thousand incumbents who responded living in their parishes.[32] Yet a contemporary vouched for his pastoral diligence: 'Although away so much Mr. Pemberton did not neglect his parish, and I cannot tell all the good work he did in it. His beautiful grounds, which were very extensive, were always open to his people; he knew every parishioner personally, and never missed visiting every house at least once every year'.[33]

It was in Pemberton's middle years at Stretton that the national reform movement gathered impetus and culminated in a series of important acts in the late 1820s and early 1830s. The Test Act was repealed, giving greater rights to Nonconformists, and Catholic Emancipation carried before the Whigs came to power in 1830. Two years later the Great Reform Act extended the franchise and effected some redistribution of Parliamentary seats; Stretton Town Hall was soon to become a polling centre for the constituency of South Shropshire. There followed the abolition of slavery and the Poor Law Amendment Act. But it was the projected reform of tithes and church rates that generated some of the greatest interest in rural areas and was most likely to affect the church in Stretton. 'The regressive nature of tithe was particularly burdensome at a time of depressed agricultural incomes'.[34] The Tithe Commutation Act of 1836, which converted the great tithe of grain into a money payment calculated at about two-thirds of the gross value of the tithe, was therefore welcomed by those who had to pay, and accepted readily by most clergy who knew that often they were able to collect only half the due amount. The collection of tithe at

Stretton had been farmed out by John Mainwaring for a fixed annual sum, but the commuted tithe was now worth £505 per annum to Robert Pemberton.[35] In the same year twin acts were passed to allow marriage in licensed Nonconformist chapels or registry offices, and to appoint local registrars of births, marriages and deaths. Anglican clergy felt that both were blows to their status, to marriage, and even to baptism as formerly the parish register of baptism served as proof of birth.

The struggle over church rates was much greater. 'Until the year 1820 parishioners obeyed the law and voted money, either annually or whenever necessary, to repair the naves of their churches, to supply it with ornaments, and to maintain the churchyard and its walls or fences'.[36] Each Easter at a Vestry meeting the churchwardens presented their accounts and estimates for the coming year and a rate was fixed. All parishioners had a legal right to attend, but the rate, though it applied to all occupiers of property, was never imposed on the poor. Antagonism to the rate increased after an Act of 1818 voted £1,000,000 to build churches (especially in the new industrial areas), which led to some Dissenters having to pay rates to two Anglican churches. Annual Vestry meetings in some places became scenes of passion and strife. Some thought that the very establishment of the Church was in danger. A government bill of 1834 to abolish rates and make the repair of churches a charge on the Treasury passed the Commons and only failed to become law because the government fell. It is unlikely that there were disruptive Vestry meetings in Stretton, but in 1822 it was agreed unanimously to exclude certain items from the church rate: payments to singers and ringers at the visitation, any expenditure on organ or organist, and the purchase of candles other than the six pounds used each year to provide illumination for the bell-ringers. In an effort to keep the rates down the wardens were told in 1843 that the cost of the visitation dinner must not exceed £2. By 1845, with a growing population, the rate actually fell to 1d. in the £. Yet church rates were not to be abolished until over 20 years later.

There are no printed sermons or other writings to shed light on Robert Pemberton's theological views or churchmanship. His activities and interests, however, provide valuable clues. His concern to beautify the chancel reflects the contemporary High Church emphasis on 'mystery' and 'the beauty of holiness' as a reaction to the element of 'plainness' in Low Church circles. His enthusiasm for education and his success in developing the school in Church Stretton on the National plan echo a High Church priority for it was an inner group of such clergy who were instrumental in setting up 'The National Society for Promoting the Education of the Poor in the Principles of the Established Church' in 1811, although Evangelicals were also ardent supporters of educational progress, especially to encourage the reading of the Bible. His personal commitment to charitable giving and to sacred learning were alike typical of the High Church party. It is very doubtful, however, if he would have had much sympathy with the Oxford Movement whose *Tracts for the Times*, published between 1833 and 1841, leaned to the academic rather than the practical and were seen to play down the differences between the Church of England and the Church of Rome. Pemberton lived just long enough to see Dr. Hampden, Regius Professor of Divinity at Oxford and the '*bête noire*' of the Tractarians, consecrated as Bishop of Hereford.

Robert Pemberton was a wealthy man. A map of his estates in Church Stretton in 1834[37] shows 76 different holdings: 19 belonged to the living, but the rest were his by freehold or copyhold and stretched from the Rectory Field to Crossbanks, besides other land along Shrewsbury Road and on the east side of Watling Street. From the church he drew an income, from commuted tithe and the glebe land, of £565 per annum, at a time when the schoolmaster was paid £40, but his income from other property was far greater. His rent-books[38] show a half-yearly income from his estates at Church Stretton, Llandrinio, Roddington, Halston and New Mills, Millichope and the Roden Estate which varied, in the years 1833-48, between £2,100 and £2,500. So his annual income was about £5,000. As patron he also owned the rectory and had inherited Millichope Park where he built his stately home.

The rector was not only non-resident in the 1840s but often absent from his cure. Three licences for absence still exist.[39] Perhaps Pemberton sometimes offici-ated at Munslow Church, near Millichope, where the east window is very remi-niscent of the one at St. Laurence's and almost certainly given by Pemberton who is commem-orated by a monument. In any event, the diocese rewarded him in November 1846 with the gift of the prebend of Moreton and Whaddon. It was two years later, and while he was attending the confirmation service at Church Stretton, that he was suddenly taken ill. Although no doctor was called immediately as it

Commemorative plaque to Rector Pemberton near the spot where he was buried on the north side of the church

seemed to be no more than a bilious attack, his condition deteriorated rapidly and he died at Millichope Hall on 7 October 1848. He was only 57. In his will he asked to be buried in a vault on the north side of St. Laurence's under a nave window that disappeared when the aisle was built, but where the commemorative plaque can still be seen.

Pemberton had made his will in 1834, shortly after inheriting Millichope, and when he still had hopes of children to succeed him. These hopes had disappeared by the time of his death and, although he left his wife a substantial income and his personal effects, the estates were bequeathed to a distant cousin, Charles Orlando Childe. It was stipulated, however, that his heir must assume the name of Pemberton, either simply or linked with another surname, and bear the arms of Pemberton and More. If this were not done within a year the estate would go to the next named heir. One senses here the great sadness that he had no son to succeed him and the strong desire to perpetuate the family name.

Pemberton did his utmost to keep the living within his family. On his death, the will laid down, any qualified son of Edward Cludde or of Sir John Salusbury Piozzi-Salusbury, who were other distant cousins, should be presented to Church Stretton. Even if another clergyman were appointed he would have to resign if a son of one of the above became qualified to succeed to the incumbency. Such a son would receive as rector the income of Pemberton's estates at Church Stretton and Acton Scott as well as all his divinity books. In the event, the advowson went with the estate to the renamed Charles Orlando Childe-Pemberton. A sum of £200 was bequeathed to the Trustees of the National School at Church Stretton to be invested for the benefit of the school, and a further £200 if a school were established at Munslow. The £20 left to each of his head gardeners was increased to £100 in a codicil of 1842.

Pemberton's affluence is revealed by the evaluation of his belongings.[40] His wife received all his carriages and jewels except the diamond ornaments that had belonged to the Mores. Fittings, furniture and other items at the rectory specifically bequeathed as heirlooms were valued at over £2,000; furniture, plate, china and glass at Millichope at nearly £5,000. Among the bequests to his successor at the rectory were three dozen bottles of sherry, ten dozen of port, four dozen of Madeira and 38 dozen of Tawney Port, of a total value of over £100! The valuations afford, too, a fascinating glimpse of his personal interests: the rectory dining room was home to a large organ, while display chests in dining and drawing rooms contained his collections of minerals, shells and coins; Millichope boasted a library, gallery and music room.

Robert Pemberton was clearly a gentleman of culture and learning. He beautified the church and could have delivered a weighty sermon. He was also a man of expensive tastes—and able to afford them. Yet the personal quality highlighted in his obituary in the *Shrewsbury Chronicle* was his generosity.

'Endeared by his kindness and cordiality to everyone, his loss will be felt even wider than his generosity extended. No-one could boast of a more extensive circle of acquaintance since his benevolence extended to all. His kindness to his poor parishioners will be remembered with gratitude, and will raise a monument to his memory more lasting than the marble sepulchre since it emanated from a pure desire to alleviate the distresses of unprovided age or the undeserved pangs of destitution'.[41] Such eulogies are not uncommon in obituaries, but to put a figure on his munificence is unusual and the amount extraordinary: 'He was accustomed to spend about £4,000 annually in paying old and decayed parishioners to take care of his grounds who were otherwise unable to support themselves'. Such a sum, even for one so wealthy, must surely be greatly exaggerated, but generous he clearly was—as well as, according to the paper, unassuming, kind, affable and truly beloved. A parishioner later wrote: 'I well remember his kindness on the Coronation Day of Queen Victoria. In addition to feasting all the children on the lawn in front of the Rectory, it was thrown open to visitors and lunch provided. Mrs. Pemberton played several pieces on the organ in the dining room', before presiding at a dinner in the Market Hall for women of all classes. The same parishioner, a doctor's wife, described Mr. and Mrs. Pemberton as liberal subscribers to every good cause. 'One was a Dorcas Society which was carried on by several ladies and garments given to the poor. Mr. Pemberton started a Clothing Club shortly before his death, putting a donation into the Savings Bonds as an emergency fund'. Another of Mrs. Pemberton's charitable acts was to 'purchase stores in large quantities, such as flannel etc., and sell them to the poor at half price'.[42]

St. Laurence's debt to the Rev. Robert Norgrave Pemberton is expressed by Sir Stephen Glynne in his notes on the church[43] made on his visit in about 1830: 'The interior of the church presents a beautiful appearance, being very handsomely fitted up in the best taste by the present rector'. Hardwick shortly afterwards singled out his most striking gifts and his most permanent memorial in words still echoed by perceptive visitors who arrive early in the day when the sun is in the east: 'A new approach from the west into the nave was completed in the month of August 1831 with large handsome folding doors from whence the grand eastern window is seen to the greatest advantage and unexpectedly strikes the beholder at first view with amazement and pleasure at its imposing and illumined effect'.[44]

11
VICTORIAN RESTORATION AND GROWTH

In the mid-nineteenth century Church Stretton was clearly changing in character. It remained a small market town with one principal street, and the sharp increase in population in the previous 50 years had slowed down, but it was attracting growing numbers of visitors. *Bagshaw's Gazetteer* of 1851 reads like a travel brochure:

> The secluded and romantic situation of Church Stretton, the grand majestic character of the surrounding scenery – its proximity to scenes of great and historical interest – the mildness and salubrity of the air, which is at the same time peculiarly bracing – its general exemption from contagious and epidemic disease, and the excellence of the water, all conduce to render it peculiarly attractive to parties in pursuit of health and pleasure. During the summer months it is a very favourite resort of visitors from the neighbouring towns, the great variety of the scenery rendering it almost impossible to weary the most fastidious taste. When it has become more easy of access by railway it will no doubt become a favourite retreat for persons from all parts of the kingdom.

The advent of the railway in Stretton was already within sight when that was published. Work on the Shrewsbury and Hereford Railway had begun in January 1851 and was proceeding fast on the completion of the line through Strettondale and the building of a station in Church Stretton. The day when the first train would come through Stretton was fixed for Tuesday, 20 April 1852. Pealing church bells greeted the great day and the Union Jack was unfurled on the tower of St. Laurence's. People poured into the town from the neighbouring settlements and outlying farms. The procession to the station down what was still called Lake Lane, but would become Station Road and then Sandford Avenue, was led by the Dorrington brass band. The original station was on the opposite side of the road from its present day successor, with sidings, goods warehouse, coal wharf and cattle landing near where Polymer Laboratories now stands. The first train steamed in from Shrewsbury shortly after noon with 25 carriages pulled by two locomotives, suitably festooned with flags and greenery, and an open truck carrying a brass band and a battery of small cannons which announced the train's approach. When it had left for Ludlow, then the end of the line, the celebrations began with children's games, followed by a community tea, with roast beef, plum pudding and a due proportion of ale for the inmates of the workhouse, and concluded with an evening dance in the Town Hall.

Church Stretton would never be the same again. As *Bagshaw's Gazetteer* had forecast, more and more visitors came and the residents travelled more widely. Church Stretton went on growing slowly, but the days of the remote market town were finally over. For good or ill its future was now irrevocably linked with the world beyond its hills.

These exciting developments challenged the church to keep abreast of change. It was an opportunity that a new young rector might have grasped eagerly. Unfortunately Pemberton's successor was in no position to do that. As his will had laid down, that successor was a distant relation, the Rev. Charles Arthur Salusbury, second surviving son of Sir John Salusbury Piozzi-Salusbury, himself the son of an Italian merchant and former High Sheriff of Flintshire who had married Harriet Pemberton in 1814. The new rector, who came from the Winchester diocese, was 25 years of age and a graduate of Jesus College, Oxford, where he had taken his B.A. in 1846. He was instituted at Stretton on 10 January 1849, on the presentation of Robert Pemberton's executors. Records show, however, that the curates, Preston Nunn and William Day, continued to conduct all baptisms, marriages and funerals; the register of other services has not survived. Perhaps Charles Salusbury was too ill to undertake church duties for he was described as 'far gone in consumption'.[1] He died on 9 July, just six months after his institution.

All Robert Pemberton's hopes of keeping the living in the family were dashed. The new patron, Charles Orlando Childe-Pemberton, who had coupled the former rector's surname with his own in order to inherit his estates, turned to a friend he had known since boyhood and with whom he had lived 'almost like brothers'.[2] On 10 October 1849, just three months after Salusbury's death, he presented the Rev. Hugh Owen Wilson to the living of Church Stretton. It was to prove a good choice. Wilson was, like his predecessor, 25 years old, but of more robust constitution. He was the second son of Charles Townshend Wilson, a gentleman of Shrewsbury, and grandson of the Ven. Hugh Owen, Archdeacon of Salop and the celebrated historian of Shrewsbury. He was educated at Shrewsbury School and Worcester College, Oxford, where he graduated B.A. in 1846, M.A. in 1849. He was ordained deacon in 1848, priest 1849, and had served briefly as a curate at Prees. In 1851 he is recorded as leading a bachelor existence in the rectory with three servants, but 10 years later he was married with three children.[3] The first child of Hugh Wilson and his wife Charlotte Elizabeth was born on 26 April 1856 and named Harriet Elizabeth Jane; she is commemorated in the window on the south side of the

*Window on the south side of the chancel
dedicated to the first child of the
Rev. Hugh Owen Wilson
who died in infancy*

chancel, for sadly she died in infancy on 4 February 1857. His wife was to bear him, however, over the next 20 years, a further eight daughters and seven sons— though it was he who died young. Of their succeeding offspring, one son died in infancy and another at the age of 15. Their eldest surviving child, whom he baptised on 20 June 1858, was Harriet Catherine; their last, baptised on 3 June 1877, was Constance Douglas, who throughout her life had to bear the name of the brother who had died six weeks before she was born. She is of particular interest to Church Stretton people of today, for she left the C.D. Wilson Bequest which since 1972 has provided an honorarium for one or two Parish Visitors to the elderly and lonely.[4]

The new rector was quickly immersed in his church duties, conducting his first baptism and first funeral in November 1849. He continued to share these responsibilities with Preston Nunn, 'who was well known to all the people and knew their wants'.[5] Gradually he allowed the curate to conduct about two-thirds of the baptisms, marriages and burials recorded in the register; no doubt they shared the preaching and reading of services. These were held at 11. a.m. and 3 p.m. on Sundays, with a sermon at each service; Holy Communion was administered every month 'and at other stated times'. The nationwide Census of Church Attendance in 1851,[6] which gave St. Laurence's seating capacity as 500, recorded 300 as the average morning attendance, with 120 in the after-noon. There was also an average of 53 worshippers on Sundays in the work-house where the chapel could seat 65. An invitation issued by the Loyal Caradoc Lodge of the Independent Order of Odd Fellows names the rector as the preacher at their Triennial Meeting on 13 August 1850,[7] their service in the parish church following a procession through the town.

The church from the north-east by John Homes Smith c.1850. The door east of the tower door must have been the entrance to the old small vestry

In their responses to the archdeacon's articles of inquiry prior to his visitation in 1851,[8] the churchwardens stated that they regarded the rector as a person of sober and exemplary life and that all the services were conducted properly and in accordance with the Prayer Book. The church was reported to be clean and in good repair. The only change noted, and presumably a recent one, was that 'the small robing room in the chancel' had been taken down by the rector and the stone removed to the rectory. There were some minor exchanges of glebe land, particularly as a consequence of the building of the railway.

If little of note was happening in the church, the first two decades of Wilson's rectorship witnessed important developments in the town. In 1853 Samuel Glover Bakewell arrived in Church Stretton, bought up the Talbot coaching inn, in decline since the coming of the railway, and developed it as Stretton House, an asylum for upper and middle class gentlemen. After his death the business was sold to William Hyslop and later passed to his son, William Campbell Hyslop, under whom Stretton House prospered, the accommodation being extended and gardens laid out. The prospectus said that, 'Many inmates attend the parish church, while the chaplain also conducts services in the house and visits patients'. An asylum for ladies had been opened by Bakewell at Grove House in All Stretton. In the 1870s this was bought by Dr. McClintock and run by three generations of his family. Another significant new

Grove House, All Stretton, a mental asylum for ladies. It was owned by
Samuel Bakewell, who also owned Stretton House, an asylum for gentlemen.
Grove House was later run by three generations of McClintocks, doctors
and leading figures in the village (by kind permission of David Bilbey)

building was the Endowed Free School in Church Street to replace the
outgrown Burway House. It was erected in 1861 at a cost of £1,500 on land
donated by Charles Orlando Childe-Pemberton, the church's patron and Robert
Pemberton's legatee. The new school for boys and girls—now the public
library and information centre—had classrooms to accommodate 144 pupils

Church Stretton School, Church Street, opened in 1861.
It is now the Public Library

and a master's house, where the curate lives in 2002. Shortly afterwards the old Crown Inn was rebuilt and extended, reopening in 1865 as The Hotel where the more affluent visitors stayed; Joseph Chamberlain, then Lord Mayor of Birmingham, was to be among the guests in 1880.

But the development that most closely concerned St. Laurence's was the building of a nonconformist church in the town. Since the decay of the chapels at Minton and Womerton, near the southern and northern extremities of the parish, in the sixteenth and early seventeenth centuries, there had been no place of worship other than the parish church, apart from the short-lived noncon-formist meeting-houses like those registered in 1725, 1808 and 1833. But from the 1830s Primitive Methodists of the Bishop's Castle circuit had been at work in Church Stretton. The town 'was not fertile ground, but the northern and southern parts of the parish were, and meetings just beyond the parish boundary were probably accessible to the remoter parishioners'.[9] Primitive Methodist meetings were held in the northern part of the parish at All Stretton and Lower Wood, where a chapel was eventually opened in 1876, and in the southern part at Little Stretton and Minton. It was the Congregationalists, however, who built their chapel first. In 1858 some friends connected with the Congregationalists in Shrewsbury, Ludlow and Dorrington, 'who were inter-ested in the spiritual welfare of the town of Church Stretton, became anxious to hold services there'.[10] As there was no room available, they started outdoor services in the market area under the Town Hall. In the winter of 1858-59 they attracted 70 or 80 people to worship held in a carpenter's shop. They also established a

The United Reformed Church in High Street.
It was opened as a Congregational Chapel
in 1866

service and a Sunday School at All Stretton. On 14 February 1860 a church of seven members was formed under the auspices of Castle Gate Chapel and their minister, the Rev. E. Hill. For some years services in Church Stretton continued to be held in confined spaces, but then a site for a chapel in High Street was procured and the foundation stone laid in August 1865. The chapel, opposite the bottom of Cunnery Road, was completed at a cost of a little over £1,000 and opened for divine worship on 29 May 1866, when the service was led by the minister, the Rev. J. McKiddie, and the sermon preached by the renowned Rev. R.W. Dale of Carrs Lane, Birmingham.

*

No great initiatives in the church had been taken by Hugh Owen Wilson in his first decade and a half as rector. Perhaps he had been pre-occupied bringing up his large family and establishing himself in local society where he was a considerable landowner and magistrate. When he first thought of restoring St. Laurence's, he later confessed that the obstacles appeared too great. Whether or not he was influenced in any way by the progress on the Congregational church, it was early in 1866 that he decided it was 'Now or Never'.[11] He there-fore contacted Samuel Pountney Smith, a Shrewsbury architect already well known as a restorer of churches, and requested him to examine St. Laurence's to suggest how accommodation might be improved without altering the building and what 'restoration' he would propose. Pountney Smith paid a visit and drew a plan of the church but, as he explained in his letter dated 22 September 1866,[12] he found the rector's proposed condition too restrictive: 'I could not make up my mind what to recommend for without going beyond the present area of the building nothing in the way of improved arrangements, such as the present age demands, can be made'. However, he took a second look at it, with the aim of getting 'proper Church Order and if possible more accom-modation for worshippers, and this without destroying any interesting features of the ancient building'. This time he produced a plan which he thought worth carrying out and yet, considering that the church had to be wholly refitted, at a minimum cost. His chief proposals were:

1. To clear away all the wood fittings, except the gallery and the easternmost stalls in the chancel, and to put in new pews.
2. To remove the plaster ceiling from the nave, north transept and chancel, and to construct a new ceiling between the oak 'couples'.
3. To clear the walls of plaster or to repair it, taking steps to counter the damp at the foot of the walls.
4. To lower the floor of the church by a foot, filling or stopping down graves or vaults, and covering with nine inches of concrete, with extra concrete in the warming channels to prevent exhalations from below.

5. To cover the whole area with encaustic tiles.
6. To clean and varnish the roof timbers.
7. To remove the ringing floor of the tower and to adapt the clock-floor for the bell-ringers.
8. To build new aisles to both transepts, one for the children so that the gallery could be removed, and one to provide additional seating for general use.
9. To create an organ aisle on the north side of the chancel.

He recommended using as much as possible of the timber from the old pews, but 'the grotesque, incongruous and unsuitable carving' and the 'old Bedheads and purely domestic work', probably used to repair the oldest pews, would have to go. Clearly the seating was very different from the uniform pews of today.

His proposal to restore the tower lantern, 'the most interesting feature of the church', was imaginative. He knew that the ringers would oppose the loss of their floor and the shortening of the bell-ropes, but maintained that 'the additional height of wall over the tower arcade is necessary to the proportion of the aisles and the general interior'; the original ceiling would be restored to view and the 'ancient loop lights' would afford light and ventilation.

Another idea for which he had produced a detailed drawing[13] and probably discussed with the rector, was to extend the chancel on the north side, building a new outer wall to enclose the staircase and to provide a new Choir and Sacristy. The Choir, 12 feet square, would have been entered through an arch where the organ now stands, and the Sacristy through a door on the step before the communion rail. He went as far as proposing windows in both rooms, and planning a new external door in the east wall of the Sacristy. The idea seems never to have gone beyond the drawing-board.

In the initial report to the rector he set out reasons for some of his suggestions and answered possible questions. He argued that tiling was better and cheaper than wooden flooring for the pews; he proposed to shut the south door and to provide access to the new south aisle from the transept; any windows removed would be reused; the arcade openings of the new aisles would be harmonised with the old design; the chancel fittings would be separately designed; and the existing reredos preserved or replaced with unmistakably superior work. He concluded by asking for the rector's opinion and instructions, and promised to furnish detailed estimates and drawings.

Hugh Wilson's reply was clearly positive, for on 14 November Pountney Smith duly sent estimates, that for the restoration of the church,[14] excluding the cost of a new aisle or improvements to the heating system, came to £751 4s. 6d. The work on the floor, walls and ceiling of the chancel, with two new oak stalls, was estimated to cost £115 16s.

The church's response, at a Vestry meeting attended by Pountney Smith on 11 January 1867, was to agree unanimously on the desirability of restoring the church and to appoint a committee to raise funds for the improvements. It consisted of the rector and churchwardens, the curate, the patron and 13 church members who were substantial local figures. They also requested the architect to provide an estimate of the cost of adding a new aisle to the south transept but, probably to limit expense, they declined his proposal to build a north aisle and to remove the gallery. Certainly when the additional estimate was sent on 16 February it was for a south aisle only and amounted to £320 13s. 5d. He enclosed drawings of the arcades for the new aisle.

At the Vestry meeting on 12 April Pountney Smith's estimates were considered and it was resolved to omit the removal of the ringing floor and to opt to have the wall plaster repaired and coloured rather than stripped down to the masonry. These modifications may have been for financial reasons or on account of opposition. There was concern, too, that the churchwardens should 'appropriate the several sittings in the transepts to the present occupiers of them as near thereto as circumstances will permit'. But they did determine to employ Pountney Smith as architect and to draw up a proper contract. He replied promptly, accepting the appointment, outlining his responsibilities, and setting his fees at 5% of the total cost. The rector counter-signed this agreement on behalf of the committee.

A newspaper advertisement was placed inviting tenders for the work from builders and the plans and specifications displayed in the School House. Only one reply was received by the deadline of 15 May: William Jarvis of Shrewsbury costed the restoration of the church and chancel, but not the new aisle, at £1,190. The committee now sent the plans to the Incorporated Society for the Enlargement, Building and Repairing of Churches and Chapels for their approval and to solicit grant aid. The committee, at its meeting on 7 June, was clearly concerned at the Society's response which pointed out omissions from the plans and said further consideration must await their return, for the rector at once wrote back expressing the disappointment at any delay that would be felt by those who had subscribed liberally. The revised plans were dispatched a fortnight later and a rapid response received on 4 July. The Society now insisted that the width of free sittings must be 2 feet 9 inches (not the 2 feet 6 inches proposed) and the seats 13 inches deep; they also said that the pitch of the new aisle's lean-to roof was not steep enough and suggested a gable, that original masonry should not be chiselled, and that the planned access to the new aisle seats through the vestry, was objectionable. The architect sent a compliant reply, stating that he would remove one pew to give the greater width, and defending the proposed access to the aisle through the vestry as 'this has been done to suit ultimate restoration of the south porch', with a new vestry to be built by the priest's door when funds permitted. The rector advised the

Society that he would also like to remove the gallery, but the consequent loss of accommodation would be very unpopular in the parish.

The Society was satisfied and the revised plans bear their seal and the date 16 July.[15] Three days later the committee, which properly affirmed that 'free seats ought to be like other seats in size and form', agreed to ask the architect to seek new tenders from five builders, the architect accepting the wardens' request that the plaster ceiling should be removed before tenders were invited. On 7 October the committee unanimously resolved to accept the tender of Mr. Thomas Pugh of Corvedale, subject to the architect's approval.

Things then moved quickly. On 21 October 1867 the bishop gave his approval for the use of the schoolroom to accommodate up to 300 for divine service on Sundays at 11 and 3 during the restoration and enlargement of the church. Five days later Pountney Smith produced further detailed drawings and specifications for the builder, and work was able to begin, no doubt initially on the interior during the winter months. The first task was to dismantle and remove the old box pews, retaining any serviceable timber that could be reused. It is very likely that former occupiers claimed or purchased their pews, as some found their way into the Raven Inn at the corner of the Square and another to Greengates in High Street.

The existing 'stone, wood and brick flooring over the whole area of the church' was dug out to a depth of 18 inches. Any remains found were rein-terred, and graves and vaults stopped down with solid earth. (Since no record was made, or none has survived, of the memorials then in the church, it is fortunate that the antiquarians Williams and Hardwick made their earlier records—though David Parkes had noted, 'There are fewer monumental memorials in this church than any with equal magnituide I have visited'.[16]) At this stage the hot and cold air flues and grates of the warming apparatus were repaired, the channels corrected and, with foresight, provision made for 'a ventilating gas main'. The whole floor was then covered by concrete to a depth of six inches, with the base in the passages built up to be ten inches above the level under the seats. Although he had argued initially for tiling the whole floor space, the architect had now agreed to construct wooden flooring under the pews, and so it was only in the passage ways that encaustic tiles, six inches square and one inch thick, in chocolate, black, red and buff, were laid, protruding under the wooden flooring. The area just inside the west door, that is behind the pews, was not tiled. A stone step was made to the chancel.

The roof and walls were also transformed. The semi-circular plaster ceilings in the nave, chancel and north transept, which perhaps dated back to the sixteenth or early seventeenth century, were removed. The exposed rafters were cleaned, treated and varnished, and the area between them covered with laths and whitened with mortar and lime. The roof tiles were taken off to complete this work and damaged tiles replaced when they were put back. 'Everything required to make the roof sound and weather-proof was to be done'. The bottom of the walls, cleared of plaster to a line level with the top of the new seating, was specially treated with cement to repel damp. Above this line the intention was to clean the walls down, repair the plaster where necessary, and apply a thick coat of white distemper. But it seems, from two pieces of evidence, that there was a last-minute change and that the walls were stripped of plaster to gain the appearance that is seen today. First, in his speech at the reopening of the church the archdeacon said in praise of the churchwardens: 'They had not left them mere plaster but good stone walls – and that is what I like'.[17] Second, on a visit to Stretton by the Cambrian Archaeological Society in 1882 the interior walls of the church were strongly condemned: 'The plaster has been entirely removed, leaving exposed the original rubble work which, from the nature of the stone, not admitting even an approximation to courses, has a singularly bad effect'.[18] They also considered that the dark colour of the stone gave the building a very gloomy appearance. It seems then that the architect's initial preference was finally adopted.

The new seats—they reserved the description 'pews' for what we call box pews—were all to be, the architect emphasised, 'well and truly worked and firmly put together'. In addition to today's pews, there were three facing east where the pulpit now stands, and 11 in the new aisle. The north door, closed since 1819, was now bricked up, and the font, complete with base and drain, positioned on the south side of the nave just west of the vestry door.

The inside of the south aisle, built in 1868, as it is today

The Jacobean pulpit was retained in its position on the south side of the chancel arch but lowered: the desk remained in front of it and, to avoid crowding, a projected pew immediately in front of the desk was struck from the plans. 'The rectory pews west of the chancel door'—obviously used by the growing Wilson family—were removed and replaced by two new oak stalls with carving superintended by an approved artist. The two pews nearer the east end were retained and the reredos untouched.

The only new building executed at this stage was the additional aisle to the south transept. Significant changes had been made in its design since the first plans were drawn up. The church committee had opted for a gable roof and this meant alterations in the siting of windows: the end one, now the Leighton window, was almost certainly the 'modern window' that had to be taken from the nave when the arch to the new aisle was inserted and above it the gable now included a new small window. On the west wall of the aisle the lancet window from the former transept wall was placed just beyond the end of the then vestry. A two-light dormer window, planned to be above the roof line of the vestry, was excised from the plans. The seating plan was also altered because the architect had bowed to the objections to access only through the vestry by means of a door to be inserted in its east wall. Instead, access was to be from the passage in the south transept. Because this meant removing the third pew from the rear

The exterior of the south aisle, between the end walls of the south transept and the vestry. It juts out because they wanted to accommodate an extra pew to compensate for the one lost to create a passage to the pews in the new aisle

on the west side of the transept, and the consequent loss of precious seating, the end wall of the aisle was pushed further out by over two feet and supported by buttresses. This is the reason for the rather ugly external line of the south side of the church. One further modification was made while building was in progress: whereas all the arches in the new arcade had been planned in Gothic style, with a slight point echoing the Transitional arches of the crossing, it was now decided that the arch to the nave should be semi-circular in keeping with the Norman doorways.

In erecting the new aisle the builders had to take great care when dismantling the west wall of the transept and inserting the central pillar of the new arcade. When the ground was lowered, as in the church, any remains were reinterred and the soil removed to the rectory field. Four inches above ground level a damp course was laid. The steps to the warming chamber (sometimes referred to as 'the crypt' as it was under the vestry) which were on the east side disappeared; new steps had to be cut on the more readily visible west. The material from the old transept wall was to be used where possible but the new outer walls were faced with the best burr stone from Soudley. The interior masonry was of Grinshill and red Mansfield stone. A 12 inch fireclay flue pipe was built within the new wall and the vestry chimney pot placed on its summit. Best Staffordshire tiles were laid on deal or pine roofing timbers framed in couples as in the nave.

It often happens that when major building alterations are in progress a suggestion is put forward that while the contractors are on site some further change can be effected. This was the case at St. Laurence's. In early 1868 the suggestion was that the gallery should be removed and a new aisle added on the north side, as Pountney Smith had originally proposed. Whether the idea came from the architect, the rector or one of the committee, there was full support for it when the committee met on 21 April 1868. At the Vestry meeting six days later the architect produced drawings[19] which were inspected and approved and a resolution passed to remove the gallery and adopt his plans for a north aisle — again to be financed by voluntary subscriptions.

The north aisle, now the Emmaus Chapel, restored the symmetry of the church, but differed in some particulars from the south aisle: it is slightly shorter, has a lean-to roof, and has just one large arch on to the transept. When it was erected the Early English priest's door became internal and superfluous but was rightly preserved. The old two-light window from the north side of the nave was placed at the end of the aisle, and the old lancet window from the west side of the transept was reinstated on the west wall of the aisle. A second lancet nearer the nave is marked 'new' on the plans. Initially pews were not placed in this aisle although the gallery seats had gone.

The magnitude and permanence of the changes brought about by Pountney Smith's 'restoration' can best be appreciated by studying the church of the present for, as David Bilbey wrote in his booklet on St. Laurence's, 'it is basically his church which we see today'. For a start, the two aisles are the only significant extensions to the building since the early thirteenth century, other than the raising of the tower. The tiled floor and wooden flooring under the pews remain and the pews are so well made that they could last as long again. The attractiveness of the exposed oak rafters and couples fully justifies the action that he took, although opinions are divided on the bare stone walls. The chancel is the area most changed since the restoration. In the church we may lament the disappearance of some of the original memorials and the total loss of the old box pews—and have reserva- tions about the masonry of the new aisles—but he

The inside of the restored church today. It shows the pews and the encaustic tiles which were both new in 1868

created an attractive interior and increased the accommodation at a time when that was a pressing concern. And had his wish to raise the height of the tower lantern been supported the proportions of the church would have been enhanced, even if the ringers lost out. Whatever charges may have been levelled against Victorian restorers—and some have been denounced as vandals—it would be unfair to Pountney Smith to conclude that he spoiled St. Laurence's Church.

The total cost of the work on the church was almost exactly £2,000. The cost of restoration in the chancel, £245 4s. 6d., was met by the rector; the remainder came to £1,759 4s. 4d. The Diocesan Church Building Society made a grant of £100, the Church Building Society one of £25, and £14 came from Jane

Norton's West Window Fund (perhaps improperly as that was not altered). The rest was raised by personal subscriptions: the rector headed the list with £220, Edward Gibbon, Esq., gave £210, the patron £100, the lord of the manor £50. Indeed, the two grants and the 11 leading donations raised half the total cost. The Congregationalists, struggling to pay for their new church, must have reflected ruefully on the wealth of the Anglicans. But altogether 154 persons are named in the subscription list, besides those who put money in the boxes in church or contributed to the tremendous total of £116 11s. collected at the reopening of the church. When that list[20] was printed they were still £100 17s. 10d. short, but late gifts and the sale of oak from the gallery reduced this to £69 17s. 4d., which was paid off by the rector. If we add to this his donation of £220 and the cost of the work in the chancel, the Rev. Hugh Owen Wilson had contributed over £500, a sum which would need to be multiplied perhaps at least two hundredfold to appreciate its value today. A carved oak eagle lectern was presented by Dr. H. Griffiths, a member of the

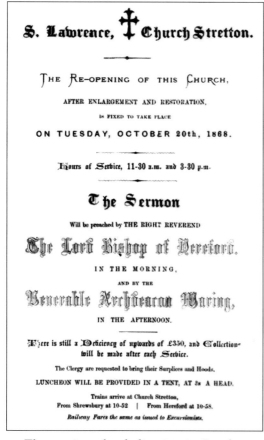

The service of rededication in October 1868

initial restoration committee who had just left Church Stretton.

The church was reopened on Tuesday, 20 October 1868, having been closed for a year. It was an exciting and memorable occasion. 'The town generally presented a very animated appearance', reported the *Shrewsbury Chronicle*,[21] 'from the great number of visitors who arrived during the day by railway and other conveyances. The church bells pealed forth their merry music at intervals, the people generally were dressed in holiday attire, and everything wore a most jubilant appearance'. Excursion fares were available on the trains arriving from Shrewsbury at 10.52 and Hereford at 10.58. The main service began at 11.30 with the clergy and choir—one of Wilson's innovations but of which this is the first mention to survive—entering to the processional hymn 'All people that on earth do dwell'. The rector led the prayers, the choir sang an anthem, and the Bishop of Hereford preached on the text from Ephesians 3:14-16. They also sang 'Holy, Holy, Holy Lord God Almighty' and, as a recessional, 'Jerusalem the golden'. The collection raised over £83. Lunch at 3s. a head was served in a marquee, but 150 sat down to a lunch in the Town Hall, followed by innumerable speeches and toasts. The most interesting comments came from the patron, who related how he had grown up with the rector; from Archdeacon Waring, who was glad to see the old and unsightly gallery go and welcomed the stone walls; and from the rector himself, who told how he had visited the church daily during the restoration and seen every stone of the new parts laid. Mr. Wilding expressed what was probably a majority view: he had mourned the disappearance of the gallery and many other features associated with the old church, but now it was done neither he nor any parishioners regretted it. Several speakers referred to the importance of the union of Church and State, for they were concerned at the possibility of disestablishment if Gladstone and the Liberals triumphed at the forthcoming election. For Jasper More, M.P., Church Stretton with its new hotel, artillery range and restored church was becoming notable. The archdeacon preached at the 3.30 service when the collection raised over £30.

*

While the restoration was being planned and implemented, the church and community were engaged in purchasing an additional burial ground as the churchyard was full and clearance or burial on top of existing graves, as in former centuries, were no longer acceptable. In March 1867 a Vestry meeting agreed to buy an acre of land in the former Talbot meadows, at the bottom of Cunnery Road and within sight of the church. A subsequent Vestry meeting in April 1868 approved the purchase cost of £450—£220 for the land, £200 for its enclosure, and £30 for legal and consecration expenses. The money was borrowed at 5% interest and was to be repaid over 20 years by a charge on the parish rates and an assurance policy till 1882. The effective, though not official, closure of the churchyard means that the tombs and gravestones we see today are predominantly of the nineteenth century.

The month before the Vestry agreed how to pay for the new burial ground, Parliament had passed Gladstone's bill to abolish compulsory church rates, although voluntary levies like the burial rate continued to be legal. The same Vestry, however, resolved to introduce a weekly offertory at the morning service to cover necessary church expenses. At first the weekly offering brought in about £2, but it soon fell and only £30 was raised in the year 1870-71. A final resolution at the meeting was that 'the church ought to be provided with gas as soon as possible'. But it was not until 1874 that subscriptions

The churchyard through the ornamental eastern gate

were invited to provide gas lighting in the church. The chancel was fitted with standards in 1875 at the expense of the rector. With nearly £60 raised by donations it may be presumed that the church was fitted at that time too. In 1871-72 £9 9s. was spent on a new window, but the reglazing of the large window in the south transept in 1873 made no financial demands as it was the gift of Edward Gibbon, the 'squire' of Little Stretton, who had also headed the list of subscribers for the gas lighting and been a major contributor to the restoration fund.

By the mid-1870s more money was being raised by collections: in 1873-74 the offertories tabled in the wardens' accounts add up to £40 but they were recorded as £65 6s. 7d., which suggests that there were late or separate contributions. By 1875-76, after collections were introduced at the evening service and the newly-introduced 8 a.m. communion, and as agricultural prices made some recovery after a slump, the final sum reached £107 5s. 10d. Even after payments to the clerk, sexton and organist, for a notice-board outside the church, for the usual repairs and, from 1876, for gas bills, there was a surplus. It is heartening to note that this was given to the poor, (through the Rev. Preston Nunn, now chaplain to the Union Workhouse), to Salop Infirmary and the Eye and Ear Hospital, to the Society for the Propagation of the Gospel and, in 1877-78, to relieve the famine in India.

Preston Nunn, the senior curate, was now an old man. There had been only one assistant curate in Rector Wilson's time, William Beaumont, who had stayed only from 1858 to 1860. Nunn had been a widower since 1849 and was now looked after by his one surviving daughter. It was as a venerable figure of 87 that he took his final baptism in November 1876, after 55 years of service in the parish. He died in February 1877 and was buried, 'deservedly loved and respected',[22] in the new burial ground.

Early in the previous year the Rev. Matthew Bower had arrived as an assistant curate. Within months he had gravely offended the rector. In a sermon in aid of the fund to provide the organist's salary, he had 'intimated that the organ and choir were not located in their proper position in the church, and that it would be better had they occupied the chancel from the time of the church restoration'.[23] Since the gallery had been removed the only places they could have been were at the very back of the church or in the new north aisle, since everywhere else was pewed. Be that as it may, a fortnight later the Rev. Hugh Owen Wilson demanded Bower's resignation for a 'breach of faith'. Bower refused. The bishop intervened and the rector eventually had to withdraw his charge unconditionally, although it remained clear that he expected the curate to resign. 'This he has done', reported the *Hereford Times*, 'and, as a result, general dissatisfaction is felt throughout the parish'. He did not actually leave until March 1877, but he was still under a cloud, and his parting gift, presented at Mrs. Bakewell's in All Stretton, was, the paper reported, inscribed, 'Presented by a few friends as a mark of the respect and esteem in which he is held throughout the parish'. In his response, Bower maintained he had only tried to do his duty faithfully and conscientiously.

The incident was more than a clash between a new, incautious curate and a long-serving rector prickly about his authority, especially within the chancel which was his domain and where his family sat. It was, too, a dispute over churchmanship and gives us a rare insight into the attitudes of clergy and congregation, a view of church life beyond the recorded details of personnel, finance and building development. Change filtered through slowly to this rural parish, where contemporary issues were not in daily debate. It is unlikely that the advance of scientific research, and specifically the publication of Charles Darwin's *Origin of Species* in 1859—which fuelled a protracted controversy between science and religion—had had much impact on the Stretton congregation. Similarly, the development of historical criticism of the Bible, and the bitter struggle through the 1860s following the publication of *Essays and Reviews* by a group of liberal churchmen, would have gone over the heads of most of those who sat in the pews of St. Laurence's, although 'no educated Christian could fail to feel the disruption, caused by new knowledge, to the faith of his childhood'.[24] But what did cause a stir was the threat of change in customary practice. People were content with their inherited forms of worship: what had been good enough for their fathers was good enough for them. The curate may have had his 'few friends' and respect throughout the parish, but most at this time were probably behind the rector for, as Mr. Wilding observed at the Buck's Head housewarming party in the Town Hall at Christmas 1877 in proposing the toast of the Bishop and Clergy, coupled with the name of the Rev. Hugh Owen Wilson, 'there appeared to have been in many places much uneasiness respecting the recent innovations introduced into the services of the Church, which he was pleased to note was not the case in Church Stretton'.[25] These innovations were chiefly the work of High Churchmen who believed that, especially in the towns, more ceremonial and colour would attract the working class, and who wanted to teach reverence by eye as well as by word and to deepen the sacramental sense of their people. A particular feature of this movement was the introduction of robed choirs into the chancel. There was to be another manifestation in Stretton of the opposition to this revival of ritualism shortly after a High Church rector was appointed.

After Bower's departure and Preston Nunn's death, the Rev. Noel Colley arrived in 1877, to be joined by the Rev. Leighton Hope-Edwards the next year. With the church restoration completed, gas lighting installed, a healthy financial position, and two young curates, everything seemed ripe for a period of action and expansion. Yet it had hardly been agreed that the first project should be the repair of the roof of the church tower when suddenly, out of the blue, the rector was taken seriously ill and died. He had been well enough to baptise Dr. and Mrs. McClintock's baby in January 1879, but he died on 20 February. He

The grave of Hugh Owen Wilson in Cunnery Road Cemetery

was only 54 years of age, and had served as rector for nearly 30 years. The *Shrewsbury Chronicle*[26] wrote: 'His death has created a gap which it will be difficult to fill up, whether as rector of the parish, as a county magistrate or as Chairman of the Board of Guardians', a post he had held for 20 years. 'In his daily life the reverend gentleman was courteous, unostentatious, kind and charitable in the best sense of the word. In business he employed but few words, was prompt and decided, and very seldom gave an opinion which did not command the respect, if not the assent, of the inquirer'. The obituary in Eddowes' *Shropshire Journal*[27] also emphasised his personal qualities and praised him for the manner in which he discharged his magisterial duties: 'If he erred, it was on the side of mercy, and he usually advised an amicable settlement of quarrels and disputes in preference to an appeal to law'. Newspaper reports on court cases when he was on the bench support this tribute to his merciful disposition. But it is extraordinary that neither obituary made further reference to his achievements as rector nor to the restoration of the church in which he had been the moving spirit. The *Wenlock and Ludlow Express*[28] was worse, for the one detail of his funeral which it included was that a horse slipped outside the church and damaged the vicar of Woolstaston's carriage. Wilson was buried with two of his children who had predeceased him in the north-west corner of the new graveyard.

The church and local community realised the magnitude of their loss. At the Vestry meeting in March a message of 'heartfelt sympathy and condolence' was sent to Mrs. Wilson and the family. In May a committee was set up to arrange for the installation of a new organ as a memorial to the late rector. Although they were to have second thoughts about the nature of the memorial, all knew the church's great debt to Hugh Owen Wilson. He had been a minister of energy and commitment who had carried through the greatest building programme in the church since the thirteenth century. He was also Stretton's last 'squarson', combining the role of parson with that of squire—wealthy landowner, justice of the peace and, since he chaired the Board of Guardians of the Poor and was very active in the development of the town's drainage, a pillar of the community.

Mrs. Wilson's position was particularly difficult for she had 13 surviving children between the ages of 20 years and 18 months. It proved fortunate that the next rector instituted on 10 June 1879, on the presentation of C.O. Childe-Pemberton, came from a local and well-connected family. He was Charles Noel-Hill, older son of the Hon. Charles Arthur Wentworth Noel-Hill of Shrewsbury and a grandson of the 4th Lord Berwick. It would seem that he was able to arrange for Mrs. Wilson and her family to move to a residence on the estate at Atcham, because as early as August the choir of St. Laurence's had an outing to see her new home, with dinner, singing and a tour of Lord Berwick's estate.[29]

*

Charles Noel-Hill was another Oxford graduate, admitted to Exeter College in 1867 and awarded his B.A. 1871 and M.A. 1874. He had proceeded to theological training probably at Cuddesdon, where he would have come under the influence of the then Principal, Edward King (later Bishop of Lincoln), a ritualist of saintly life revered as an outstanding exemplar of pastoral care. Ordained deacon in 1873 and priest 1874, Noel-Hill served as a curate for two periods at Abingdon, 1873-74 and 1875-79, with a year at Clifton Hampden in between. He was 31 when he came to Stretton, still a bachelor, and a man of faith, energy, experience and High Church inclinations.

He had early opportunities to display these qualities and beliefs, and changes came thick and fast. Within three months of his arrival in September 1879 he introduced a daily service at seven o'clock in the evening, with special sermons on Fridays. There was, initially at least, an encouraging attendance and the service was thought to be a great boon. Another novelty was carols sung by the choir from the church tower on his first Christmas Eve; they failed to get a harmonium up the winding stair and instead were accompanied by a violin. Christmas Day services were 8 a.m. Holy Communion, 11 a.m. Matins and 6.30 p.m. part-choral Evensong. Noel-Hill was very keen on decorating the church on special occasions, and at Christmas there were hot-house flowers and plants on each side of the chancel, holly entwined on the pulpit, lectern and pillars, and the text, 'The Word was made flesh', displayed above the altar, as the communion table was increasingly described. At Easter the features were a floral rood screen, an altar cross of scarlet and white azaleas on a background of green moss and an illuminated text, 'I am the Resurrection and the Life', above the altar. Every encouragement was given to the Sunday School: numbers rapidly increased 'chiefly through the exertions of the rector and the coming forward of a number of ladies and gentlemen to act as a staff of teachers'.[30] The Sunday School Christmas treat ended with a magic lantern show in the Town Hall; by summer 1883 they had graduated to high flier swings in the rectory garden. The development that will have brought greatest joy to the rector was the appearance, for the first time on Easter Sunday 1880, of the new church choir 'composed entirely of boys' and robed in surplices. They were surely seated in the chancel—which would have rejoiced Matthew Bower's heart.

The pace of change was too much for some. In April 1880, only seven months after Noel-Hill's arrival, the *Shrewsbury Chronicle* published a letter from 'Old Inhabitant' expressing the dissatisfaction with the new rector that was said to exist among parishioners. The writer complained about the surpliced choir, the novel practice of standing when the rector entered the church, the time spent on decorating the church instead of being around the parish, and even about moving the announcement of banns from its traditional place after the second lesson. 'Little attention is paid to old customs, and none to the wishes of the inhabitants'.

In the next week's issue James Walker, a local solicitor, sprang to the rector's defence. He condemned the previous letter as unchristian, unseemly and scandalous, full of old-fashioned notions. He maintained that Noel-Hill was valued and much respected, and that people liked everything done decently and in order and 'in accord with the times'.

The correspondence concluded with a letter the following week from 'A lover of peace', who deplored the raising of grievances in the press. The writer considered that many of the changes in the church were minor and non-doctrinal, and praised the rector's untiring energy and industry. There were suggestions, however, that there had been insufficient consultation with the congregation and that frequent communions kept the rector away a little from the parish. What this correspondent condemned was not the decoration of the church but the paintings suspended above the communion table 'highly offensive to many sensitive individuals who regard their introduction as an attempt to familiarise us with the imagery and surroundings of the Church of Rome'. This was another echo of the great Ritualist controversy that divided the Church of England in the later Victorian period.

Noel-Hill would not have been prepared to relinquish his High Church convictions, but he seems to have gone out of his way to pay more attention to the parish. This was made possible by the appointment of the Rev. Vernon Carter as curate in the place of Noel Colley and Leighton Hope-Edwards who had both moved on. The rector gave his enthusiastic backing to the project for a Working Men's Club and Reading Room, although he made clear he was not an advocate of total abstinence. He was also instrumental in founding a Choral Society and then a Ringing Society in the spring of 1880. 'Clothing clubs, coal clubs, and existing charities of all kinds, have had fresh vitality infused in them'.[31] Social improvement was important, but the rector's greater concern was the religious and moral welfare of all his parishioners. Visiting was now efficiently organised and mission services conducted in outlying districts so that the aged and infirm were not cut off from the church. Right from his institution the rector had become chaplain to the workhouse—where his predecessor had been Chairman of the Board of Guardians. People were struck by his moral earnestness. But there were lighter moments. In his first summer he entertained a huge party from his former parish in Abingdon who had chartered a special train, and followed this up with a garden party in the rectory grounds for his new parishioners, with tea for 280 and dancing on the lawns.

In spite of criticism from some quarters, Charles Noel-Hill was held in high regard. 'The rector possesses, in a marked and unusual degree, all the qualifications of a minister of God. His singular charm of delivery, his clear musical voice, his intense earnestness, and the dramatic power of his sermons so fill the church that additional accommodation is required in it, and the offertories will be devoted to that purpose'.[32] Those offertories had continued to increase—the total in 1879-80 was £118 11s. 9d.—but the only extra seating was in the new north aisle, and the chancel screen he desired did not materialise for nearly 20 years.

But there were several other building projects. Back in September 1878, in response to a request from Rector Wilson, the architect, Pountney Smith, had submitted a detailed drawing of his proposals for the repair of the roof of the tower and the renewal of the corner stone pinnacles. A pyramidal structure was

The pyramidal tower roof and renewed pinnacles

proposed to direct the flow of rainwater to the downspouts. It was to be topped by an elaborate weather vane with the pointing arm balanced by a small-scale gridiron, the symbol of St. Laurence; the design of the pinnacles displayed intricate carving. Hugh Wilson's death put the project on hold, but his successor appealed for support at a Vestry meeting: 'We should not like to sleep in our beds with a sound roof over our heads and know that the roof of the House of God let in the rain'. In September 1880 it was resolved to go ahead with the work, employing Pountney Smith as architect and Richard Pace of Shrewsbury as contractor. The rector was offered special thanks 'for his exertions in this matter'. It was completed before February 1881 when heavy snow blew into the belfry and damaged the clock, and a hurricane caused serious damage to the new roof, lifting the tiles at the corners. And so the top of St. Laurence's tower came to have its familiar conical shape. In the long run the pinnacles have suffered more than the roof from the effects of the weather.

Two other building projects both related to the late rector. It seems that the committee established to install a new organ in his memory had quickly changed its mind, probably because the building extension required by a good organ would have made the scheme too expensive. Instead, they elected to go for a new pulpit. The Rev. E.D. Carr, Rector of Woolstaston (and survivor of a night in the snow on the Long Mynd, having lost his way home after taking a service in Ratlinghope in January 1865), supported the revised proposal because he said Hugh Wilson had often complained to him how unfit the existing pulpit was after the church had been so beautifully restored. Within a month over £184 was raised through subscriptions. Designed by Pountney Smith, the pulpit was erected in the summer of 1880 by Landuccis of Shrewsbury on the north side of the chancel arch where it still stands. It is of Caen stone enriched with various marbles. Its installation involved raising the cornice and adding a plinth and further steps which, like the pulpit itself, were carpeted. The total cost, including the removal of the Jacobean pulpit on the other side of the arch, and the refitting of the desk and seat, was about £150. While the memorial pulpit, described as 'light, graceful and harmonious',[33] was generally praised at the time, many must have lamented the dismantling of its historic predecessor. Fortunately, some of its panels were fastened to the wall in the south-west corner of the church, where they can still be admired.

One of the first occasions when the new pulpit was used was on Harvest Sunday 1880. 'The church was beautifully decorated, and the fairy-like structure of flowers, fruits, grasses, ferns and grain which now spans the entrance to the chancel conveys some idea of the additional beauty which will be lost to the chancel when the

The new pulpit in memory of the Rev. Hugh Owen Wilson, Rector 1849-79

proposed screen is erected'.[34] On that day Communion at 8 a.m. was followed by Matins at 11, with a sermon by the curate, a service for children at 3 p.m., and finally Choral Evensong at 6.30 with a robed choir and a sermon by the rector. Another of Noel-Hill's innovations was the Watchnight Service to welcome in the New Year of 1881. It began at 11.30 and proceedings were suspended at 11.55; as the congregation prayed silently, the great tenor bell boomed out each minute until on the stroke of midnight all the bells rang out to hail the New Year.

Before that year was out other building developments were afoot. Pountney Smith's drawing dated December 1881 of the planned extension of the vestry[35] shows it doubled in length to its present size, although there is only a narrow entrance from the original vestry into the extension and no external door. It appears, however, that the plans of 1881 were not carried out, probably because other appeals for funds were pending. The extension had to wait until 1913.

The organ project, however, had certainly taken off. Donations rolled in and a Grand Fancy Fair or Bazaar held in the rectory grounds on two days at the end of July 1881, with bands, dancing and stalls, raised the extraordinary sum of over £372. Pountney Smith was able to produce his final drawing of the

External arcading on the organ chamber

The organ installed in 1882

proposed organ chamber in January 1882. The chamber was just over 11 feet square. The walls were to be of local stone with masonry dressings from Grinshill, and the gable roof finished with Broseley tiles to match the church roof. Externally the north wall would show a small circular window above mock round-arched arcading enclosing two narrow lancet windows. Thomas Pugh, contractor at the restoration 15 years earlier, tendered for £209 and the work was completed at the end of May 1882. Unfortunately when cutting the opening in the north wall of the chancel the workmen damaged the east window and nine panes had to be repainted. The old organ continued to be used while the chamber dried out. The new two manual and full compass pedal organ was installed by Nicholsons of Worcester to the design of the distinguished musicologist the Rev. Dr. Sir Frederick Gore Ouseley, Professor of Music at Oxford, 'who perhaps did more than any other person to raise the standards of Victorian church music'.[36] When the organ was officially opened by him on 24 April 1883 he gave a recital and also preached. The plaque on the organ names Mr. George Bailey as the organist at the time; he was succeeded in 1887 by Mr. Jonathan Hugh Chester, A.R.C.O., who was followed by Mr. F.J. Butler in 1893.

*

213

The Stretton served by the renovated parish church of these years was itself a curious mixture of the old and the new. 'In the '80s Church Stretton was still rural, little more than a large village. Droves of cattle and marketing country folk, a few of the older men in smock frocks, were familiar sights in its single street way, and farmers' wives led back laden panniered ponies up the Burway and over the Long Mynd to Ratlinghope and Medlicott and other distant farms and hamlets'.[37] There was much poverty. Some tried to make ends meet by picking whinberries on the Long Mynd each September; the more enterprising emigrated. The news of a former resident's death in Australia prompted the *Shrewsbury Chronicle* to comment: 'The little mountain-girt town of Church Stretton has sent many of its sons to far distant countries to help to build up new colonies'.[38] Yet the snippets of news about Church Stretton in the pages of the same weekly newspaper record events and organisations that have quite a modern ring about them: football and cricket matches featuring the local sides, the Bowling Club on the green by The Hotel, the Annual Flower Show and Athletic Sports at Stretton House on August Bank Holiday Monday, and amateur dramatic presentations. The Choral Society's regular concerts in the Town Hall included performances of 'Judas Maccabaeus' and Haydn's 'Creation', as well as an evening in aid of Dinah Parton, a local blind girl. Even the Football Club presented an annual concert in order to raise funds.

In other ways, too, it is clear that the social life of the town was developing. The Loyal Caradoc Lodge of Odd Fellows, to which Noel-Hill was admitted, met at the King's Arms; once a year, led by a brass band, they marched in procession to the parish church for a special service. Other public houses in the town centre were the Buck's Head, the Raven, the Plough, the Red Lion, the Queen's Head and the Britannia. Perhaps it was their popularity that caused Charles Noel-Hill to head the movement to set up a Working Men's Club and Reading Room and in 1886 to become President of the new Church Stretton branch of the Church of England Temperance Society. He declared that drunkenness was a vice 'eating like a canker into social life and gnawing at the root of national greatness'.[39] Children enrolled in the Band of Hope. Certainly drunkenness figured prominently in the cases brought before the magistrates in Petty Sessions; other regular misdemeanours included larceny, breaches of the peace, assaults, trespass, highway offences like straying cattle or drunk in charge of a horse, and, more occasionally, wife beating or arson. A few received a summons for travelling on the train without a ticket or even smoking in the booking office at the station.

George Windsor's novel *Laura Heathjohn*, based on life in Church Stretton, suggested that the church service on Sunday and the weekly market were the only occasions to enliven the uneventful existence of the town, but there were also six fairs in the course of the year. The hiring fair on 14 May was the biggest, for it was not only the place for hiring labourers or servant girls, but a

Horse fair near the church

funfair too, with swingboats, hobby horses, waxworks, peepshows, acrobats and shooting galleries. The main horse and sheep fair fell on 25 September. Circuses paid regular visits. In 1887 a scheme was proposed to create two artificial lakes in the Carding Mill valley for swimming, boating and fishing, but although an engineer gave initial approval nothing more was heard of it. (The notice about depth of water by today's car-park is evidence that there was a pool to feed the mill-race.) The idea may have been prompted by the great flood of May 1886 when, after days of unremitting rain, holes appeared in the road caused by geysers from the culvert, the station was flooded up to the platform, houses inundated, gardens washed away, the streets littered with debris and a great lake formed at World's End at the southern end of the town.

New buildings were all the time springing up among the old, including the two redbrick houses next to the Buck's Head in 1880, and the terrace of timber-framed cottages in Church Street in 1886. But much the most significant development was the creation of Sandford Avenue. It is named after the Rev. Holland Sandford, Vicar of Eaton-under-Heywood, who was the moving spirit behind the planting of lime trees along Station Road from The Hotel to the railway station. Sandford himself donated the trees and planted the first one in a little ceremony on 19 December 1884. In all, 153 trees were planted, eventually taking the avenue up the new road to the east of the town as far as the Hazler turnpike. The trees were individually dedicated to a whole array of local dignitaries and more famous figures who gave their permission, including Queen Victoria, the Prince of Wales, Disraeli and General Gordon.[40] It is sad, but noteworthy, that several of the first trees planted were vandalised within days.

Sandford and the avenue were hailed by the town's great publicist, George Windsor, who in 1885 published his *Handbook to the Capabilities, Attractions, Beauties and Scenery of Church Stretton*. He compared Stretton favourably with Switzerland and paradoxically quoted Canon Lloyd's opinion that he had never seen a town so like Jerusalem. Windsor, who was the postmaster at the time, was also the editor of the *Church Stretton Times and Visitors' List* launched in September 1881 but which ran for just two issues. Even without George Windsor, Stretton's attractions were becoming widely known. This was partly the consequence of the development of the Long Mynd as an artillery firing range. The 1st. Shropshire Artillery Corps had been formed in 1860; 20 years later the Church Stretton Battery was commanded by William Campbell Hyslop, soon to succeed his father as proprietor of the Stretton House Asylum. As the years passed more and more artillery units held summer camps in Church Stretton, and the sound of firing could be heard from morn till night. In October 1877 misdirected shells, fortunately filled with sawdust, fell on Minton without causing casualties, but in 1880 a man from Little Stretton was killed. The range ceased to be used in the last years of the century, but it had brought trade to the town and the glamour of military bands playing in the evening outside the officers' mess in 'The Hotel' and for church parades to St.

The church from the bottom of Burway Road, late nineteenth century (SRRC)

Laurence's. But it was the hills that drew the visitors and a curfew was rung at 8 p.m. to advise walkers of the direction of the town. The Birchfield Bicycle Club came from Birmingham, and hundreds of trippers arrived by rail on Bank Holidays—over a thousand on Whit Monday 1880 and four excursion trains on Easter Monday 1887.

The parish church flourished, too. Windsor recorded in his 1885 *Handbook* that seats had been placed in the new north aisle on account of the large congregations, and commented that the introduction of gas lighting had made it possible to hold the evening service at the more convenient hour of 6.30 p.m. Churchwardens' accounts show that offertories largely met the church's expenses, although gas bills at over £20 per annum accounted for 25% of expenditure, while for five years the organist's annual salary was reduced from £20 to £15. It is interesting to compare the annual aggregate collections at the three services: in 1885-86 they amounted at the 8 a.m. Holy Communion to £19 19s. 9d., at the 11 o'clock Matins to £47 19s. 6d., and at 6.30 Evensong to £38 9s. 4d.. There is no record of the size of the congregations, but it is clear that the evening service was almost as well attended as Matins, and that many came to the early Communion. The total giving, with

offertories on Good Friday and Ascension Day, was £107 13s. 4d. The collections for that year, which reveal what was usually put on the plate, contained 5 farthings, 3,516 halfpennies, 5,271 pennies, 962 x 3d. pieces, 2 x 4d. pieces, 907 sixpences, 489 shillings, 46 florins, 22 half-crowns, 7 half sovereigns, 1 sovereign and 1 £5 note.[41] Special collections were held for the poor, the Church Building Society, Salop Infirmary, the Seaman's Mission, and for a new window— could this have been the otherwise unrecorded stained glass window in the nave portraying the Virgin Mary with the

The nave window with Victorian glass within the Norman wall

*Right: Flemish roundels in the chancel
lower side window*

accompanying figures of Isaiah, St. Gabriel
and St. John the Baptist? Another possibility is
that the collection helped to pay for the
roundels and panels which were fitted into the
north side and low side windows in the
chancel.[42] The roundels date generally from
the late sixteenth or early seventeenth century;
many are thought to be of Flemish origin.[43]
They probably came to England after the
Napoleonic Wars and may have been
purchased by Robert Pemberton, the rector at
that time, though Glynne in 1832 made no
reference to them.

The purchase in 1881 of new chant books
and psalters, presumably for the choir, is
indicative of Charles Noel-Hill's efforts to
raise the standard of services. In this he had the
assistance of successive curates—David
Llewellyn Davies (1882-87), Howard
Whitehouse
(1887-90), and
Owen Kyffin
Williams (1890-
93). He was also supported by a venerable parish
clerk, John Lucas, who served for 56 years until
his death in 1884, and by two of St. Laurence's
longest-serving churchwardens: John Edward
Proffit, whose draper's shop stood in the Square
near the church gate, succeeded his father as
Rector's Warden in 1881 and served until his
own death in 1910, and David Hyslop, coal
merchant and proprietor of the posting establishment at the bottom of Burway Road, was
People's Warden from 1887 till he died in 1907.
Mrs. Andrews, the widow of Hyslop's predecessor Thomas Andrews, presented, on Easter

*Left: The eagle lectern presented in 1888 in
memory of Thomas Andrews, churchwarden*

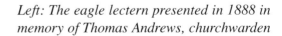

The rectory at the end of the nineteenth century

Sunday 1888, the brass eagle lectern still in use today in memory of her church-warden husband, although a carved oak lectern had been given only 20 years earlier on the completion of the restoration. That same day, another lady, name unknown, presented the medieval style amethyst-studded chalice, again still used today, and a paten with a Paschal Lamb design. The rector's personal contribution to the development of the church and his high standing were recognised in 1889 by his appointment as Rural Dean.

Queen Victoria's Golden Jubilee in 1887 prompted the setting up of a committee chaired by the rector to organise the town's celebrations. On Jubilee Day, 21 June, there were decorated arches at the church gates and rectory gates as well as other strategic places. A special choral service was followed by athletic sports, an open-air fête, a promenade concert in the rectory grounds, a torchlight procession led by a band, and bonfires on all the local hills. The rector sent a message to the queen—and saw that the workhouse folk enjoyed a roasted ox. The next day, at his sole expense, he threw a party for all the children, including those from the workhouse, in the rectory garden. The town marked the Jubilee by erecting a drinking fountain on land given by Squire Benson at the junction of Burway Road and High Street; it was later moved 80 yards up Burway Road and later still, because of increasing traffic, dismantled altogether.

It was perhaps the Jubilee that revived discussion of the state of the church bells, for the safety of the wooden beams to which the bells were attached had first been questioned in Hugh Wilson's time. The small fund for the repair of the bells that had since accrued was substantially augmented by a grand bazaar in August 1890 which raised nearly £450. At a Vestry meeting later that month the rector was thanked for hosting the event and, following the installation of a larger boiler and improved under-floor heating conduits, 'for providing for the comfort of worshippers in St. Laurence's Church by a sufficient warming apparatus for the sacred edifice'. It was then resolved not only to rehang the six old bells but also to add two more to complete the octave. When work began it was soon apparent that further expense was necessary: one bell was found to be cracked and it was decided to have all of them recast; the extra weight also necessitated new floors. The initial estimate of £208 must have been greatly exceeded. One of the new bells was inscribed 'Te Deum laudamus' and the other 'Laudate sum in excelsis', and on the tenor bell, 'To the greater glory of God these bells were re-hung, and the peal increased, Christmas 1890. Gloria in excelsis Deo. C. Noel-Hill, rector, J.E. Proffit and D. Hyslop, churchwardens'. The bells were dedicated at a special Friday Evensong in February 1891. During the evening 'a most competent band of ringers from Welshpool and Whitchurch made the hills and vales of Church Stretton re-echo to sounds which they had certainly never heard before, by a peal of Grandsire Triples, 5,040 changes on the lines of Holt's ten-part peal, the time being two hours and fifty minutes, during which not a single error or mistake was made'.[44]

At the same dedication service the rector presented a new clock, the work of Messrs. Smith & Co. of Derby. The old clock, installed at an unknown date in the previous century but which had needed a new dial plate in 1779, had been made by a Mr. Roberts at a cost of £120, and 'did good work for many years'. The rector dedicated the new clock with its Cambridge chimes 'to the greater glory of God and to the use of the people of this parish', a use still gratefully acknowledged more than a hundred years later. As he finished speaking the clock chimed the fourth quarter and struck the hour of three. A brass plaque on one of the crossing piers records: 'The clock in the tower of this church of St. Lawrence was given in the Year of Salvation 1891 by Charles Noel-Hill Rector. The day and the hour knoweth no man. Watch and pray'. It is of note that 'Lawrence' is here spelled with a 'w', the English form, which continued in use well into the twentieth century, as opposed to the Latin form, 'Laurence' ('Laurentius'), which had been used for centuries and has now been restored as the church's name.

The rector's clock may have reminded him of the passage of time in his own life for later that same year, at the age of 42 and after 12 years in the parish, he took a wife! His bride, Edith Mary, was the daughter of the Rev. Riou Benson, Rector of Hope Bowdler and brother of Squire Ralph Beaumont Benson, now lord of the manor of Stretton. The wedding took place on 6 October 1891 at St. John's, Kensington, where the bride's uncle was rector. The marriage was very popular in the parish and on their return from honeymoon, in a rerun of

*Noel-Hill's clock given in 1890
and still keeping time*

the celebration of Robert Pemberton's homecoming with his bride in 1820, their carriage was pulled through the streets and up to the rectory by willing young men. Triumphal arches spanned the main street, the bells rang out and a volley was fired by soldiers of the local artillery. Dinner was served to 700 in a giant marquee. For Charles Noel-Hill the most touching moment was the presentation of the first posy to his bride by a girl from the workhouse. 'Nothing could have been more in harmony with his own feelings than that the poor of the parish should have been made happy', read the report on his reply to the toast of the new couple.[45]

Just a year later their first child, Monica, was born; Katherine Mary followed in 1894 and Charles Michael Wentworth in 1897. Their son was only two months old when, once again, the town was festooned with decorations, this time for the Queen's Diamond Jubilee. Charles Noel-Hill had always looked after his church people, annually demonstrating his gratitude and generosity by entertaining the choir and church officers to dinner and a social evening at the rectory, and ensuring that the Sunday School children enjoyed treats at Christmas and in the summer. On this occasion he and his wife cast the net wider: they invited all parishioners over the age of 16—the children's festival was the next day—to a garden party at the rectory. Six hundred came. They were entertained by a band, sketches, songs, refreshments and a free pint of ale for all men who wanted it. As in 1887, bonfires were lit on the hills and 65 were visible from Caer Caradoc.

To mark the Jubilee at the church subscriptions were invited towards the cost of erecting a permanent chancel screen: the temporary framework for decoration at Christmas, Easter and Harvest had prepared the way for a feature clearly close to the rector's heart. The screen of carved oak, surmounted by a cross, was the work of H.R. Franklin from a design by G.F. Bodley, A.R.A. It was erected in 1898 at a total cost of £180 and dedicated at the morning service on Whitsunday. Its erection involved moving the choir stalls and removing a

The chancel screen erected in 1898 to commemorate Queen Victoria's
Diamond Jubilee the previous year. It was removed in 1983

wing wall of the pulpit. The two prayer desks were placed immediately behind the screen—which still allowed a clear view of the choir and the east end. There must have been some who were concerned at this significant change in the internal order of the church, as it was nearly 350 years since the medieval rood screen had been demolished at the Reformation, but it was reported that its appearance gave 'general satisfaction'.[46]

The chancel screen was not the only internal embellishment in the late 1890s. A two-light stained glass window featuring St. Augustine and St. Paulinus was dedicated 'to the glory of God and in memory of the departed members of her family' by Katharina Haverkam in 1898 and placed at the end of the north aisle (now the Emmaus Chapel). The death of one Anna Katharina Haverkam at the age of 78 is recorded on 25 March in that year, so the window must have been one of her final gifts. She lived at The Hall, All Stretton, and was the daughter of William Haverkam who had kept The Talbot 50 years earlier and acted as Stretton's postmaster. The family of another All Stretton resident, Constance Cordelia Wimberley, whose address was The Grove and who died in May 1898 aged 58, may have been prompted by the Haverkam memorial to present a stained glass lancet window in her memory. Entitled Faith, it is to be found on the west wall of the south aisle and is now an internal window visible also on the extended wall of the vestry.

*The Haverkam window now in the
Emmaus Chapel*

Of far greater promi-
nence than the Haverkam
and Wimberley windows is
the Leighton window at the
end of the south aisle. This
window was put in place in
1899 by Stanley Leighton,
M.P., in memory of Lord
Leighton of Stretton, a
Victorian painter of considerable renown who was
President of the Royal
Academy from 1878 to
1896. When he was created
a baron in the New Year
Honours of 1896 he chose
Stretton as his title on the
suggestion of a distant relative, Sir Baldwyn Leighton
of Alberbury in Shropshire.
Lord Leighton had never
been to Stretton, but his
kinsman would have been
aware that his forebears
had been the leading
family of the parish in the
fifteenth century and
perhaps important benefactors of St. Laurence's. The
two stained glass panes commemorate, on the left, Edward Leighton who died
in 1455 and for whose soul we are, in Latin, asked to pray, and, on the right,
Frederick Lord Leighton himself, President of the Royal Academy, born 1830
and died 1896—'He past [*sic*] a soul of nobler tone'. Around the edges of both
windows the family motto, 'Dread Shame', is enscrolled numerous times.
Above the two panes are three smaller lights with dates and heraldic shields: in
the centre, A.D. 1428, and the Leighton coat-of-arms impaling Cambray, for
John Leighton who died in that year had married Maud, daughter of Watkyn
Cambray in 1383 and come to live in the Cambray manor-house in Stretton; on
the left, A.D. 1455, and the Leighton coat-of-arms impaling Stapleton, for
Edward Leighton, who died in that year and was buried in the church, had
married another heiress, Elizabeth Stapleton; and on the right, A.D. 1896, with
Lord Leighton's coat-of-arms, a variant of the principal Leighton arms. The

Right: The Leighton window given in 1899 in memory of Lord Leighton, President of the Royal Academy

title 'Lord Leighton of Stretton' has the distinction of being the most short-lived in the history of the peerage: his patent bore the date 24 January 1896 and he died the following day, unmarried and without an heir. He was buried in St. Paul's Cathedral.

The church was not only being beautified but appears to have been flourishing, for in 1896 no fewer than 400 copies of the Prayer Book with Hymns Ancient and Modern were purchased, together with 20 music copies for the choir. Mrs. Noel-Hill had put on three 'entertainments' to help raise the necessary funds. The new books were first used on Easter Sunday 1896. There were nearly 200 communicants on Easter Day 1900, and the Bishop of Hereford that year confirmed 70 candidates from Church Stretton and the neighbouring parishes.

The church may have been thriving, but by 1899 its rector was not. Charles Noel-Hill seems to have suffered a very long illness. The timing of its onset could not have been worse for the church as the only curate had recently left. William Ashburner and Charles Custance, curates between 1893 and 1895, had been followed by Harold Mason who stayed only briefly, and it was his successor, Reginald Bolton, who departed in August 1898. When the rector fell ill, therefore, services and occasional offices had to be taken by neighbouring clergy until a new curate, Richard Dansey, arrived in May 1899, just after Noel-Hill left for the continent to recuperate. At the beginning of 1900 the Rev. George Ellis, fresh

Left: The Rev. Charles Noel-Hill, Rector 1879-1904 (SRRC)

Church Stretton from the east c.1900. The church, with rectory behind, is in the centre, and Stretton House on the extreme left (SRRC)

from mission work in London, was signing himself 'priest-in-charge'. Yet at the end of February the bells rang out to welcome the rector after a nine-month absence. He took some services but when he appeared at the anniversary of the Foresters in August he told them that his health had been bad and that he would have to go away again. By the end of September, however, he was well enough to go on the choir outing to Hawkestone and to preach at Harvest on the appropriate text, 'It is good for us to be here'. He must also have been involved in the mission services conducted over a long week-end by the Diocesan Missioner, who led a service for communicants on the Saturday evening, preached on 'Following Christ' on the Sunday morning, addressed the men in the afternoon on the theme of 'The Armour of God', took as his text in the evening the parable of the Good Shepherd, and on the Monday talked to the children about 'The Good Soldier'.

As the century drew to a close the town witnessed the first signs of imminent and dramatic development. There was a boom in building. William Campbell Hyslop built Woodcote in 1896 and four years later the Hydropathic Establishment, soon to become the Longmynd Hotel, was erected. Roads were laid out to give access to the lower slopes of the surrounding hills, with building plots offered in Madeira Walk, Trevor Hill, Clive Avenue, Watling Street and Brockhurst. New leisure facilities became available with the founding of the Church Stretton Golf Club in June 1898 and the opening of a second bowling green opposite to the Buck's Head. The Church Stretton Water Act, given Parliamentary approval in 1899, led to the construction of the new and much larger reservoir off Carding Mill Valley.

The town's growing status seemed to be confirmed by the replacement of the Parish Council at the end of 1899 by the new Urban District Council. The *Church Stretton Advertiser*, in the second month of its publication, prophesied, 'Surely Church Stretton has a splendid future before it'. Even as the curtains were drawn on the Victorian era by the death of the queen in January 1901, the scene was already changing and a new act about to begin in the saga of Church Stretton and its parish church.

12

THE CHURCH IN PEACE AND WAR

The bells of St. Laurence's have, down the centuries, rung out not only to summon the faithful to worship or to mark local festivities but also to celebrate major national events. The new octave was in great demand in the final years of the nineteenth century to herald the Diamond Jubilee and, during the Boer War, to celebrate the relief of Mafeking in May 1900—when they pealed out all afternoon as a big crowd gathered at the fountain—and on the queen's birthday in June when an effigy of Kruger was paraded through the streets before a ceremonial burning on Longhills to the accompaniment of patriotic songs. They rang out again to welcome the new century. But three weeks later it was a muffled peal that conveyed the news of the queen's death.

The accession of King Edward VII was the signal in Stretton for 'a burst of building activity probably unparalleled since that presumed to have followed the 1593 fire'.[1] For years George Windsor and Holland Sandford had been talking up Church Stretton as a place to visit—Windsor's newspaper included a list of visitors to the town and where they were staying, and Sandford, after turning Station Road into a tree-lined avenue, dreamed of Swiss chalets on the Long Mynd. Now, at the turn of the century, the aim was not just to attract a good class of visitor but permanent residents to what the new *Church Stretton Advertiser* (which also published a visitors' list) delighted to call 'the Highlands of England'. The Church Stretton Land Co. Ltd. was formed in 1897, followed two years later by the Church Stretton Building Co. Ltd. What followed was little less than a smash and grab raid on field, lane and hedgerow. New roads were laid out on the slopes of the hills to take full advantage of Strettondale's scenic beauties for the intention was to develop the town as a superior residential district. Already by 1901 Cunnery Road, Madeira Walk, Trevor Hill and Clive Avenue had been laid out. At first plots sold slowly, but within ten years the urban district's rateable value had doubled and large villas had been built upon the lower slopes or in the valley—Overdale in Clive Avenue, Mynd Court on Longhills, Denehurst on Shrewsbury Road, Arden House in the road to Carding Mill Valley, The Rowans and Scotsmansfield on the Burway, and other large houses in Sandford Avenue and Watling Street.

Photograph of the development of Longhills and Trevor Hill
early in the twentieth century

Less expensive properties were erected in Watling Street South and in the Crossways area where Tower Buildings was the imposing precursor of a planned new shopping precinct. In the town centre the brook was culverted and Sandford Avenue widened, while Henry Salt gave his shop a handsome new frontage. Between 1901 and 1911 the population of the Urban District of Church Stretton rose by 78% from 816 to 1,455. Yet although 186 houses were added in the first five years of the century, by 1905 the momentum of development was slackening, many plots were still vacant, the Land Co. went into receivership, and even the smaller building plots laid out by Squire Benson on his lands in the area immediately north of the newly widened Sandford Avenue remained largely unsold. An ambitious scheme to develop the town as a spa, with water from a saline spring at Wentnor on the western side of the Long Mynd piped to a Pump Room near an enlarged Long Mynd Hotel, came to nothing.

The church was not slow to recognise the significance of the development in the early Edwardian years. A rising population called for additional accommodation, and Rector Noel-Hill had sufficiently recovered from his illness to be the moving spirit behind the building of St. Michael's in All Stretton. The village had already witnessed increasing church activities as mission services were held there in 1888 and probably other years. When the mission room was acquired in 1892 as a place where young people could meet to read or play music, the *Shrewsbury Chronicle* delivered an extraordinary verdict: 'The inhabitants of the picturesque little hamlet of All Stretton will, on Wednesday evening next, emerge from that quiet, out-of-the-world existence in which they have for generations luxuriated, and make an effort to place themselves on a level with their metropolis, Church Stretton'.[2] It is hard to decide who would have been most astonished by this comment—the bucolic villagers of All Stretton, the metropolitan inhabitants of Church Stretton, or the young people who were to spark this revolution!

The decision to build a church at All Stretton must have been taken early in 1901 for by September plans had been drawn up. When in November the rector appealed for help in the erection of 'a small supplementary church' in the village, he had already purchased the site. Parishioners and others promptly promised £700 towards the estimated building cost of £1,600. The *Chronicle* stated that 'the undertaking has become necessary because of the many visitors in search of health who have recently come to Church Stretton',[3] but there must have been strong support from local residents. By January 1902 the rector was able to report, in the earliest known issue of a parish magazine, that £1,000 had been raised and the tender of Mr. Bowdler from Shrewsbury for £1,570 accepted. Since the contract was due to be completed by the end of September, work on clearing the ground began at once. The phenomenal success of previous bazaars guaranteed the establishment of a committee to organise another in August. In the June magazine, which also reported that the last shot

St. Michael and All Angels, All Sretton, consecrated 24 October 1902

had been fired in the Boer War, it was announced that 'the walls of the vestry and nave are now ready for the roof'.[4] By late July the roof was going on and the plasterers moving in. The £700 still needed in August—the overall cost had risen to over £2,000—was reduced to £300 by the success of the bazaar.

Because of its rocky site the church[5] could not be built on a true east-west axis. It was possible, nevertheless, to construct a nave 57 feet long and $21^{1}/_{2}$ feet wide, with a semi-circular apse as the chancel, a small extension at the west end for the font, and a south transept measuring 21 feet by 18 feet for use as a vestry and a meeting-place for the Sunday School. The church—built of stone from the local quarry (carted along the road on a dray belonging to the Yew Tree Inn), with Grinshill dressing, and a red Ruabon tile roof—was given a miniature tower with a pyramidal roof. It could seat 155 in the nave and 50 in the transept. The floor was of wooden blocks with tiled passages; there was gas lighting and hot air circulated from a stove in a chamber under the vestry. Apart from the American organ and the oak pulpit, almost everything in the church was given, including the Grinshill stone font made and presented by Mr. Joseph Jones, and the bell, the gift of a Mr. William Healey.[6] The south door entrance was approached through a lych-gate.

The church was dedicated to St. Michael and All Angels by the Bishop of Hereford on Friday, 24 October 1902. His sermon was based on the Lord's words to Solomon in 1 Kings 9:3 – 'I have heard thy prayer and thy supplication that thou hast made before me: I have hallowed this house which thou hast built, to put my name there for ever; and mine eyes and mine heart shall be there perpetually'. On the following day Stretton rejoiced again at the opening of the 15,000,000 gallon reservoir in Carding Mill Valley. This chance juxtaposition of the opening of church and reservoir caused one wag to remark that cleanliness was still next to godliness.

Events earlier in 1902 testify to the patriotic and loyal character of the Stretton community. On St. George's Day the flag was flown from St. Laurence's tower and the schoolchildren went in their annual procession to the Jubilee Memorial Fountain where they sang the National Anthem and gave three cheers for the king. Yet at a public meeting to consider how to celebrate the coronation, Charles Noel-Hill was bold enough to say that he did not have the same admiration for the private life and character of Edward VII that he had had for Queen Victoria. Nonetheless, the coronation was celebrated in style in August with a children's procession and sports, decorations and illuminations, and a torchlight procession in the evening with refreshments and a dance. The children received coronation mugs and the king a loyal telegram. To commemorate the occasion an oak was planted at the foot of Burway Road and the fountain moved near to it.

The building of St. Michael's, the confirmation of 107 candidates (90 from Stretton) in St. Laurence's by the bishop in April 1903, the 322 Easter communicants, the highest ever offertories in the year 1902-03, the appointment of six sidesmen at St. Laurence's, and record congregations at Harvest are all evidence that the church still flourished. Further expansion beckoned. But if 24 October 1902 had been All Stretton's red letter day, Tuesday 20 October 1903 was to be Little Stretton's, for on that day 'this commodious mission church' was formally dedicated to All Saints by the Bishop of Hereford. The *Shrewsbury Chronicle*'s reporter seized the opportunity to blow Stretton's trumpet:

> With the increasing appreciation of the charm of Church Stretton and its recognition by experts as one of the finest health resorts in the kingdom, a result largely brought about by the far-seeing and enterprising policy of the Land Company, the town is rapidly outgrowing its old clothes. All around are evidences of commercial activity on the part of those who are ministering to the wants of the larger community; the village is rapidly being surrounded by a network of picturesque habitations ... There has also been a spiritual development. With the growth of the neighbourhood the mother church also has grown and expanded her influence, under the fostering care of the rector. When the venerable parish church became inadequate to meet the needs of the larger flock from an ever-expanding area she showed her vitality by building a new church at All Stretton, and later developments having more affected Little Stretton she has with equal zeal hastened to make provision for the spiritual needs of the growing community there.[7]

All Saints', Little Stretton, consecrated 20 October 1903

In fact, the initiative for the erection of All Saints' Church came principally from Mrs. Gibbon, the widowed daughter-in-law of Mr. Edward Gibbon, a great benefactor of St. Laurence's. She gave both the site and the building. She lived at the Manor House and had the church built next door to match the black and white half-timbered style of her own dwelling. The church was, however, a fully wooden structure, whose framework arrived early in September. Initially it had a corrugated iron roof covering an interior of deal timber illuminated by two large candelabra. There was a carved reading desk, but at first no pulpit. The windows were frosted except to the east where clear glass afforded a view of the hills.

Barely three weeks after the consecration of All Saints', Charles Noel-Hill announced that he would be leaving in the new year after 24 years in the parish. The news cannot have come as a total surprise to his congregation because they were only too well aware that for three or four years he had struggled with ill-health. It must have been with justifiable pride that, with the help of his curate, he took the Christmas service in each of his three churches. In the New Year issue of the parish magazine he wrote: 'It is not for me to enumerate the various improvements and additions which have been carried out in our parochial life, in divine service, in increased accommodation, in the foundation and support of the various institutions which are essential to the proper working of a large parish in these days'.[8] It had all been possible, he continued, through the support of curates, wardens, church workers and all the people of the parish. They had had, he told them finally, 'the benefit, such as it has been, of my best years'. He preached his farewell sermon on 10 January 1904 before leaving to become Rector of the much smaller parish of Stockton near Shifnal.

A committee set up in December had the unusual task of inviting donations to a farewell presentation to the rector and his wife instead of to a memorial, for Charles Noel-Hill was the first rector not to die in office since Henry Maurice left in 1671! They presented him with an antique mahogany writing desk and a Chippendale chair and Mrs. Noel-Hill with an antique dressing-table and Chesterfield settee. A parishioner expressed her sense of loss thus: 'I can only write of Mr. Noel-Hill and his excellent wife in the highest terms'.[9] The rector was 55, but their three children were still only eleven, nine and six years of age.

Charles Noel-Hill's departure brought to an end a period of over 50 years during which two remarkably energetic rectors, Hugh Owen Wilson and himself, had presided over the restoration and growth of the local church. It was, it is true, a conspicuously religious age. In the Church of England baptisms, confirmations and the number of Easter communicants continued to rise until the First World War. Over three million children attended Church, mainly Anglican, schools. Yet over the country as a whole church attendances were declining. Of course there never was a time, at least since the seventeenth century, when nearly everyone went to church regularly. 'During the last three centuries an ever smaller number of the inhabitants of the British Isles have been subjected to social, cultural or legal pressure to adopt active membership of a church not of their choosing. In this geographical and historical context, therefore, churches have come to be voluntary associations whose members join and leave them at will'.[10] As has been noted, in the 1830s, before there were any Nonconformist churches in the Strettons, the archdeacon's inquiry asked if the church building could accommodate *half* of the population, while the 1851 Inquiry recorded only 300 in the morning congregation at St. Laurence's. National statistics show that in spite of the dedicated attitude and mounting efficiency of the late nineteenth-century clergy, the size of congregations was steadily diminishing, particularly in the industrial areas of the North and Midlands. Yet what was new in the Edwardian age was less the Church's loss of the working class because the poor had never really belonged to it, than the unmistakable decline in Christian belief of the middle class.[11] As Charles Masterman wrote in his contemporary survey, *The Condition of England*, 'It is the middle class which is losing its religion; which is slowly or suddenly discovering that it no longer believes in the existence of the God of its fathers'. Among the reasons for this was the accumulated effect on educated people of Darwin's theory of evolution, the onward march of science, and the historical criticism of the Bible which had punctured the simple scriptural faith of the Victorians. Certainly the signs of decline were much clearer in the towns than in the countryside, although as early as 1889 Noel-Hill had welcomed spokesmen of the Church Defence Association, formed to counter the political challenges to the Church stemming from the decline in faith, and become secretary of its new branch in the deanery. The church in Stretton, as in most rural areas, continued to hold a central place in the life of the community. At the start of the twentieth century probably a majority of the inhabitants attended a Sunday service in one of the churches, but such attendance remained the socially acceptable practice, and for some church membership did not signify a deep commitment. Further challenges to church allegiance came from the economic, social and political development of the community, which had seen functions once performed by parish organisations, and especially the church-wardens, transferred elsewhere, so that the parish as such had lost much of its importance in people's daily lives. Finally there was the erosion of church attendance caused by the mushrooming of secular recreational activities. Even in the pages of the conservative *Shrewsbury Chronicle* the references to Church Stretton in the late nineteenth century were increasingly of council meetings, the development of roads, water and gas supplies, sports, concerts and other social occasions, while the only items of church news reported were the services at Christmas, Easter and Harvest. 'Where once they had been central to the life of Victorian Britain, religious issues and controversies were, by the last two decades of the nineteenth century, well on their way towards a new location somewhat nearer to the periphery of national life'.[12]

What Charles Noel-Hill achieved in the Strettons, by an active and dedicated ministry spanning a quarter of a century, was to enhance the spiritual life of the church, as well as increasing the congregation, improving the building, and opening new churches in All Stretton and Little Stretton. On his arrival his High Church ways had not pleased all, and his single-minded devotion to the church— he did not, for instance, become a magistrate, like his predecessor and his future father-in-law—left him, particularly at first, somewhat socially isolated, but by the time he left his views had broadened and he was held in esteem and affection. The bishop called him, 'A high-minded, unselfish, humble, devout Christian English gentleman ... One of the high types of parish priest'.[13]

*

Since Noel-Hill's appointment to the living, the patronage had changed hands twice. After the death of Charles Orlando Childe-Pemberton in 1883 the advowson was bought by W.N. Heald, Esq., of Parr's Wood, Lancashire. Early in the new century he came to an agreement with the Church Patronage Society, on the Evangelical wing of the Church, that they should become patrons but he would make presentations in his lifetime. The candidate he now presented, and who was inducted at Church Stretton on 27 May 1904, was the Rev. Alexander Roberts. Born near Bristol, he had been admitted to Wadham College, Oxford, in 1870 at the age of 19. Following his graduation he was ordained deacon in 1875, and priest in 1876. After three years as a curate in Bath he became Rector of Kimberley, Nottinghamshire, in 1878. During his 12 years there he married Alice Mary, daughter of Major-General Herbert Jacob, and they had one son. Vicar of St. Peter with St. Owen, Hereford, from 1890 to 1893, Alexander Roberts was then appointed Secretary of the National Protestant Union for seven years. When offered the living at Church Stretton he had been Vicar of Christ Church, Leicester, since 1900.[14] It was therefore as an experienced parson of Evangelical sympathies, in contrast to the High Church Noel-Hill, that Alexander Roberts came to Church Stretton. An even greater contrast was their age on appointment, for Noel-Hill had arrived at 31, Roberts at 54, only one year younger than his predecessor who had completed almost a quarter of a century in the parish. The similarity of their ages as one succeeded the other in 1904 may have disguised from parishioners the significance of the change. And it was a change that continued—the average age on appointment of the ten rectors of the twentieth century was to be 51 and the average length of their rectorship nine and a half years, just half the average duration of their nineteenth-century predecessors. Gone were the days of young men appointed for life; clergy now tended to move on to obtain wider experience and to build a career. Many of those who were to come to Church Stretton were on the final stage of that progression. Gone, too, were the days of rectors with very substantial private means; their twentieth century successors, like their church, were sometimes to face financial exigencies.

The congregation will have been made sharply aware of the change of leadership in the church by the new, simpler style of worship and the evangelical emphasis of the ministry. In his first sermon on Whitsunday 1904, the new rector appealed for support from the laity for the church's work and invited members of the congregation to ask themselves, 'What can I do for the Lord?' One visitor who in the future would respond positively to that chal-

The Rev. Alexander Roberts,
Rector 1904-1911 (SRRC)

lenge might have been discerned in the congregation in September that year, for a party of undergraduates staying at The Hotel was led by Mr. Temple of Queen's College, Oxford, the future Archbishop William Temple.[15] Alexander Roberts quickly showed himself willing to be involved in the life of the community: a Cake Fair was held in the rectory grounds to raise funds to assist the Barn Owls' Dramatic Society to build public recreation rooms; he led the annual service for the Ancient Order of Foresters; and he showed his keen interest in educational matters by serving as chairman of the local trustees and school managers and of the Church Stretton District School Attendance Committee. A new, perhaps diocesan, venture was a Missionary Exhibition and Sale of Goods, with African and Chinese melodies sung by children in native dress.

Rector Roberts was assisted by two curates: the Rev. Charles Bryant replaced Richard Dansey in 1904, and the semi-retired Rev. Vincent Higgins came in place of George Bainbridge, who also left in 1904 after only a year—did Noel-Hill's men not find themselves at one with the new Evangelical rector? That he needed two curates is evident from the details of services published in the earliest surviving copies of the parish magazine which are for the months of October 1906, September 1907 and July 1909:

Parish Church of St. Laurence

Sundays -   Morning Service at 11.00. Evening Service 6.30.
             Holy Communion on 1st.& 3rd. Sundays of the month at Morning
                 Service; on other Sundays and Saints' Days at 8.00 a.m.
             Children's Service on 1st. Sunday at 3.00 p.m.
Week-Days - Wednesdays – Evening Service with Sermon at 7.00 pm.

St. Michael's and All Angels', All Stretton

Sundays -   Morning Service at 11.00. Evening Service 6.30
             Holy Communion on 1st. Sunday of the month at the Morning
                 Service, and on 3rd. Sunday at 8.00 am
             Children's Service on the 2nd. Sunday at 3.00 pm
Week-Days - Shortened Evening Service with address at 7.00 pm on Tuesdays
                 during the winter months.

All Saints', Little Stretton

Sundays -   Evening Service 6.30
             Holy Communion on 1st. Sunday in the month at 8.00am
Wednesdays - Evening Service at 7.00 pm

Published monthly, the magazine contained two or three pages of parish information and news together with an inset of 24 sides. Local advertising, particularly by church members, kept the initial cost to 1d. per copy. Each month recent births, marriages and deaths and details of offertories were included and the next month's hymn numbers displayed. Individual issues provided details of working parties, sales, outings, the annual garden party and sale of work, and expressions of sympathy on the deaths of local people. Its homely contents would seem to confirm what national statistics in the Edwardian era reveal: that the Church of England was becoming already noticeably a church of women, although positions of responsibility were still held almost exclusively by men.

An interesting item appeared in the September 1907 issue: a meeting of clergy, churchwardens and sidesmen of the parish church had approved the rector's proposal that a Church Council should be formed consisting of themselves and sidesmen from St. Michael's and All Saints'. At the inaugural meeting it was agreed to obtain expert advice on heating the church and to support the Mission arranged for the next month particularly, and significantly, by arousing interest among men. It was further agreed that the existing Additional Curate Fund should be renamed The Assistant Clergy Fund and managed by a committee. This was the upshot of a long discussion at the 1906 Easter Vestry on how a second curate was to be financed. Rector Roberts said he would continue to pay one curate but, after it was pointed out that he was paying less than his predecessor, he had to plead that his emolument was comparatively small and there was a limit to what he could contribute. Someone signing himself 'Churchman' had then written to the *Church Stretton Advertiser* setting out the rector's income —£350 from commuted tithes (half a century earlier, according to *Bagshaw's Directory* in 1851, this had been £505), £150 supplement from the Ecclesiastical Commissioners, £75 from three chaplaincies, £45 rent and £40 fees, giving a total of £660 per annum plus a house and 30 acres of glebe. It was an income still well above the average for Anglican livings. The letter concluded: 'It is not a huge endowment, but most people would hardly call it a small one. But perhaps the above is not a perfectly accurate account and, if so, I think the Rector would do well to take the parishioners into his confidence by stating the exact facts'.[16] This is clearly what the rector then did with his new Church Council. He agreed to pay into the Assistant Clergy Fund the stipend he currently paid to one curate—£160—and he hoped that other donations and funds raised would support another curate and any occasional extra need. The Rev. Charles Bryant remained as curate until 1908. He was followed, for brief terms, by Alfred Osman, Gifford Johnson and Francis Tattersall. The two long-serving wardens both died during the Roberts' rectorship: David Hyslop in 1907 and John Proffit in 1910. A brass plaque in the nave commemorates the service as warden of John Proffit and his father Thomas.

It was in the Edwardian years that the Methodist Church was built on the intended, though never completed, Crossways development off Watling Street. At its opening in 1906 Mr. Pace of Stretton assured those present that it was not built in a spirit of opposition to the other churches, with whom they wished to co-operate, but because they believed they could do their own work best in their own way.[17] There was, in fact, both competition and co-operation between the different denominations. The Congregationalists built up a reputation for good musical services and reached out with their 'Popular Evenings for the People' featuring choral and instrumental items, while the Wesleyans held a two-week mission in the Town Hall in 1905. Yet the Nonconformists joined the Anglicans for a watchnight service on 31 December 1900 to greet the new century and, even though the Education Act of 1902 caused controversy over religious teaching in rate-supported schools, the denominations worked together in unsectarian gospel missions in the Town Hall and Carding Mill Valley.

With two Nonconformist churches endeavouring to expand their membership, and new leisure pursuits increasingly drawing people away from church, the Anglicans sought new means of outreach. The mid-week addresses back in 1902 on 'Some Aspects of Sin' may not have had outsiders crowding in, but the men's services introduced by the new rector on Sunday afternoons in the Town

The Methodist Church, consecrated 1906

Hall in the winter months seem to have attracted a good number with their non-liturgical format and a band to provide the music. The ten-day evangelistic mission in November 1907, which included services in the daughter churches, has a special interest as it was led by the Rev. Robert Catterall, 'an eloquent preacher' from London, who was to be welcomed back as the next rector four years later. Even the workers on the sewerage scheme had a special service organised for them in the Barrack Room at World's End; they were afterwards presented with tobacco or cigarettes.

The local church was making a positive response to fears of diminishing attendances, especially among men, but like the national Church it failed to appreciate the fundamental changes in social attitudes. A Roman Catholic mission in Ludlow encountered 'dogged indifference' to religion, and in Stretton, for all their missionary activity, the churches were fighting a losing battle against rival attractions. There were sporting clubs early in the century for football, cricket, bowls, hockey, golf, tennis and rifle-shooting, besides the Barn Theatre, the Glee Society, pigeon-racing and the meets of the United Hunt. The Sunday opening of the Golf Club in 1905, at which the rector protested, was an indication of the way things were going. The public houses, too, remained popular, although the Temperance Movement rejoiced at the closure of the Britannia and the Lion in High Street, the Grapes at World's End and the Crown in Little Stretton. The appearance of the motor-car was another portent of the future and, although there were frequent protests at their speed, especially after the first fatality on the road to All Stretton in 1904, the car, as Councillor Sherratt observed, was 'here to stay'. In the same year there are the first references to the telephone and electric lighting in Church Stretton.

More irregular church attendance may explain the wide fluctuations in church offertories; but there was always generous support for special collections for causes as diverse as the dependants of those lost in the Boer War, the Seaman's Mission, the Girls' Friendly Society, Indian Famine Relief, and the Salop Infirmary and Eye and Ear Hospital. There was also enough for the repair of the tower and roof, when a pinnacle fell during morning service, and for the levelling of the churchyard in 1908. However, when the annual £20 grant from the Curates' Aid Society stopped, and Mrs. Gibbon's three-year grant towards a curate ended, they had to have a special collection for the Assistant Clergy Fund.

Although he had been a keen athlete at university and became an ardent golfer, it was apparent by 1910 that Alexander Roberts's health was failing. He struggled on for 18 months and was able to celebrate George V's coronation – another oak tree planted—but died on 25 September 1911 at Aberdovey where he had gone to recuperate. He was 61. A memorial was erected on the north side of the nave to him and his sister in 1923, with a later one to his wife and son.

*

Within a month of the rector's death, the Rev. Robert Catterall was named as his successor. The speed at which he was appointed is explained by the fact that he was married to the daughter of Mr. W.N. Heald in whose gift the parish remained, although the official patrons were now the Church Patronage Society. He was also familiar with Stretton as he had led the 1907 mission. Robert Catterall was aged 54 and a Salopian from near Whitchurch. He did not attend university, but trained at St. Aidan's Theological College, Birkenhead, where in 1883 he was awarded a First Class in the Preliminary Theological Examination. His lack of a university education sets him apart from all the other rectors from the early seventeenth century to 1974, 13 of whom were Oxford men and six from Cambridge. On the other hand he had had some academic theological training, a sign that the age of the 'gentleman priest' was passing. He was ordained deacon in 1883 and priest a year later. After four years as curate and vicar in Manchester, he served as Diocesan Missioner there from 1887 to 1889. Twelve years as a rector in Crumpsall, a suburb of Manchester, were followed by eight in London before he returned to Manchester as Rector of Middleton in 1909.[18] In a farewell message to his Middleton parishioners Catterall wrote, 'To go to Church Stretton is, in a measure, to go into retirement from the heavier, more strenuous life of the north. But you will see that there is plenty of work to be done in a parish like that, and that in retirement I shall never be idle'.[19]

The Rev. Robert Catterall,
Rector 1912-1914

Robert Catterall came to Stretton with wide experience and a reputation as an extempore preacher, an enthusiastic evangelist and a gifted organiser.[20] Before he was inducted in January 1912, his immediate predecessor had been followed to the grave by Squire Benson and Charles Noel-Hill, the latter commemorated in three stained-glass windows in the apse at St. Michael's All Stretton, donated by his widow. Catterall himself was not in the best of health, but he tackled his new responsibilities with energy and skill. The parish magazine for January 1912 carried a New Year greeting and introductory letter from him, in which he admitted that all his experience had been in parishes with large and crowded populations, and therefore asked them to set up a Voluntary Church Council which he could consult; perhaps the one formed in 1907 had lapsed. 'The churches are yours, not mine', he tactfully reminded his new parishioners. But he went on, 'No clergyman can take the benefice of Church Stretton, as it now is, and maintain the rectory and its grounds unless he has very considerable private means'. As his gross income would be only £625, he proposed to continue defraying the stipend of one curate through the Assistant Clergy Fund but would rely on the parishioners to support another. (He had obviously heard of Alexander Roberts's problem.) Even then there would be only three clergy for three churches and he asked if they would also fund one half-Sunday assistant; the alternative would be to reduce services at All Stretton and Little Stretton. His promise to 'talk out this whole matter with your Church Council' was successfully fulfilled because three curates were appointed before the end of the year: Cuthbert Birley, Robert Catterall Worsley—surely a relative or godson—and the part-time Arthur Holmes, a mature ordinand. This enabled him to restore the Sunday morning service at Little Stretton.

The record of the Vestry meeting on 11 April 1912, which began with all standing in memory of the previous rector, illustrated Catterall's managerial experience. There were printed copies of the audited accounts for all present and a properly minuted account of the meeting. He raised questions about the church heating and ventilation and suggested the vestry might be enlarged as a memorial to the two late rectors. By the time of the next Vestry meeting in 1913 the rector was able to announce the exciting news that there would soon be a Parish Hall in Church Street opposite to St. Laurence's. He was personally largely responsible for this important development: he and his wife contributed £300, his father-in-law and former patron, Mr. Heald, £300, and his friends £200. At the same meeting the Church Council was instructed to consider enlarging the vestry, a task completed in 1914 when it was extended to its present size and the plaque dated 1831 attached to the new end wall.

The rector had meanwhile demonstrated his skills as an evangelist. On Good Friday evening in 1912, in the Barn Theatre, he gave an address illustrated by lantern-slides on 'The Story of the Cross' to a large audience. He introduced Hospital Sunday in August 1912 with a procession through the town led by the Longden Prize Band, with uniformed organisations invited to join, and a collection in the streets before he preached at a special afternoon service. He gave an illustrated talk in the Town Hall for the British and Foreign Bible Society and enthusiastically supported Church Missionary Society lectures. Everything seemed to have gained new vitality: the number of communicants at Easter 1913 was a record-breaking 369; the Sunday School treat included a conjurer and ventriloquist; there is the first reference to a Mothers' Union; and the Garden Fêtes, opened in successive years by the widows of Hugh Owen

The Parish Hall completed in 1913 and extended in 1927

Wilson and Charles Noel-Hill, were exceptionally successful. The second Hospital Sunday was an ecumenical venture. One Sunday in July 1913 there were children's services in all three Anglican churches, with collections for the School and Sunday School. It is true that the bell-ringers went on strike over Christmas 1912 and the New Year, when a new sexton replaced Ned Marston who had served for 50 years, but it was soon sorted out. So much was going on that church activities forced their way back into the local newspaper.

The pinnacle of achievement was the opening of the Church Hall by the Bishop of Hereford just in time for Christmas 1913. He described it as 'the symbol of what one might call the gospel of social service. It meant they were giving more thought to the whole life of the people amongst whom they were living, and to the Christian duty of doing something to serve them'.[21] The hall, which was to be extended in 1927, provided accommodation for a multitude of church and parish activities for three-quarters of the century. Sadly, this special occasion was the first time Robert Catterall had been in the parish for six months on account of ill-health, and the rejoicing was muted by the news that he was having to resign.

Tributes at once flooded in: from the Bible Society of which he was a life governor; from his curate who remarked that 'everyone knew how hard he had worked for the good of the parish ever since he came among them'; from Dr. Higginson who believed that 'no parish could possibly have had a better rector. He was a good business man as well as a good preacher'. After less than two and a half years he left a forward-looking congregation, a healthy financial position, a new hall and an enlarged vestry. What is more, he was held in such

The prayer-desk presented to Robert Catterall by the men of the church in 1912

affection that the men's group had presented him with a prayer desk after only three months as rector. A similar prayer desk was presented in 1914 in memory of a 14-year-old girl, Winnie Lewis Grier. Both are still in use today. Robert Catterall remained in the parish, but was too weak to come to the Garden Party and died in August of acute anaemia. His *Gospel Messages for the Times* was published posthumously in 1915.

One of the first tasks of the Rev. Sidney Woods, the new rector, was to assist at his predecessor's funeral. His induction on 19 June 1914 had been made more memorable by the unveiling and dedication of the lancet window in the south transept to the memory of Hesba Stretton, the local authoress renowned particularly for *Jessica's Last Prayer*, which had been a Victorian best-seller. She had worshipped at St. Laurence's.

Sidney Woods had been a student at Pembroke College, Cambridge, graduating in 1889. After a year at Ridley Hall, an Evangelical Theological College in Cambridge, he was ordained and served as a curate in Tunbridge Wells. Incumbencies in Great Yarmouth and Guildford were followed by three years as Chaplain to the Seamen's Mission. Before coming to Stretton he had been Vicar of Holy Trinity in Stockton-on-Tees for 12 years.[22] He was 44 and married with children.

His first Garden Party on 29 July 1914 was particularly spelndid. The large crowd was entertained by the band of the King's Shropshire Light Infantry and could choose between the sale of work, with its six stalls in a marquee, and a range of entertainments including hoop-la, a coconut shy, a shooting range, bowls, putting and croquet, with ices and refreshments available. The whole was illuminated in the evening.[23] But the occasion was overshadowed by the news that Robert Catterall was close to death and the nation even closer to war. Hostilities with Germany were declared on 4 August.

Over the next four years services and activities continued in much the same way, but everywhere there were reminders that the country was at war. Soldiers were camped near the town, recruiting meetings were held in the Town Hall—by Easter 1915 there had been a hundred volunteers from the Strettons—part of the Harvest offertories went on comforts for the troops, a small hospital for the sick and wounded was set up at Essex House, and the ladies of Stretton were thanked by the queen for the hundred pairs of socks and hundred woollen belts they had knitted for the soldiers at their Monday working sessions.[24] The new rector was in the thick of it: in the chair at recruiting meetings, President of the Rifle Club, compere at the concert in aid of Belgian refugees, leading the memorial service to Lord Roberts. In January 1915, at a men's meeting, he tackled the sensitive topic of 'The Bible and German Theology', lamenting the death of Christian devotion in Germany, and praying that at home 'the old evangelical spirit of their forefathers might be again revived in the ministry'. In some respects life carried on as normal, with 68 candidates from the parish at the Confirmation Service in May 1915, the official opening of the town's Recreation Ground and tennis courts in the same month, and the Garden Party in July. Yet the sight of wounded soldiers from the local hospital sitting in the chancel on Whitsunday brought home the reality of war; even more grim was the occasional heart-breaking news of local men killed in action, including Second Lieutenant Guy Barnett, whose memorial plaque is in the nave, and Second Lieutenant F.H. Butler, the son of the head-master and organist, who played at the memorial service for him and Sergeant Preen.

Memorial in the nave to a local man killed in the Great War. He was the son of the Medical Superintendent at the Stretton House asylum

And yet in the midst of the daily reminders of the titanic struggle across the Channel a plan was drawn up in 1915 for a comprehen-

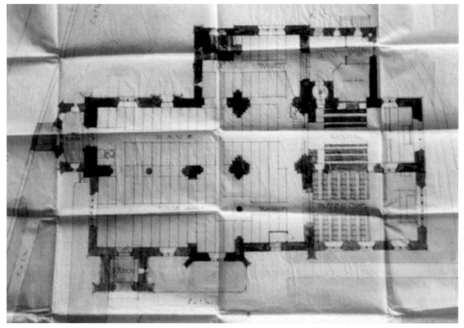

Plans for a great church extension, 1915—never implemented

sive enlargement of St. Laurence's! The project was an ambitious one. The plans, dated December 1915 and the work of architects Naylor and Sale of Derby and Nottingham, feature a new aisle on the south side of the nave, with the vestry pulled down and a new small porch added; a morning chapel as large as the chancel on its south side; a choir vestry and clergy vestry beyond the organ chamber, extending outward as far as the north wall of the transept and incorporating the entrance to the tower; and a substantial new west porch.[25] The intended extensions were far greater than the aisles added to the transepts in 1868 and would have been the biggest building project since the thirteenth century. Yet who authorised the submission to the architects? There is no mention in the churchwardens' accounts, the diocesan archives, the parish magazines that have survived nor the newspapers of the time. Indeed, our only source of information is the plan itself. On the envelope containing it is the cryptic comment, 'Not implemented'. That the project had got as far as a ground plan suggests that the church was still pressed for space and that it was anticipated that extension would be needed as the population continued to rise. The gradual decline in congregations, other than on special occasions, since the Great War, however, indicates that it was a wise decision not to proceed, although the immediate reasons are likely to have been the cost and the rector's heart attack at the end of 1915.

Sidney Woods was well enough again to preside at the Annual Vestry in May 1916 and at the local launch of the 'National Mission' at a crowded meeting in the Parish Hall in June. Two of their speakers came to Stretton and 'did much to brighten our lives'.[26] One of the curates, the Rev. Robert Stockdale, had already gone to be an Army Chaplain, and at the 1917 Vestry the rector announced that he was leaving for a year 'to go to the soldiers, which I had always wanted to do'.[27] His place was filled by a pro-Rector, the Rev. G.M. Davies, who stayed for 12 months, and then, after a short period under the senior curate, Leslie Morton, by the Rev. D.W. Whincup, who also served for a year as Woods did not resume his position as soon as the war ended.

Roll of Honour 1914-1918

Armistice Day, 11 November 1918, was a day never to be forgotten. 'Very soon after the momentous news reached Stretton the whole place was adorned with flags, the bell-ringers mounted the church tower and rang out merry peals, cannon were fired, and the townspeople gathered round the memorial fountain',[28] on which was hung the roll of honour. That roll, reproduced in the church today, contains 49 names. The pro-Rector expressed the universal mood when he said that feelings of joy mingled with feelings of sorrow. In the evening the parish church was filled to overflowing for a United Service of Thanksgiving with the Nonconformists. Afterwards there was a bonfire on Burway Hill and an impromptu social at the new Silvester Horne Institute. This had been built in memory of the celebrated Congregationalist leader and preacher, who had been one of the first clergymen to become an M.P. on his election in 1910, and had lived briefly at the White House in Sandford Avenue before his death in 1914.

*

Peace brought new problems to the country and the local church. 'The world has gone through a tremendous upheaval that has shaken it to its depths', wrote Rector Woods in the magazine on his return after two years away, 'Naturally there is sure to be a mighty reaction'. He instanced 'the fantastic rise in prices' and 'the mad race for this world's materials'. Turning to the parish, he promised to respond to the call for a return to the full pattern of services as before the war (Little Stretton had been reduced to a fortnightly service), but warned, 'I am certain that under existing conditions no Rector of Church Stretton can expect to have on his staff more than one priest and one deacon. It is all very well for the people to tell me that the money will be forthcoming for more. IT WILL NOT'. He was aware that stipends would have to rise and that it would be difficult to maintain even his two curates, Charles Pratt and Martin Custance. As a temporary measure Mr. Frank Butler, brother of the organist, would assist with services at St. Michael's and All Saints'; he proved to be the first of the lay readers who have contributed so much to the life of the church ever since. The rector told the Garden Sale committee how crucial their success would be to the church, 'We cannot expect assistant clergy to live on what has always been a miserable pittance and much less than the average worker was obtaining. Now, with wages going up 50%, and with food going up 100%, how can we keep our clergy on the old scale? … We shall have to budget for a much larger Assistant Clergy Fund'.[29]

Fortunately the installation of electric light in St. Laurence's and an electric blower for the organ had been agreed and paid for by subscription in 1919, for church finances were to remain a problem for the remainder of Sidney Woods' rectorship. Indeed, they presented an immediate challenge to the first Parochial

Church Council (PCC). This came into being in 1920 as a result of the passing of the Enabling Act which established the Church Assembly, giving the Church a measure of administrative independence from Parliamentary control. A meeting was convened in April to elect members to the Stretton PCC. The earlier Voluntary Council had consisted of the wardens and sidesmen; now the members were chosen by the 634 who had been placed on the new Electoral Roll—385 for Church Stretton, 132 for All Stretton, and 117 for Little Stretton. It was decided to elect 20 members—ten for St. Laurence's and five each for the daughter churches. The elected members held their first meeting on 28 May 1920 with the rector in the chair, two curates (Martin Custance and Selby Lennie), the churchwardens and three representatives to the Ruridecanal Conference ex officio, and two co-optees: a total of 30. This first PCC included three senior army officers and five women. Mr. Frank Butler was elected secretary. They agreed to meet quarterly, and established the following committees: Assistant Clergy Fund, Standing and Finance, Parish Hall, Sunday School, Magazine, Garden Sale, Missionary, and Coal and Clothing Club (a long-standing charity for the poor), some with co-opted, non-PCC, members.

Under the terms of the 1920 Act all PCC members were responsible for the parish finances, a change which was initially resisted by the churchwardens. In its first year the PCC agreed to start a freewill offering scheme in 1922. A successful garden sale and the introduction of offertory schemes at the daughter churches helped to keep them solvent, but they were slow to launch the scheme in St. Laurence's. When the PCC met on 20 January 1922 Sidney Woods warned them of the dire financial situation. There was talk of curtailing services and reducing the staff, with the rector declaring that he would ask his newly-priested curate, Selby Lennie, to move on. Members pinned their hopes on the next garden sale, but the rector refused to undertake another without more backing. After a heated discussion he concluded: 'There would be only one head in the parish and as long as he remained he intended to be head. The duty of each one was to go home and try to save our parish from bankruptcy!'

Sidney Woods did not remain as head much longer. Although in May 1922 he felt there was a better spirit abroad, two months later he told the PCC he was leaving, adding that what the church needed was a man of God who would build up the Church of Christ in the Strettons—and a man with money. He also made the important suggestion that perhaps the rectory could be sold to augment the parish income. When one possible successor turned the living down because the rectory would be too expensive to maintain, the PCC realised it would have to go. Dr. Cranage, a PCC member famed for his work on *The Churches of Shropshire*, said that anyone taking the living would be making an annual gift of £500 to the parish. At the end of the year Woods departed to become Schools' Secretary of the Mission to Seamen.

Mynd Court, the new rectory in 1923

At a preliminary meeting with his eventual successor, the PCC agreed to sell the rectory at a future date when prices had risen, but meanwhile to sell the glebe and woods and to purchase, as the new rector's residence, Mynd Court on Longhills at a cost well below its real value. 'Whilst not being too large, it maintained somewhat the dignity of the position of the Rector of Church Stretton'.

That successor, who was instituted on 19 January 1923, was the Rev Dr. Henry Thomas Dixon, D.D. Born in Cumberland in 1874 he had proceeded to Merton College, Oxford, graduating in 1897. After his ordination the next year, he served curacies in Nantwich, Birkenhead and Blundellsands, during which time he gained his B.D. In 1907 he began four years as a vicar in Oxfordshire during which he was awarded his D.D. From 1911 to 1915 he was a vicar in Taunton, being made an examining chaplain to the bishop and a prebendary of the cathedral. After a further five years as a vicar in Clifton and three in Bridgwater, where he became Rural Dean, he arrived in Church Stretton.[30] He had published three short devotional works: *Have Miracles Happened?* in 1909, *The Power of the Cross* in 1911, and *The Life of the Spirit* in 1919. They testify to his belief in the literal inspiration of the Bible, in the power of the cross and the forgiving love of Jesus in the life of the Christian, and in the power of the Holy Spirit 'to deepen the spiritual life of church members, to guide them into all truth, and to inspire them to attempt great things for Christ'.

In his introduction to Dr. Dixon's second book, the Bishop of Liverpool had written: 'The writer has gained his spiritual experience on the banks of the

The Ven. Dr. Henry Dixon,
Rector 1923-37 and Archdeacon
of Ludlow 1932-39 (SC)

Mersey and among the Cotswold Hills. He has ministered to souls in a great city suburb and in the quiet of the country. He has found everywhere that the words of the Lord Jesus appeal alike to the townsman and the villager, and meet the deepest needs of their spiritual nature'. This rich experience, his academic distinction and his record of achievement commended him to the patrons and to the church in Stretton; the Bishop of Hereford, who had known him for 16 years, felt sure that God had guided him to Stretton.[31] He was 48 years old, and his marriage to Evelyn Mary Lambart had produced two sons and a daughter. Mrs. Dixon, a grand-daughter of the Eighth Earl of Cavan, was also related to the Archdeacon of Salop. They took up their residence at Mynd Court, and the rectory, woods and land were let.

The church's financial problems seemed to melt away. This was immediately due to the Freewill Offering Scheme, with church members pledging regular gifts, and the letting of the old rectory, but it was undoubtedly affected by the high regard in which Dr. Dixon was held from the start. Over the next four years some major expenses were incurred on the maintenance and improvement of St. Laurence's and St. Michael's but the bills were paid promptly. As early as 1925 there was a substantial credit balance in the Assistant Clergy Fund. When, years later, Henry Dixon announced that he was leaving, Mr. T.R. Thornes said that never during the 30 years he had been associated with the parish finances had they been in a more satisfactory state, 'but, more than that, we have had the benefit of the rector's able, kindly and peaceable ministrations'.[32]

No sooner had he arrived in 1923 than the new rector was demonstrating that he was also a man of vision and energy. The first necessity was to staff the services—on Sundays two at 8. a.m. (alternate weeks at All Stretton and Little Stretton), three at 11 a.m. and three at 6.30 p.m.; on the third Sunday Holy Communion was celebrated at St. Laurence's at 12 noon after Matins. That meant eight services each Sunday to be conducted and six sermons to be prepared. To assist him the rector had two curates, initially William Wallace and Charles Warren, retired clergy and, after 1927, two lay readers, R.P. Marshall joining F.W. Butler. But the church's teaching role went further. Dr. Dixon told one of his first PCCs that he wanted their meetings to tackle issues of current interest in the inner life of the church, and one of the curates proceeded to read a paper on the revision of the Prayer Book and the next year on the role of the laity. The rector revived the Sunday afternoon men's meetings on 'subjects of current interest, educational and helpful'—and limited to 45 minutes. The Mothers' Union prospered with Mrs. Dixon as its enrolling secretary. There were appeals for more Sunday School teachers and a training week in 1926. Dr. Dixon 'urged all the loyal and willing helpers to keep before them the common aim to extend the Master's Kingdom in the parish'.[33] An Evangelistic Committee was set up and, although the rector encouraged church members to attract others by their 'silent witness and good example', he and the curates (from 1927 Reg. Griffiths and John Bartleet) introduced open-air

meetings in the churchyard and at Minton and Lower Wood. A United Service on Hospital Sunday continued as an annual summer event. In the parish of Church Stretton the tide of decline seemed to have turned, as indeed perceptive observers believed that it had for the wider Church which began to display a new confidence with modern men like William Temple, now Archbishop of York, among its leaders, a fresh concern for social problems like unemployment, and an intellectual fight-back against the 'modernism' of the 1920s.

When he proposed at the 1934 Annual Meeting that, as usual, the rector should receive the Easter offertories, the treasurer remarked that it was 'a mark of our esteem and appreciation of his ministry among us'. This was also reflected in the remarkable growth in the number on the Electoral Roll

The south transept window given by Mr. W.A. Sherratt

which reached its peak at 1,180. There was, moreover, a social as well as a spiritual side to parochial life: the Summer Garden Fête and Sale proved just as successful at Mynd Court as in the more extensive grounds of the old rectory, and a Social Fellowship Committee organised events through the year.

The expansion of young people's activities led to the addition of extra rooms and cloakrooms to the Parish Hall in 1927. Three years later, the builder, Mr. W.A. Sherratt, a former churchwarden, donated the new stained glass window in the south transept, portraying Jesus, St. Luke and St. Laurence, as a thank offering for his recovery from an operation. His family was to give, in 1955, the large stained glass window of the north transept in memory of his wife. The east window, the gift of Robert Pemberton, needed repair in the 1930s and someone offered to meet the cost if the faces were changed! Fortunately the PCC decided to preserve the original and to foot the bill — although at some time, perhaps when the window was damaged at the installation of the organ in 1882, new glass had been inserted at the head of Jesus which lacks the halo enjoyed by Peter and John. The only other window added in these years, in the east wall of the north transept, commemorates two deep personal tragedies for the rector: the deaths of his six-year-old son Joey in 1928 and of his wife Evelyn in 1930.

Other improvements at St. Laurence's included work on the heating and drainage, the addition of umbrella racks and troughs to many of the pews in 1926, the preparation and framing of the list of rectors, and the return of the stone coffin 'and other relics' from Rectory Wood before the rectory was eventually sold in 1934. Several old lime trees were felled in the churchyard after an expert's report that they were in a dangerous state. A churchyard committee, created in 1923, supervised the planting of new trees, including probably the Douglas firs that have today reached undesirable heights. At St. Michael's the roof was mended, heating improved and electric lighting installed in 1926; All Saints' had to wait until 1933 for Mr. Gibbon's gift of electric lights.

The really big building project was restoration work at the parish church. The state of the tower had been the cause of some anxiety for years and in 1930 it was resolved to commission an architect to inspect both tower and south transept. A special meeting of the PCC in October 1931 was advised that, owing to interments made too close to the walls over the centuries, there were bad cracks in the walls of the transepts, the chancel and the organ chamber and that these weak foundations jeopardised the security of the tower. A comprehensive programme of regrouting the walls and underpinning the foundations was required. The initial estimate was for £1,300, but they were advised that if the tower had moved the cost would have been £20,000. Work began in 1932 and by December they had spent £800 and were running out of money. Appeals for contributions were stepped up, a diocesan grant applied for, fundraising events organised, and a request made for interest-free loans from the congregation. Within a month more than £1,000 had been guaranteed and work continued. Costs went on rising as further work on the tower and parapet was agreed and the clock face regilded while the scaffolding was in place. The rector left no avenue unexplored that might yield something for the building fund. His letter of appeal in *The Times* brought only one response but the cheque for 40 guineas from a gentleman from near Bournemouth made it worthwhile. Dr. Dixon's pamphlet on the parish church produced at this time was the first of its kind for St. Laurence's.

The work was finished at last at a total cost of over £4,000 and a Thanksgiving Festival was planned. The Bishop of Hereford duly came on 15 October 1933 for the service of rededication, followed the next Sunday by the Bishop of Lichfield in the morning and the former Bishop of Bristol in the evening. Finally, on 29 October, they staged a belated Harvest Festival with Dr. Cranage, now Dean of Norwich, as the guest preacher.

In the year the restoration began Dr. Dixon was appointed Archdeacon of Ludlow. He remained a very active rector, although more will have been taken on by the curates, who in the early 1930s were Thomas Wilkinson, Reginald Leathley, Eric Serjeantson and Thomas Chisholm. One of the parish's outstanding areas of achievement then, and indeed throughout the early twentieth century, was its support of overseas missions. The December 1927 magazine shows that the Missionary Committee had no fewer than 23 members including the local secretaries of 12 societies. Principal among these was the Church Missionary Society (CMS) which held an annual festival in Stretton. In 1918 there had been 18 CMS subscribers and eight box-holders. A magazine article that year had called for 'intelligent enthusiasm' and the sort of commitment that was soon to triumph in the Great War. There was strong backing, too, for the Society for the Propagation of the Gospel, the British and Foreign Bible Society, the Bezwada Mission to Indian outcasts, and the Zenana Mission supporting Indian Christian teachers. The ladies of the Missionary Guild met at Scotsmansfield with Miss Bartlett to make goods for sale. In October 1926 20 undergraduates were hosted during a missionary rally and in 1933 a three day missionary campaign was held in Church Stretton.

The church was not, of course, without its problems, though the differences revealed in the PCC minutes were minor and parochial—disagreement over dancing in the Parish Hall or hesitation about granting permission for cinema shows there (a sub-committee was formed to vet the films). At various times they were divided over the addition of Woolstaston or Hope Bowdler to the parish, proposed changes in diocesan boundaries, and the revision of the Prayer Book. But fundamental issues like the marginalisation of the Church in much of society since the war, the spread of agnosticism, poverty in mining areas and the General Strike of 1926 were not discussed in the PCC, though they may have been in the men's meeting. And they had in Mrs. Robinson—as most parishes do—a specialist in complaining: she grumbled about the banging of the hall door, about ponies in the churchyard, and about open-air services. At one meeting she expressed the view that it was 'very necessary that the uneducated people should have the commandments read to them at every communion service'.

The great ecclesiastical debate of the late 1920s was centred on the revision of the Prayer Book, which incorporated changes in the liturgy, including the prayer of consecration, that were in line with the dominant Anglo-Catholicism in the Church of the day. It has been noted that Dr. Dixon asked his curate to read a paper to the PCC on the question; at a later meeting members voted in favour of revision with only one dissentient. This response in what was an 'Evangelical' parish shows how far Anglo-Catholic sacramentalism had become accepted practice in the Church of England, although at one time the controversy over the reserved sacrament had threatened to tear the Church apart. The large majorities in all three houses of the Church Assembly in favour of replacing the 1662 Book of Common Prayer with the 1928 revision confirm how far the Church had drifted from its Protestant moorings. But when the question came before Parliament, the Commons twice rejected the new Prayer Book, reflecting the nation's remaining fears of Romanism. Some bishops authorised the use of the '1928 Prayer Book' in their dioceses, and it came to be used sometimes in Stretton, but it was never legalised. Meanwhile 'the country as a whole would continue its slow slide away from organised religion'.[34]

The issue that came to prominence in Dr. Dixon's later years was the development of education in Stretton. At first the church had to decide its response to the Local Education Authority's request to lease rooms in the Parish Hall for cookery and handiwork classes. Agreement in 1935 to let the rooms was ensured by the saving of the £1,000 it would have cost to add rooms to the school and by the £30 annual income from the lease. There was anxiety, however, about the children's safety because of the narrowness of Church Street, and 28 square yards of the churchyard was given up and the wall moved so that the road could be widened by a yard. In the end the local council agreed that it should become a one-way street and dropped their insistence on a footpath with a rail by the hall. A bigger issue emerged in 1936 with the announcement that three senior schools were to be built in South Shropshire at Bridgnorth, Pontesbury and Church Stretton. The bishop and Archdeacon Dixon were determined that the one in Stretton should be a Church School.

Discussions were still at an early stage when the rector announced that he had been offered a residentiary canonry at Hereford and that he would be leaving the next year. It came as a great blow to the parish but not one entirely unexpected. He had been outstanding as a rector and the church had flourished under his leadership. Mr. Rowland Clegg, J.P., vice-chairman of the PCC and chairman of the County Education Committee, expressed the general view as recorded in the minutes: 'We in this parish were very grateful for the very happy position in which we found ourselves financially and spiritually. We owed a great debt to Dr. Dixon for the beautiful services we had enjoyed. He was so broad-minded that he gave to everyone exactly what they needed'. On his departure in March 1937 he was presented with a handsome cheque.

*

Before Dr. Dixon left the PCC had been in touch with the Church Patronage Society and agreed to the appointment of the Rev. Herbert Edward Whately who had impressed them when he came to their meeting in February to speak and answer questions. He was inducted on 19 May 1937, just a week after Church Stretton, in carnival mood, had celebrated the coronation of King George VI. Herbert Whately was a native of London. After three years at Trinity College, Oxford, he had undertaken theological training at Wycliffe Hall and was ordained deacon in 1900. Following two short curacies he served as a rector in Liverpool from 1904 to 1916. In the middle of the war he moved to London to become Vicar of St. Michael's, Blackheath, for 14 years and at Honor Oak until 1937. He came to Stretton as a man of 60 with experience of nearly 40 years in two great cities. Both the curates he inherited left within a year—Robert Lansdale in September 1937 and Gerald Gardner-Brown in April 1938. They were replaced by Harry Woodford and Eric Maddock.

The proposed new senior school was the most pressing issue facing the new rector. A fundraising committee was set up and an appeal launched for £2,000. Reluctantly it was decided to leave the provision of a new cemetery to the Urban District Council as the church could not afford that and the school. Contributions began to come in from the many who wanted the school to be a Church of England foundation. Sadly it all came to naught, for in November 1938 the Ludlow Voluntary Schools Association had to confess that they could not afford the six church schools planned for the archdeaconry; Church Stretton and Condover were the ones to be dropped. The PCC agreed to return gifts where the donors could be identified.

Already church and nation faced a much greater crisis. Although the PCC had congratulated Mr. Chamberlain on the 'wonderful deliverance' achieved at Munich, the threat of war with Germany remained. It was brought home to the church when the A.R.P. demanded a new door and proper black-out in the Parish Hall. Monthly services of Thanksgiving and Intercession were organised with the Free Churches. They created, the rector believed, 'a feeling of fellow-ship deeper and stronger than before'. He had also approached the Roman Catholic priest at St. Milburga's Church which had opened in Watling Street North in 1929. As the war clouds gathered through the summer there came the

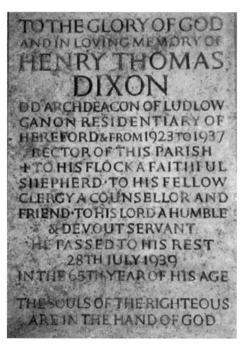

Memorial tablet to Dr. Dixon

further sad news of the death of Archdeacon Dixon on the golf course on 28 July 1939. The Rector of Ludlow, who had been Dixon's curate in Somerset, spoke of his gentleness and patience, of the quiet persuasiveness of his preaching and of his pastoral gifts. 'Whatever his personal care, sorrow or trouble, his heart was ever open to the many who came to him with their perplexities'. The feelings of the parish towards him were expressed on the memorial tablet in the north transept that was to be dedicated in 1942: 'To his flock a faithful shepherd – To his fellow clergy a counsellor and friend – To his Lord a devout and humble servant'.

On 5 September 1939 an emergency meeting of the PCC was summoned, not on account of the declaration of war two days earlier, but because the bishop wanted the rector to succeed Dr. Dixon as archdeacon while remaining in the parish—and would not take 'no' for an answer! Herbert Whately had already won the affection of his people by his assiduous visiting, 'his splendid sermons which all had so much enjoyed', and his personal kindness. At Easter 1939 there were no fewer than 536 communicants. He had given spiritual leadership, too, promoting missionary work, encouraging Bible reading, and persuading the Bible Reading Fellowship to present the new lectern Bible. Taking advantage of the spirit of ecumenism which had seen the World Council of Churches set up in 1938 (the British Council of Churches followed four years later), he had built up good relations with the Nonconformist churches whose people joined in the study circles now held after the monthly united services. In June 1939 a United Open-Air Service was held in the Carding Mill Valley amidst the cars, cyclists, hikers and picnickers. The rector now responded positively to the bishop's call, although his dual role was to prove exceptionally demanding in wartime conditions and with a wife suffering from a debilitating illness.

Fear of air attack in that first winter of the war led to the suspension of Sunday School and to Evensong being brought forward so that people could get home in daylight. At the request of the police, the bells were not rung and the clock was silenced. But when the 'phoney war' continued into the spring,

Sunday School, service times, bells and chimes were restored. The young people had in any case gone on meeting on Sunday evenings in the hall. There were, however, other effects of war: the Garden Sale in July 1940 was replaced by a Day of Prayer and Gifts—for which some had pressed for years and which raised nearly as much—and the magazine was reduced to a single sheet. 'All seemed to agree that new blood was required on the PCC', though sensibly they voted down the proposal to double the size to 50. Conflict in the choir was defused by the rector who asked the choirmaster to resign; women and girls in the choir were seated in the body of the church to lead the congregation. Throughout the war monthly united services continued, held in the new Regal Cinema (now the site of Spar) in the winter months one year. At St. Laurence's there were daily war intercessions at 11 a.m. and evening services every week-day at 6.30 p.m.

Signs of war were everywhere in the town. There were soldiers billeted in private houses and the A49 by-pass, construction of which had begun in February 1939, was used as a giant military vehicle park. Sandbags appeared at the church and an air raid shelter was erected behind the Parish Hall. Dr. McClintock thought women could be included on the rota of fire-watchers if they were of good physique. Children evacuated from industrial areas went to local villages because in 1940 St. Dunstan's, the national charity for the blind, decided to make Church Stretton their wartime headquarters so taking up much

of the available accommodation. From their centre at the Longmynd Hotel wires were strung out down to the town so that blinded servicemen could find their way. Workshops for the blind were set up in temporary huts behind the present fire station. Every Sunday there was a St. Dunstan's service in the parish church at 9.45 a.m. The St. Dunstan's memorial in the north transept was placed there in 1987 to commemorate the 700 blinded servicemen and women who were helped in Church Stretton to come to terms with their injuries.

The rector, whose responsibilities grew with the swelling numbers in the parish and the anxieties that people were suffering, told the Annual Meeting in 1941 that the

*The St. Dunstan's plaque
in the north transept*

previous 12 months had been very hard for him. As archdeacon he had met with 120 incumbents to discuss their problems, and even the leading of parade services had fallen to him as acting local padre. He was assisted by two curates, Harry Woodford and Eric Maddock, but the former went to serve as an army chaplain in 1942. Welcome help was also forthcoming from two retired clergy, R.C. Purton and J.H. Kidson, who was to continue to lead services till his 90th year. Miss Dorothy Bartlett in 1942 became the first woman to serve as church-warden at St. Laurence's, and ageing church officers like the Butler brothers, organist and lay reader, stayed in their posts. The parish was fortunate to acquire a new boiler for St. Laurence's after heating failure in early 1943 caused services to be held in the Silvester Horne Institute. More important was the consecration of the new cemetery at Greenhills in May 1942. But there were growing difficulties. Petrol shortage curtailed visiting in the villages, the commandeering by the army of the main room of the Parish Hall restricted young people's activities, and there were heating problems at St. Michael's. Sometimes no-one turned up for the daily intercessions or Evensong, numbers at the Sunday evening service plummeted, and in Dr. McClintock's opinion 'there was nothing attractive to children in the church services'.[35] Public morale was being sapped by the apparently interminable war, by rationing, by news of the death of local men in the forces, and by the arrival of more and more sightless servicemen and women in the town.

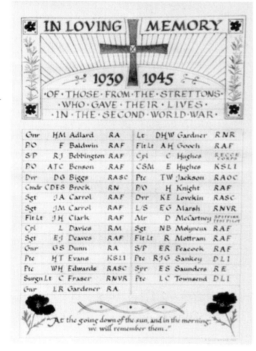

Roll of Honour 1939-1945

A change of mood was apparent in 1944 when D-Day opened the long-awaited second front. The Beveridge Report, published in 1942, had already turned thoughts to the future; now there came the passage through Parliament of Butler's great Education Act. As the inspiring leadership of Winston Churchill had steeled the nation's resolve in its darkest hour, so now the rousing and forward-looking leadership of Archbishop William Temple evoked a positive response nationwide. Even his untimely death in October 1944 did not destroy the hope he had generated. Only a few days later, in Stretton, Archdeacon Whately called a special PCC to discuss spiritual revival, and he endeavoured to organise inter-denominational occasions on the lines of the 'Religion and Life' meetings that were being held all over the country.

As the opening months of 1945 passed, hopes rose of an early end to the war. Yet peace came suddenly—and with a universal sense of relief and joy. Herbert Whately wrote of 7 May in the magazine: 'It was inspiring to see how the Parish Church filled up that afternoon, half an hour after the Prime Minister's official announcement of the German surrender, and equally so when we all gathered on the Sunday for Thanksgiving and Dedication. And how fine was the contribution of our bell-ringers!'

But the war had taken a heavy toll. The Roll of Honour for 1939-45, which hangs in the north transept alongside that for 1914-18, contains 31 names from the parish. The country as a whole had suffered much. Post-war recovery was slow and there was severe hardship for many. The Church, too, faced fundamental problems with a continuing fall in attendances, baptisms and confirmations. The effects on the church in Stretton were still cushioned by the town's rural setting, but they were nonetheless clearly discernible. Old Mr. Crofts, church treasurer for many years, put his finger on it when at a PCC meeting shortly before the war ended he exclaimed: 'All churches have attendance problems. Men say they have no time and use for it ... A different spirit seems to be in the world today'.

13

THE CHURCH IN A WORLD OF CHANGE

A fresh spirit was indeed abroad in the world in 1945. Peace brought hopes of a fresh start, of social justice, and of international co-operation through the United Nations Organisation. In Britain the new Labour government, though confronted by post-war dislocation, pursued policies of economic and social reform. The Church, too, faced up to the need for change. Archbishop Temple had rightly sensed the mood of the nation. When he addressed rallies around the country in 1944 the packed audiences had responded enthusiastically to the 'increased hopefulness for some resurgence of social idealism within the Church'.[1] His premature death was a devastating blow for the Church, but he had set it in the right direction.

Before 1945 was out the Church of England Commission on Evangelism produced its much-debated report *Towards the Conversion of England*. It has been described as 'a damp squib', but it had the merit of recognizing that the Church had to act to bring people back to the faith. The Bishop of Hereford at once established an Evangelistic Committee which organised meetings to prime the clergy and to seek to deepen spiritual life in the parishes. The bishop's Pastoral Letter was read in all churches and copies distributed to every family. Picking up the theme of the bishop's campaign, the rector, Herbert Whately, told the Stretton PCC, 'We want a real movement towards others who do not attend churches, and we ought to see that our own lives are a good advert for the Christ-like life'.

Under the aegis of the Bible Reading Fellowship parish discussion groups had already been set up to consider '(i) Problems of our own; (ii) Fellowship within the congregation; (iii) Fellowship with the churches; (iv) How can we reach outside? (v) Fellowship within the nation; (vi) Fellowship between the nations'. They reported to a special meeting of the PCC on 15 February 1946. This generated an interesting if somewhat rambling and inconclusive discussion to which most of those present contributed. Unsurprisingly, but sadly, for it betokened a narrow outlook, parochial issues dominated. Services more appropriate for young people were requested as they were said to find church dull and gloomy; the congregation preferred hymns they could sing and which were not pitched too high; there was a need to do more to welcome newcomers and 'to move up in our seats', inviting others to sit alongside. Considerable support emerged for Family Communion every Sunday, though there were differences about time and hesitation from those who preferred a 'fasting Communion'. Positive comments were offered on the united services with other churches, and on the willingness of some to help nurse the sick and, of those with cars, to take people to hospital. On social issues, concern was expressed that all houses should have upstairs bathrooms and running hot water, whereas the Sunday opening of the cinema was regarded as undesirable. The recommendations agreed were far from ambitious. They included invitations to members of the congregation to visit private gardens after summer evening services, giving a few words of explanation before reading the lesson, and, more importantly, encouraging younger people returning from the war or war work to take their part in the church and older ones to withdraw. Ideas left in the air were a 'Religion and Life' week, outdoor services in the summer, and a monthly service for young people. In summing up, the rector reminded the PCC of their role in evangelism, and made clear his own concern to reach out beyond regular churchgoers by announcing a Lent course of sermons asking 'What am I? Why am I? Who is God? How does God work? Why the Cross? and Where do I come in?' He agreed to a mid-week evening get-together to discuss the previous Sunday's sermon. It was clearly a valuable meeting for at least there was a real opportunity to examine openly the life of the local church and the freedom to make suggestions for change. Yet it also revealed the Council's inability to comprehend the magnitude of the challenge that the Church was facing.

Ideas not immediately adopted by the PCC were considered further by a new Group Suggestions Committee. Their reports to the PCC in July supported the creation of a Guild of St. Mary and St. John for younger communicants aged 15 to 25, a five-minute talk for children once a month in the morning, and a Debating Society not confined to religious subjects. The question of an evening Communion was left to the rector. At Christmas that year the Midnight Service on Christmas Eve was introduced. After the success of the Welcome Home Social for those returning from war service, a Social Committee was set up to organise a Summer Fête and Harvest Home in 1947.

If revitalisation were to be more than a pious hope the Church of England faced an immediate manpower problem, though the good news was that there were 5,000 candidates for the ministry from those leaving the armed services. To fund the training of those selected an appeal for £650,000 over five years was launched. Church Stretton readily exceeded its designated share of £123. Similarly they were able to meet the 1946 increase in the Diocesan Quota from £73 10s. to £108 to assist clergy and to make grants for Religious Education, Social Welfare and Church Building. But because of post-war inflation income could not keep pace with rising costs for curates' stipends, repairs and insurance. Indeed, the rector reported that the number in the Freewill Offering Scheme had fallen from the original 182 to 39 in 1945. The amount raised by annual Days of Prayer and Gifts—about £400—failed to rise significantly. When the treasurer forecast a deficit for 1947 another committee was set up to expand Freewill Offerings.

What was really needed was new blood in positions of leadership, and quite suddenly the opportunity for such a transfusion was presented. Frank Wilford replaced Eric Maddock as curate and was joined by Harry Woodford returning after five years as an army chaplain. Eric Burn, a lay reader, died at the end of 1945, followed a few months later by the Rev. J.H. Kidson at the age of 90. Then in 1947 Mr. Hayes retired as warden and treasurer, Frank Butler's health forced him to give up after 26 years as PCC secretary and 35 as a lay reader, and his brother Fred, who had resigned as the local headmaster some years before, announced that he would stand down after 53 years as organist. They were rightly praised for their enormous contributions to the life of the church. But replacements of like commitment were not readily found, though Graham Jukes, appointed as a temporary organist, held the post for 25 years. Finally, just before Christmas 1947, the rector, who had recently resigned as archdeacon after eight years on account of his health, died of cancer. His final

watchword, from Psalm 62, in the magazine of November 1947 was: 'Put your trust in Him always ye people, and pour out your hearts before Him for God is our Hope'.

At an emergency PCC meeting a few days after the funeral, Harry Woodford expressed the feelings of all when he said that Herbert Whately had been greatly loved and was a true Christian. He had carried a huge responsibility as archdeacon right through the war, but it was as a deeply caring pastor that he was remembered in the

The Ven. Herbert Whately, Rector 1937-1947 and Archdeacon of Ludlow 1939-47

parish. In his sermons and writings he displayed a gift for words to express his inner faith. The Rector's Letter in the magazine of December 1941, the month of Pearl Harbour, had hailed the advent of the Prince of Peace and reflected on the causes of war and strife: 'In this strange, adventurous voyage we call human life God has left the helm of my ship in my own hands; and if I neglect to watch the sun and stars of His Heaven in my navigation of untried seas, or recklessly steer contrary to their guidance, should I blame Him when ship-wreck follows – or myself?' The parish had been blessed to have such a rector at such a time.

*

As the next rector the PCC asked the patrons to present 'a Broad Churchman, who will carry on the traditions of our late rector', preferably a married man, energetic, and not to be Archdeacon of Ludlow as well as rector. As early as 18 February 1948 they interviewed the Rev. Reginald Wragge Morley, Vicar of St. Peter's, Hereford, who said he believed a parson should be a real leader but no dictator. His views, he claimed, were very similar to those of the late Archdeacon Whately. He received their unanimous approval.

The new rector, a churchman of wide experience, was instituted on 10 May 1948. In his youth he had been a good amateur soccer player on the books of Preston North End. A graduate of Selwyn College, he had stayed in Cambridge for his theological training at Ridley Hall. Following ordination in 1912 he had served as a curate in Reading till 1917. He had probably then gone as a padre to the forces, because it was two years later, when the war was over, that he became CMS Organising Secretary for the dioceses of Ely and St. Albans for two years. There followed terms as a vicar in Birmingham, the East End of London and Bournemouth before going in 1942 to St. Peter's, Hereford, where he acted as Rural Dean for three years prior to his move to Stretton.[2] He was to be made a Prebendary of Hereford Cathedral in 1950 in recognition of his services to the Church, but having reached his late 50s when he arrived in Stretton he would find it increasingly difficult to relate to a world of rapid change.

The post-war years saw the country gradually recover from shortages and rationing. In the 1950s social change accelerated, with many more women going out to work, an ever-swelling demand for material improvements and the appearance of a television set in almost every home. The Church had at the same time to adapt to this different world and contend with rising costs. Imaginative, dynamic leadership was required at the head of the Church, but the strength of Temple's successor as archbishop, Geoffrey Fisher, lay more in administration. In Stretton, too, the rector was a good man of business. Yet although he kept the church solvent and maintained the regular services, there was a failure to respond to the needs of an expanding community and particu-larly of the younger generation. For in Wragge Morley's time, while the overall population rose only slowly, council houses were going up apace in Essex Road, Lutwyche Road, Central Avenue and, finally, Brooksbury, with scattered private housing development. Successful 'maintenance' of attendances and collections, which was what the rector claimed year after year at the Annual Church Meeting, was therefore not enough. Moreover, his regular plea, on the same occasion, for a spirit of fellowship to be spread in the community, was heard by only a faithful nucleus because, while for most of his 16 years as rector the Electoral Roll contained over a thousand names, the average atten-dance at the Annual Meeting was a mere 36. People came to services but were not keen on meetings and there was little attempt to reach those outside the regular congregation.

It is true that it was an achievement to keep the books balanced. Since only a minority supported the Freewill Offering Scheme, the church had to rely on the proceeds of the Annual Fête and the Day of Prayer and Gifts to supplement collections. The root of the problem was ever-increasing expenditure. Apart from the maintenance of the fabric of the three churches and the hall, there were rising bills for heat, light and insurance. More demanding still were the growing Diocesan Quota, clergy expenses—especially as these came to include help with the running of cars —and the obligation to augment curates' remu-neration and to provide them with proper living accommodation. Of the two curates when Wragge Morley arrived, Harry Woodford soon left and Frank Wilford assumed responsibility for St. Michael's, with an increase in stipend to £350 per annum. By 1963, the year before Wragge Morley retired, the new curate, married and with three children, was receiving £675 plus expenses and the Whitsunday collection. The rector's own stipend was now paid by the Church Commissioners, though the church paid his expenses and presented the Easter offering. Accommodation was a bigger problem still. In John Morgan's time—he took Wilford's place in 1951 and stayed till 1962—the plan to build a curate's house on a plot next to St. Michael's was abandoned and 47 High Street purchased instead. At the same time 16 Church Street was bought for the verger, Mrs. Overton, who had succeeded Mr. Lewis, verger for 25 years. 47 High Street was sold during the curacy of Morgan's successor, John Duffie, and a bungalow bought in Oaks Road on the new Battlefield estate.

With costs rising everywhere, many parishes hired a professional group to conduct a Stewardship Campaign in which all those on the Electoral Roll were visited in an effort to persuade them to commit themselves to regular giving. PCC members were divided when addressed on the subject in 1959 by a vicar from Hereford. Some wanted a representative from such an organisation to speak to the PCC, but those opposed to the idea carried a motion by thirteen votes to six to await the long-term results in parishes that had gone ahead with campaigns.

The monthly meetings of the Standing and Finance Committee as compared with quarterly meetings of the PCC are evidence of the disproportionate attention given to business matters in Wragge Morley's time. With only one curate for much of the time he was hard-pressed just to keep the church going, especially as he had to care for a sick wife. There were occasional efforts by PCC members to extend the church's horizons, but the rector was reluctant to promote new initiatives. Miss Cadman gave the PCC an 'excellent account' in January 1950 of the address on 'Evangelism in the Parishes' at the Diocesan Conference that recommended Young Wives' Groups; more teaching of the laity, especially after confirmation; lively Communicants' Guilds for Young People; an effort to make churches more beautiful and less Victorian; and encouragement to church members to 'show more real interest and love for others'. However, her report was only accepted and no follow-up discussion held at subsequent meetings, although an extraordinary meeting was called in September to consider the replacement of a grate in the rectory! Perhaps this is why Miss Cadman asked in April 1951 what had happened to the 'suggestions' made after the extended discussion five years earlier. It was a good question.

Initially the rector was prepared to accept some change. He told the Annual Meeting in 1950 how pleased he was that the Sunday School 'had been started up afresh'. When Miss Beaumont pressed for a fuller part for youth in church life it was agreed to revive the monthly Children's Service and to introduce a monthly Evening Service for Young People since a majority on the PCC reckoned they would not come to a Family Service. The rector himself suggested a question-and-answer session in place of the sermon. The first such service in March 1951 was 'fairly well attended', and subsequently Miss Beaumont formed a Youth Fellowship. But she left the area and in Wragge Morley's later years activities among children and young people feature little in PCC minutes. Evangelism made even less progress: the formation of a sub-committee was agreed in 1954—the year of Billy Graham's remarkable 'Greater London Crusade' at Harringay—but the rector did not want decisions on its composition to be hurried and nothing more is heard of it. A later proposal for a committee to organise sick-visiting was also lost without trace. As befitted a former CMS Organising Secretary, he was more enthusiastic about missionary work, encouraging support for a CMS Missionary Exhibition in 1960, hosting the Diocesan Missionary Festival in 1962, and proudly announcing at his final Annual Meeting that the year's missionary gifts amounted to £477, the second highest in the diocese.

Social activities changed little. Each New Year began with a party, the summer highlight was the Fête, and the autumn was marked by the Harvest Supper. The Mothers' Union was well served by a succession of 'enrolling members'. Ladies and girls were reintroduced into the choir in 1954 to bolster the singing and, although they could not afford robes for them, it was felt that musical standards improved.

The on-going life of the church was dependent not simply on the clergy but also on the willingness of a number of individuals to give generously of their time. The staffing of the services was more demanding than ever. Weekly Parish Communion, a practice spreading widely at this time through the Parish and People movement, was not adopted, but there was Communion weekly at 8 a.m. at St. Laurence's, fortnightly at St. Michael's, and monthly at All Saints'; 11 a.m. Matins and 6.30 p.m. Evensong at all three churches; 12 noon Communion twice a month at the parish church and monthly at the daughter churches; and a monthly Children's Service. All services, of course, used the Book of Common Prayer and *Hymns Ancient and Modern*. During periods when there was only one or even no curate, services were maintained with the help of the lay readers—Major Morris, Mr. Newton and Dr. Johnson—and retired clergy. The ladies in 1952 formed the Guild of Church Workers to care for the linen, but the church offices were filled by men, some of them serving as churchwardens, treasurers or PCC secretaries for extended periods. The outstanding example was Mr. J.H. Crofts who continued year after year as deputy warden and treasurer of the parish church until the age of 100! The prevalence of long service meant that the leadership of the church was increasingly in the hands of the elderly, the rector himself carrying on till he was 73. Back in 1943 the Annual Meeting had agreed to elect the whole PCC each year 'to bring in new blood'; in 1952 they voted to revert to electing one-third of the Council each year—again to bring in new blood! Yet with a membership of 42 it was too unwieldy a body to get things done, and the smaller Standing and Finance Committee concerned itself almost entirely with business matters and maintenance. Still more serious, the cry for new blood was really a plea from some members for more innovative leadership.

During Wragge Morley's rectorship St. Michael's and All Saints' celebrated both their Golden and Diamond Jubilees. Each had its faithful congregation who attended regularly and whose giving covered all but extraordinary expenditure. In 1958 the diocese took over the freehold of All Saints' from the Gibbon family, with the PCC becoming responsible for maintenance. The former Congregational Chapel in Little Stretton became a village hall let to the community at a peppercorn rent.

The maintenance of St. Laurence's was costly. Regular minor repairs were needed and, after the 1961 Quinquennial Inspection, treatment for woodworm and dry rot in the roof timbers. But heating problems caused the most trouble, affecting attendances during two cold winters. Complaints of noisy boosters making it difficult to hear caused a change to oil-fired heating in 1955. The church, it was then said, was still not warm enough and even after electric tubular heaters were fixed to the walls there were grumbles about downdraughts in the south aisle. A new, larger oil-fired boiler was fitted in 1960. Illumination had been improved by the installation of concealed lighting in 1950 as a memorial to the late rector, Archdeacon Whately. The stained-glass window in the north transept (see p.52) was donated by the Sherratt family in 1955 and complemented the one in the south transept given by Mr. W.A. Sherratt 25 years earlier. The new window, 'in grateful memory of Daisy Emilie Sherratt, devoted wife and mother', appropriately includes the figures of the Virgin Mary, Ruth and Naomi. The smaller representations of David, Jesse and Obed echo on a miniature scale the medieval Jesse Tree windows in St. Mary's, Shrewsbury, and St. Laurence's, Ludlow. Above them remain the coats-of-arms inserted 130 years before by Robert Pemberton. Repairs to the stonework of the west window were paid for from the Widow Owen's Fund, which was wound up in 1959 when Messrs. Curry, who now owned the property in Mardol, Shrewsbury, from which the annual income of £1 was derived, gave £30 which when invested produced a like income.

The management and maintenance of the Parish Hall loom large in church records. In 1952 the Local Education Authority asked if one infant class could be taught in the hall as the closure of schools in Hope Bowdler and Acton Scott had led to overcrowding. The PCC was equally divided on the issue, but the rector used his casting vote to defeat the proposal, as his wife feared it would disrupt the Mothers' Union working party, although one parent claimed his child's health and education were suffering. 'Major Morris asked the PCC to consider whether, as a Christian body, it was satisfied to leave things as they were'.[3] Soon afterwards the use of an upper room was sanctioned and came into use in 1954, the year in which the school accepted Voluntary Controlled status. When the new Secondary School opened in Shrewsbury Road in 1961, the Primary School moved into their vacated premises in the former St. Dunstan's huts off Essex Road, and the L.E.A. ended its lease of the room in the hall. Now nearly 50 years old, the hall urgently needed renovation. By 1963 rewiring, improvements in lighting and heating, the insertion of a false ceiling and redecoration throughout meant, the rector claimed, that they had a hall to be proud of.

Prebendary Wragge Morley announced his impending retirement in April 1964. Two months later he was presented with 'a delightful case' and a handsome cheque. He proved to be Stretton's longest serving rector in the twentieth century and in some ways he personified the last stand of the traditional order against the irresistible currents of modernity. He is remembered as a forceful preacher—with a voice that boomed down the church—and a kindly pastor, with a wry sense of humour. His middle-of-the-road churchmanship was welcomed by many long-standing residents and newcomers alike. His expressed wish that 'the Church should be at the centre of community life', however, remained a somewhat forlorn hope. As in so many parishes, congregations were middle-class, ageing and slowly diminishing. Surviving copies of the monthly magazine reflect the unexciting church which issued it. A single, folded A4 sheet, with the current copy of an insert called *Home Words* enclosed, it contained times of services, a short letter from the rector, a few details of recent collections and forthcoming events, entries of baptisms, marriages and funerals, and hymn numbers for the coming month. The parish desperately needed new and vigorous leadership.

*

Within weeks of Wragge Morley's departure the candidate of the Church Patronage Trust had visited the parish, been 'very taken' with Church Stretton, and been judged by Major Morris, lay reader and warden at St. Michael's, to be 'most suitable in every way'. His appointment was quickly agreed. The new rector was the Rev. William Herbert Wilson from London. He was 56 years of age, an Exhibitioner of Clare College, Cambridge, who had read History and Theology and been awarded his B.A. in 1931. Ordained after a year at Westcott House, Cambridge, he then served curacies in Handsworth (Birmingham) and Chelsea. Through the war he was a vicar in Southall, moving in 1947 to Maida Vale where he stayed for 18 years. He was instituted at Stretton on 15 December 1964. The bishop sent him a message saying that his arrival was the best news he had had since he came to the diocese.

To those who wanted change the initial omens seemed good. Bill Wilson obviously came from a lively church, staying on in London to see through a Parish Mission. He thanked his first PCC meeting for their warm welcome, told them he saw tremendous opportunities, and sought their help and co-operation in solving the problems ahead—'What was to be done for our children, the needs of youth, young mothers in our community, and in facing up to the prob-

lems of the world?' And the words were followed by action: a creche in the hall during services, with young mothers involved; Sunday School children coming into the service for the first 25 minutes; Parish Communion at 11 a.m. on the first Sunday of the month; a Mothers and Toddlers Club; and a Youth Club in the Parish Hall in the summer months—albeit one run by the Shropshire Youth Service.

The 1960s, a decade remembered for rising standards of living—'You've never had it so good'—as well as for changing moral attitudes, the 'permissive society', rioting students and the Beatles, also saw radical ideas and change in the

The Rev. William Wilson,
Rector 1964-1971,
from the first Focus

Church. In one of his last Rector's Letters in the magazine Wragge Morley had written, 'No-one can say that the Church as a whole is not busily engaged in thinking out afresh its way of life'. He had singled out Bishop John Robinson's *Honest to God*, whose importance he thought had been much exaggerated, and the ecumenical movement that had been given an extraordinary boost by Archbishop Fisher's visit to the Pope and by John XXIII summoning the Second Vatican Council. This has been called 'the most important ecclesiastical event of the century, not just for Roman Catholics but for all Christians'.[4] In England, it was, however, the movement for Anglican-Methodist union which promised more immediate success.

Bill Wilson arrived in Stretton eager to encourage ecumenical progress. He appealed for strong support for the Week of Prayer for Christian Unity in January 1965 and a joint service with the Methodists that received the unanimous approval of the PCC. Joint services were held in the Congregational and Roman Catholic churches in 1966. There was even support on the PCC for inviting communicants of other churches to a shared Holy Communion. Six representatives were elected to the reconstituted Council of Churches which led the way in a collection that raised £400 in Stretton for the 'Feed the Minds'

campaign which aimed to complement food aid in under-developed countries. Since there was general dissatisfaction with the current magazine, the proposal of a joint publication with the other churches was welcomed. This quickly evolved into 'Focus', a new Inter-Church and Community Newspaper, edited by Rosaleen Whately, daughter of the former rector, and a pillar of St. Michael's. The first issue was in February 1967, with a circulation of 750. The church magazine ceased publication. There must have been great disappointment, if not dismay, in Stretton when the General Assembly of the Church of England and, finally, General Synod (which had replaced the Assembly in 1970) failed to achieve the 75% majority required for union with the Methodists.

Front page of the first Focus,
February 1967

Bill Wilson was alive to the changing world of the 1960s, and to the changing outlook for the Church, with the sharp decline nationally in baptisms, confirmations and ordinations—but also the fresh opportunity offered by the cultural revolution. 'In the world of today', he wrote, 'there is much questioning of established authorities. Domination will no longer be tolerated by men and women who, through education and technological advance, are able to control the circumstances of large areas of their life. In this situation there is much to rejoice at. A new freedom to serve is offered to Christians'.[5] He went on to urge church members to get involved in 'The People Next Door', a study programme followed by eleven house groups in Lent 1967. The aim was to promote inter-denominational dialogue and then to continue the discussions with non-churchgoing neighbours. He also launched Sunday evening discussion groups for young people. Both initiatives were all the more urgent as the town went on expanding and a new youth culture emerged. After the council house developments of the '50s, the next decade saw the building of the private Battlefield estate. Young people's life-style was changing ever faster as a result of enhanced educational provision and more immediately under the influence of television and pop music .The churches' response was to open a Combined Youth Club which met in the 'Combo' room in the Parish Hall. Nineteen teenagers were given financial help in 1966 to attend the Diocesan Youth Congress; two became members of the parish Social Committee. The fruits of this new trust became apparent as young people organised Youth Services in St. Laurence's and the Congregational Church. Of course, other agencies extended the range of provision for the young: the L.E.A. ran an Open Youth Club and the Scout Hut was erected near the Parish Hall. When the Combo Youth Club leader left in 1971, to be succeeded by the curate, Kenneth Newbon, assisted by Leslie Penny, there were 70 on the club's books, with 35 attending regularly and an active committee of seven. Younger children were catered for by Sunday Schools in all three churches, and in September 1970 a Family Week was organised for children by some Church Army sisters. The wider need outside the parish was brought home to some when annual camps shared by Oxford undergraduates and Borstal boys were held in All Stretton, with the participants 'sharing in the work and worship of village and church'.[6]

These burgeoning activities made demands on funding as well as manpower. Since Robert Hannay, curate from 1965 to 1969, was able to afford his own property the curate's house in Oaks Road was sold. But for his successor, Kenneth Newbon, Trefrie in Carding Mill Valley had to be purchased, and the additional outlay of £1,500 put further pressure on resources stretched by a Quota now over £1,000, on top of rising expenses, higher running costs, and improvements to the verger's house when Mr. and Mrs. Higgins succeeded Mrs. Overton in 1968. But the introduction of weekly envelopes for the Freewill Offering was so successful that there were hopes of a substantial surplus in future. Miss Kenyon's munificent legacy in 1966 was recognised as a long-term investment, and when a sound amplification system was installed in 1967 it was paid for by donations.

The greatest threat to the church's solvency came again from the Parish Hall. The building Wragge Morley was so proud of in 1962, five years later required major repairs to a leaking roof and a new floor on account of rising damp. Not surprisingly a visit to the modern Harlescott Youth Centre prompted pleas for a new hall. Instead, the architect produced a plan in 1970 to extend the church to the west and south-west to incorporate a porch, a narthex, small meeting rooms, a kitchen and toilets at an estimated cost of £20,000. The PCC gave its approval in principle.

Bill Wilson's years as rector witnessed important developments in the Church of England. The avalanche of change in the 1960s had not only rocked society, but caused the Church to seek renewal through innovation. The first steps were taken in liturgical revision and, in 1972, Synodical government introduced. In Stretton it was agreed by the PCC in 1969 to use the experimental Series 2 forms for the Confirmation Service and for baptisms for 12 months, and the next year Series 2 Holy Communion for three months. By a narrow majority in 1971 it was decided to use the Prayer Book and Series 2 for Communion in alternate months for a year. *Hymns Ancient and Modern Revised* was adopted. After the opinion of the congregation had been sounded out, Evensong at the parish church was moved from 6.30 to 6 p.m. in 1970. More significantly, Parish Family Communion on the first Sunday morning and third Sunday evening were replaced by an additional Family Service weekly at 9.55 a.m., which became very popular with families whose children had gone to Parents and Toddlers. The rector, who started an ecumenical group for clergy, doctors and other health professionals and social workers, discreetly conducted a healing ministry in individual homes. Missionary support remained strong: besides personal contributions the PCC made annual donations to the C.M.S. and the United Society for the Propagation of the Gospel, and St. Michael's began its fund-raising for a church in Mokhotlong in Lesotho. Christian Aid and other good causes benefited from special collections on certain Sundays.

The administration of the parish improved in various ways. Secretarial help for the rector, clearer presentation of the accounts and, from 1968, typed and duplicated minutes all appeared. The PCC met more frequently, while Standing and Finance Committee meetings were reduced to bi-monthly. Churchwarden Henry Horrocks produced the first guide to the parish church since Dr. Dixon's little leaflet 35 years earlier.

Strangely, it was an incident unconnected with the church that led to the most striking change in the internal appearance of St. Laurence's in the Wilson years. Three young boys, Korwin, Alastair and Jonathan Goulder, whose

*The Goulder Memorial to the three young brothers who died
in The Hotel fire in 1968*

family was staying overnight at The Hotel prior to moving into their new home, perished in a fire on 2 April 1968. The whole community was shocked. In time the parents, who went to live elsewhere, expressed a wish to present a permanent memorial to their sons in the parish church. 'The Symbol of St. Laurence', by sculptor John Skelton, won much praise and still attracts appreciative comments from visitors. It takes the form of an iron grille with copper flames, clearly representing the nature of the death of the church's patron saint and recalling how the boys died, and symbolizing the tongues of fire at the first Pentecost.

The following year the church was riven by the rector's decision to close the Mothers' Union. His wife Margaret, (who had served on the Central Committee of the M.U. in London), found the group, one suspects, too exclusive to introduce some of the young wives who were being drawn to the Family Service. At the Annual Meeting in March 1970 when Miss Cadman, a long-standing member of the church, spoke against its closure, the rector assured her he was meeting Mothers' Union members to ensure that 'nothing of value was lost'. In response to expressions of support for the Mothers' Union at the PCC, the rector said he thought it was divisive and 'hoped for a wider fellowship based on understanding and Christian Fellowship'. At a later meeting, however, one member expressed his dismay, averred that on this issue he had lost confidence in the rector, and walked out. Bill Wilson, who was not a man to make contentious decisions, expressed his regret at the damage to the fellowship, saying he would note the feelings of members. Shortly afterwards the Women's Fellowship was launched with a more open membership.

The rector, who was in his early 60s, announced his resignation in August 1971 and left on 31 December. He and his wife sailed for Israel where he served as a chaplain in Tel Aviv; they became St. Laurence's new mission partners. Bill Wilson is remembered as a gentleman and scholar, 'a lovely man', even as a very keen gardener, and also for his healing ministry. He undoubtedly made a real impact on the church, for many of his initiatives were taken up by later incumbents. He was a man of spiritual stature, somewhat reserved, but 'a good, academic preacher', and, above all, a gifted pastor. His love of music led him, with a talented teacher of dance and a composer, to stage a number of striking 'music and movement' presentations with the aid of secondary schoolchildren. One young lad playing the part of Christ was converted through this experience. Bill Wilson's musical abilities and dignified presence — he was always addressed as 'rector' — also raised the standard of church worship. But his attempts to awaken a slumbering church had not pleased all. Divisions appeared in the church community over the use of Series 2, the future of the Parish Hall, and the Mothers' Union, and there was some tension between the older members of the congregation and the young people he had set out to reach.

Feelings had been sufficiently aroused for the PCC to demand that they, and not just the churchwardens and lay readers, should meet one of the patrons before the new appointment. They also laid down what they required of the next rector, including his views on the Mothers' Union, visiting, and methods of money raising. They made a point of recording their wish to see the spirit of ecumenism maintained in Church Stretton. When they met Canon Wade of the Church Patronage Trust he concluded that 'a married man of broad evangelical outlook seemed to be needed'.[7]

By February a candidate had been selected and met the PCC after initial discussions with the wardens and curate. The Rev. F.P.B. Ashe and his wife were approved, he accepted the living, and he was inducted on 13 May 1972. Pat Ashe came after eight years at St. Mary's, Leamington. Born in 1915, and a graduate of St. John's College, Cambridge, he had proceeded to Westcott House in 1937 and was ordained in 1940. Following four years as a curate at Woolwich, he had spent two years doing relief work in war-torn Greece. The Bishop of Southampton made him his Chaplain to Youth in 1946, and four years in this role were followed by appointments to livings in Southwark and Otley before he went to Leamington.[8]

Pat Ashe's arrival electrified the parish. In personality he was much more out-going than his predecessor and, though a man in his later 50s, had four children in their teens or younger and an adopted daughter of Asian origin. When they were not away at school, the youngsters kept open house at the rectory for their teenage friends in the town. Both Pat Ashe and his wife Marion were the children of missionaries and the whole family lived out the gospel. The rector himself, a man of uncompromising faith, had a strong sense of God's presence and leading. He sent a tremor through his congregation when he called on them to take Ugandan Asians into their homes at the height of the Idi Amin crisis. His disorganised life-style shocked his more staid parishioners, who were embarrassed when the *Daily Mail* published an account of a wedding he had forgotten to turn up to.

Ashe had barely settled in when Constance Douglas, the youngest daughter of Hugh Owen Wilson, rector at the time of the Victorian restoration, died in 1972 at the age of 94. In her will she remembered her father's old parish even though he had died and the family had moved out when she was only an infant. She had, in her declining years, valued the visits and kindness of others when she was in a home in Ludlow. In her will, therefore, she left a substantial sum to provide an income for a Parish Visitor who would similarly bring comfort and friendship to the elderly and lonely people of Church Stretton. The first Visitor appointed was Sister Winifred Henry of the Church Army who arrived in September 1973. In the same month the Rev. Paul Burgess came to assist the rector. Among other new faces in the leadership of the church were the readers Tom Wheeler and John Joyce, Norman Owen who joined Henry Horrocks for their 13-year partnership as churchwardens, Gordon Skinner who began a 14-year spell as treasurer, and Emlyn Ephraim who took over as organist from Graham Jukes after his 25 years in the post.

The previous rector's enthusiasm for youth work was outdone by Pat Ashe whose own children attracted others to the inter-church Combo Club. This met in the hall in a room they decorated in psychedelic colours. The club eventually closed because of a shortage of leaders, but youth groups met in the rectory and at the school in the lunch-hour. What the rector really wanted was a café-style meeting place for the young. He followed his predecessor, too, in his eagerness to forge ecumenical links and to try out the revised Series 3 services. The Family Service was brought forward to 9.45 a.m., sometimes with guitar accompaniment, more people took part in evening worship, and there were experiments with a nave altar under the crossing for up to 70 communicants. The plans for a narthex and additional rooms were continually being altered but never finalised.

Strong backing continued for missionary societies and Pat Ashe interested a number of people—none more so than Edith Flynn—in Project Vietnam Orphans that he had launched just before leaving Leamington. It absorbed much of his time and became a full-time operation when he left Stretton and settled in Godalming; today, as 'Christian Outreach', it still draws support from St. Laurence's. Pat Ashe's announcement of his resignation came out of the blue early in 1974. He told the PCC that he and his family had been very happy in Stretton but 'he felt his style of ministry was not suited to the needs of the parish'. At his last meeting with them in June he recommended perseverance with Series 3 Holy Communion and his style of evening service with its warmer fellowship; he asked them also 'to bear very much in mind the provision of an open space under the tower to enable services to be conducted from there' — still a matter of debate in the church. He departed in June 1974, requesting no formal leaving ceremony. It had been a whirlwind couple of years, but though Pat Ashe had made many feel uncomfortable the church had been given a further shake into life.

14
THE CLOSING YEARS OF THE MILLENNIUM

The reawakening of the local church, and particularly the efforts to draw in young families and teenagers in the time of Rectors Wilson and Ashe, came not a moment too soon, for the population of the Strettons, only 3,000 in 1961, rose to over 4,000 in the next 30 years. The haulage vehicles of Swains of Stretton Ltd. carried the town's name near and far and some diversity of employment was offered by the development from 1976 of a small industrial estate on land between the A49 and the railway line. Building development in the parish continued apace. The 1960s and 1970s saw not only the completion of the council house programme and the Battlefield estate, but building on the lower slopes of Ragleth Hill, the linking of Essex Road and Churchill Road, new houses in Woodcote Edge and, after the demolition of Stretton House in 1976, the building of the Stretton Farm estate. There was infilling in Burway Road, Clive Avenue and Shrewsbury Road as well as more houses and bungalows in All Stretton and Little Stretton. The nature and extent of these developments were among the concerns that led to the founding of the Stretton Society in 1974-75 and the declaration of the town centre as a conservation area in 1986. More recent developments in the 1980s and 1990s include Rectory Gardens, more houses in Churchill Road, King's Court, Hazler Orchard and other large properties further up the hill to the east of the town, and at last some affordable housing for first time buyers in Swain's Meadow. The construction of a supermarket in Lion Meadow in 1994 has brought the further benefit of opening up the centre of the town. For the church the imperative has been not just to provide for its members but to welcome young families and newcomers, who include many recently retired, at a time when across the country the fall in attendances has continued.

The church had its own building pressures. Even before Pat Ashe left, discussions had taken place on the future of the rectory and the curate's house. Indeed, consideration had been given to a new rectory back in 1964 but the Wilsons had preferred improvements to Mynd Court. The incoming rector and his wife were to regret that earlier decision as for years they struggled with a large, cold house. One proposal, abandoned for lack of funds, was to build a

School House bought in 1975 for the curate's use

new rectory on the site of the Parish Hall. There was better progress with the curate's accommodation. Trefrie was sold for £13,000 when Paul Burgess left in 1974, and School House in Church Street bought for £5,000 before Tony Burdon arrived the next year—although a similar amount was spent on renovations and a new heating system. Gas central heating was installed in the parish church, at a cost of £3,000, in the autumn of 1974 in time for the new rector's institution.

The PCC had again chosen to be consulted over the appointment, but the Patrons' candidate seems to have been readily agreed. He was the Rev. John Woodger, 38 years of age and trained at Tyndale Hall, Bristol, a leading Evangelical theological college. After his ordination in 1963 he had served as a curate at St. Peter's, Hereford, and at Macclesfield. He came to Church Stretton from the rural parish of Llangarron where he had been vicar for five years. He and his wife, Rose, had two young sons.

John Woodger was instituted by the Bishop of Hereford on 11 November 1974. He quickly demonstrated why he was the patrons' choice. A man of prayer, a good communicator and a skilled organiser, he had a common touch that enabled him to relate readily to all sorts of people. His open personality and sense of humour balanced his drive to get things done. What he wanted was a live church with a sense of mission, but he recognised the need to carry people with him. At only his second PCC meeting he proposed a series of open meetings on Wednesday evenings in Lent to discuss major areas of church life like worship and giving. Lent lunches were introduced on Thursdays. Over a hundred attended his first Annual Meeting at which he paid tribute to Pat Ashe for his ground-breaking work, praised the Lent discussions, and invited them to speak their minds. His own view of the church's priorities a year later reads like a mission statement: 'The main task of the Church in Church Stretton is to build up a Church family and to make God known by its love and the effectiveness of its faith'.[1]

The rector lost no time in setting about his task. One immediate need was to ensure that the church's structures assisted the realisation of its aims. He wished the PCC to be the forum for the discussion of major issues, leaving maintenance and money matters to the Standing and Finance Committee. Council members were invited to join one of four groups set up to consider and suggest ideas for the development of worship, evangelism, stewardship and fellowship; others with specialist knowledge could be co-opted. Existing committees were reduced in size.

John Woodger was looking to establish a five-year plan for the church, but this required a period of discussion and preparation. In the meantime he wanted particularly to develop outreach to children and young people and to enhance the quality of worship. By 1976 he could report that the Mothers and Toddlers group had 34 on the register, while a Pathfinder group for 11-15 year-olds led by Leslie Penny numbered 37, with boys and girls in almost equal numbers. The rector was an advocate of liturgical development, too. Series 3 services for Holy Communion, Marriages and Funerals were in regular use by 1977, and the new forms of Morning and Evening Prayer under consideration. These were to be used experimentally at St. Michael's, whose later verdict was that they were 'not keen'.

By Easter 1977 the rector believed they were ready to tackle the formulation of a Five Year Plan. The previous autumn the PCC had reviewed its evangelistic, social, ecumenical and pastoral roles; the fruit of such meetings was apparent at the next Annual Meeting. Whereas in the preceding two years the invitation to ask questions or make recommendations had elicited no response, in 1977 areas suggested for the PCC's consideration included evangelism, meetings for prayer, the stewardship of time and talents, 'anything to build up the common life of the community', prayers for the elderly and Pathfinders, and 'the improvement of the spiritual life of Church Stretton generally'. Such breadth of concern augured well for the whole-day PCC Conference at All Stretton Hall on Sunday, 15 May, at which a five-year plan was adopted. The day ended with a service to 'show the PCC to the congregation'. The acclaim of John Woodger's leadership and inspiration at the close of the Annual Meeting was indicative not just of the support he enjoyed but of the unity and enthusiasm for growth now at the heart of the church. Nonetheless, his final comment was a challenge to all—'to bring the love of God to all who do not know it'.

The rector received strong support from his curates, Tony Burdon, 1975-78, and Barry Brewer, 1978-81, from Sister Winifred and from the lay readers; perhaps the Rev. Fred Legge spoke for all the retired clergy when he declared that the older men were delighted to help. With so many services to conduct in the three churches, John Woodger needed all this assistance. Yet he and the PCC groups continued to generate ideas for further advance. Mission, prayer, education, pastoral care, Church union, baptism policy and stewardship were all on the agenda. To involve the wider membership of the church, question-naires were distributed to all on the Electoral Roll inviting their views on parish affairs and church life. For those who could remember the church 20 years earlier, the transformation was remarkable.

Recommendations from the discussion groups did not always reflect the rector's thinking. The Worship Committee favoured uniting the Family Service and Matins and holding the service earlier than 11. a.m. This was tried out in August 1978, with the service at 10.30, but when the committee pressed for its permanent adoption some PCC members objected that this was premature—ten years too soon, the rector thought. When a large majority of the congregation still voted for the single service at 10.30 it was introduced in June 1981. In the same year the Alternative Service Book (ASB) Rite A was first used for Holy Communion. John Woodger continued to have misgivings about the single service since 'very few children and fewer parents with children had been attending'. He proposed a reconsideration after the coming Mission.

For all the emphasis on spiritual priorities, finance and fabric could not be ignored. In a period of rapid inflation the Diocesan Quota rose from £2,400 in 1975 to £14,600 in 1985. Expensive repairs caused all other proposed alter-ations, like the narthex and vestry, to be abandoned. The verger's house at 16 Church Street was sold, but the proceeds went to augment the pay of the next verger, Brian Hazeldine. Gift Days, Summer Fêtes, May Fairs and Autumn Sales were all tried in the late '70s, but the real value of their takings fell way below earlier years and they became more social occasions. The idea of a Stewardship Campaign was revived after the repair of the south wall of the churchyard in 1979 had cost £2,500, but the PCC decided instead to appeal to members to covenant and, if possible, increase their donations. In the light of the knowledge that the average weekly offering per person in the Hereford Diocese was at that time 30p.—the lowest in the country—Council members were divided on whether advice should be offered on how much to give: in the end they resolved that the church should state that it upheld the standard, not the rule, of 'tithing', while recognising that the interpretation of this should be left to the individual. The response to the appeal was encouraging. The rector was able to announce that the target of doubling the church's income by 1980 set in the five-year plan had been achieved in three years. Yet by 1984 the word from the treasurer was that a 25% increase in giving was needed, on top of which he thought that they should build up a contingency fund and launch a special appeal for a new hall.

During John Woodger's rectorship there were two major building developments at St. Laurence's. The first was planned for 1977 to mark the Queen's Silver Jubilee. The aim was to restore the west wall and window, insert a new inner west door, and at the east end to enlarge the sanctuary. The west end work was completed in 1978, the date which is displayed high on the outside of the wall together with 1619, the year of Jane Norton's original gift. Her Widow Owen's Fund was still able to pay £910 towards the total cost of £2,700; the inner door was an anonymous gift. A plaque on a choir pew records the extension of the sanctuary in 1978 'in memory of former choristers, Erica Doreen Bower, 1922-76, and Nora Bower, 1889-1978'. The other development began with a proposal to move the chancel screen erected to commemorate Queen

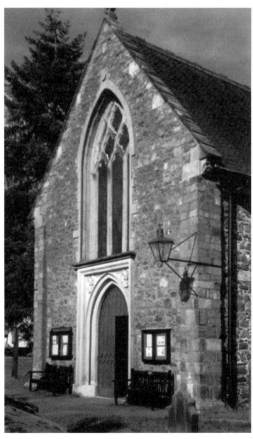

Victoria's Diamond Jubilee. Dropped after advice from the archdeacon, the proposal surfaced again in 1978 linked to the idea of a side-chapel. When it was revived once more in 1982 it formed part of a wider plan to transform the aisle added to the north transept in 1868 into a side-chapel, with the chancel screen moved to form a glazed partition separating the chapel from the transept. The architect drew up plans, diocesan approval was secured, and an estimate of £4,700 from Mr. Morris of Pontesbury accepted. The work was undertaken in the summer of 1983 and the Emmaus Chapel— Sister Winifred's suggestion for a name was adopted—was dedicated by the Bishop of Hereford on 1 July 1984. It was enhanced by an oval oak table given in memory of Henry Horrocks, churchwarden for 19 years who

The west end of the church, restored 1978

The north aisle became the Emmaus Chapel in 1983,
with the former chancel screen forming its eastern side

had recently died. The chapel was intended as a place for quiet prayer and has so remained, serving today also as a point of administration for Communion and the venue for Thursday morning Holy Communion, although it remains an under-used resource. The removal of the screen and the subsequent extension of the platform to facilitate the erection of a handrail went some way towards realising Pat Ashe's final plea, ten years earlier, to provide an open space under the tower so that services could be conducted from there.

Alterations within the church were not the only building items on the agenda. There was regular discussion of the need for a new rectory and a new hall. With the first John Woodger was successful. In 1981 Mynd Court was sold and Norfolk Lodge in Carding Mill Valley Road purchased as the rectory; it remains so to this day. The Parish Hall dilemma was not so readily resolved. Many thought that the cost of restoration was prohibitive. The architect's alternative proposals to make additions to the church had already been abandoned, and another suggestion to convert the former school building, now leased as a library, was only briefly entertained. A new hall was to be the achievement of a new rector.

*

The climax of John Woodger's ministry in Church Stretton was the Parish Mission of 1983. He had first suggested this in 1979, knowing that it would

The new rectory in Carding Mill Valley Road, 1982

require much preparation—and, for some, persuasion. He himself delighted to preach the gospel and throughout 1978 he had conducted an evangelistic service on the first Sunday evening of the month. Two years later the 'Meeting Point' sessions he had introduced were replaced in spring and autumn by Bible studies with monthly social gatherings. With more young people being drawn in, the rector used the fourth Sunday evening to hold an informal service with a longer address. What he really wanted, like Pat Ashe, was a place for teenagers to drop in without being preached at. He brought three of them along to a PCC meeting to talk about how they were fitting into church life and how things could be improved. They must have been very persuasive because the PCC agreed to underwrite a Pop Group Concert in April 1982! It was significant that the bishop chose to launch the Nationwide Initiative in Evangelism in Shropshire from Church Stretton. John Woodger followed this by inviting the Rev. Daniel Cozens (now leader of Through Faith Missions) to lead a mission. But there was still much to be done if the church was to be ready to welcome new Christians. To improve pastoral care 'area visitors' were appointed, and the rector challenged the PCC by asking how they could best be a caring church and if people slipped through their pastoral net. Pathfinders and CYFA (Church Youth Fellowships Association)—to cater for older teenagers and led by John Woodger himself—were well established and in 1981 Climbers and Explorers were introduced.

By the end of 1981 it had been decided that Daniel Cozens should come in May 1983. The PCC was unanimous in its support, the local Council of

Churches agreed to join in and a working party was set up. Unfortunately after Barry Brewer left in October 1981 there was no curate during some exceptionally busy months, with a course of Bible studies after Easter and prayer groups formed. With the arrival of Mike Harries as curate preparations moved into top gear. St. Laurence's Day 1982 was declared a Day of Prayer and Gifts for the Mission. Prayer cards were prepared, and it was agreed to visit all non-churchgoing homes with a copy of Luke's gospel, though St. Michael's wanted a different approach. The rector provoked a lively PCC discussion by asking what new Christians would find in the church and if changes needed to be made. Three youth events were held in the Silvester Horne Institute to arouse interest in the Mission and the Combo Room transformed during the Easter holiday.

The Mission began on Saturday, 14 May, and finished on Sunday, 22 May. Daniel Cozens brought with him a small team, mainly of men, who led meetings each morning in the homes of church members. The emphasis in the mission was on adults and young people rather than children. Daniel Cozens was a forthright speaker and many remember the power of his messages, especially at the men's breakfast held in The Hotel and at the supper and rally on the final Saturday evening. Some found his appeal too emotional, but others were enthusiastic and some current church members date their Christian conversion from this week. Yet not as many as had been hoped made a response of faith during the mission; as with many such events the greatest effect was on those who already had some link with the church. One very positive consequence was the starting up of a number of regular house groups.

Just before the mission the PCC had listed their three priorities for the coming year as children and young people, lay ministry, and provision for families in Sunday morning worship; other leading concerns included catering for new Christians, a review of the use of the ASB, a second five-year plan, giving, Mission England, Bible study, and the influence of the Holy Spirit in worship. This agenda is a measure of what John Woodger had achieved in the parish. There was already graduated provision for the young, a principal area of lay ministry that David Janes with help from his wife Loveday was shortly to combine with his new duties as a lay reader alongside Tom Wheeler and John Joyce. In the autumn the congregation voted decisively to retain one morning service, with the proviso that special attention be given to the teaching of children.

But by early 1984 the church's finances had again become a priority—indeed, the situation was so serious that thought was given to dispensing with a verger. The rector planned a series of sermons on giving. He decided, too, to devote one evening service a month to missionary societies at home and abroad. This was a timely move. The parish had long maintained interest in and support for missionary work. There were currently nine link missionaries and teachers: St. Laurence's particularly supported CMS, St. Michael's the church of the same name in Mokhotlong, and All Saints' the Rantisis with their Boys' Home at Ramallah in Palestine. The proportion of the church's income given to missions, which over some years had fluctuated between 8% and 13%, had in 1983 fallen to a mere 5%, chiefly on account of a big increase in the diocesan quota. This caused great heart-searching. In the end it was accepted for that year, but 10% was agreed for the future.

Four extra priorities emerged in 1984—Prayer, Pastoral Care, a Men's Meeting, and the future of the Parish Hall. But these were to be issues for a new incumbent because in May John Woodger announced his impending resignation. He had turned down the offer of St. Peter's, Hereford, in 1982, the year in which he had been made Prebendary of Gorwall, but now after ten years in Stretton he believed it was time to move on. They had been ten fruitful years. The church was now much more outward-looking and enjoyed lively worship, the rector himself sometimes playing the piano to add gusto to the singing. The building, too, had been enhanced by the removal of the chancel screen, the opening of the Emmaus Chapel, the extension of the sanctuary and platform, and the restoration of the west end—not to mention the newly-embroidered altar frontals and kneelers, and the processional cross in memory of Canon Young, one of the retired clergy who assisted with services. It is interesting how many of today's practices originated in John Woodger's time: joint services with the other denominations on August Sunday evenings; corporate Communion before the first meeting of the new PCC; a parish office; the use of a modern Bible translation—then the Good News Bible—in all three churches; and regular house groups, of which there were seven, with about 70

The Rev. John Woodger, Rector 1974-1984, with church leaders and the choir

members, when he left. This record of achievement was the more praiseworthy since it occurred in years when the Church as a whole was contracting.

John Woodger had been a charismatic, up-front leader, too much so for some, although the sharp fall in the number on the Electoral Roll was misleading for revisions caused it to consist largely of those who attended church regularly. Throughout a decade of change he had tried to carry people with him. Annual away-days with the PCC helped them to work together, and occasional parish weekends drew more widely from church members. But it was through his challenging, Bible-based preaching and his presence about the parish that John Woodger reached most people. He made a practice of walking the streets on market days and Saturday mornings and visited the church primary school weekly. All recognised his dedication and energy, appreciating, too, how much was owed to his wife, Rose, who led the Women's Fellowship and kept open house while bringing up a young family. The church family's gratitude and love were reflected in the very generous presentation at their farewell on 13 October 1984.

*

Only ten days after the rector's farewell the bishop approved the invitation to John Woodger's successor. The Rev. Michael Stedman and his wife had impressed the PCC on a visit in September, prompting churchwarden Norman Owen to expedite the appointment. At 50 years of age slightly older than his predecessor, Michael Stedman had been priest in charge of a group of small parishes in Norfolk and Rural Dean for the previous ten years. He had trained at Clifton Theological College and after ordination in 1965 had served as curate in the Chichester and Chelmsford dioceses. His professional qualification as a chartered surveyor was no doubt a feature of his *curriculum vitae* that attracted a PCC eager for a new Parish Hall.

The new rector was markedly different from his predecessor, less out-going in personality and more consensual in his leadership style. Yet Michael Stedman had the spiritual depth and ministerial dedication to begin consolidating the pioneering advances of his predecessors, complementing the 1983 Mission with a number of initiatives to deepen the faith of church members. Given the prevailing culture this was no easy task. In Church Stretton the gospel was faithfully proclaimed, and frequent efforts made to attract the young—with a measure of success, but not enough to turn the tide of numerical decline caused by changes in the way we live, the ever-increasing secularism of society, and what has been called 'the privatisation of religion', the growing desire of individuals to choose their own set of beliefs. Between the early '80s and the mid '90s morning congregations slowly declined from an average attendance of 176 to one of 138.

The rector found himself at once facing severe staffing difficulties. Only weeks before his institution on 29 March 1985, the senior churchwarden, Norman Owen, had died suddenly after 15 years in office. John Hughes was elected to join Norman Powell, who had himself succeeded Henry Horrocks two years earlier. The curate, Mike Harries, was seriously ill and needed prolonged hospital treatment, and two lay readers, John Joyce and Tom Wheeler, as well as Sister Winifred, retired. Problems over duties then led to the resignation of the verger, a position Ron Hughson came to fill in 1986.

With two teenage sons of his own, but still a predominantly elderly congregation, Michael Stedman was eager to develop activities for young people and children. United Youth Services and social events were organised, and a CYFA representative (later two) was co-opted to the PCC; some CYFA members visited the Rantisis on the West Bank. A Christian Fellowship was formed at the school and invited to share in the Education Sunday services; and there were two successful Holiday Clubs before Colin Stephenson of Scripture Union in spring 1988 presented 'Break-out'. This included children's meetings, a Family Fun Evening, a Men's Night at the Stretton Hall Hotel, and a Teenage Event. Further advances were hampered by the poor accommodation and a shortage of leaders.

The rector wished also to foster spiritual growth in the church and to review the pattern of worship. On one occasion the PCC discussed 'Allowing in the Holy Spirit to lift our worship', the Evangelism Committee raised questions about spiritual maturity, and a Quiet Day was held to listen to what the Holy Spirit was saying to the church. On another 'away-day' it was resolved that the prayer life of the church should be strengthened. As a result Leslie Harrison and Beryl Shedden became Prayer Secretaries, prayer groups were formed, a prayer diary circulated, and more lay people led intercessions. After Michael Stedman aired the idea of a Healing Service, the laying on of hands with prayer came to be offered monthly at an Evening Communion and the Thursday Communion. The suggestion of an additional hymn-book provoked protracted discussion. In the end, in 1987, 200 copies of *Songs and Hymns of Fellowship* were bought. In an attempt to provide for all, morning services on the four Sundays of the month came to include Holy Communion (twice), a Family Service and Morning Prayer; both the Book of Common Prayer and the Alternative Service Book were used.

Repairs and building developments were inevitably on most PCC agendas. Plans to move the font to the north transept and to develop the back of the church as a memorial to Norman Owen failed to gain diocesan approval, but it was agreed to remove two rear pews and to erect bookshelves at the west end, separated from the seating area by glass screens. The memorial books were introduced in 1986 and displayed in a glass case near the entrance. The next year repair of the organ became imperative; over £12,000 was raised with the aid of a Day of Prayer and Gifts.

But the topic that dominated the second half of the decade was the replacement of the Parish Hall which was well past its 'sell by date', although it had recently featured in a BBC film 'The Combination'. The sub-committee set up in 1985, and chaired by Gordon Skinner, rejected the proposal to use the former schoolroom (leased as the Library), but estimated that a new hall could cost £150,000. A special meeting of the PCC the next April, which heard the existing hall described as 'the worst-looking building in the town', agreed to invite Philip Eaton, a local architect, to draw up plans for a new hall with better facilities for children and young people and a car park. The prospective cost, however, was daunting at a time when the Diocesan Quota had reached £20,000 and the treasurer had announced that a 25% increase in giving was needed. Repairs to School House at a cost of £3,000 when Tim Price arrived as curate added to the burden.

Early in 1988, when feasibility studies had been completed, the PCC voted in favour of a new building rather than renovation or an addition to the church. The rector ruled that 75% of the members of the Electoral Roll must give their approval and that, after taking into account the sale of the land at the rear of the plot, half of the cost of the project must be pledged before they could proceed. Two other steps that had to be taken were the removal from the site of the Luccombe Oak, which had a tree preservation order, and the termination of the County Council's lease on the Youth Room at the rear of the hall. The support of the Parish Council for the project and the good offices of County Councillor Reggie Lloyd, long-standing deputy churchwarden at St. Michael's, helped eventually to persuade the County to grant planning permission, which included the removal of the oak tree; they agreed also to vacate the Youth Room by the end of May 1989.

With warm support for a new hall expressed at a public meeting in December 1988 attended by 120 people, the way was open to confirm Messrs. Onions and Rowley of Shrewsbury as the building contractors and to get down to the serious business of raising the money. The signs were encouraging. Members of the PCC had responded generously to the rector's letter and there were hopes of a substantial contribution from the Central Board of Finance. Further good news emerged in March 1989 with the builders' offer of £100,000 for the land at the rear of the hall so long as they could build five bungalows. It was still considered necessary, however, to modify the plans and to scale down the basic cost to £180,000, as there would also be V.A.T., fees and perhaps price increases. Indeed, it was to avoid such increases that a letter giving the go-ahead was sent to the builders in April.

When demolition of the old hall began at the end of June £70,000 had been raised, but it was considered that perhaps as much again would be needed. Fortunately the cost of the initial work was covered by the payment for the building land. A great variety of fundraising events was planned: sales of 'nearly-new' items, of holiday gifts and of miniature models of the church, coffee mornings, CYFA events, and brass and silver cleaning; a sponsored walk up Snowdon failed to materialise. The most successful was the 'buy-a-brick-and-lay-a-brick' day on Saturday, 19 August. By October the builders were two weeks ahead of schedule and almost ready for roofing. December's heartening disclosure was that the total building cost would be only £216,000 and that with £105,000 raised, the sale of the land for £100,000 and £11,000 promised in interest-free loans the whole sum could be paid off! A further £10,000 was deemed necessary for furniture and equipment, but with donations continuing to come in this was exceeded, making available valuable extra funds for the future.

It had been readily agreed that the new housing area should be called St. Laurence Close. What proved much harder to decide was the style of the large cross that all believed should feature on the east-facing wall of the new Parish Centre, as it was to be known. Members on the Electoral Roll were exactly equally divided in their support for a plain cross or a modern design. It was agreed that the views of Ted Owen, treasurer of the Appeal Fund who had just died, should finally decide: his wife said he had favoured the plain cross. In the event an anonymous donor gave £1,000 and the result was a metal cross, almost plain but skilfully incorporating the shape of a shepherd's crook.

The Parish Centre was completed in February 1990 and dedicated on 25 March by the Bishop of Ludlow. The thanksgiving collection at the service was sent to the Boys' Home in Ramallah. The centre's construction and the prompt settlement of the cost were terrific achievements. It has been, and is, a wonder-

The new Parish Centre, opened in 1990

fully valuable resource in the parish. With a main hall large enough for a wide range of meetings and activities and even for services, a well-equipped kitchen, a comfortable lounge known as the Owen Room in memory of Ted Owen, and spacious rooms upstairs, the Centre provides accommodation for church meetings and children's activities and is let to innumerable outside organisations. However, the 'great need' recognised at the time 'for the provision of an evening youth club to keep youngsters off the street and to provide the facilities to attract leaders and youth to form a club where they can meet to play games, talk and drink coffee'[2] has not been fully met, and some in the town still lament the loss of the old Youth Room. The inclusion of an office was an early decision and this has become the hub of parish administration, with ever more sophisticated technology and equipment and, in Nancy Cleaton, an ever-busier parish secretary.

*

By the time the Centre opened, Michael Stedman had been rector for five years, five busy years, for in 1988 he had also become Rural Dean for the Condover Deanery. The momentum was to be maintained throughout the succeeding decade. Not only were there parish innovations; responses had also to be made to diocesan and national initiatives as the Church endeavoured to keep up with the ever-accelerating pace of change in society. Within the parish ideas for development came from the rector and from the five 'departments' created in 1991 after the 'Mission Audit'—Worship, Discipleship, Pastoral Care and Evangelism, Families and Young People, and Standing and Finance. There were, in addition, Missionary and Social Committees. The organisation and activity of all these elements of church life—more numerous than ever before—were dependent on the willing involvement of a host of lay people.

The departments' areas of responsibility provide a helpful framework for an account of the church in the last ten years. Worship remained the centre of church life. There were signs, however, of polarisation between the adherents of the traditional and the modern. The proposal in 1988 to phase out the use of the Book of Common Prayer had led to a PCC debate which concluded with agreement that 'a gentle approach to change was required'. Nonetheless, although it was recognised that it would cause anxiety to some people, the use of the BCP for the third Sunday morning Holy Communion in alternate months was discontinued in 1989. With numbers of children and young people dwindling, in spite of the rising population, the greatest concern was to attract more families. It was decided not to revive the separate Family Service; instead, 'Family Focus'—a short talk early in the morning service before the children went out to Sunday Club—was introduced. Evening services were sometimes held in the more relaxed setting of the Parish Centre, and a group was formed to organise occasional informal services. To sound out wider opinion a questionnaire was distributed to those on the Electoral Roll, but it was, as always, impossible to please all of the people all of the time. This was as true of the music as of the liturgy. Adrian Cleaton, who took over as organist from Ted Newson in 1990, compiled a varied collection of hymns under the title *Worship the Lord*, which virtually ended the use of *Ancient and Modern Revised*, but some wanted more traditional hymns and others greater use of modern choruses.

Even the provision of services of worship was difficult at times because of the staffing demanded by the three churches. When David Janes was ordained as a part-time non-stipendiary minister in 1989, Stella Barnes was left as the sole lay reader until Doreen Hall arrived in 1994 and John Hughes and Philip Bytheway completed their training. It did mean, however, that there was a second ordained minister when Tim Price moved on and before the new curate, Derek Waller, arrived in 1991. Yet it was still impossible for a time to maintain weekly services at Little Stretton.

The situation at All Stretton was different. In 1984 the dilapidated state of the United Reformed Chapel there had prompted St. Michael's to invite that congregation to share the use of their building. Within a couple of years ecumenical co-operation was being explored. Long discussions ensued within the parish and with the diocesan and U.R.C. authorities. Finally, after a covenant and constitution had been approved, the Local Ecumenical Partnership (LEP) came into existence in 1994, with both Anglican and U.R.C. services but a mixed congregation and a joint committee.

The organisation of services presented the problem of how to meet the widely differing expectations of congregations that included retired people with experience of a whole range of churchmanship (and even from other denominations) and at the same time to attract young families. The solution adopted of providing a variety of services—BCP, ASB, Holy Communion, Morning and Evening Prayer, informal, All-age—has the disadvantages of complexity and perhaps of encouraging selective attendance. Yet the alternative of greater uniformity may succeed in satisfying fewer. So when in 1997 75 people gathered at a congregational meeting on worship and different views were expressed—although questionnaire responses showed strong core support for ASB and Family Worship—it was generally agreed that the range of services should continue. The most important change at St. Laurence's was at 10.30 on the second Sunday of the month when in addition to Morning Prayer in the church, an All-age service was to be held simultaneously in the Parish Centre. This innovation has brought more young families regularly to worship, but voices have been raised against the division of the congregation. At All Saints' the Prayer Book has been more frequently used, drawing a few away from the parish church. As an LEP St. Michael's had its own pattern of services. At both All Stretton and Little Stretton one service continued to be held each Sunday, though at differing times.

Michael Stedman wished not just to achieve consensus on the pattern of worship but, more importantly, to nurture discipleship. Series of sermons, the monthly healing services, house groups, biennial parish weekends at the Quinta Conference Centre on the Welsh border, PCC away-days, and the encouragement of Christian reading from the church bookstall or library were all means to assist this. He encouraged attendance, too, at retreats which commended the Ignatian discipline of prayer. The Discipleship Group examined a variety of materials for studies in house groups that were also envisaged as centres of prayer life. But corporate prayer failed to flourish. Only the faithful few came to the Prayer Support Group or Parish Prayers on a Thursday, although the new Prayer Chain and the Prayer Request Board seemed to meet real needs. 'Praise and Prayer', a monthly ecumenical (though largely Anglican) gathering with a 'Charismatic' influence, which had begun in 1989 under John Hughes' leadership, went on attracting considerable numbers.

The launch of the national Decade of Evangelism, in the year the Parish Centre opened, focused attention on another aspect of the Church's mission, one in which the parish had a worthy record. The year after the Daniel Cozens' Mission three coach loads had gone from Church Stretton to hear Billy Graham at a Mission England meeting at Villa Park, and in 1989 the church had supported the Shrewsbury Link of Billy Graham's London Mission. Halfway through the Decade the Churches issued a challenging review entitled 'Signs of Life'. In considering their response and the parish's performance on 'five marks of mission', the PCC agreed that the pursuit of social justice was too low on the church's agenda, but on evangelism were able to point to the 'Person to Person' training programme in the house groups, the newly-adopted mission statement emphasising the call to share God's love, and the 'On Fire' weekend in 1994 organised by Derek Waller. In September 1996 a team from 'The Walk of 1,000 Men on Offa's Dyke' (organised by Daniel Cozens' 'Through Faith Missions') stayed in the parish for a few days visiting homes, schools and pubs, preaching and telling of their Christian experience. Immediately afterwards the church took part in J. John's Mission to Shrewsbury, coach parties attending several of the rallies. That same autumn the first Alpha course attracted about 50 people for ten weeks, though mainly from existing church members. Alpha, which began at Holy Trinity, Brompton in London, has become a world-wide movement; the course is now an annual event in the parish and promises to be a crucial element in the church's mission to reach outsiders with the gospel. Derek Waller's successor as curate in 1996, Tony Cannon, proved himself an ardent advocate of personal evangelism, as well as leading the revival of CYFA.

Pastoral Care was another department's responsibility. The Pastoral Committee advocated training and commissioning for visitors to the bereaved, the housebound and newcomers, as well as a co-ordinator to follow up baptisms. Holy Communion was taken to residential homes and to others unable to get to church, for whom sermons, and later complete services, were recorded. Concern for the bereaved lay behind the opening of the Garden of Remembrance in the north-east corner of the churchyard in 1994. An ambitious Pastoral Care Scheme of 1992 allocated oversight of small areas of the parish to volunteer helpers with a core of four leaders. The importance of welcoming newcomers to church was recognised and generated coffee after the morning service, welcome cards and welcome packs. The wide distribution of 'Contact', a weekly information sheet introduced by Michael Stedman, has helped to keep many in touch with the church. Everyone's enjoyment of social occasions has been enhanced by Norma Brewer and her team of ladies with their splendid meals and buffets.

In spite of the eagerness of the rector and others to provide activities for children and young people, when the facilities of the Parish Centre became available in 1990 numbers in Sunday School and Pathfinders were low. Adele Mander, the Co-ordinator of Young People's Activities in 1995, persuaded the PCC to adopt six targets, all set to bring more young families into church membership, Sunday Club and CYFA. Progress has been made, and more children attend regularly, but leaders are still hard to find. The problem stems from changes in our way of life. More mothers are in paid employment, many fathers commute long distances and work demanding hours: weekends therefore become more than ever times for families to visit, shop or simply be together. So children sometimes miss 'Kidzone', as Sunday Club has been renamed, and, like those newly retired, young parents are reluctant to bind themselves to a weekly commitment, though many are willing to join a rota. On the other hand, abundant volunteers have come forward to make the annual Holiday Club in August a striking success, thanks to the leadership of Moriel Gidney and most recently of the effervescent Captain Tony Maidment of the Church Army. Up to 100 children have come every afternoon for a week.

The effort to attract more young families and the consequent changes in the style of worship in some services have led to consideration of changes inside the church building. In 1994 the removal and sale of the pews in the south aisle created space for the font, moved from the west end, for bookshelves, and for little ones not in the crèche to play during family services. Four years later another working party proposed further reordering to open up the chancel, improve visibility and, as would have rejoiced the heart of Pat Ashe, create an open space under the crossing. This would have meant the replacement of the remaining choir stalls by chairs, and the removal of the front three rows of pews in the nave to accommodate an extension of the platform from which services would be conducted. The heating system was also to be renewed. The plans were approved by the PCC and the Diocesan Advisory Committee, but their publication provoked strong protests and letters to the press, even from some who never attended the church. A poll among those on the Electoral Roll saw a small majority against removing the choir stalls and a slightly larger majority against the changes in the crossing; only improved heating gained general approval. The PCC agreed to seek professional advice on heating and to reconsider the other proposals after three years.

Successive quinquennial reports on the church fabric attracted less attention but produced important renovations—protective guards on stained glass windows, improved lighting, the treatment of roof timbers, and the repair of the small window of Flemish roundels.[3] At All Saints' the roof was rethatched and the churchyard wall renewed. But the greatest undertaking, and the most expensive, was the reroofing of St. Michael's in 1997; fortunately nearly half the cost was met by the generous bequest of Ann Morris, daughter of the former lay reader and warden there. Successive churchwardens—Denise Houghton-Brown, Harvey Bromley and Douglas Grounds—have sought to keep abreast of repairs, to advocate reordering of the church in accordance with changing styles of worship, and to safeguard the church plate and ornaments. These were augmented by the gift in 1994 of a chalice with a Celtic cross and a paten in memory of Elaine Grounds, and another chalice in memory of Molly Purcell.

The new chalices

The churchyard is another responsibility of the wardens. At the end of the 1980s, after the Women's Institute had compiled a record of all existing memorials, 12 insecure tombstones were moved to the south wall and nearly 50 others, which had become indecipherable and hazardous, broken up. In 1997 the church joined 'Caring for God's Acre', a South Shropshire initiative with financial support from the Council and environmental groups. It was agreed to conserve an area on the north side of the church as meadow land, uncut during the summer months to allow the growth of wild flowers in which churchyards, having been uncultivated for centuries, are extraordinarily rich.

The maintenance of three church buildings and the Parish Centre, salaries for verger, parish secretary and organist, on top of a 'parish share' (formerly 'diocesan quota') that had reached £57,000 by the year 2000, meant ever increasing financial pressures. The maintenance of School House was an additional burden: £25,000 for reroofing, central heating and replacement windows was raised only with assistance from the diocese which took over 11% of the equity. An important innovation, adopted in 1989, was an annual Commitment Sunday in the spring, inviting church members to review their use of time, talents and money. Yet successive treasurers, Paul Parsons and, from 1998, Jim Reeves, were still obliged to appeal for increases in giving, especially when there was extraordinary expenditure, as in 1992 for the complete rewiring of the church, or later for sound systems in church and Centre and the extension of the office. But time and again members responded with increased gifts through the Freewill Offering envelopes and by covenanting; others made generous bequests or financed improvements in memory of loved ones, like the regilding of the clock face by the Horrocks family and of the weather vane in memory of Guy Heath.

The Missionary Committee, led for years by Margaret Carey, long-standing deputy churchwarden at All Saints', endeavoured to keep the parish's mission partners in the congregation's thoughts and prayers. In the 1990s Dr. Nigel Pearson with CMS in the Congo, Ed and Marie Brice in Paraguay and Linda McIntyre in Greece and Albania were supported by gifts and prayer, while a group from St. Michael's visited Mokhotlong to see the namesake church that their gifts had helped to build. The parish also part-financed a bursary that enabled an African clergyman to receive extra training in England. The PCC ruled that 10% of its income should go to missions and charities, while Christian Aid Week was strongly supported and an annual Christingle Service benefited the Children's Society. Missionary giving was assisted by the Annual Day of Prayer and Gifts on St. Laurence's Day.

As the church maintained its commitment to overseas mission, it sought ways to realise its mission in the local community. Besides the baptismal, marriage and funeral services and counselling for the large though declining number who requested them, it distributed 'welcome packs' to newcomers, and hired out the Parish Centre facilities to local organisations. There was a Lunch Club in the Parish Centre on Mondays. A popular Parents and Toddlers group met on Thursday mornings, with 'Tots' Praise' once a month. Church members ran the 'Trackers' Christian Club in the Primary School. But the days when the Church was the guardian of social tradition and churchwardens were important figures in the administration of poor relief were long past. Nor does the Church or the local congregation have the staff, finance or expertise to become heavily involved in social action. However, in addition to the regular visiting by clergy or the pastoral care team, many individual church members in Stretton offered their services to Good Neighbours and the Mayfair Community Centre, and formed an important contingent on the 'Focus' team. Others served on the Parish (now Town) Council or had roles in the annual Stretton Arts Festival or Fringe Festival, while for two years a float was entered in the revived Church Stretton Carnival. Yet such individual commitment cannot disguise the fact that the church has lost its once dominant influence in the community.

Michael Stedman saw an opportunity to unite church and community in the preservation of the town's most historic building through the launch of the Friends of St. Laurence in 1997. Under their first chairman, Michael Edmunds, the Friends have raised large sums which are held by a trust for the long-term

A view of St. Laurence's from the south-west

294

benefit of the church building. Its first action was to finance the repair of the sixteenth-century Flemish roundel window (see p.218).

If Michael Stedman had encountered staffing problems in his early years as rector, the position was strong as his rectorship came to a close. When Philip Bytheway was ordained as a local non-stipendiary minister in 1997 there were three curates (two part-time), two lay readers and several retired clergy, like George Jennings, willing to take services. A third reader was added in 1999 with the licensing of Mervyn Williams, who had taken over as verger in the previous year on Ron Hughson's retirement, and the parish secretary, Nancy Cleaton, began reader training. The musical element in worship was broadened in range when David Hotton became Director of Music in 1998 for he balanced 'the good old hymns' with more contemporary songs and music from the Taizé and Iona communities. Mention must be made, too, of Tom Reece, who in 1993 completed 73 years as a chorister and 70 as a bell-ringer.

The Church of England's staffing problems have been eased by the ordination of women. Controversial though that was in some quarters, the Church Stretton PCC expressed its support for the change at the end of 1990. Later in the decade the Diocese of Hereford sought to ease its own difficulties and to encourage fuller lay participation in the mission of the Church with the introduction of Local Ministry Teams. Though these were generally to include more than one parish, the Team commissioned by the Bishop of Hereford in St. Laurence's in 1997 was for the Stretton parish only. The ten members included the four clergy, two lay readers, two wardens and two others. Subsequent difficulties suggested that it may have been set up too hastily and after little more than a year it was temporarily suspended. The members continued to work together in the way they had previously, for Michael Stedman, like John Woodger, had done much to encourage the active participation of the laity.

Early in 1999 Michael Stedman advised the PCC of his impending retirement. The diocese had shown its appreciation of his worth four years earlier when he had been made Prebendary of Moreton Parva. At his farewell in September the esteem and love of the church family were generously demonstrated. As the second longest-serving rector of the century — just exceeding Dr. Dixon but not Prebendary Wragge Morley — Michael Stedman had striven in his quiet way to steer the parish through the rapids of late twentieth-century change. As members of a more church-going generation passed on, attendances at worship, particularly in the evening, had fallen, but in the last years more young families were being attracted, especially to the monthly All-age service in the Parish Centre. The rector had also skilfully maintained a delicate balance between the traditionalist supporters of the Book of Common Prayer and well-established hymns on the one hand and those who favoured more informal services and modern music on the other. He was aided by the growing middle group who had come to like the ASB and enjoyed both sorts of music. He was

The Rev. Michael Stedman, Rector 1985-99, says farewell to his churchwardens, Denise Houghton-Brown and the author

held in high regard as a preacher, undemonstrative but always persuasive, scriptural, and able to lead people towards deeper spiritual understanding. He was also a dedicated visitor with an encyclopaedic knowledge of parishioners in need. In this he was assisted by his wife, Gill, who had led and built up the Women's Fellowship, acted as a pastoral care leader, and become a Parish Visitor, with a growing interest in counselling. Visiting together on occasion, they had brought comfort to many in distress. The rector was rightly remembered, too, for the building of the Parish Centre, as chairman for many years of the Governors of St. Lawrence's Primary School, and for important initiatives like the healing services, the LEP at All Stretton, the Alpha courses and the Friends of St. Laurence. He had supported the Council of Churches, or Churches Together as it became, establishing good personal relations with the other ministers who, to general astonishment, all retired or moved on in the same year as himself.

Church Stretton, which has a very high proportion of elderly inhabitants, has encountered, like everywhere else, an increasing reluctance among younger people in our over-busy and mobile society to take on long-term commitments to leadership in the church or other organisations. Fortunately town and church have benefited from the steady influx of those who have taken early retirement but have wide professional experience and enough energy left to more than hold the fort. The town has an enviable range of cultural and leisure-time organisations, and the church, at a time when the media have continually published figures of declining church attendances in all denominations, has fared remarkably well. And as the century ended there were fresh gleams of hope for St. Laurence's: more young families in the congregation, a revived CYFA, Alpha courses and more house groups.

For the Church as a whole, too, there was light amidst the encircling gloom. While religion ceased to feature in so many lives that the Archbishop of Canterbury once declared that 'a tacit atheism prevails', more and more people were finding that material wealth, consumerism and technological progress do not bring deep and lasting satisfaction. Many were searching for their own brand of spirituality. This led some to experiment with drugs or the occult, others to seek the transcendent through music, New Age movements or concern for the environment. Yet this search for something deeper in life has presented Christians with a new opportunity. As the millennium ended, the great question for the church in Stretton, as for the wider Church, was this: is it sufficiently faithful, imaginative, daring, and open to the needs and aspirations of modern people and to the promptings of the Holy Spirit to rise to the challenge of a new age?

EPILOGUE

The new millennium was greeted throughout the country and all over the world with enormous excitement. The bells ringing out at St. Laurence's to welcome 1 January 2000 heralded the beginning of its second millennium. It is an awesome thought that there has been an active church in Stretton for half the time since Jesus walked the earth. The occasion was marked by the planting of the Millennium Yew, itself propagated from a tree four thousand years old.

It is fitting that the new millennium witnessed the arrival of a new young rector. The Rev. Jonathan Millard, with degrees in Management and Law, five years' experience as a barrister in Manchester, and a Three-Year Certificate in Theology from Wycliffe Hall, Oxford (where he met his American wife, Jill), was ordained in 1992. There followed a short curacy in Buckinghamshire and then five years as Rector of Trinity Episcopal Church in Washington, Pennsylvania, where what had been a run-down church was transformed into a thriving congregation that opened a splendid new building in the year of his departure. He was instituted at Church Stretton by the Rt. Rev. John Oliver, Bishop of Hereford, on 5 May 2000.

It is fitting, too, that in the millennium year the Church of England introduced 'Common Worship' which appropriately looks back and forward, incorporating both the 1662 Book of Common Prayer and services in modern language to appeal to the broadest possible spectrum of Christian believers.

One of the rector's first acts was to win approval of a crisper mission statement committing the parish afresh to 'Growing in Faith, Hope and Love; Sharing the Good News of Jesus with all'.

Jonathan Millard has quickly proved himself a dynamic leader and the 'broad Evangelical' that the PCC had sought: he has accepted the wish of the people of All Saints' to continue to use the 1662 forms of service included in '*Common Worship*', supported an ecumenical future for St. Michael's in its centenary year, and built up the congregation of St. Laurence's with lively services and thoughtful, challenging sermons. Assisted from 2001 by the new curate, Jon Hutchinson, he has made children, families and all newcomers feel genuinely welcome. The appointment in 2002 of Claire Nagioff as Youth

*The Rev. Jonathan Millard, Rector since 2000,
with his wife Jill and their children*

Minister, financed directly by the gifts of church members, heralds action in an area of strategic importance. A large Pastoral Care Team, trained and headed by Doreen Hall, is already active. The thriving Women's Fellowship, led by Sue Polents, has been matched by a rapidly-growing Men's Meeting organised by John Hughes. Members of a slimmed-down PCC together with others from the congregation are to form four 'commissions' to give a lead in the areas of Worship, Discipleship, Fellowship and Outreach. There is an air of excitement as morning congregations expand and many experience a renewed sense of commitment.

Building as well as renovation is back on the agenda, but instead of the limited reordering proposals of 1997 or a piecemeal response to the Quinquennial Inspection of 2000, a more fundamental review of the church and Parish Centre is underway to fit them for the new century. The '20/20 Vision Project', in borrowing a term that denotes perfect sight, acknowledges in its hinted date that major developments will take time. Yet the emphasis is rightly on future needs as St. Laurence's stands poised on the threshold of the second thousand years of its history.

*

The church's first thousand years have seen it develop from an isolated Saxon foundation to a central place of worship with two daughter churches within the parish; from a simple, probably wooden, structure to an impressive stone building, extended and embellished over the centuries; from an outpost of the Catholic Church where the Latin Mass was celebrated, to a Protestant church using an English Prayer Book, and finally to a Christian centre of worship with modern liturgy drawing on both Anglican and more ancient traditions.

Yet for all the myriad changes that have occurred, Stretton and its church remain in some ways remarkably the same. By the standards of today Church Stretton is still a small settlement, nestling among the same lovely hills in the gap through which the Romans once laid down their road. It remains an historic market town, its market place and high street the centre of commercial activity for about eight hundred years. And the church, standing where the Normans—and quite probably the Saxons—placed it, is still at the heart of the community and still proclaims the timeless message of God's love and redemption through the Lord Jesus Christ.

RECTORS OF THE PARISH OF CHURCH STRETTON

1214-22	Ralph de Neville
1222-27	Walter de Brackley
1227- ?	William Friland
1237- ?	William de Pinu
1246-65	Bonettus de Pinibus
1265- ?	William de Ippele
? -1276	David, son of Griffin
1277	Walter, son of William
1277-1309	Master Philip le Waleys
1309- ?	William de Cleobury
1316- ?	Roger de Kynlet
1321- ?	Ralph de Snelleston
1327- ?	William de Hardishull (I)
1331-35	William de Hardishull (II)
1335-47	John de Watenhull
1347-58	'Sir' John Sprot
1358-61	Master Nicholas de Chaddesden
1361-64	Robert de Astmede
1364-69?	William de Wolverton
? -1388	'Sir' Richard Cloppe
1388- ?	Robert Pobelowe
? -1393	William Baron
1393-95	Walter Clyfford
1395- ?	William Smythecote
1402- ?	Alan Thorpe
1405-17	Master William Corve, D.Th.
1417-39	Thomas Oswestre
1439-54	John Fox
1454-59	Master Richard Norys
1459-65	Master David Haliwelle
1465-1514	'Sir' William Hugyns
1514-15	Master Edward Higgons, D.Cn.L.
1515-49	George Dycher, B.Cn.L.
1549-79	John Marett
1579-1621	'Sir' William Harries

1621-52	Anthony Hawkes, M.A.
1654?-67	Peter Dormer, M.A., D.Med.
1668	George Roberts, M.A.
1668-71	Henry Maurice, M.A.?
1671-1725	Henry Clayton, M.A.
1725-48	Rowland Tench, M.A.
1749-1807	John Mainwaring, M.A., B.D., Lady Margaret Professor of Divinity
1807-18	Thomas Coleman, M.A.
1818-48	Robert Pemberton, M.A., Prebendary of Moreton and Whaddon
1849	Charles Salusbury, B.A.
1849-79	Hugh Owen Wilson, M.A.
1879-1904	Charles Noel-Hill, M.A.
1904-11	Alexander Roberts, M.A.
1912-14	Robert Catterall
1914-22	Sidney Woods, M.A.
1923-37	Henry Dixon, M.A., D.D., Archdeacon of Ludlow
1937-47	Herbert Whately, Archdeacon of Ludlow
1948-64	Reginald Wragge Morley, M.A., Prebendary of Inkberrow
1964-71	William Wilson, M.A.
1972-74	Patrick Ashe, M.A.
1974-84	John Woodger, Prebendary of Gorwall
1985-99	Michael Stedman, A.R.I.C.S., Prebendary of Moreton Parva
2000-	Jonathan Millard, B.Sc., Barrister-at-Law

CURATES OF THE PARISH OF CHURCH STRETTON

The thirteenth-century 'curates' were called vicars. Later, dates of appointment are recorded but not always dates of departure. Second curates of course became more common after the daughter churches were opened.

1227	Walter de Mora
1252-53	Ralph de Cestreton
1255	Gilbert
*c.*1560	John Felton
*c.*1587	William Childe
1621	William Haile
1626-27	Thomas Hennant
1630	John Swetnam
1636	Thomas Taylor
1664-68	Samuel Paddy
1671	Charles Farrer
1674	John Bowdler
1678	Vincent Hicks
1747	Henry Meredith
1752-71	Richard Wilding (I)
1771-78	Thomas Piazza
1779-1807	Richard Wilding (II)
1816-19	John Nunn
1821-77	Preston Nunn
1834	" " + William Harries
1837	" " + Sebastian Gambier
1841	" " + Thomas Atkinson
1843-48	" " + William Day
1858-60	" " + William Beaumont
1876-77	" " + Matthew Bower
1877	Noel Colley + Leighton Hope-Edwards
1880	Vernon Carter
1881	David Llewellyn-Davies

1887	Chavasse Whitehouse
1890	Owen Kyffin-Williams
1893	William Ashburner + Charles Custance
1895-98	Reginald Bolton
1896	Harold Mason
1899-1904	Richard Dansey
1903	" " + George Bainbridge
1904-08	Charles Bryant + Vincent Higgins (1904-11)
1908-09	Alfred Osman + " "
1909-10	Gifford Johnson + " "
1911	Francis Tattersall + " "
1912	Cuthbert Birley, Robert Worsley + Arthur Holmes
1914-15	Robert Stockdale
1915-19	Leslie Morton
1919	Martin Custance
1920-23	Charles Pratt + Selby Lennie
1923-27	William Wallace + Charles Warren (to 1926)
1927-29	Reginald Griffiths + John Bartleet (to 1931)
1931	Thomas Wilkinson
1932	Francis Young
1933-34	Reginald Leathley + Eric Serjeantson
1934-36	Thomas Chisholm
1935-37	Robert Lansdale + Gerald Gardner-Brown (to 1938)
1938-41	Harry Woodford + Eric Maddock (to 1945)
1946-48	Harry Woodford + Frank Wilford (1945-50)
1951-61	John Morgan + M.W. Smith (1949-54) + H. Lane Davies (1954-58) + T.W. Doherty (1958-61)
1963-64	John Duffie
1965-69	Robert Hannay
1969-72	Kenneth Newbon
1973-74	Paul Burgess
1975-78	Tony Burdon
1978-81	Barry Brewer
1982-87	Michael Harries
1987-91	Timothy Price + David Janes (1989 NSM part-time)
1991-95	Derek Waller
1996-2000	Tony Cannon + Philip Bytheway (1998 LNSM part-time)
2001-	Jon Hutchinson

CHURCHWARDENS OF THE PARISH OF CHURCH STRETTON

There are many gaps in this list before the Churchwardens' Accounts are available from 1776. In some years since then one warden has been chosen by the rector and one elected by the Vestry Meeting, but this has not been a consistent practice. At times St. Michael's and All Saints' have had their own churchwarden; at other times one or two deputy churchwardens each.

1553	Thomas Walker, Thomas Rawlyngs
1661	Walter Brooke, Thomas Hawkes
1664	John Oates, Richard Minton
1665	John Harrington, Edward Berry
1666	Edward Berry, William Sherry
1667	Edward Minton, David Jones
1668	John Posten, Giles Edwards
1669	Thomas Tomlins, Edward Floyd
1670	Richard Minton, John Clee
1671	Edward Mason, William Bowdler
1672	William Minton, Thomas Minton
1673	Edward Lownes, Philip Lucas
1674	Joseph Paddy, Samuel Minton
1675	William Davies, Matthew Stephens
1676	Richard Minton, Randolph Jones
1677	Stephen Garbett, John Posten
1678	Roger Butler, Edward Williams
1679	Thomas Hawkes, Thomas Minton
1680	Richard Medlicott, Henry Jarrett
1681	William Davis, Thomas Phillips
1684	Edward Berry, Thomas Parr
1691	Thomas Bright, Richard Botvyle
1709	Benjamin Baldwin, John Harrington
1710	Elias Bennett, Uriah Kyte
1711	Thomas Brookes, Randolph Jones
1713	Thomas Waring?, John Williams?
1715	Thomas Tomlins
1716	James Botfield, William Rea

1717	William Tomlins, Thomas Bright
1718	Thomas Croft, John Bridgman
1719	Samuel Phillips, Aaron Eaton
1721	Francis Jarrett, John Lewis
1726	Thomas Waring, George Groom
1727	Samuel Phillips, Richard Hadsall
1737	John Oliver?, Samuel Phillips?
1739	Thomas Bridgman, John Phillips
1742	John Phillips, Moses Eaton
1751	James Metcalfe, Edward Robinson
1752	James Metcalfe, John Francis
1753	John Jones, John Corfield
1758	Thomas Waring, William Davies
1771	Moses Luther, J. Reynolds
1772	" " , " "
1773	John Edwards, Benjamin Bridgman
1774	Thomas Waring, " "
1775	" " , Richard Phillips
1776	John Holmes, John Bridgman
1777	John Bridgman, Thomas Beddoes
1778	Thomas Harrison, Thomas Lucas
1779	Richard Pinches, Richard Minton
1780	" " , " "
1781	Edward Thomas, Thomas Mills
1782	" " , " "
1783	John Northwood, Thomas Watkis
1784	" " , John Bridgman
1785	John Bridgman, William Waring
1786	" " , " "
1787	Benjamin Bridgman, Thomas Gough
1788	" " , " "
1789	John Bridgman, Thomas Harrison
1790	" " , Thomas Robinson
1791	" " , " "
1792	" " , " " , William Waring
1793	John Broome, Stephen Jarrett
1794	" " , " "
1795	Mr. Colley, John Corfield
1796	" " , " "
1797	Richard Beddoes, William Baldwyn
1798	" " , " "

1799	Richard Pinches, William Jones
1800	″ ″ , ″ ″
1801	John Davies, Francis Bridgman
1802	Francis Bridgman, James Walters
1803	Stephen Jarrett, Thomas Beddoes
1804	Benjamin Bridgman, Richard Broome
1805	John Bridgman, George Corfield
1806	John Nicholls, ″ ″
1807	″ ″ , Edmund Childe
1808	John Phillips, Richard Minton
1809	″ ″ , Edward Mansell
1810	Thomas Gough, Francis Bridgman
1811	Thomas Robinson, Richard Heighway
1812	Thomas Waring, George Davies
1813	John Robinson, Edward Lockier
1814	Thomas Smith, Benjamin Reynolds
1815	John Belton, William Jones Hill
1816	Richard Child, Robert Glover
1817	John Phillips, William Corfield
1818	George Corfield, Martin Luther
1819	John Robinson, Benjamin Bridgman
1820	Samuel Wilding, John Broome
1821	John Robinson, Francis Bridgman
1822	″ ″ , Joseph Corfield
1823	Richard Beddoes, Thomas Heynes
1824	″ ″ , John Bridgman
1825	Francis Minton, George Corfield
1826	Richard Home, William Tomlinson
1827	Robert Craig, John Mansell
1828	Benjamin Colley, William Hall
1829	John Speake, James Edwards
1830	″ ″ , ″ ″
1831	George Davis, William Lewis
1832	Edward Medlicott, ″ ″
1833	John Wilding, ″ ″
1834	Thomas Oakley, William Langford
1835	″ ″ , William Corfield
1836	William Corfield, John Lucas
1837	John Belton, Richard Minton
1838	Arthur Phillips, William Craig
1839	John Craig, John Phillips
1840	John Robinson, Edward Lloyd

1841	David Evans, William Beddoes
1842	William Griffiths, Thomas Parker
1843	″ ″ , William Corfield
1844	John Stedman, Richard Minton
1845	″ ″ , ″ ″
1846	John Robinson, John Bridgman
1847	William Barrett, Samuel Bowdler
1848	″ ″ , Thomas Hotchkiss
1849	James Robinson, Timothy Smith
1850	John Beddoes, George Davies
1851	William Lewis, Richard Minton
1852	James Robinson, William Hide
1853	William Bridgman, William Corfield
1854	″ ″ , John Hide
1855	″ ″ , ″ ″
1856	Henry Wood, John Speake Jnr.
1857	″ ″ , ″ ″
1858	Richard Home, Timothy Smith
1859	Thomas Gibbon, Richard Minton
1860	″ ″ , ″ ″
1861	Thomas Andrews, Edward Heighway
1862	″ ″ , ″ ″
1863	Robert Craig, Francis Minton
1864	″ ″ , John Hoggins
1865	Richard Wilding, William Simpson
1866	James Robinson, Richard Edwards
1867	″ ″ , ″ ″
1868	Robert Craig, ″ ″
1869	George Robinson, Edward Andrews
1870	″ ″ , ″ ″
1871	William Jones, Edward Heighway
1872	″ ″ , ″ ″
1873	Thomas Proffit, William Lewis
1874	″ ″ , John Speake
1875	″ ″ , Edward Jones Gwilliam
1876	Richard Edwards, William Hyde
1877	″ ″ , ″ ″
1878	″ ″ , Thomas Andrews
1879	″ ″ , ″ ″
1880	″ ″ , ″ ″
1881	Thomas Proffit, ″ ″

1882-86	John Proffit, Thomas Andrews
1887-1906	John Proffit, David Hyslop
1907-09	John Proffit, Henry Salt
1910-11	Lancelot Squarey, Henry Salt
1912-14	W.J. Roberts, Henry Salt
1915-16	T.R. Thornes, Henry Salt
1917-18	T.R. Thornes, H.E. Gunn
1919	G. Bateson, W.A. Sherratt
1920-21	F.E. Burden, W.A. Sherratt
1922-23	W.T. Boughey, G.H. Birbeck
1924	W.T. Boughey, H. Billson
1925	H. Billson, F. Plimley
1926	H. Billson, J.H. Evans
1927-28	J.H. Evans, M.R. Barron
1929-30	J.H. Evans, A.B. Nock
1931-34	A.B. Nock, Luke Smith
1935-40	A.T. Farquhar, Luke Smith
1941	A.T. Farquhar, M.R. Barron
1942-44	Miss D. Bartlett, L. Atack
1945	Miss D. Bartlett, T. Hayes
1946	W. Jukes, T. Hayes
1947-48	W. Jukes, R.A. Page
1949-51	W. Jukes, A.O. Jones
1952-53	W. Jukes, H.C. Hooper
1954-59	M.J. Spier, H.C. Hooper
1960-61	A.O. Jones, H.C. Hooper
1962-69	Henry Horrocks, H.C. Hooper
1970-82	Henry Horrocks, Norman Owen
1983-84	Norman Powell, Norman Owen
1985-91	Norman Powell, John Hughes
1992	Denise Houghton-Brown, John Hughes
1993-96	Denise Houghton-Brown, Harvey Bromley
1997-2001	Denise Houghton-Brown, Douglas Grounds
2002	Douglas Grounds, Camilla Aston

Sources and Bibliography

Abbreviations

Bodleian	Bodleian Library, Oxford
H.R.O.	Herefordshire Record Office
P.R.O.	Public Record Office
S.R.R.C.	Shropshire Records and Research Centre
W.S.L.	William Salt Library, Stafford

Primary and Principal Sources

Bagshaw	*Bagshaw's Directory & Gazetteer*
Bishops Registers	(Listed individually)
Blakeway MSS	Blakeway MSS, Bodleian Library
Bye-Gones	*'Bye-Gones'* (bound news items & reminiscences — SRRC)
C.Ch.R.	Calendar of Charter Rolls
C.C.R.	Calendar of Close Rolls
C.D.S.P.	Calendar of Domestic State Papers
C.I.M.	Calendar of Inquisitions Miscellaneous
C.P.R.	Calendar of Patent Rolls
Camden	Camden Society publications
Charity Comm	Report of Commissioners on Charities in England & Wales, 1839
Church Archives	Documents still held by St. Laurence's Church
Cranage	D.H.S. Cranage, *An Architectural Account of the Churches of Shropshire* (1895)
Crockfords	Crockfords Clerical Directory
C.S.A.	*Church Stretton Advertiser*
D.B.	Domesday Book
D.N.B.	Dictionary of National Biography
Eagle	*The Eagle*, magazine of St. John's College, Cambridge
Eddowes	*Eddowes' Shropshire Journal*
Emden	Emden's *Biographical Register of the University of Oxford to 1500*
Eyton	R.W. Eyton, *Antiquities of Shropshire*
Foster	J. Foster, *Alumni Oxonienses*
Glynne	Sir S. Glynne, *Church Notes from Shropshire* ed. D.C. Cox (1999)
Hardwick MSS	Hardwick's *MSS Collections for the History of Shropshire* (WSL, 350/5/40)
Heralds	Heralds' Visitation Records of Shropshire, 1623
Leland	*The Itinerary of John Leland in England, 1535-43* (1907)
Maurice	The Rev. Henry Maurice's Shropshire diary, 1672 ed. J.V. Cox in *Shropshire Historical Documents: A Miscellany* (2000)
Parish mag.	Parish magazine of St. Laurence's Church
Parkes	D. Parkes, Drawings of Shropshire Churches (1806-24) - SRRC Mic. 60 from British Library Add. Mss.
P.C.C.	Minutes of Parochial Church Council, Church Stretton
Peace Roll	*'Shropshire Peace Roll, 1400-14'* (1959 ed.)
Pigot	*Pigot's Directory*
Shreds & Patches	*Salopian Shreds & Patches* - bound news extracts (SRRC)
S.C.	*Shrewsbury Chronicle*
T.S.A.S.	*Transactions of the Shropshire Archaeological Society*
Valor Ecc.	*Valor Ecclesiasticus*, 1535
V.C.H.	*Victoria County History of Shropshire*

313

Venn	J. & J.A. Venn, *Alumni Cantabrigienses*
W.L.E.	*Wenlock & Ludlow Express*
Williams	E. Williams, Drawings of Shropshire Churches (SRRC Mic 122)

Bibliography

Acton F.S.	*The Garrisons of Shropshire during the Civil War, 1642-48* (1867)
Arkwright D.L. & Bourne B.W.	*The Church Plate of the Archdeaconry of Ludlow*
Aston M.	*Thomas Arundel* (1967)
Auden H.M.	*The Parochial History of Church Stretton* in *Church Stretton* vol.II (1904)
Auden T.	*The Church & Parish of St. Juliana in Shrewsbury* (1887)
Bailey B.	*Churchyards of England & Wales* (1987)
Baker T.	*A History of St. John's College, Cambridge*
Barlow F. (1979 A)	*The English Church, 1000-66* (1979)
Barlow F. (1979 B)	*The English Church, 1066-1154* (1979)
Barlow F. (1988)	*The Feudal Kingdom of England, 1042-1216* (1988 cd.)
Bassett S.	'Church and Diocese in the West Midlands: the Transition from British to Anglo-Saxon Control' in *Pastoral Care before the Parish* eds. J. Blair & R. Sharpe (1992)
Bilbey D.	*Church Stretton* (1985)
Blair J. (1985)	'Secular Minster Churches in Domesday Book' in *Domesday Book: A Re-Assessment* ed. P. Sawyer (1985)
Blair J. (1988 A)	'Minster Churches in the Landscape' in *Anglo-Saxon Settlements* ed. D. Hooke (1988)
Blair J. (1988 B)	'Introduction: From Minster to Parish Church' in *Minsters and Parish Churches* ed. J. Blair (1988)
Blakeway J.W.	*Sheriffs of Shropshire*
Bp. Bothe	*Register of Bishop Bothe* ed. A.T. Bannister (1921)
Botfield B.	*Stemmata Botevilliana* (1858)
Brooke C.	*Medieval Church and Society* (1971)
Calamy E.	*The Nonconformists' Memorial* (1752)
Bp. Cantilupe	*Register of Bishop Cantilupe* ed. W.W..Capes (1907)
Carpenter D.A.	*The Minority of Henry III* (1990)
Chadwick O.	*The Victorian Church* (2 vols. 1971 & 1972 eds.)
Bp. Charlton	*Register of Bishop Charlton* ed. W.W. Capes (1912)
Cole W.	*A Catalogue of Netherlandish & North European Roundels in Britain* (1993)
Collinson P.	*The Religion of Protestants, 1559-1625* (1982)
Cong. Church	*Church Stretton Congregational Church: A Short History published for the Centenary*, 1960
Cradock J.	*Literary and Miscellaneous Memoirs* (1828)
Cragg G.R.	*The Church and the Age of Reason, 1648-1789*
Cranage D.H.S. (1952)	*Only a Dean* (1952)
Croom J.	'The Fragmentation of the Minster Parochiae of South-East Shropshire' in *Minsters & Parish Churches* ed. J. Blair (1988)
Cross C.	*Church and People, 1450-1660* (1976)
Currie R., Gilbert A. & Horsley L.	*Churches and Churchgoers* (1977)
Darby H.C. & Terrett I. eds.	*The Domesday Geography of Middle England* (1971)
Davies R.R. (1978)	*Lordship & Society in the Marches of Wales, 1282-1400* (1978)

Davies R.R. (1995) *The Revolt of Owain Glyn Dwr* (1995)

Dawley P.M.   *John Whitgift and the Reformation* (1954)

Deanesly M.   *The Pre-Conquest Church in England* (1961)

Dickens A.G.   *The English Reformation* (1964)

Dickinson J.C.   *The Ecclesiastical History of England in the Later Middle Ages* (1979)

Duffy E.   *The Stripping of the Altars* (1992)

Eales J.   *The Harleys of Brampton Bryan and the Outbreak of theEnglish Civil War* (1990)

Faraday M.   *Ludlow, 1085-1660* (1991)

Faraday & Cole   *A Calendar of Probate & Administration Acts, 1407-1547 in the Court Books of the Bishop of Hereford* (unpublished)

Farrow W.J.   *The Great Civil War in Shropshire, 1642-49* (1926)

Fisher G.W.   *The Annals of Shrewsbury School* (1899)

Foss E.   *The Judges of England*

Gelling M. (1992)   *The West Midlands in the Early Middle Ages* (1992)

Gelling M. (2000)   'Place Names' in *The Gale of Life* ed. J. Leonard etc (2000)

Harper-Bill C.   *The Pre-Reformation Church in England, 1400-1530* (1989)

Hastings A.   *A History of English Christianity, 1920-2000* (2000)

Heath P.   *The English Parish Clergy on the Eve of the Reformation* (1969)

Hillaby J.   'The Early Church in Herefordshire: Columban and Roman' in *The Early Church in Herefordshire* ed. Leominster History Study Group (2001)

Howard R.   'Unrest in the Marches, 1280-1485' in *The Gale of Life* ed. J. Leonard etc. (2000)

Hudson A.   *The Premature Reformation* (1988)

Hutton R.   *The Restoration: A Political and Religious History of England and Wales, 1658-67* (1985)

Hylson-Smith K.   *The Churches in England from Elizabeth I to Elizabeth II vol. I, 1558-1688* (1996)   (1996)

Hylson-Smith K.   *Christianity in England from Roman Times to the Reformation vol. I, To* (1999)   *1066* (1999)

Iremonger F.A.   *William Temple* (1948)

Jacob E.F.   *The Fifteenth Century* (Oxford History of England, 1961)

Jones A.   *A Thousand Years of the English Parish* (2000)

Kemp B.   'Some Aspects of the Parochia of Leominster in the 12th Century' in *The Local Church in Transition, 950-1200* ed. J. Blair (1988)

Leonard J.   *Shropshire Parish Churches* (1991)

Loyn H.R.   *The English Church, 940-1154* (2000)

Bp. Mascall   *Register of Bishop Mascall* ed. J.H. Parry (1916)

Bp. Mayew   *Register of Bishop Mayew* ed. A.T. Bannister (1919)

McFarlane K.B.   *John Wycliffe and the Beginnings of English Nonconformity* (1952)

McKerrow R.B.ed   *A Dictionary of Printers and Booksellers in England, Scotland and Ireland, 1557-1640*

McKisack M.   *The Fourteenth Century* (Oxford History of England, 1959)

Mercer E.   *English Architecture to 1900: The Shropshire Experience* (forthcoming)

Moorman J.   *Church Life in England in the 13th Century* (1945)

Morgan R.   *The barony of Powys, 1275-1360* in Welsh History Review 1980-81

Morrill J.   *The Nature of the English Revolution* (1988)

Morris R.   *Churches in the Landscape* (1997 ed)

Bp. Myllyng   *Register of Bishop Myllyng* ed. A.T. Bannister (1919)

O'Day R. &
   Heal F. eds.   *Continuity and Change: The Personnel and Administration of the Church in England, 1500-1642* (1976)

Bp. Orleton   *Register of Bishop Orleton* ed. A.T. Bannister (1907)
Owen & Blakeway *A History of Shrewsbury*
Pevsner N.   *The Buildings of Shropshire* (1958)
Phillips J.   *A Guide to Church Stretton* (1869)
Plymley J.   *A General View of the Agriculture of Shropshire* (1813)
Pounds N.J.G.   *A History of the English Parish* (2000)
Powicke Sir F.M.   *The Thirteenth Century* (Oxford History of England, 1962)
Pretty K.   'Defining the Magonsaete' in *The Origins of the Anglo-Saxon Kingdoms*
                          ed. S. Bassett (1989)
Ray K.   'Archaeology and the Three Early Churches of Herefordshire' in *The Early
                          Church in Herefordshire* ed. Leominster History Study Group (2001)
Richards & Shadwell *The Provosts and Fellows of Oriel College, Oxford*
Roope H.E.G.   'Church Stretton Memories of the 1880s' in *Shropshire Magazine*, June
                          1962
Rupp E.G.   *Religion in England, 1688-1791* (1986)
Scard M.A.   *The Building Stones of Shropshire* (1990)
Shrewsbury Abbey *The Cartulary of Shrewsbury Abbey* ed U. Rees (1975)
Skinner R.F.   *Nonconformity in Shropshire, 1662-1816* (1964)
Spinka M.   *John Hus and the Council of Constance* (1985)
Spurr J.   *The Restoration Church of England, 1646-89* (1991)
Stacey R.   *Politics, Policy and Finance under Henry III, 1216-45* (1987)
Bp. Stanbury   *Register of Bishop Stanbury* ed. A.T. Bannister (1918)
Stroud D.   *Capability Brown* (1984 ed)
Suppe F.C.   *Military Institutions on the Welsh Marches: Shropshire 1066-1300* (1994)
Swanson R.W.   *Church and Society in Late Medieval England* (1989)
Bp. Swinfield   *Register of Bishop Swinfield* ed. W.W. Capes (1909)
Thomas K.   *Religion and the Decline of Magic* (1971)
Thompson A. Hamilton *The English Clergy and their Organisation in the Late Middle Ages*
                          (1947)
Toghill P.   *Geology in Shropshire* (1990)
Tout T.F.   *Chapters in the Administrative History of Medieval England*
Trabert-Cussac   *L'Administration Anglaise du Gascogne sous Henri III et Edward I, 1254-
                          1307*
Bp. Trillek   *Register of Bishop Trillek* ed. J.H. Parry (1910)
Trinder B.   *The Industrial Revolution in Shropshire* (1981)
Vallance A.   *English Church Screens* (1936)
Ward W.R.   'The Tithe Question in England in the Early 19th Century' in *Journal of
                          Ecclesiastical History*, 1965
Warren W.L.   *King John* (2nd ed 1978)
Webb J.   *The Civil War in Herefordshire* (1879)
Webster G.   *The Cornovii* (1991)
Whalley T.S.   *The Journals and Correspondence of Dr. Thomas Sedgwick Whalley D.D.*
                          ed. H. Wickham (1863)
White R.& Barker P. *Wroxeter: The Life and Death of a Roman City* (1998)
Windsor G.   *A Handbook to the Capabilities, Attractions, Beauties and Scenery of
                          Church Stretton* (1885)
Windsor G.   *Laura Heathjohn*
Woolley C.   *Church Stretton and District* (1905)
Zaluckyj S.   *Mercia, The Anglo-Saxon Kingdom of Central England* (2001)
Ziegler P.   *The Black Death* (1991 ed)

REFERENCES

For abbreviations and titles of works referred to by authors' names see the previous list entitled Sources and Bibliography.

CHAPTER 1
1. Gelling M. (2000), p.45
2. Gelling M. (1992), p.28
3. *Ibid.*, p.123
4. Bilbey D., Introd.
5. Hardwick MSS, (WSL 350/5/40), 'Church Stretton', p.18
6. White R. & Barker P., p.123
7. Ray K., p.109
8. *Ibid.*, p.117
9. Bassett S., p.39
10. Quoted in Zaluckyj S., p.46
11. Gelling M.(1992), p.49
12. Hillaby J., p.48
13. Zaluckyj S., p.43
14. Bassett S., p.35
15. Kemp B., p.85
16. Blair J. (1985), p.130
17. Bassett S., p.36
18. Croom J., p.68
19. Blair J. (1988 B), p.8
20. Pounds N.J.G., p.29
21. Morris R., p.163
22. Blair J. (1988 A), p.57
23. Morris R., p.75
24. Zaluckyj S., pp.241, 262
25. D.B., Shropshire, f.254a
26. VCH, Shropshire, I p.484
27. D.B., Shropshire: 'A hide was a unit of measurement, generally reckoned at 120 acres, but often different in practice; a measure of tax liability, often differing in number from the hides actually cultivated'.
28. TSAS, 1939-40, pp. 31-34
29. Darby H.C. & Terrett I. eds, p.127, suggests multiplying by a factor of four or five to calculate the total population.
30. D.B., Shropshire, f. 258b
31. 28 churches in Shropshire appear in DB, but 27 other priests are mentioned, making a possible 55 churches.
32. Barlow F. (1988), p.131
33. Leonard J., p.10
34. Quoted by Morris R., p.147
35. Scard M.A., p.69, and information given personally by Mrs. S. Beale
36. Hardwick MSS (W.S.L. 350/5/40), 'Church Stretton', p.50
37. Barlow F. (1988), p.26
38. Morris R., p. 287

CHAPTER 2
1. Eyton, II, p.82
2. Jones A., p.49
3. Blakeway MSS, Shropshire Parochial History O-W, p.103
4. Barlow F.(1979 B), p.3
5. *Ibid.*
6. Hundred Roll of 1255, quoted by Eyton, XII , p.6
7. Bilbey D., Introd.
8. Eyton, XII, p.20
9. Morris R., p.213
10. Barlow F. (1988), p.401
11. Eyton, XII, p.20
12. Warren, p.145
13. Cranage, II, p.80-83
14. Moorman J.R.H., p.68
15. Glynne, p.113
16. Eyton, XII, p.29
17. Morris R., p.283
18. Toghill P., p.82
19. Hardwick MSS (WSL 350/5/40), Church Stretton, p.50
20. Pevsner N., p.100
21. Parkes
22. Hardwick MSS, Church Stretton, p.25

CHAPTER 3
1. Stacey R., p.17
2. DNB
3. Moorman J.R.H., p.164
4. Carpenter D.A., p.408
5. Quoted in DNB
6. CPR, 1216-25, p.353
7. Shrewsbury Abbey, I, p.159
8. Quoted in Jones A., p.118
9. CChR, 1226-57, p.103
10. Suppe F.C., p.109
11. In 1287 Strettondale was able to provide

100 armed men – PRO, Calendar of
Various Chancery Rolls, 1277-1326
12. Eyton, XII, p.5
13. Calendar of Liberate Rolls, 1226-40,
p.218
14. The Prior was one of the leaders of the
rebellion in 1253, together with Gaston
de Bearn and the del Soler family who
headed the opposition to Simon de
Montfort in Bordeaux – Trabut-Cussac,
p.4
15. CPR, 1247-58, p.206
16. *Rotuli Hundredorum*, II, p.84
17. CPR, 1247-58, p.337
18. Eyton, XII, p.27
19. *Ibid.*, XII, p.22
20. TSAS, LVII, p.67
21. CPR, 1258-66, p.508
22. CPR, 1272-81, p.193
23. Heralds, 1623, I, p.104; Morgan R. p.6
24. Bp. Cantilupe, p.119
25. Swanson R.W., p.40
26. Moorman J.R.H., p.224 – 'Often enough
children were appointed who had to
wait long years before they could
qualify for holy orders'.
27. CCR, 1272-79, p.475
28. CPR, 1272-81, p.302
29. Bp. Swinfield, pp.3-6
30. *Ibid.*, p.89
31. Eyton, XII, p.29
32. Swanson R.W., p. 4
33. Moorman J.R.H., p.32
34. *Ibid.*, p.21
35. CIM, I (1219-1307), No. 2277
36. Powicke Sir F.M., p.485
37. Moorman J.R.H., p.167
38. Camden, 1855, (vol. 62), p.cxc –'The
Household Roll of Bishop Swinfield'.
39. Camden, 1854, (vol. 59), p.79
40. CCR, 1302-07, p.77
41. CPR, 1307-13, p.186

CHAPTER 4
1. CPR, 1307-13, pp.190, 196
2. *Ibid.*, pp.240, 283
3. *Ibid.*, p.196
4. Eyton, XII, p.27
5. CPR, 1313-17, p.397
6. Bp. Swinfield, p.543
7. Charlton eventually became Bishop of
Hereford in 1327.

8. Bp. Orleton, p.391
9. CPR, 1327-30, p.133
10. Bp. Charlton, pp.89, 44
11. CPR, 1327-30, p.484
12. *Ibid.*, p.494
13. CPR, 1330-34, p.39
14. CCR, 1330-33, pp.579, 582
15. CPR, 1330-34, p.339
16. CPR, 1334-38, p.4
17. Bp. Charlton, p.83
18. CCR, 1330-33, pp.65, 592
19. CCR, 1333-37, p.730
20. CPR, 1334-38, p.391
21. CPR, 1343-45, p.533
22. CChR, 1327-41, p.353
23. *Ibid.*, p.421
24. TSAS, ser 3 vol iii (1903), p.290
25. Eyton, XII, p.29
26. Parkes
27. Hardwick MSS, Church Stretton, p.10
28. CIM, vol 3, 1348-77, No. 988
29. Ziegler P., p.151
30. Bp. Trillek, p.390
31. Emden
32. Thompson A. Hamilton, p.108 –
'Everyone who has attempted to
compile lists of incumbents of parish
churches from episcopal registers
knows how frequent the gaps become,
even where the registers are quite
complete, in the last quarter of the
fourteenth century'.
33. Register of Archbishop Langham
(Canterbury & York Society), p.40
34. Davies R.R. (1988) p.190
35. Hair P.E.H., 'The Mobility of Parochial
Clergy in the Hereford Diocese *c.*1400'
in *Transactions of the Woolhope
Naturalists Field Club*, 1980, p.175
36. HRO, Bishop's Visitation 1397
37. Thompson A. Hamilton, p.107
38. *Ibid.*, p.107-8
39. McFarlane K.B. p.29
40. Swanson R.W. p.55
41. Thompson A. Hamilton, p.108. Gehazi
and Simon Magus are Old and New
Testament characters who respectively
sought financial gain or to buy spiritual
power for selfish ends - see 2 Kings
ch. 5 & Acts ch. 8.
42. Duffy E.

CHAPTER 5

1. Davies R.R. (1995), p.112
2. Howard R., p.126-7
3. Peace Roll, Introd, p.10
4. *Ibid.*, p.10
5. CPR, 1391-96, p.606
6. 'Peace Roll', pp.56, 83, 90
7. Details from Bp. Mascall, pp.171, 188, and Emden
8. Richards and Shadwell, p.17
9. Spinka M., p.169
10. *Ibid.*
11. TSAS, 1st Ser vol VI (1883), p.319
12. It is possible that he was related to Alan Thorpe, Rector of Stretton 1402-04. Owen and Blakeway, pp.202-4, say he was 'probably connected with this neighbourhood'.
13. Faraday M., pp.68-9
14. Blakeway J.W.
15. Faraday & Cole, 53/159
16. Botfield B., p.25
17. Faraday & Cole, 68/128
18. Bp. Stanbury, p.112
19. Harper-Bill C., p.50
20. Eyton, VI, p.30
21. Bp. Myllyng, pp.120, 123; Bp. Mayew, p.63
22. TSAS, 2nd ser vol XI (1899), pp.19-21
23. Dickinson J.C., p.450
24. SRRC, 6001/6865
25. Vallance A., p.71
26. Dickinson J.C., p.446
27. TSAS 1st ser vol VI (1883), pp.320-1
28. Faraday & Cole, 534/204
29. PRO, c 66/1083/2463 m 17
30. HRO, Woodard Index 9/2/7
31. TSAS 3rd ser vol IV (1904), pp.6-8
32. Harper-Bill C., p.64
33. Duffy E., p.117
34. Indulgences were remissions by the Church of temporal penalties still due (on earth or in Purgatory) after penance and absolution.
35. Quoted by Duffy E., p.98
36. Botfield B., p.dxxiv
37. Hardwick MSS, Church Stretton, p.73
38. Details from Emden
39. Botfield B., p.28
40. Bp. Bothe, p.114
41. Hardwick MSS, Church Stretton, p.54
42. Leland, V, pp.80-81
43. Valor Ecc., Salop (1535), p.208
44. Bp. Bothe, p.369; Harper-Bill C., p.45

CHAPTER 6

1. Quoted by Duffy E., p.432
2. Quoted by Dickens A.G., p.72
3. PRO, E 117/8/17
4. HRO, Woodard Index 8/3/40
5. TSAS ser 4 vol XI (1927-28), p.186
6. *Ibid.*, p.201
7. Hardwick MSS, Church Stretton, p.52
8. HRO, Woodard Index, 21/2/70, 21/1/64
9. TSAS, ser 3 vol IV (1904), p.116
10. Botfield B., p.70
11. PRO, Prob 11: 61 q 48 records an earlier benefactor named Thomas Vaughan who on 3 December 1578 left five marks for the poor, but this seems to have been a one-off payment.
12. VCH, Shropshire IV, p.131
13. Hardwick MSS, Church Stretton, p.5
14. See below, p.99
15. TSAS, vol XLVI (1931-32), p.44
16. Foster
17. Heralds
18. TSAS, ser 3 vol IV (1904), pp. 115-129
19. HRO, Box 17 vol 68 f233
20. HRO, HD 2/14/17
21. SRRC, 'Bye-Gones', 1 Feb 1911
22. Dickens A.G., p.46
23. Hardwick MSS, Church Stretton, p.77
24. SRRC, 3365/2621
25. Hardwick MSS, Church Stretton, p.52
26. Dawley P.M., p.205
27. Glynne, p.25
28. Thomas K., p.721
29. Collinson P., p.232

CHAPTER 7

1. TSAS, ser 1 vol X (1887), p.132
2. SRRC, 2956/1
3. Introduction to Onibury Parish registers
4. DNB
5. Foss E.
6. 'Transcripts of the Royal Company of Stationers', II, p.10
7. SRRC, 2956/1
8. Mercer E.
9. *Ibid.*
10. Windsor G. (1885), p.89

11. Morris R., p.406
12. Hardwick MSS, Church Stretton, p.50
13. Chancery records quoted in The Library, 1901, p.357
14. McKerrow R.B. ed., p.202
15. Domestic State Papers, Charles I, vol 169, nos. 5, 6, 7, 20, 21 and vol 175, nos. 123, 124
16. 'Transcripts of the Royal Company of Stationers', IV, p.283
17. TSAS, vol LIV (1952-53), pp.36-42
18. Blakeway MSS
19. PRO, C 2/ Jas I/ T 12/ 17
20. Auden H.M., p.188
21. Collinson P., p.93
22. Ibid., p.94
23. Oxford details from Foster
24. O'Day R.& Heal F. eds, pp.71-72
25. Collinson P., p.96
26. HRO, HD 4/1 vol 36 Acts of Office, 1534, p.124
27. Rev. Thomas Froysell, Vicar of Clun, quoted in Collinson P., p.164
28. Eales J., p.12
29. George Widley in 1604 – quoted by Collinson P., p.204
30. Reproduced in TSAS ser 3 vol I (1901), pp.351-58
31. Thomas K., p.722
32. Morrill J., p.37
33. Eales J., p.196
34. Ibid., p.144
35. TSAS, ser 2 vol VII (1895), p.241
36. Ibid., p.244
37. Letter quoted in Acton F.S., p.9
38. Webb, I, p.383
39. TSAS, ser 3 vol I (1901), p.331
40. Ibid., p.332
41. TSAS, ser 2 vol VIII (1896), p.239
42. CDSP, 1644, p.283
43. Webb, II, pp.72-3
44. TSAS, ser 3 vol I (1901), p.334
45. TSAS, ser 3 vol VII (1907), p.251
46. Bodleian, 4/D/62/Th
47. Farrow W.J., p.27
48. TSAS, ser 3 vol VII (1907), p.270
49. Hylson-Smith K.(1996), p.187

CHAPTER 8
1. Hutton R., p.125
2. Ibid., p.143
3. Ibid., p.172

4. Spurr J., p.42
5. The Agreement of the Presbyterian-dominated House of Commons with the Scots in 1643.
6. Foster
7. Lipscomb, County of Buckingham, I, p.415
8. Hardwick MSS, Church Stretton, p.52
9. Ibid., p.92
10. TSAS ser 4 vol II (1912), p.214
11. HRO, HD 5/11
12. Hutton R., p.176
13. TSAS, vol L, (1939-40), p.180
14. Skinner R.F., p.2
15. Spurr J., p.43
16. Auden T., p.37
17. HRO, HD 7/8/30
18. HRO, HD 7/11/17
19. Calamy E., p.338
20. Maurice
21. Quoted in Skinner R.F., p.114 , from Campion MSS in Transactions of the Congregational History Society, vol 19/71
22. Transcribed in Blakeway MSS
23. HRO, HD 7/14/293
24. HRO, HD 7/14/31
25. SRRC, C 63
26. Staffs R.O., D (W) 1788, p.46
27. HRO, HD 7/15/81
28. HRO, HD 4/1 Box 40 vol 173, 75R
29. HRO, HD 7/15/137
30. Refs in this paragraph – HRO, HD 7/9/122; HD 7/11/77; HD 7/11/203; HD 4/1 Box 40, vol 173, pp 89, 119; HD 7/19/28; HD 7/21/264
31. HRO, HD 7/21/332
32. SRRC, D 34.6
33. Cross C., p.231
34. Spurr J., p.70
35. Skinner R.F., Appendix 3
36. HRO, HD 2/15/1
37. Spurr J., p.163
38. Bodleian, MS English Letters E 29 Folio 176v
39. HRO, HD 7/21/265
40. HRO, HD 2/14/18
41. Spurr J.,p.196
42. HRO, Woodard Index 28/2/2 and 33/3/6
43. HRO, HD 7/19/165, HD 7/20/409, HD 7/20/333, HD 7/20/347
44. Charity Comm.

45. HRO, HD 5/14/164 (1719 –
      HD 5/15/156)
46. Skinner R.F., p.27

CHAPTER 9
1. HRO, HD 4/1 Box 41 vols 153/154
2. Rupp E.G., p.278
3. Fisher G.W., p.203
4. Eagle, vol 23, pp.144, 158-9
5. See the plaque in St. Mary's erected on
      the school's quatercentenary
6. Hardwick MSS, Church Stretton, p.52
7. Berridge J., *The Christian World
      Unmasked*, p.335
8. Trinder B., pp.15, 90
9. TSAS, vol LIV (1951-53), pp.41-42
10. Venn
11. Plymley J., p.148
12. Cradock J., pp.228-29
13. *Ibid.*, p.189
14. Whalley T.S., I, p.10; II, p.367
15. 'Pakenham Correspondence', quoted in
      Stroud D., p.172
16. SRRC, 6001/6865
17. Cradock J., p.147
18. SRRC, P 67/B/1/1
19. TSAS, ser 3 vol IV (1904), pp.6-8
20. SRRC, 6001/6865
21. Currie R., Gilbert A., and Horsley L.,
      p.23
22. Bye-Gones (SRRC), 1 February 1911
23. SC, 28 November 1772
24. SRRC, 6001/6865
25. VCH Shropshire, X, p.78
26. Rupp E.G., p.493
27. Bye-Gones, 1 February 1911
28. Hardwick MSS, Church Stretton, p.53
29. SRRC, Williams E., Mic. 122
30. Hardwick MSS, Church Stretton, p.53
31. SRRC, 6001/6865
32. Parkes
33. SRRC, P 67/B/4/1
34. Parkes
35. Woolley C. ed. (1905)
36. Baker T., II, p.736
37. St. John's College, Cambridge,
      Admissions, part III

CHAPTER 10
1. SRRC, 802/51
2. SRRC, 807/172
3. SC, 7 August 1818

4. SRRC, 2563/123
5. TSAS, ser 3 vol VII (1907), p.137
6. SC, 17 November 1820
7. Church archives
8. SRRC, 1045/537-38
9. SRRC, P 67/B/3/2
10. SRRC, P 67/B/3/1
11. Church archives
12. Phillips J., p.18
13. See below p.251
14. Glynne, p.24
15. Woolley C., (1905), p.21
16. Bagshaw, 1851, p.526
17. *Gentleman's Magazine*, July 1820, p.91
18. Church archives
19. Hardwick MSS, Church Stretton, p.51
20. Windsor, (1885)
21. Hardwick MSS, Church Stretton, p.50
22. *Ibid.*, p.50
23. *Ibid.*, p.51
24. Glynne, p.25
25. SRRC, 6001/6865
26. Pigot, 1822-23
27. Bagshaw, 1851
28. SRRC, P 67/A/9/1
29. Bagshaw, 1851
30. SRRC, P 67/W/1/1-2
31. TSAS, ser 3 vol VII (1907), p.136
32. Chadwick O., I, p.34
33. Bye-Gones, 1 February 1911
34. Ward W.R., p.69
35. Bagshaw, 1851
36. Chadwick O., I, p.82
37. SRRC, P 67/F/1/1
38. SRRC, 1011/1048
39. HRO, HD 8/17, 22, 24
40. SRRC, 1011, Box 241
41. SC, 13 October 1848
42. Bye-Gones, 1 February 1911
43. Glynne, p.25
44. Hardwick MSS, Church Stretton, p.51

CHAPTER 11
1. Bye-Gones, 1 February 1911
2. SC, 23 October 1868
3. Population Census, 1851 & 1861
4. See below
5. Bye-Gones, 1 February 1911
6. PRO, HO 129/354 No. 6
7. SRRC, 1672
8. HRO, HD 5/45
9. VCH, Shropshire, X, 116

10. Cong. Church
11. SC, 23 October 1868
12. Church archives
13. SRRC, P 67/B/2/2
14. Church archives
15. SRRC, P 67/B/3/4
16. Parkes
17. SC, 23 October 1868
18. SC, 20 January 1882
19. SRRC, P 67/B/2/2
20. Church archives
21. SC, 23 October 1868
22. Bye-Gones, 1 February 1911
23. SC, 27 October 1876
24. Chadwick O., II, p.124
25. SC, 28 December 1877
26. SC, 28 February 1879
27. Eddowes, 26 February 1879
28. WLE, 1 March 1879
29. WLE, 23 August 1879
30. SC, 22 April 1881, 2 January 1880
31. SC, 1 June 1880
32. WLE, 16 October 1880
33. Eddowes, 25 August 1880
34. WLE, 16 October 1880
35. SRRC, P 67/B/2/3
36. Chadwick O., I, 519
37. Roope H.E.G.
38. SC, 15 March 1889
39. SC, 23 April 1886
40. Windsor (1885)
41. SC, 7 May 1886
42. VCH, Shropshire, X, p.113
43. For details see Cole W., pp.60-62
44. Shreds and Patches, 11 February 1891
45. SC, 9 October 1891
46. SC, 3 June 1898

CHAPTER 12
1. VCH, Shropshire, X, p.80
2. SC, 2 December 1892
3. SC, 22 November 1901
4. *St. Michael & All Angels, All Stretton: The Story of a Village Church, 1902-77* (75th Anniversary booklet)
5. SC, 31 October 1902
6. St. Michael's 75th Anniversary booklet
7. SC, 23 October 1903
8. SC, 8 January 1904
9. Bye-Gones, 1 February 1911
10. Currie R., Gilbert A. & Horsley L., p.116

11. Hastings, A., p.41
12. Parsons, *Religion in Victorian Britain,* II, 13 (quoted by Hylson-Smith K., *The Churches in England from Elizabeth I to Elizabeth II,* III, p.94)
13. CSA, 2 June 1904
14. Crockfords
15. F.A. Iremonger F.A., p.64; CSA, 8 September 1904
16. CSA, 26 April 1906
17. CSA, 9 August 1906
18. Crockfords
19. CSA, 9 November 1911
20. SC, 21 October 1911
21. SC, 19 December 1913
22. Crockfords
23. CSA, 30 July 1914
24. SC, 13 November 1914, 11 December 1914
25. Church archives
26. SRRC, P 67/B/1/2
22. *Ibid.*
28. SC, 15 November 1918
29. Parish Mag., July 1919
30. CSA, 25 January 1923
31. SC, 26 January 1923
32. Annual Parochial Church Meeting, 1936
33. *Ibid.*, 1930
34. Hastings A., p.208
35. PCC Minutes, 7 May 1943

CHAPTER 13
1. Iremonger F.A., p.582
2. Crockfords
3. PCC Minutes, 16 May 1952
4. Hastings A., p.525
5. Parish Mag., January 1967
6. St. Michael's 75th Anniversary booklet
7. PCC Minutes, 5 December 1971
8. Crockfords

CHAPTER 14
1. Annual Parochial Church Meeting, 9 April 1976
2. PCC Minutes (Special Meeting), 8 April 1986
3. For details of the roundels see Cole W., pp. 60-62

INDEX

Entries under Church Stretton and St. Laurence's Church, Church Stretton are very numerous and are sub-divided into various categories.
R. stands for Rector, C. for Curate.
Page numbers in italics indicate illustrations.

INDEX

INDEX

Cleobury Mortimer (Shrops) 17, 46-7, 94
Cleobury, William de (R. 1309- ?) 46-7
Clifton Hampden (Oxon) 208
Clive, Robert (Archdeacon of Salop) 142
    Lord Robert (of India) 145
    Hon. R.H. 182
Cloppe, 'Sir' Richard (R. ? - 1388) 54
Cludde, Edward 187
Clun (Shrops) 47, 106-7, 113
Clungunford (Shrops) 56
Clyfford, Walter (R. 1393-5) 55
Coalbrookdale 138
Coke, John 67, 71-2, 80
Coleman, Ann Gregory 163, 165-6, 168, 172, 183
    Thomas 163
    Thomas Bernard (R. 1807-18) 163-6, 173, 179,
      183
Colley, John 86
    Noel (C. 1877-79) 207, 210
Collins, Sir Walter 52
Commons, House of 102, 107, 115, 185
Common Worship 299
Compton Census 125, 126
Condover (Shrops) 5, 63, 94, 98, 102, 254
    Deanery 288
    Hall 172
    St. Andrew's 102-3
Congregationalists (*also see* Independents, Church Stretton
    Churches – URC – All Stretton Chapel and Little
    Stretton Chapel) 118, 125, 237, 246
Constantine, Emperor 40
Conventicles 125 (for Act, *see* Parliament)
Cook, Ann 161
Corbett (formerly Plymley), Joseph (Archdeacon of Salop)
    146, 150, 152, 162-3, 165, *169*, 170, 179
Corfield, Thomas 123
    Thomas *173-5*
Cornelius 143
Cornovii 1
Corve , Master William (R. 1405-17) 58-60
Corvedale (Shrops) 5, 10, 93, 183, 198
Council of Constance 58-60
Council of Lyons 42-3
Council – Vatican II 268
Courtenay, William (Bp. Hereford & Abp. Canterbury) 56
Cowper, John 122
Cozens, Daniel 281-2, 290
Cradock, Joseph 141, 144, 146-8
Cranage, D.H.S., Dean of Norwich 247, 252
Cranmer, Thomas (Abp. Canterbury) 71, 78, 82
Croft, Herbert (Bp. Hereford) 124
Crofts, J.H. 258, 265
Cromwell, Oliver 108
    Thomas 78
Cuddesdon Theological College 208
Custance, Charles (C. 1893-5) 224
    Martin (C. 1919) 246-7

Daily Mail 273
Dale, R.W , 195
Dansey, Richard (C. 1899-1904) 224, 235
Darby, Abraham 138
Darlington, Earl of 182
Darwin, Charles 206, 233
David, son of Griffin (R. ? – 1276) 40, 44

Davies, Mr.(organist) 167
    David Llewelyn (C. 1882-7) 218
    G.M. (Pro-Rector 1917-8) 245
    William 123, 126, 133
Dawes, Thomas 111
Day, William (C. 1841-3) 184, 190
Decade of Evangelism 290
Declaration of Independence (USA) 143
Declaration of Indulgence 118-9, 125
Declaration of Sports 102
Dee, James, 115
Defoe, Daniel 134
Despenser, Hugh 48
Diddlebury (Shrops) 3
Disraeli, Benjamin 216
Dissent (*also see* Church Stretton – Churches, and
    Nonconformists), 116, 126, 185
Dixon, Evelyn 249, 251
    Henry (R. 1923-37; Archdeacon of Ludlow,
      1932-9) 248-*55*, *249*, 295
    Joey 251
Domesday Book 1, 6, *8*, 19
Dormer, Anne (née Shepherd), 111
    Sir Fleetwood 111
    Judge 111
    Peter (R.1654? – 67) 110-11, 113, 115-7, 137
Dorrington (Shrops) 189, 194
Dover, Earl of –*see* Carey, Henry
Drayton Manor (Staffs) 139
Dudesley/Dudgeley (Shrops) 73
Duffie, John (C. 1963-4) 263
Dycher, George (R, 1515-49) 74, 76-8, 81

Eadric the Wild 7, 8
Easthope (Shrops) 3, 134, 140, 172
Eaton, Moses 137
Eaton-under-Heywood (Shrops) 45, 134, 215
Ecumenical Movement 254-5, 268-9
    Council of Churches (British) 255
    (Stretton – Churches Together) 268, 281, 296
    (World) 255
Edmunds, Michael 294
Edward I, King 41-2
    'The Lord Edward' 38, 40
    at Stretton 41
Edward II, King 46-8, 52,
    at Stretton 48
Edward III, King 49, 52
Edward VI, King 68, 78-9
Edward VII, King 227, 230,
    as Prince of Wales 216
Edwardes, Humphrey 106
    Sir Thomas 102, 106
Edwards, James 167, 175-6
Edwin, Earl of Mercia 7, 8
Elizabeth I, Queen 67, 82-3, 85, 89, 98
Elizabeth II, Queen 279
Elizabethan Poor Law 153
Elizabethan Religious Settlement 82, 89
Ellesmere (Shrops) 38
Ellis, George (Priest-in-Charge, 1900) 224
Engelard de Pitchford (later, de Stretton) 17, 22
Ephraim, Emlyn 273
Essays and Reviews 206
Ethelbert, King of East Anglia 175
Evans, John 162
Exclusion Crisis 126

Onibury (Shrops) 94
Onions & Rowley (builders) 286
Oratory (private chapel) 63
Origin of Species 206
Osman, Alfred (C. 1908-9) 237
Oswestre, Thomas (R. 1417-39) 60
Oswestry (Shrops) 1, 47, 57, 62
Otley (Yorks) 272
Ottley, Sir Francis 105
Ouseley, Sir F. Gore 213
Overton Mrs. (verger) 263, 269
Owen family of Condover 172
    Jane (*also see* Norton, Jane) 94
    Thomas 94
    Sir William 104
Owen, Hugh 190
    Norman 273, 284-5
    Reginald 137
    Ted 287
Oxford, Diocese of 121
Oxford Movement 186
Oxford, University of 239
    All Souls' College 100
    Brasenose College 100
    Christ Church 73, 121-2, 166
    Exeter College 208
    Jesus College 117, 137, 190
    Magdalen College 111
    Merton College 117, 248
    New College 99
    Oriel College 58-9, 121-2
    Queen's College 235
    St. Edmund Hall 99
    St. John's College 100
    Trinity College 100, 117, 254
    Wadham College 234
    Worcester College 163, 190
Oxford, Wycliffe Hall Theological College 254, 299

Pace, Mr. 237
Pace, Richard 211
Paddy, Joseph 123
    Samuel (C.1664-8) 116, 121
Paganism 3, 4, 13
Paris, Matthew 34, 45
Parishes, evolution of 6
Parker, James 115
    Matthew (Abp. Canterbury) 81, 91
Parkes, David (artist) 52, 169, 198
    Sarah 158
Parliament 102 (*also see* Commons & Lords, Houses of)
    Acts of –
      Abolition of Slavery (1833) 184
      Burial in woollens (1678) 128
      Burning of Heretics (1401) 60
      Catholic Emancipation (1829) 184
      Church Building (1818) 185
      Church Stretton Water (1899) 225
      Conventicles (1664) 115
      Education (1902) 237
      Education (1944) 257
      Enabling (Church, 1919) 247
      First Fruits (1535) 75
      Five Mile (1665) 116
      Great Reform (1832) 184
      Poor Law (1601) 153
      Poor Law Amendment (1834) 154, 181, 184
      Six Articles (1539) 78

Test (1673) 126, (Repeal) 184
Tithe Commutation, (1836) 184
Toleration (1689) 126-7
Uniformity (1549) 79
Uniformity (1559) 82
Uniformity (1662) 110-1, 113, 115, 120
Cavalier Parliament 109
Convention Parliament 109
Long Parliament 103
Short Parliament 103
Parliamentarians 104, 106-7
Parrs Wood (Lancs) 234
Parry, Humphrey 137
Parsons, Paul 293
Parton, Dinah 214
Patronal churches 5, 6
Pearson, Nigel 293
Pecham, John (Abp. Canterbury) 42-3, 45
Pechell, Augustus 166, 172
Pemberton, Caroline (*née* Pechell) 166
    Harriet 190
    Robert 160, 166
    Robert Norgrave (R. 1818-48) 166-88, *186*,190, 193, 218, 221, 251, 266
    Thomas 166, 183
Penelope, H.M.S. 160
Penny, Leslie 269, 277
Percy, Lord Henry (Hotspur) 57
Phillips, Ann 158
    Edward (apothecary) 133,137, 153,157
    Edward, (apothecary) 153, 157-8
    Francis 98
    John 137
    John (parish clerk) 150
    Mary 157
    Richard *158*
    Samuel 137
    Thomas 123
    Thomas (churchwarden) 122
    Thomas (school trustee) 133
    Thomas (Shrewsbury) 139
    Thomas (parish clerk) 150
    Thomas 158
    William 105
Phipps, Roger, Grace, Ruth 103
Piazza, Thomas (C. 1771-8) 140
Picklescott Hill 180
Pierson, Thomas 101
Pilleth (Radnor), Battle of 57
Pinches, Maria 122
Pinibus, Bonettus de (R. 1246-65) 36-7, 39, 43
Pinu, William de (R. 1237- ?) 36, 43
Piozzi, Mrs. 145
Piozzi-Salusbury, Sir John Salusbury 145, 187, 190
Plimley, Anne 137
Pluralism 45, 50, 54, 58, 81, 140
Plymley, Joseph (*see* Corbett)
Pobelowe, Robert (R. 1388 - ?) 54-5
Pole, Reginald (Cardinal) 82
Poll Tax 122
Pontesbury (Shrops) 37, 46, 58, 253, 279
Poole, William 133
Poor rate 114
Popish Plot (1678) 126
Posterne, John 128
    Thomas 123
    William 88

INDEX